Studies in Ibo
Political Systems

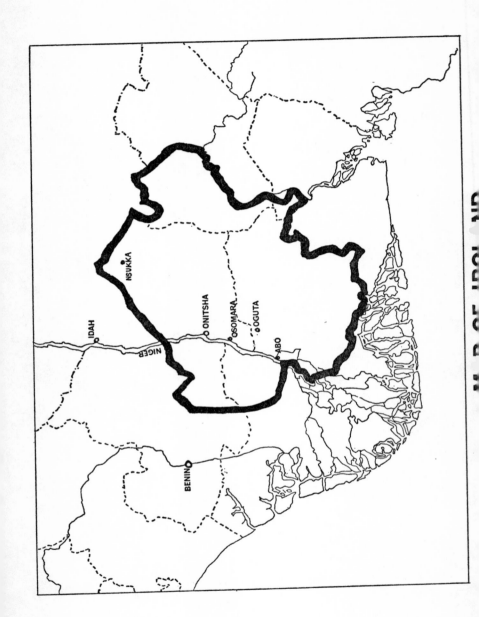

MAP OF IBOLAND

NSUKKA

ONITSHA

OSOMARA

OGUTA

ABO

IDAH

NIGER

BENIN

Studies in Ibo Political Systems

Chieftaincy and Politics in Four Niger States

Ikenna Nzimiro
D. Phil. (Cologne), Ph.D. (Cantab.)

Department of Sociology and Anthropology,
University of Nigeria, Nsukka

UNIVERSITY OF CALIFORNIA PRESS
Berkeley and Los Angeles
1972

0743602

38006

UNIVERSITY OF CALIFORNIA PRESS
Berkeley and Los Angeles, California

ISBN: 0–520–02228–9

Library of Congress Catalog Card No: 79–187745

Printed in Great Britain

For

G. I. Jones,
Lecturer in Social Anthropology, Cambridge

for his contributions to the
Study of Ibo Sociology

and

In Memory of My Late Cousin,

Dr. P. Nwanzuluahu Ada Nzimiro,
on whose academic path I trail

Contents

			Page
	Foreword		xi
	Preface		xiii

PART I			
	1	Ethnography and History	3
	2	Social Organisation	21
		Social Structure 21	
		Rank and Status 23	
	3	The Framework of Government I	41
		Onitsha 41	
		Abo 56	
	4	The Framework of Government II	65
		Oguta 65	
		Osomari 76	
	5	The Functions of Government I	94
		Policy Making and the Legislative Process 94	
		Onitsha 100	
		Abo 109	
		Oguta 110	
		Osomari 113	
	6	The Functions of Government II	118
		The Judicial Process 118	
		Maintenance of Order 128	
		War Organisation 134	

PART II			
	7	The Notion of Kingship	147
		Myths of Origin 147	
		Prerogatives of Kingship 147	
		Ritual Duties 149	
		National Festivals 151	
		Rituals of Kingship 156	
		Palace Organisation 157	

Page

8 Rituals of Kingship   162
   Installation Rituals 162
   Mortuary Rituals 181
9 The Dynamics of Kingship I   194
   The Succession
10 The Dynamics of Kingship II   226
   The King and His Chiefs
11 Summary and Conclusions   255
   Common Characteristics 255
   Special Characteristics 264

Bibliography   277
Index   283

Tables and Diagrams

		Page
A	State Officials	37
B	Onitsha Social Structure	*At*
C	Abo. Structure of the Umudei Clan	*end*
D	Oguta Social Structure	*of*
E	Osomari Social Structure	*Book*
F	Osomari Political Hierarchies	
G	Stages in Installation Rituals	80
H	Emblems and Regalia	162
I	Succession to the Office of Obi of Onitsha	177
J	Succession to the Office of Obi of Abo	196
K	Distribution of the Office of Iyase (Onowu)	214
		228

Illustrations

Map of Iboland	*Frontispiece*
1 Iyasara Uzoka of Oguta performing the ceremony of Ibe Odu	*Between pages 126–127*
2 Ngbiligba imi na anya, the bell with human features	
3 Iyase Onowu Anatogu of Onitsha	
4 Obi Oputa II of Abo	
5 Igbudu Ezeukwu: the funeral effigy of the deceased Ezeukwu guarded by acolytes	*Between pages 142–143*
6 The late Uzoma Ossai II, Ezeukwu of Oguta, the principal kingmaker, with his acolytes	
7 Udom Ezeukwu of Oguta	
8 Obi Ndokwu Mberekpe of Oguta	

ix

Foreword

This book is an enlarged form of my Ph.D thesis which I developed when I was at the Department of Social Anthropology, Cambridge. My four years' connections (1962–66) with the staff of the department were periods of great intellectual stimulation and I owe my gratitude to many persons. Professor Meyer Fortes's interest in the research was consistently maintained throughout this period and I am greatly indebted to him for the inspiration and encouragement I derived from him. Mr G. I. Jones, who was my supervisor throughout the period, proved a worthy one, and his criticisms of the original draft thesis and this enlarged version enabled me to set out my ideas lucidly. He carried into this assignment a personal interest in all aspects of the work and as a respected ethnologist of Ibo Society, I profited immensely from his observations. The book is dedicated to him for his contributions to the study of Ibo Sociology.

The Department's post-graduate seminars enabled me to benefit from the criticism and observations of the members, and the questions raised by the staff and Research Students when I presented papers on aspects of the work were very useful. The seminars themselves were sources of my intellectual orientation and for this I will always be indebted to them, and in particular, to Dr Edmund Leach, Dr Jack Goody, and Dr Audrey Richards.

This study was made possible by three sources: the Federal Ministry of Education (in particular its then Minister, Mr Aja Nwachukwu) and the officials of the London Office, who deserve my gratitude for the financing of this project; the former Director of the Institute of African Studies at the University of Ibadan, Dr K. O. Dike, to whom I offer my sincere thanks for offering me a year's Visiting Research Fellowship in the Institute during 1963–64; and finally, Dr Eni Njoku, former Vice-Chancellor of the University of Nigeria, on whose recommendation I was able to obtain a fellowship grant from the then Eastern Nigeria Government to supplement my Federal Government grant.

I am grateful to the many important people from the communities that I studied for their assistance in introducing me to their communities, and enabling me to obtain co-operation from their kings and chiefs. Notable among these are Mr R. Olisa, the king elect of Osamari; Mr F. Oranye of Onitsha, a one time interpreter to the government anthropologist C. K. Meek; Chief Mbanefo, the Odu of Onitsha; and prominent Ndichie including the late Obi Onyejekwe, the Akpulosu (Prince Oputa), and the Olilinzele of Abo, especially the late Obi Oputa who gave me comforts in his palace. I owe a debt of gratitude also to the family of the late Charles Olisa of Abo, for allowing me to use his documented *History of Abo*, which was not published until after his death.

My thanks are especially due to Professors Rene Koenig and Helmut Petri at the University of Cologne, who encouraged me to continue this work at Cambridge so that I might work with the distinguished Africanists I have mentioned above.

Lastly, I thank Miss Judith Elton, formerly of New Hall, Cambridge, who with painstaking effort drew from my rough plans most of the diagrams illustrating this book.

Ikenna Nzimiro

Nsukka
1971

Preface

The search for a scientific understanding of the Ibo political system is not of recent date. It has its historical roots in the early 1930s. Interest was awakened by the women's demonstration against the Warrant Chief System in 1929, and the widespread opposition which this demonstration reflected brought about the decision to study in depth the social organisation of Ibo societies. Over two hundred Intelligence Reports were written by administrative officers, and their reports were written according to specific guide lines given by the then government anthropologists at Lagos. On the basis of these reports a series of Native Administrative Organisations were established and the foundation of modern local government was laid.

In 1950 two modern trained anthropologists, Forde and Jones, made an ethnographic survey of Ibo society and classified the people into five cultural groups. The study revealed the extent of these cultural areas; and though the Ibo people possess common characteristics, the differences in the cultures of these ethnic areas which the survey showed brought to the attention of social anthropologists the fact that these Ibo cultural groups are different in size and scale from the cluster of small groups that anthropologists have been used to studying.

There is a widespread belief that Ibo societies are acephalous. This belief does not take into account the differences between cultural areas revealed by Forde and Jones. Hence it has loomed in the minds of some social anthropologists that all Ibo cultural groups fall within this classificatory type, in which case the belief becomes a misconception.

What this study sets out to do is to show that to understand the political system of the Ibos, each of these cultural areas should be investigated in detail and the pattern of its political structure described and defined. Studies of other cultural areas can provide us with similar empirical data, and from those data, we can by comparative analysis formulate our generalizations and hypotheses.

The study I have made is in keeping with this methodology, and it is a study of the political system of one of the Ibo cultural areas, the riverain Ogbaru people who live along the banks of the Niger and its tributaries.

Six of these communities (Abo, Onitsha, Osamari, Oguta—discussed here, and Asaba and Aguleri, to constitute a further work) were singled out for investigation, and the characteristic features of their political system show marked differences on the one hand and marked similarities on the other. A generalization about the political structure of any particular community becomes possible only by understanding how each community's political organisation works. Kings, titled chiefs, title associations, age grades, are all found in these communities, and a particular community combines these elements in its political structure in its own particular way, as we shall show in the study.

Kings and titled chiefs might rule in one area, as in our present sample; while in others, such as Asaba and Aguleri, titled personnel and age grades combine, so that qualification for political office depends not on lineage but on age and title. In Western Ibo areas we find kingdoms which, though akin to the areas we are concerned with, differ from these Niger areas in details of structural organisation. In some other Ibo areas, such as at Nri, Ndi Nze (title associations) and heads of lineages (elders) combine in the rulership.

Because of these varieties, our methodology should be followed in future, so that Ibo cultural areas can be studied with the social anthropologists' scientific objectivity, and so that abundant data can be made available for comparative studies and theoretical formulations.

* * *

The field work for this study was carried out between July 1963 and September 1964. Between October 1964 and the time that I returned to Cambridge, I made further visits to some of the six communities.

In 1960 and 1961 I carried out field work in two of the communities, Onitsha and Oguta, but was concerned mainly with aspects of their kinship and marriage systems.

During the latter period, two political incidents occurred in the communities. One was the death of the Obi of Onitsha, which led to a succession controversy and the other was the rift between the royal lineage at Oguta on the one hand and the entire body of chiefs and the twenty-six non-royal lineages on the other. In both cases the then Eastern Regional Government appointed a Commission of Inquiry.

When I returned in 1963 the two Commissions had completed their investigations and published their reports, to which I have referred in the study, and the interest shown by the various groups in each community was to my advantage, for articles, memoranda, and write-ups of local history provided me with recorded material which was lacking in the past. Though some of the material represented embellishments of the authors, it gave me a clue to the role of interest groups and chiefs in the dynamic activities of each community. The publications of the commissioners were sources of information. These were supplemented with archival material.

For the purposes of the enlargement of the scope of the inquiry, I had to include Abo, Osamari, Asaba, and Aguleri in the field study, and with the experience gained by my first research in Onitsha and Oguta, I had little difficulty in carrying out field studies in these areas. However, for lack of space, the information from Asaba and Aguleri cannot be included in this study.

The period spent in each community varied. Attention was concentrated in the new areas as well as in the areas of my former experience. Because of difficulties of communication it was not possible to make early visits to Osamari and Abo. Moreover, since most of the people who are still resident in the towns are farmers, they would return to the farming hamlets and only come into the towns at particular periods. Because of this, the tours of these towns were made to coincide with the period when the farmers returned to the town for their political, social and ritual activities.

This timing enabled me to witness the Obi's annual festival at Abo, which was the occasion to observe the chiefs and title associations and various groups performing their duties. In both states meetings were held with the different political segments in the community. Interviews were held with the chiefs, and with important persons who possessed knowledge of the culture, and the amazing knowledge of some of the women, particularly those from the royal lineages, was fully exploited. Where difficulties were encountered they were mitigated by the help of certain educated persons who wished to see their culture recorded, and they helped to influence some of the chiefs to give information that was relevant to the work. By participation, observation, and all the available means that I employed, I did everything possible at my disposal to note all an observer can record. What I have written in the following chapters concerns essentially aspects of their political systems—the place of the chiefs and kings in the day-to-day politics of the states. Their kinship, lineage, marriage, religion, and other social institutions are left out, and are brought in where appropriate to the theme. The rest will be fully dealt with in later publications.

In this book, which is divided into three parts, I have tried to do two things.

The first is to reconstruct the political organisation as narrated to me by the people and as I observed it myself. In the first part, therefore, I have briefly described the political structure of each state and have shown how the structure is used as an instrument for the carrying out of the purpose of each state. I have tried to show how the personnel of office, the kings and their chiefs, carry out the governmental functions of (a) policy making, (b) adjudication of justice, (c) execution of laws and (d) the defence of the state. These activities are the concern of all the governments and the way the political class and the elite perform their duties are of equal interest to the members of the community who constitute the various interest groups which are the sources of pressure in the system.

In the second part, I have discussed kingship as an institution, and as the enduring focus of political values. The notion of the sacredness of kings is expressed in the various ways that the life of a king is limited by the rituals that confer on him the status of a ruler and endow him with the sacredness of his office. This sense of kingly sacredness is also expressed in those rituals that send his soul to the other world only to continue to maintain, from this spirit world, a relationship with the living, thus entrenching their concept of the continuity of the office which is elaborated in the rituals of his installation and of his burial. Though the king is considered sacred, I have shown that he is not above the law however, and that the rules of the office separate him from it if he breaks them. Though sacred he is a politician and can be challenged, either by his chiefs on behalf of the people or simply for personal aggrandisement on the part of an individual chief. In these conflicts, the protagonists (the king and the chiefs) modify the rules and establish new norms and ideas about the office.

In the final chapter, I have tried to examine the whole theme of the study as discussed in Parts I and II. This appraisal of the system is to enable us to examine the common characteristic features of the whole political system, as well as to show the similarities between particular states.

I have suggested that they all possess basic common politic structures; they have kings who are endowed by myth as t spiritual force behind the office and as secular heads of th these kings appoint some or all of the chiefs; these chiefs are allo-cated specific functions and roles commensurate with the status of their offices and all of these states base the organisation of their political structure on their unilineal descent groups. On top of these structural units—Obodo, Ebo and Ogbe—the highest structure is the state system dominated by their kings and their chiefs. But they vary also in the degree of power and authority located at the centre or in the peripheral structure of the state. The administration of justice and defence of the state, however, are controlled at the centre; and furthermore, the kings are the symbol of their states. The life cycle of every king which we have described contains aspects which represent common ritual and political interests in the community.

External cultural contacts have affected the political institutions of the states. The first is the contact arising from their migration which, as recorded in their traditions, shaped the structure of their kingdoms. Second, at the other end of the change (mostly dictated by European contact as already explained) the people have recognised that the modern epoch (enu oyibo) which has brought about changes in the general framework of modern governments also requires change in their system. What is important to emphasize is that the present generation, though prepared to modify, does not intend to abandon these institutions.

At a reconciliation meeting organized by the former Premier of the Eastern Region to settle the chieftaincy dispute at Oguta, the Premier wondered how the two political blocks consisting of leaders with university training, professional men, such as lawyers, doctors, engineers and also wealthy businessmen, could dissipate their energies over an institution he regarded as 'anachronistic' in the modern society. Someone, however, retorted, "You do not understand what kingship means in our life, because not being a member, you have not been nurtured in the emotional streams of life that pervade the office".[1]

It is this emotional attachment to its values that enables the institution of kingship to remain the focus of political unity.

NOTES

1 The premier comes from a part of the Ibo country which does not possess the office of kingship.

B

Postscript

Between the completion of the field research and the publication of this book, the four Obis referred to—Obi Oputa I of Abo, Obi Onyejekwe of Onitsha, and Obis Mberekpe and Ojiako of Oguta—have died. Regents are acting in two of the communities: the Odua at Abo, and the Udom at Oguta. Succession to the throne is now being contested at Abo since there is no definite rule for choosing the next Obi, all successions, as indicated, being by contest.

At Onitsha, the dispute about the succession to the throne of the late Obi Onyejekwe, as reported in the book, has been resolved. The Obi's death helped to resolve the issue, as the Iyase and some senior Ndichie Ume had remained by their decision not to recognise him on the grounds that the Obi crowned himself, and according to the tradition bequeathed to them by their ancestors, the Iyase is the only person who can legitimately crown an Obi. Since the coronation was not performed by him, they refused to recognise his position.

The 1932–33 pact reported in the book stated that succession to the throne should rotate between the two royal divisions of Umuezearoli and Umudei. The throne has passed to the Umudei, who selected a new Obi Ofala Okagbue and presented him to the Iyase and Ndichie. The new Obi was crowned by the Iyase.

The two Obis at Oguta have died and regents are on the throne. They come from two royal lineages of Ngegwu, an original royal lineage restored after the dispute between Obi Ojiako (of Umudei) and the Ndichie and non-royal wards, and Umudei who have been the royal lineage for a long period.

When the period of regency expires, the question of which of the two royal lineages will continue to supply the Obi will be determined.

April, 1971   I.N.

PART I

Chapter 1   **Ethnography and History**

ETHNOGRAPHY

The Ibo, numbering about seven million,[1] are people who speak a common language which forms part of the Kwa group of West African languages. Their territorial distribution covers the Niger Cross River area, with Ibibio and Cross River people to the east, Ijaw to the south, Edo speaking peoples to the west, and Igala Idoma speaking peoples to the north.

They have similar cultural features, possessing an agricultural economy, with fishing in the riverain areas carried out particularly by those living along the River Niger. Their physical environment is mainly tropical rain forest and marginal savanna in the extreme north.

Their religious philosophy is essentially based on the ideology of animism and a belief in a High God—Chukwu or Chineke. Society and morality are bound together by their cosmological concepts, and the social organisation of their institutions is sustained by their metaphysical views about life and the universe. Their religious beliefs provide support for law and order, and in particular ani (ala), the deity of the land, is the supreme moral sanction. As they are an agricultural people, land is the basis of their material existence. Communities and their subdivisions are very largely defined in terms of ownership of land which is governed by three cardinal principles: (*a*) that land belongs to the community and cannot be alienated from it without its consent; (*b*) that within the community the individual shall have security of tenure for the land he requires for his compound, his gardens, and his farms; (*c*) that no member of the community shall be without land.[2]

Forde and Jones have divided the Ibo into five cultural divisions —Northern or Onitsha Ibo, Southern or Owerri Ibo, Western Ibo, Eastern or Cross River Ibo, and North-Eastern Ibo. The Niger Ibos are part of the riverain group of the Western Ibo. They are known by other Ibos as Oru and are generally referred to as Ndi Ogbaru, meaning those people living along the bank of the river Niger who follow the downward current (omumu) to their towns. They are small communities bound by a common riverain culture but politically autonomous, each constituting a small kingdom and resisting political domination by any neighbouring group.

The whole area, with the exceptions of Onitsha and Oguta, is very low-lying, and during the rainy seasons—June-July to September—the land where yams are cultivated is covered with water. The farm hamlets situated outside the dwelling towns become flooded, and the populace move to the town, returning to the farm hamlets after the recession of the flood.

Farming is the predominant occupation and yams are cultivated in alluvial plains along the Niger and its numerous tributaries. After the flood has receded, which is about late November, the men cutlass the forest growth and when it has dried they burn it; they also break-up the soil into mounds in which they plant their yams and other crops. These mounds retain enough moisture to support their growth during the dry season.

The seasonal farming activities determine the people's festival calendars, for they have to clear the farm (Isuolu) by cutlassing the undergrowth, burn it when it is dry (Ikpa-oku), plant the yams (Ikoiji), tend the young shoots and support them with poles (Ima Oni), carry out the first and second weeding (Ikpa Olu), and harvest the yams (Igwuiji). There is an early harvest of a special variety of yams, while the general harvest marks the end of the farming period when they repair to the towns (Iputa uno iju). Most of the annual festivals are held after the harvest and before the next farming season begins. This is a period for taking titles and for other social and ritual activities in the community.

Interspersed with farming is fishing, the produce from which they sell. The various streams and ponds provide the Ibo with considerable fishing resources and their techniques of fishing are highly developed. Nets of different types—ugbu, elili and ochokolo—are used. Women build temporary dams (agbo) in order to trap fish when the dams are drained or dried up. All the Niger kingdoms are conversant with these fishing techniques with the exception of Onitsha which is not accustomed to riverain activities. Here they do not use canoes, and only farm on dry land; hence the other riverain (Ogbaru) people refer to them as Ibo, a term which Onitsha people reject, insisting that they are Ogbaru not Ibo.

Throughout the area cassava is cultivated on dry land unaffected by flooding. In between the yam mounds women plant maize which is harvested before the yams are ripe (ijiokika), and they depend on this maize and on cassava until the yams are harvested.

Their agriculture is highly developed, and in their technique of farming they know the different types of yams, and the depth that must be dug for a planted seedling of any type to yield large tubers (ilunne). They know the correct time to plant each type, the soil fit for their growth, and the time for their harvesting. They follow the seasons of the year in the planting, weeding, and harvesting of their crops; they know that they must dig canals (unamiri) to drain water from the farm, and if this technological knowledge seems to fail, they have the deities of the yam (ufeshioku) and of the farm land (aniubi), to appeal to in any period of hardship due to a drought or any other conditions which make farming difficult.

They cultivate yams for sale to non-yam cultivating areas in the Niger Delta. Oguta supplies yams to all the Ijaw people along the Delta coasts, Port-Harcourt being one of their markets. The yams are transported by water in large canoes. Today they are also taken by road for sale in the inland urban centres.

At the beginning of the eighteenth century markets in the Niger Ibo area became increasingly important for the supply of slaves and wealth was greatly increased through this trade. It later became the centre of early European enterprises. Niger Ibos became middlemen who bought oil from the hinterland Ibo producers and sold it to the trading companies which had established trading factories along the Niger in the following places: Abo 1843, Onitsha 1857, Asaba 1863, Osomari 1877, Oguta 1884, Atani 1884, and Aguleri 1884.

Of the various Niger Ibo communities, this study is concerned with four—Onitsha, Abo, Oguta, Osomari—which have been chosen for the following reasons.

Firstly, they are the most important communities today and, in the past, they dominated trade and politics along the Niger prior to the arrival of the British.

Secondly, when the Trotter expedition entered the Niger, the three communities on the Niger became important centres for trade and commerce and mission activities, and remained so for some considerable time until trade shifted to the mainland, when Oguta became an important trading centre while Abo and Osomari lost their positions. The administrative headquarters of the Abo Division were removed from Abo to Ashaka, while the Osomari divisional office was transferred to Atani.

Thirdly, the trading, governmental and missionary activities led to a migration of people to these places, particularly to Onitsha, and eventually resulted in modern urban development, though this varied considerably. The net result was that the patrilocal descent groups which controlled the traditional 'urban' community were exposed to the new forces of social and political influence. Aware of these forces, each of the communities resisted from the beginning the intrusion of 'aliens' into their traditional community and separate urban areas developed along the waterside 'beaches', where land was allocated to the trading firms, the government, missionaries, and to the migrant population from other parts of Nigeria.

In spite of this influence the people have nevertheless continued to preserve the political institutions of their society, and kingship still endures as the axis of moral and legal norms.

Fourthly, because of the persistent efforts to preserve the institution of kingship, there are kings at Oguta, Onitsha, Osomari, and Abo, and the communities are thus the only places where we are able to study the working of the traditional political institutions, to reconstruct them, and to create a basis for the study of the way they have changed. In the other communities, kingship as an institution is waning, and most of them no longer have the office of Obi (king) but only other subordinate offices. These four communities are therefore the areas where we can study the continuity of their political system over several centuries.

Onitsha and Osomari are situated on the left bank of the Niger, as are a number of other small communities. From Osomari a waterway leads to the Ulashi (Ulasi) river and to Oguta town, which occupies the north side of the lake of the same name, and which Oguta people call Uhamili. Further to the south, Abo on the right bank of the Niger commands the northern exit of the Niger Delta.

HISTORY

The history of these states can be divided into three early periods referred to only in local oral traditions and a later period when oral sources and European historical sources come together and which the Niger Ibos call 'enu oyibo', the white man's epoch.

The first, which can be termed the distant past, is concerned with the founder or founders who live in the original home, either Benin or Igala, and occupy a particular area there. Then comes the period of unrest in this kingdom which leads to conflict between these founding fathers and the head of the state. The second is the period of migration following the conflict, and this is filled with legends of settlements at successive places until their arrival at their present home. In the course of these migrations, kinsmen break away or are left behind, and become the founders of communities with whom the kingdom claims political relationship today. The third stage is the period of settlement in their present abode. It is marked by the conquest or absorption of the people already living there, some of whom flee to other communities, whilst others remain.

The fourth dates from the time of European penetration into the Niger in 1841. This revealed to British traders, missionaries, and colonial officers, the form and nature of these kingdoms whose rulers were later to enter into treaties with Queen Victoria. Once centres of the slave trade, these places later became important commercial river ports for the palm oil trade when 'legitimate trade' replaced the slave trade. The slave trade era had introduced gunpowder and cannon into these kingdoms and such was the power of the war chiefs that they were able to mobilise their fleets, attack each other, subjugate small villages, and take slaves, some of whom were sold at a comfortable profit whilst others were retained in the service of the kings and chiefs. The fortunes of kings and chiefs did not disappear with the abolition of the slave trade, as most of the trading companies had at first to pay subsidies and later rents for their factories which they established ashore. The final stage was the taking over of the administration of the Royal Niger Company by the Imperial Government, and its subsequent penetration, through Onitsha, Asaba and Abo, into the interior of Eastern and Western Nigeria, leading to the consolidation of British administration in the country. The system of native administration introduced between 1927 and 1935 dove-tailed into the reforms of 1950, and eventually led to the establishment of local government in these communities by the regional governments.

ONITSHA

Onitsha oral history begins with the myth of the Umuezechima clan who trace their ancestry to Chima, the great father who lived at Ado na Idu (Benin). Onitsha, like the other Umuezechima people in the West (namely Onicha-Ugbo, Onicha-Ukwu, Onicha Olona, Obamkpa, Isele, Obio, and Ezi) state that their ancestor Chima left Benin because of a dispute which he had with Asigie, the mother of the Oba of Benin, who had been assaulted when she trespassed on his property. The Oba sent his military chief Obugwala to attack Chima and his people, and to avoid this, Chima and his group left. (Abo tradition claims relationship with Onitsha by asserting that Esumei Ukwu and Chima Ukwu were brothers, and that the two left together, separating at Agbor.)

They left Benin and each son of Chima had an ufie gong, a symbolic wooden drum used by the king. It was agreed that wherever the ufie of any group happened to fall, the group would settle there, and that the person whose gong fell first should become king. In the course of the journey, different gongs fell at different places and each leader settled with his people and founded a kingdom.

The founders established the Benin type of kingship, and went to the Oba of Benin to receive the sword of office known as ada; hence, I style them the ada kings, for example the Onicha, Isele and other Umuezechima towns of the Asaba divisions.

Several of these kings, who came to be known as Obis, were made governors of a single town or of a town with its scattered quarters. They swore fidelity to the Oba, and for many years paid him tribute in the form of slaves and cattle, also providing warriors when called upon to do so. However, being separated from Benin political influence (for Benin never crossed the Niger) Onitsha adopted a system of succession different from the hereditary primogeniture of Benin. The sons of Chima, who became the ancestors of the present Onitsha Mili (the Onitsha we are concerned with here), continued their journey. The traditions of Onicha Olona and some of the other Umuezechima towns assert that Chima did not cross the Niger to the present place, and that Oreze and his brothers led the migration; Onicha Olona tradition explains that the founders of Onitsha Mili first settled at Onicha Olona and then moved down to Illa, whence they made their final move to Onitsha.[3] Oreze ordered all gongs to be destroyed. This was done so that the people inhabiting the area they wished to occupy would be taken unawares, for if they heard the sound of the ufie, they would resist their landing. It was agreed that new gongs should be made on landing, and the person whose ufie sounded most like that of their father Chima would be king. Oreze, however, hid the original ufie Chima and did not destroy it. On reaching Onitsha, he brought out his gong, played it, and it sounded exactly like that of Chima. Another version says that Oreze ordered that whoever landed first and played his gong should be the leader. According to this version, as they were nearing the shore Oreze smuggled his servant into the river and he swam to the shore with the ufie and sounded it first. The people exclaimed "Ufie Oreze has sounded!", and thus kingship passed to his division known today as Umuezechima.[4] Whichever of the above versions of the founding of the state is correct, the significant point is that the Oreze (or Umuezechima) division, which eventually grew into the two sub-divisions of Umudei (or Okebunabo) and Umuezearoli, became the royal division, while the other division, Ugwunaobamkpa, became the non-royal division. These myths explain this segmentation into two primary divisions.

Oze people, the original inhabitants, were defeated, and Chima's people occupied their present abode about three miles from the Niger. They expanded further into the Oze territory and this became the farm land of different Onitsha lineages. They did not adopt the riverain economy of other Oru, but concentrated on farming away from the river, and intermarried with their 'Ibo' neighbours. Legends reveal several wars with these neighbours—namely Obosi, Awkuzu, and Ogidi—during this expansionist period.

In 1857, Macgregor Laird and Samuel Crowther, on their journey up the Niger, established a Mission Station at Onitsha, and from this time onwards, the kings of Onitsha (Akazua and his sons Diali and Anazonwu) were involved in economic and diplomatic relationships with the trading companies, missionaries, and the British government. On 12th October 1863 a "Treaty between the king and chief of Onitsha and Her Majesty the Queen of Great Britain for the suppression of the Slave Trade, prevention of Human Sacrifices, and the opening and encouragement of legitimate trade" was signed by "Obi Akauaza King of Onitsha, Wabuvo, a King, Arikabue, Head chief, Igive, chief, Owanusa, chief, Eperepu, chief, Abijoma, chief, Owwatari, chief, Onyaka-ohn, King's brother, F. G. Gambier, Lt. Commanding H.M.S. *Investigator*, J. G. Cruikshank, Assistant Surgeon, H.M.S. *Investigator*."

Clause III of this treaty provided that in the event of its provisions being broken and any opposition made to legitimate trade, the British Government "may take such measures as may be found necessary to compel the king and chiefs of Onitsha to faithfully carry out the letter and spirit of the treaty".[5]

On October 15th 1877 a further treaty was signed by Ha Na Eze Oun (Anazonwu), the king of the Onitsha, Agei, chief, Amodi-Amrafaro, chief, and Mejuru, king's messenger on the one side and Henry Chester Tait, acting Consul, S. A. Crowther, Bishop of Niger Territory and seven other gentlemen on the other. In this treaty the king and chiefs of Onitsha also agreed to cede to "the owners of the present factories" and to "the Church Missionary Society all right and title to the land on which the church and mission station stand, and the British trading stations occupy" and it provided that, should the consul receive a favourable report at the beginning of the 1878 trading season that its various provisions had been carried out, the Consul "may suggest to Her Most Gracious Majesty Queen Victoria the desirability of making suitable presents to the King and his principal chiefs".[6]

By 1879 the four principal trading companies had amalgamated to form the United African Company under Mr (later Sir) George Goldie. This combination did not suit the Onitsha people and one of the grievances of the King was that the prices of goods sold were higher than before. The relationship between them and the company deteriorated and eventually they attacked and broke its factories. In retaliation Onitsha was bombarded and partly demolished on 29th October 1879 by British naval forces. Captain

Bury, narrating the incident, stated that "we marched to the inner town about three miles distant and burned it; and, on 30th October, we levelled all the walls left standing in the lower town".[7]

In 1881 the Company changed its name to the National Africa Company and applied unsuccessfully to the British Government for a charter. In 1884 to forestall any French attempts to extend their influence to the Lower Niger, treaties were made between the British government and all the African states along this river including Onitsha, the Onitsha treaty making specific reference to the National Africa Company (Ltd.) and to a treaty between the king and chiefs of Onitsha and this Company in which, in recognition of the benefits obtained through intercourse with it, they ceded "the whole of their territory to the company and to its administrators for ever". The company bound itself not to interfere with any "native laws or private property and not to take possession of any land without payment for the same"; but it reserved the right to exclude "foreign settlers other than those now settled in the country".[8] Obi Anazonwu disregarded the treaty, however arguing that he did not understand the monopolistic clauses which specified that he must trade solely with the National Africa Company. He allowed a rival British company, the Liverpool Company, the right to trade at Onitsha. The National Africa Company retaliated by closing their wharf at Onitsha and blockading the town.[9]

In 1886 the Company, now known as the Royal Niger Company, was granted a charter by the British government which gave it the right to administer the Niger from Abo northward as far as Nupe. This continued until 1900 when its charter was revoked and the British protectorates of Northern and Southern Nigeria were established, with the Niger Ibo area being included in the latter.

The Royal Niger Company did not interfere with the internal government of Onitsha and the administrative officers of the British Protectorate were mainly concerned with Onitsha township, the new urban area which included the trading and mission concessions and which became the headquarters of the Province and district of the same name.

The introduction of indirect rule produced a reorganisation of local government with the Obi and council being recognised as Native Authority with jurisdiction over both the "inland town" (the original Onitsha town) and Onitsha waterside (the African section of the township) which now in population considerably outnumbered the inland town but which had till then remained separate from it. The local government reforms of 1955 altered this, combining the waterside and inland town and township into municipality with a municipal council, the majority of whose members were elected from electoral wards, most of which were in the former township and its waterside expansion. The Obi was *ex officio* the president of the council and there were a limited number of 'traditional' (i.e. *ex officio*) members who were the Ndichie Ume titled chiefs. This was the position before the civil war.

ABO

The dominant section of Abo trace their origin to Benin City. According to their tradition, their father Obazome, alias Esumai-ukwu, founded Ebo, now called Abo; he was a son of the Oba Ozolua (who is said to have been the Oba who was visited by John Alfonso d'Aveiro in 1485).

According to the tradition, Oba Ozolua was harsh, and in his attempt to build a great empire, he levied heavy taxes. This and other acts of oppression (one of which was the murder of a woman, Enahen, a great diviner from the Obi's harem, who had been bold enough to caution the Oba on his harsh measures) led to unrest and bloodshed in the city. The village heads of Ebo decided to migrate for fear of this unrest.

Prince Obazome (Esumaiukwu) left, accompanied by his brothers Oputa, Ezoma, Akilini, Osimili, Etim, Chima Ukwu, and their people. During the journey a division was formed on their arrival at Ologodo (Agbor). One part took the Agbor-Asaba direction under the leadership of Prince Ugbo together with the company of Chima Ukwu (the Umuezechima clan already referred to) and with many other Bini people. They stopped at different places, and in each place some members of the party chose to remain behind and settle there. The second part, led by Esumai, moved from Agbor in the direction of Ukwuani and stayed at a site they call Ologwu, where they settled for several months. When they continued, the different leaders dropped out, and Oputa founded the town of Usoro, Ezoma founded Ashaka, Etim founded Afor, and Osimili founded Osissa. All these constituted the Ukwu clan.[10]

Esumai continued and arrived at Osimilinta. There they made efforts to cross the river but they met fishermen from Iwelle who, instead of ferrying them, capsized the canoe (called "gbamiyoko") and many Abos were drowned. In their efforts to find a shallow place to cross they found what they thought to be a ford, which in fact was really the back of a manatee (emei) that was helping them. After they had crossed by walking on its back the animal raised its head above the water and then dived and disappeared. Whereupon Esumai struck his ofo on the water and declared the manatee their "totem" animal and this has been observed up to this day. After crossing, they attacked the Iwelle people, burnt their villages and looted their property. They settled at Afobo and then moved further on until they arrived at the present settlement which was then occupied by the Akiri people; and they pitched their camp at Ugboko Ukwu, a mile distant from Akiri land.

This was the spot that was destined to be the end of the journey, for according to them they had shot an arrow (ufere) into the air at Benin before their departure, and it was divined that where this arrow fell would be the stopping place and the end of their journey; so it happened that this was the place. Esumai met Akiri people, and negotiated with their head (Ogene); negotiations broke down however, and the Abo people defeated Akiri. (Akiri people do not accept this account.)

Esumai established the kingdom, became the Obi of Abo, and when he died his two sons, Ogwezi, senior, and Ugbo, junior, contested the succession. According to their principle of inheritance Ogwezi was to become the first Obi, but his junior brother Ugbo usurped the throne because he was wealthier. Ogwezi retreated, but later, becoming wealthy, he returned and defeated his brother and occupied the throne.

The followers of Obi Ugbo migrated and some are found in Kwale District. Ogwezi was established as the Obi (praise name Obonwe), and he had four sons—Ojigbali, Ogwezi, Ossai and Ozegbe—who became the founders of the four quarters (ebo) of Abo. When Ogwezi died, the office of Obi did not fall to the senior son, but was open to competition from all the descendants of Esumai, who are known as Umudei. Later migrants into the town became absorbed within the lineages of these four descent groups, their descendants being known as Ndichie.

In time, Abo gradually came to dominate the Lower Niger. Wars were waged with neighbouring people and villages were subjugated, particularly during the time of the slave trade from the middle of the eighteenth century onwards.

The kingdom of Abo became known to the European world in 1831 when the Lander brothers, captured at Asaba, were sent to the king of Abo, Obi Ossai, who, on being paid a ransom, released them to the British traders on the Delta Coast. The tracing of the Niger to the coast opened the way to English merchants. First the expedition of Laird and Oldfield in 1832, and then the Trotter-Allen expedition of 1841, entered the Niger. Both reached Abo, and this was the beginning of a permanent relationship between Abo and Great Britain. Captain Trotter and Captain Allen brought to the notice of English merchants, missionaries, and the British government, the real political and economic position of this city, and their comments on Abo give a clear picture of the city, the power of the king, the military organisation, trade activities, and the extent of the kingdom.

According to them "Aboh is much the largest town in the Delta of the Niger, though we consider seven or eight thousand to be the extreme number of its inhabitants. Obi Osai, the King of Ibu, is therefore one of the most powerful and influential rulers on the banks of the river, which is aided much by the position of the town, Aboh, at the upper part of the Delta, enabling him to control very much the trade towards the sea; even King Boy, of Brass, is in some degree tributary to him".[11]

The economic activities of this city state impressed the members of the expedition and they remarked that "The people cultivated rice, Indian corn, cassava, bananas, oranges, cocos, ground-nuts, yams abundantly and of good quality, pappaws, Guinea-peppers, etc. There is reason to hope the trade in palm-oil, ivory, etc., has increased very much; we saw many large canoes from Bonny, Benin, and Brass, laden with puncheons of the former, confirming what we heard on the coast, that a great portion of oil procured in the bights is brought from the interior".[12] The Trotter expedition led to further expeditions, which eventually brought the Niger kingdoms under British commercial, and later, political control.

Trotter entered into a treaty with Obi Osai and his chiefs on 28th August 1841. It was a treaty of friendship with a preamble as follows:

"There shall be peace and friendship between the people of Great Britain and the people of Aboh; and the Slave Trade shall be put down forever in the Aboh country; and the people of Great Britain and the people of Aboh shall trade together innocently, justly, kindly and usefully . . ."

It contained seventeen articles dealing with trade, of which article 17 specified the goods to be given to the obi in return for signing this treaty. It was countersigned by H. D. Trotter, First Commissioner, and three other commissioners, and witnessed by J. O. McWilliam, J. F. Schön, and by the Obi with his two brothers Aribunda and Ajeh and his eldest son Chikuma.[13] The Obi, however, did not respect the aspect of the treaty dealing with slave trade. It continued, and in 1854, to counteract it MacGregor Laird opened a factory at Abo, in the village of Isala opposite the main town. The establishment of this factory led to constant friction between the Abo people and the Company. The first open conflict arose in 1862 when the factory was looted by the people. This led to the bombardment of the town by H.M.S. *Espoir* in the same year and peace was made by another treaty signed in October of 1863.[14] Abo's wealth derived in considerable measure from the tolls it levied on trade passing between the coastal Delta and the Lower Niger but the British vessels paid no tolls and were under the protection of the British Navy. In addition the trading monopoly which the National Africa Company was later able to establish in this area seriously interfered with their trade on the Lower Niger. Matters came to a head in 1883 with the bombardment of Abo by H.M.S. *Stirling*, *Elector*, and *Flirt*. This time a landing party was put ashore in the town and the people of Abo were finally defeated.[15] Abo people love to tell this story, and I was shown round the places that had been struck by cannon shot and was told how they were able to resist the attack. They do not think that they were defeated and regard this as a myth. This was followed in 1884 by treaties signed with the National Africa Company and with the British Consul on 5th November 1884. Both treaties were similar to those made with the king and chiefs of Onitsha.[16]

These treaties led eventually to a peaceful settlement of the conflicts between the two parties, and successive obis—Imegwu, Ossai II, and Oputa—maintained good relations with the Royal Niger Company and later with the British government when it took over the administration in 1900. Missionary interests were protected and the mango tree planted by Bishop Crowther on his visit in 1841 still stands as a testimony of this contract with the kingdom of Abo, and is preserved by the Abo people in memory of this missionary.

With the establishment of the Royal Niger Company and the British Protectorate peace was established, the slave trade abolished and buccaneering activities along the Niger were brought to an end. Obi Oputa was granted a warrant in 1912, and later became the sole authority of the division named after Abo, receiving at that time an annual stipend of three hundred and twenty pounds from the British administration.[17]

OGUTA

Ugwuta (Oguta), the founder of this community, was the son of Ekenyi and Ameshi. He had a brother called Inyi. They were all settled at Benin, but because of the Asigie conflict referred to in the Onitsha tradition, Ekenyi, Ugwunta and Inyi left at the same time, according to Oguta traditions, as the Abo and Onitsha groups.

Ekenyi and his children first settled beside Igala people on the bank of the Niger. Their chief occupation was fishing and canoe-building, and they also engaged in weaving, farming and trading with the neighbouring towns on the Niger. In their government they followed the idea of the monarchy at Benin, and elected a king from among the sons of Ogwuma, one of the sons of Ugwuta. The king and his titled officials (Olilinzele) and the elders of the villages constituted the council of the town. This king, according to them, continued to foster the prestige of Oguta among the surrounding towns of Igala, Ase, Illah and Onono. Trouble arose, however, when one of the Ogwuma kings betrayed the trust vested in him by the Abo and Igala people, who were at war and wanted him to arbitrate. He accepted gifts from both states, but did nothing. Both, therefore, turned on Oguta, and the people decided to flee for safety.

First, Inyi and his people stopped and founded the town of Inyi (Oguta and Inyi people form a dispersed clan unit—the Ameshi clan). The Oguta king and his people continued their migration following the Niger south and halted at Ase Isukwa where, according to them, they fought and defeated Abo, and to avoid further conflict moved from there to Odugiri. They encountered Akiri Agidi and after this they moved downwards to Iberu and there they fought with the Egbema people. They then moved on to Ogwu where they fought and dispersed these people. Entering the Ulashi river, they continued on, and stopped at Opodo Akpurekwe.

The final episode in their migration occurred here. A man called Eneke Okitutu, son of Amam, a great fisherman, came whilst fishing to Oguta lake at the confluence of the Njaba and Ulashi rivers. He took the course leading into the lake, and at a distance he saw smoke which indicated human habitation. On going ashore he met with the Obutu people who lived at the northern end of the lake. After making friends with their head, Ogini, Eneke crossed to the present Oguta south of Umuamam, the former residence of the king of Awa whose people occupied the land. He went to the Awa market and traded his fish for food. On his return he reported what he had seen.

On the second and third trips he concluded a peace pact with the king of Awa, first making sure that he won the friendship of Obutu, and of the Obeagwa and Amozua people who were there with the Awa people. It was agreed that Eneke should settle with his people, and that none should molest the other.

But the pact was not honoured by the Oguta people, for when they arrived, each village was in its canoes and the military leaders were playing war dances (ekele). The sight of so many warriors frightened the Awa people. They fled, and their king was killed and buried on the spot where his throne (ukpo) was erected. Amam

c

occupied the palace with his people (Umuamam) and the people of the other wards as they landed took their present locations. The two brother lineages Umu-Dei and Umu-Osu lived close to Umu-Amam, the younger brother Dei occupying a site in the centre. This was also the pattern of the Eke and Alibo brother lineages. Odogwu Akpo, the friend of Amam, occupied a site close to him, and the Ngegwu, who were great fighters, were located at the extreme eastern end in order to guard the town from any attack by land.

Oguta expanded down the Ulashi River and its tributaries as far as the town of Umuanya on the Niger, occupying large areas of land which they developed as their farming settlements (Ubi).

In 1885 the Oguta Lake was discovered by the Royal Niger Company during its search for an inland port that could be used as a base for the palm-oil produce of the interior. This placed the Company in an advantageous position as it was determined to prevent its rival, the Liverpool Company, from gaining control of the interior trade. The Royal Niger Company also made treaties to exclude from the oil markets around Oguta lake the Delta traders from Brass (Nembe) and New Calabar (Kalabari).[18] Oguta was drawn into British politics and the issue about the lake and its trade was discussed in the Parliamentary Committee of the House of Commons which settled the dispute between the two rival Companies. From then onwards the kingdom of Oguta was known to the outside world. Oguta, like other Niger kingdoms, came under the administrative control of the Royal Niger Company and despite the conflict which led to the bombardment of the town in 1891,[19] it eventually settled down to the new situation and enjoyed the benefits of trade and commerce that brought prosperity to the population and made it one of the richest towns in Eastern Nigeria.

By 1930–31, the Kalabari and other Delta people, hitherto excluded by the Company, acquired a permanent settlement known as Kalabari town, on the south side of the lake, where various Companies built their trading stations, and where the Hausa, Nupe and Ogbaru Niger Ibos congregated into a new township. Like Onitsha and Abo, Oguta people avoided the encroachment of these migrants into their own traditional centres, where they continued to carry on their traditional way of life.

Under colonial rule Oguta, together with the other village groups adjacent to the lake, became organised as a Native Authority area with the Oguta township as its administrative headquarters. Under the local government reorganisation of 1955 this area became a district or county council, but separated from Oguta native town which became an urban district council.

OSOMARI

According to tradition the eight groups of Ika, Iteku, Inyamam, Inoma, Uje, Odekpe, Oko, and Osomari originally lived in a part of Idah, the capital of Igala kingdom. According to their traditions, they migrated because they were unable to pay their annual tribute to the king of Idah (the Ata), and the 'official' tax-collector had decided to take drastic measures against them. Each group, headed by its leader, stopped in the course of their downward journey along the Niger and founded the community which today bears his name. The first five of the above were the first to stop, while the three brother lineages, Odekpe, Oko and Osomari, continued farther down the Niger. Then Odekpe stopped and founded the town Odekpe; then Oko stopped while the Osomari people continued till they arrived and camped on a sand-bank which forms part of their present site.

The leaders of the three divisions of Osomari, the brothers Isiolu, Umuonyiogwu, and Ugolo, crossed to the mainland and met Ndam and Umuchi people who were already settled there. They declared their intention to come and live with them, but the Ndam leaders agreed only on condition that they should destroy both their sheep and their twins, because both were taboo for the Ndam. The Osomari people did so, and when eventually they landed, the Ndam removed and settled at Okporodum, leaving the Umuchi to take over the right of the priestship of the land deity (ani). Umuoga later arrived from Igala and these three groups—Ndam, Umuchi and Umuoga—became attached to the three Osomari descent groups of Ugolo, Umuonyiogwu and Isiolu.

The fame of Osomari extended along the Niger and its history lives in the legends of the heroic activities of its various kings (Atamanya). Osomari was considered the most important and most powerful of the Igala colonies and traded not only with the Isuama Ibo of the hinterland, but with Igala in the north, and the Abos, and Itepus (Brass men) in the south.

The Isuama Ibo occupied mainly what is now known as Orlu Division, and had a long commercial connection with Osomari through Uli and Oguta. Osomari was an important river port and goods from the interior Ibo land and from the north, such as elephant tusks, mats, and potash, were sold in exchange for palm-oil and other forest products. The connection and trade contact between Oguta and Osomari is emphasised in the trading traditions of both towns. When Abo cut off Osomari from contact with the Delta States, Osomari increased her trade with the Ibos in the hinterland, and with Oguta which was the most prosperous centre due to her favourable situation on the mouth of the Ulashi and Njaba rivers. By using the Ulashi they were able to continue their trade with the Delta States, and thus avoid the heavy tolls which Abo levied on the routes under her control.

Constant conflicts between the Abo and Osomari states led to an open warfare, in which Osomari claims to have triumphed and the two powers became the lords of the Niger. Hence arose the saying "Abo welu! Osomari welu! ani nta aha ubu", which means, "When Abo and Osomari have made their choice, the lesser towns struggle for what is left."[20]

Like the other Niger kingdoms, Osomari was an important centre for Europeans and was one of the trading posts opened up by the Macgregor Laird expedition. In 1870 Crowther described the site of the town, the commercial life of the people, and the composition of the king's council which was made up of the representatives of the nine ebos of Osomari. According to him, "its population is about six thousand divided into nine distinct villages or families in each of which there is a chief or elder viz. 1, Umu'golo is the seat of the King, Anyafuru alias Okaku, his title".[21] (This is the praise name and title of the Atamanya, the king of Osomari.)

In 1877, "the King Ocarku Okuorisha", and eight of the senior Ndichie Ume—"Odogu Abi, Anabri Ayinisere, Sanza Nouri, Isaba Aje, Odagi Oodogo, Isama G. Bemina, Osai Aje and Isama Ague" signed a treaty of trade and friendship with representatives of Queen Victoria, namely Captain J. C. Purvis, David Hopkins, the Consul, and others.[22]

The opening up of Oguta Lake affected the commercial importance of Osomari, for the palm-oil produce carried to Osomari became diverted to Oguta, and, with the aid of the river steamers, the trading companies were able to convey the produce through the Ulashi to the Delta port of Abonnema, and, by the end of the century, most trade was diverted through Onitsha and Oguta, though Osomari was made the administrative centre for the towns around her.

CONCLUSION

We are not concerned here with determining the historical accuracy of these myths. For our purpose they represent a significant social reality, namely a mythical 'charter' for the kingdoms to which they refer. Widespread knowledge of them constitutes a common foundation for the cultural similarities on which the political unity of the community depends. Except in the case of Onitsha, all agree that on leaving their respective places of origin, the communities concerned adopted the way of life of the riverain area. They indicate that these people traded amongst themselves and continued to maintain contact with each other and with the riverain districts of the Igala kingdom.

Because of their geographical position along the Niger they shared one common experience—the intrusion of European civilization. Between 1841 and 1885 none of them escaped treaties with the British nor open conflict with them, as the series of bombardments show.

When eventually they began to witness the dawn of a new era, their political institutions as time went on became increasingly affected by the forces of change. The extent to which some of their institutions, in particular those relating to the kingship, have changed over these years (1841–1964) are discussed in Chapters 9 and 10. But my concern is not only to describe their political and economic history but also to analyse and interpret the actual operations of their government as they appear both to those involved and to the anthropological observer.

NOTES

1 This is an approximate figure; the 1953 census gives 5.1 million, the 1963 over 9 million.
2 G. I. Jones, 'Ibo Land Tenure', *Africa*, Vol. XIX, 1949, p. 313.
3 At Onicha Olona, I was shown the shrine of Oreze (Ihu Oreze) which is an important ritual spot, and alongside this is the shrine of his senior servant. According to them, every Obi of Onitsha Mili came to this spot to offer sacrifice after installation and to take some of the white chalk (nzu) deposited in front of this shrine. The spot remains a sacred grove.
4 There are various versions of this ufie legend. See C. K. Meek, 1937, p. 12.
5 L. Hertslet, *Treaties*, Vol. XIII, p. 18.
6 Ibid., Vol. XIV, pp. 49–51.
7 Foreign Office, Slave Trade No. 2 (1880), Vol. LXIX, Correspondence Relating to the Bombardment of Onitsha. Presented to both Houses of Parliament by Command of Her Majesty's Government, London, 1880, p. 692.
8 L. Hertslet, *Treaties,* Vol. XVII, p. 162.
9 J. E. Flint, 1960, p. 139.
10 I. Nzimiro, 1965.
11 Allen and Thomson, 1848, Vol. I, pp. 239–40.
12 Ibid., p. 251.
13 L. Hertslet, *Treaties*, Vol. VII, pp. 22–26, and Allen and Thomson, 1848, Vol. I, pp. 253–60.
14 L. Hertslet, *Treaties*, Vol. XIII, pp. 19–20.
15 G. B. Williams, *Report*.
16 L. Hertslet, *Treaties*, Vol. XVII, pp. 178–9.

17   G. B. Williams, *Report*.
18   J. E. Flint, 1960, p. 188.
19   Lt.-Col. A. F. Mockler-Ferryman, London, 1892, p. 19. A detailed
     account of this bombardment is given in Nzimiro, 1963, Chapter 1.
20   R. N. Olisa, *Notes*.
21   Bishop Crowther, *Church Missionary Record*, Vol. XV, London 1870,
     p. 118.
22   L. Hertslet, *Treatise*, Vol. XIV, pp. 47–49. A further treaty was signed
     with the National African Company on 16th October 1884, and with
     the British Government on 9th November 1884. Hertslet, *Treatise*,
     Vol. XVII, p. 183.

Chapter 2   Social Organisation

SOCIAL STRUCTURE

In this and the three succeeding chapters we are concerned with
the social and political structure of these four communities and
with their ranking system.

A typical Ibo community, though it is often referred to as a
town, actually consists of a federation of dispersed villages (obodo
or ikoporo). These riverain communities however follow the Bini
and Yoruba residential pattern and live in compact towns which
subdivide into quarters (ebo) and these into wards (ogbe) which,
like other Ibo communities, are also patrilineages. An ogbe divides
into compounds (nkpu uno) which contain the members of an
extended family or minimal lineage.

In addition to these territorial and kinship groupings the people
of a Niger Ibo town are also organised on a basis of age and sex
into male and female age sets, the women have their system of
councils and a general assembly which parallels that of the men,
and there are a number of voluntary associations membership in
which is sought by the socially and politically ambitious.

There is also a status system which classifies people into freemen
(nwadiani) and slaves, the freemen being further distinguished between nwadiani who belong to the dominant immigrant group, and
those who are of autochthonous or stranger origin. The system
enables wealthier nwadiani of any category to acquire superior
social status through membership of title associations and through
the acquisition of chiefly political offices (Ndichie, Olinzele). We
shall refer to the last category as state officials or collectively as
the political elite.

Each state has a king called 'Obi' in Onitsha, Abo and Oguta,
and 'Atamanya' in Osomari. The office is an acquired one open
to any male agnate in either a royal clan (Onitsha and Abo) or a
royal maximal lineage (ebo in the case of Osomari, ogbe in the
case of Oguta), who is of good character and who can afford to
join particular title societies and to pay the required fees and
expenses of the installation ceremonies.

TERRITORIAL AND KINSHIP ORGANISATION

In these four states the ebo are grouped together into two primary
divisions except in the case of Osomari which has three such

21

divisions. In Oguta there are no ebo and the twenty-seven ogbe are grouped directly into two primary divisions. Ebo and ogbe are distinct residential units and so are the primary divisions except in the case of Abo where members of the two divisions are distributed between all the ogbe.

An ogbe, and in some cases an ebo, is also a corporate patri-lineage (umunna or umunne). The rule of exogamy defines such descent and a maximal lineage is the largest exogamous descent group. In some cases a maximal lineage will consist of most of the members of an ebo (the others being slaves, strangers and other unrelated elements incorporated into the ebo). At the other extreme are lineages which because of internal disputes have broken away, have installed their own ancestral shrines, and because of this have come to be accepted as separate exogamous groups and therefore as maximal lineages.

The corporate nature of all ebo and ogbe is expressed in most social contexts and most notably in political and ritual matters. Membership is primarily defined in terms of agnatic descent but is also determined by common residence. For the population of most of these Niger Ibo communities contains in addition to the dominant and immigrant group (which traces its origin to Benin or Idah), a considerable number of people of slave, stranger or autochthonous descent. Slaves are a part of their master's or former master's lineage, strangers and original inhabitants are either incor-porated as small lineages into the ogbe of the dominant element, or, if they are sufficiently numerous and cohesive they may form separate ogbe or, in the case of Osomari, separate ebo.

The smallest residential unit is the compound (nkpu uno) which consists of a number of rooms joined together and facing inward onto a cloister-like veranda which runs around a quadrangular open space. The back wall of these rooms forms the wall of the compound and is unbroken except for an entrance doorway. Facing this entrance is a raised seat of clay, the ukpo (throne) of the head of the compound, and before this ukpo are places where the ancestral cults are displayed when the lineage members meet to offer sacrifices. The rooms are occupied by the various people living in the compound and, in the case of Abo, Oguta and Osomari, these consist of a single extended family (minimal lineage) or of a number of the extended families (a minor lineage). At Onitsha each family has its own compound, and a group of such compounds, whose members constitute an extended family, will be surrounded by a large wall. Inside this enclosure will be a number of compounds opening into one another, each occupied by a wife, her family and other persons attached to her household.

Within each ogbe is a centrally situated house (oke uno) which is either a compound or a section of a compound and which represents the original residence of the founder of the ogbe. All the agnatic members of the lineage go there for lineage meetings. When a man becomes the head of the lineage (Okpala) he normally moves to this house. In cases where he does not, the residence of the Okpala, wherever it may be situated, becomes the meeting place for all political, ritual and social assemblies of the lineage. There may be a number of such oke uno in one ogbe, one for each of its major lineages. Where several ogbe combine and form a single maximal lineage which is also an ebo, as in Onitsha, Abo and Osomari, the oldest male in the ebo becomes the head of this lineage and all meetings are held at his house.

The compounds of an ogbe are built close together and the ogbe themselves are only separated from each other by open clearings (ilo), used as meeting places at Onitsha, or by a few trees. Because of shortage of land in some of these towns it is not always possible for descent and locality to coincide. It often happens that a particular maximal lineage may have some of its members resident in the territory of another ogbe. But the members so located attend meetings of their own maximal lineage held at the residence of the okpala of the lineage.

RANK AND STATUS

The status system of these Niger Ibo towns can be considered under five headings—free-born (nwadiani), slave (ohu), royal descent, wealth and membership of prestige associations (title societies), and the political elite. The first three are ascribed statuses; the fourth and fifth are acquired.

NWADIANI (FREE-BORN)

A citizen (nwadiani) is a free-born person who is a full member of the community by reason of his birth.

Three categories of persons make up this class. In the first is the free-born person who is able to trace his descent from the founder of a lineage which is a segment of a maximal lineage descended from a founder of the community. In the second are the onoru, persons whose ancestors came from other places to settle with and become attached to the founders of the community. Because of their free-born status in their place of origin, their descendants are accepted as full members of the ward, they observe its rules of exogamy and are associated with its cults and ritual activities.

In the third category are the descendants of the autochthonous groups resident in the area before the founders of the state arrived and incorporated by them into the structure of the community which they established. One of their special roles is to provide the priest, Eze Ani, of the land deity (ani). In most of these states they maintain a separate corporate identity as wards or subdivisions of wards and take part in all cultural and ritual activities except those which are specifically associated with the immigrant groups and which they are believed to have brought with them from their place of origin.

All three categories participate in the age organisation and in the membership of the title and other societies. The first category tends to be the dominant group and because of its numbers and superior position, it has incorporated any existing autochthonous groups and later arrivals into its community. The term 'nwadiani' is applied to these three categories of people who together constitute a class of free-born persons.

At Onitsha, in addition to the dominant Chima group, there is the autochthonous group of Ndi Mgbelekeke whose lineage head is the Ezeani (priest of the earth deity). There are other attached lineages most of whom were later migrants from Igala, Egbema, Obamkpa and Obio (of the Umuezechima clan of Western Ibo), and who form the bulk of the Ugwunaobamkpa residential and administrative division. At Abo, there is the migrant Benin group called Umudei, who came from Benin and founded Abo, the attached lineages collectively called Ndichie who live with them in the same ebo and include the small autochthonous group of Inwele who are attached to the Umuossai ebo. At Oguta, there are the autochthonous ogbe of Obeagwa, Obutu and Amozua, the ogbe whose founders derive from Oguta and who migrated and founded the present town, and other ogbe whose founders arrived later. The migrant group which founded Osomari incorporated the two autochthonous groups of Ndam and Umuchi and the later migrant group of Umuoga into their political system. They have allowed them to develop their own titles separately and to function as separate but subordinate political units (ebo).

The rest of the community constitute the servile class (ohu, oru, or osu), and this class division is perpetuated by a rule of a class endogamy: ohu may not marry nwadiani.

The rights and privileges of nwadiani are many. Firstly, they may intermarry among themselves and with free-born people in other towns. This intermarriage has united the three categories together in a closely knit web of kinship which has given them a strong sense of corporate solidarity. Secondly, a citizen can become the Okpala of a ward or quarter. This however does not apply in all the communities. At Osomari, an attached lineage cannot supply an Okpala of an ebo. There, when a member of an attached lineage becomes the oldest man in his ebo and thus eligible for the office, he is passed over in favour of the oldest man amongst the true descendants of the founder of the ebo. They hold that the ancestors will not accept a sacrifice made by a person who is not a true agnate. Thirdly, political offices can only be held by nwadiani. At Onitsha such offices are the gift of the king; elsewhere there are various limitations which will be discussed later. Fourthly, nwadiani alone can inherit and transfer certain types of property to their heirs. Fifthly, they have the right to participate in the ritual activities of the state and of their lineages. They can offer sacrifices to all types of shrines and particularly to the deities of the ancestors of a lineage. Certain superior ritual offices are exclusive to persons of this class. At Oguta the ritual offices of osere and ezechioha must be held by a nwadiani of the ward in which this office is hereditary. Certain ritual offices however which are considered dangerous to a true agnatic descendant can be held by a member of the servile class or of an attached lineage.

This dichotomy between citizenship (nwadiani) and non-citizenship (ohu and today, foreigners) underlies the whole social framework in these societies.

OHU (SLAVE AND SLAVE-BORN)

The origin of the servile class in these states is twofold. They were either persons who were captured in war or they were acquired by purchase. Persons who committed crimes considered by their kinsmen as an abomination (alu) were sold out of the community. In both circumstances such individuals were without kin and became kin-less. They lacked the support of a powerful group of kinsmen. This servile class (ohu or osu) constituted a numerically significant class in these Niger kingdoms. According to Trotter "the number of domestic slaves is very large, in some towns being almost equal to the free inhabitants; they are well treated, and many of them become free . . .".[1]

In most of these kingdoms slaves were renamed after they had been bought. It was a mark of wealth to purchase a slave and a person's wealth was measured in terms of the number of his slaves. Buying a slave was equated with performing an Inyama title. It indicated that the owner was a wealthy person. Wealthy chiefs used to buy many slaves in addition to those they acquired as captives during wars with neighbouring states. The concept of slavery in these states was akin to that of Aristotle. The slave was "an instrument of life" and a living possession.[2] A slave could be called 'anu ofia' (wild animal, beast of the forest), which was considered offensive when applied to a nwadiani. Today it is considered an insult when applied to anybody. They were regarded as economic commodities and were used by their masters for domestic services in the home and on the farm. They could work on their own and they traded and engaged in fishing but the proceeds from their labours could be claimed by their masters as a slave owner had the right to whatever his slave earned. The master could give him back what he considered to be sufficient for him.

The status and the rights of slaves and the amount of discrimination against them varied in the different states. In all states a second generation slave, that is a slave born in the state (amulu na uno) whose umbilical cord (ichi) was buried in a local house, was of higher rank than one who came from elsewhere. Through his parents he was a member of a group of ohu kinsfolk and a member of his father's (and his master's) lineage. A slave could also purchase another slave and give him to his master. This would free him from the obligations of domestic and farm labour which would now be performed by the slave he had purchased. He still remained however in the servile class but at least he had acquired freedom from working for a master and could earn and accumulate wealth which could be inherited by his sons and other heirs. In Abo, however, where ideas from the Delta states had penetrated, attitudes towards slaves were more liberal. A slave could obtain his freedom though he was still dependent on his former master for the land he used, and still had to pay an annual tribute of yams and livestock. As Trotter observed in 1848, "those at Aboh are liberated when they build proper dwellings, but they continue to pay a tax of forty yams each season, and in a small tithe of their goats, fowls etc".[3] According to Obi, slaves were allowed to establish their own households and to buy slaves of their own and thereby achieve the status and title of Ikwo Aka Inyama (the head of Inyama).[4]. It will be remembered that Inyama was the title which the master had acquired when he first bought the slave.

Marriage served to perpetuate the ohu status. At Oguta, Osomari, Onitsha, and originally at Abo, the distinction between free-born and slave was maintained by class endogamy. An ohu could only marry an ohu. This discrimination was carried further at Osomari where the ohu class had their exclusive residential quarters (ebo) in each division. This gave the servile quarter a sense of corporate solidarity in opposition to the free-born quarters. Elsewhere they formed part of the wards of their former masters and participated with the free-born members in their ordinary social and ritual activities. For example, they had to observe the rules of ward exogamy. They could not marry an ohu who was a member of their own ward. Through this intermarriage between members of different ogbe and ebo, the ohu of a community have developed a web of kinship which gives them a feeling of solidarity similar to that which characterises the nwadiani. Abo, however, permitted intermarriage between ohu and nwadiani, and children born of such mixed marriages had the status of nwadiani. In the other states the children of an ohu parent were always ohu. Should the father be a citizen and the mother an ohu, the child, despite the patrilineal bias of the society, would take the name and social rank of the mother's father as no legal marriage had taken place. With the increase in intermarriage between the two classes the stigma of being a member of the servile class is disappearing at Abo, though it still remains in the other three states.

In none of these states could a member of the servile class become the head (okpala) of his (that is, of his master's) lineage even though he became the oldest man in it. Since it was impossible for a slave to trace his genealogy to the ancestor of the lineage he could never serve as his representative. Slaves were also barred from various regalia. At Oguta they might not wear esuru (coral beads). Their mortuary ceremonies both here and in the other states were less elaborate and lesser animals were used for the funeral sacrifices. The ibom gong, used to announce the death of a nwadiani, could not be used in the case of a slave. At Osomari slaves might not dance the royal dance and in pre-colonial days a slave could be beheaded on the spot if he so much as moved his head in rhythm when the elegede (royal dance) was played.

Missionary reports covering the period from 1857 to the end of that century are filled with tales about the use of slaves in the funeral rites of the kings.

Slaves became members of age sets and of associations which had social rather than political functions, but they could not become holders of offices in them. At Onitsha they could not belong to the Ozo title society and thus were debarred from membership of the political elite. At Abo they could take Olilinzele titles but only those of the lower grade of Ndichie titles. At Oguta they could take the Ikwa Muo title but could not take an Olilinzele or kingly title and as they could not become okpala they were thus unable to become members of the political elite. At Osomari they could not take Olinzele, Agama or Inyakpa titles.

In all the states slaves were used by war chiefs as fighting men and as subordinate military leaders. Their duties were to fight for their masters and some of these war chiefs, as already mentioned, established settlements of their slaves to guard strategic positions along the rivers in places where they owned land. In Onitsha these slaves fought on land, and in the other states they manned the war canoes of their masters.

Except in the case of Osomari, ohu and nwadiani lived together in the various ogbe and ebo, and ohu held positions of trust in the lineages of their masters. In Osomari, however, they were excluded from the residential area of the nwadiani and in each division they lived in their own ebo.

The status of the slaves began to change when the missionaries introduced their schools and churches. The Obi and Ndichie at Onitsha did not support the missionary appeal that their sons should be sent to school; instead, these chiefs readily sent their slaves to the missionaries. This also occurred in Abo and Osomari and some other Niger kingdoms. Most of the slaves were taught to read and write and some were given further education and became the first local teachers, catechists and missionary workers. They in turn sent their sons to school and these later became employed in mercantile firms and in the colonial administration.

With the increasing mobility of labour and the income accruing from the new Nigerian labour market, the second generation of this servile class has risen well above the social and economic position of their fathers and today much but by no means all of the former social stigmas have been dispersed.

As education developed and eventually became the index of superior social status, many of the servile class who had already acquired it were able to move up the educational ladder to participate fully in the modern "open" and achievement oriented society of Nigeria, and rise to the top to occupy responsible posts in the new political and administrative institutions of the country. Paradoxically, however, discrimination still continued against them in their own communities. Wealthier and better educated ohu were able to organise their fellows and demand the removal of some of these discriminations, for example the rules prohibiting them from taking titles. At Osomari, the Osomari Improvement Society was able to recall some members of the servile class who had left the town in protest against the way they were treated. Those who returned made a new settlement, Obiofu. They now make their own titles with title names similar to those of the citizen class.

In 1956, the Eastern Regional Government passed a law prohibiting the use of the words "osu" or "oru" to describe any member of their class; it also allowed them full political rights as citizens in their communities.[5]

The rights of nwadiani prescribed for them in this bill still remain unenforced and the status of ohu persists. The bar on marriage with nwadiani still continues to be observed, and even though ohu now participate in the new organisations formed by the educated elite in these communities and hold high office in them, they are still barred from holding offices in the traditional political system and are not allowed to take those titles associated with these offices.

ROYAL DESCENT

We turn now to another type of social differentiation. In these states, as pointed out in earlier chapters, there are particular clans and lineages from which the kings are selected. They constitute the royal descendants and since any one of their male members may be king, they constitute a noble class. They are distinguished from the other lineages by their special status, and by the roles and privileges which some of their members enjoy in the state.

In the case of Onitsha and Abo, they trace their descent to a kingly origin (Benin). The history of Onitsha and Abo is basically the history of the foundation of each kingdom by their ancestral fathers who were the rulers of the states which they formed. They are therefore known in Onitsha as Umueze, that is, descendants of a king. Abo differs slightly by calling the descendants of Obi Ogweze, its founder, Umudei (collectively; singular—Nwa dei). The princes and princesses bear the praise names of 'Omodi' and 'Nwakpe' respectively, in order to distinguish them from the non-royal division which is referred to as Ndichie.

At Onitsha the royal clan of Umuezechima comprises the divisions shown in the diagrams in chapter three. The autochthonous and other non-royal lineages in this division have no claim to royalty and they are prohibited from taking the Obi title. They and the non-royal division of Ugwuna Obamkpa are alike in this, though administratively, these non-royal lineages are regarded as part of Umuezechima. At Oguta and Osomari the privileges of royalty are attached to a single ward or ebo, though two other wards at Oguta have previously enjoyed this right to provide an Obi.

The privileges attached to royal status are many and various, for example kings are buried with special royal dances. At Oguta the death of a member of the royal lineage is announced by the playing of the royal drum, opi. At Abo, as will be explained in Chapter three, the titles of the Olinzele of the royal class are distinct from those of the non-royal wards and the same applies to Osomari.

Oguta on the other hand excludes royals from taking any Olilinzele titles. At Onitsha royals and commoners are equally eligible for all titles except that of Obi.

This superior status is explained and validated in their myths of the origin of the kingship. At Onitsha the Umu-ezechima clan say that their founder Oreze became king because he was astute enough to preserve the insignia of kingship, the royal drum, ufie, as related in Chapter one. At Abo, the triumph of Ogweze in defeating his brother Ugbo in the contest for the throne is regarded as an historical event, and validates the political power of the ruling 'aristocracy'.

The Oguta royal lineages also associate the right to the throne with the heroic feats of their particular royal ancestors. However, Oguta reserves the right of the people to determine which ward may provide the Obi. At Osomari the royals claim the right to rule because of the singular loyalty of their father to the founder of the kingdom, who because of this bequeathed the ofo eze (the symbol of his authority) to him and asked him to rule. As Richards has pointed out, these mythical charters of kingship are preserved by the royal lineages. They remember and reinterpret the sequences of real or postulated events.[6] The senior royal relatives provide an informal council which the Obi can consult before making decisions. At Onitsha these Ulogoeze (the Obi's close agnates) are consulted by him whenever he wishes to award titles or to make a decision that may affect the royal lineage or clan or the officials of the state.

At Abo the Obi keeps in contact with his subjects through his sons and close agnates who act as intermediaries. At Oguta the Obi cannot be seen by any visitor without some of his agnates being present. He chooses from amongst them some who can always be at hand for private advice and consultation. The same is the case in Osomari, and in this state a special official, the Odoje Ase, is appointed from amongst the Atamanya's closest agnates to advise him and to act for him in the performance of routine rituals and other duties. At Abo, Oguta, and Osomari, where the Obis perform certain daily rituals, the close agnates assist in maintaining the continuity of these ritual acts and to see that they are properly performed.

It is this intimate connection of the royal agnates with the palace that enables them to know what occurs during each reign and to preserve the history of each dynasty. The history is retold during royal festivals when princesses recite the praises of their king. They retell the stories and epics of their ancestors. At Oguta the eldest daughter of the Obi is given the privilege of performing a special dance which is otherwise exclusive to the Obi and his Olilinzele.

The apparent harmony between the king and his close agnates is due to the fact that he is elected by them and he needs their support to continue in office. Although there may be a number of competitors for the throne, once a king is elected, all are bound to support him and to assist in promoting the duties of his office so as to maintain not only the unity of the royal lineage, but also the continuity of the office.

The question arises of how the royal class avoids an open conflict with the non-royal class. Royal agnates realise that they must preserve the royalty, for the overthrow of an Obi might affect the position they hold in the state. In their effort to preserve the royal traditions, they are exposed to the temptation of behaving as if the king represents their interests alone. As this behaviour can arouse apprehension among the community, it creates a situation of conflict. The ability of the royal lineages to maintain their position depends on a number of factors which may be enumerated below.

Numerical strength. In Onitsha and Abo the number of people in the royal group is as large as those in the non-royal. In both states the royal clan consists of a number of large corporate lineages which, when they act together, are powerful enough to disregard the interests of the non-royal groups. In Onitsha the royal clan was at one time so strong that it could monopolise the office of Iyase, which traditionally should have been filled by a member of the non-royal division. However, in both states this extreme size can be more of a disadvantage than an advantage, for the competition to control the office of Obi splits the royal division up into competing segments, each of which looks for support in the non-royal division. This is particularly the case in periods of succession when each royal segment puts forward its own candidate.

At Oguta and Osomari the royal wards are numerically small. In Oguta only one ward has been recognised as the royal ward at any one time in its history. Unless it retains the support of a substantial number of the other twenty-six it stands the risk of being replaced by another ward. The royal ward of Ogolo in Osomari is in the same position, and unless it retains the support of the other two political divisions and of the other two ebo in its own division there is nothing to prevent the heads of one or both of these divisions usurping the kingship.

Affinal ties (ogo). The second factor is the way in which affinal ties with non-royals are exploited by kings and their relatives. Kings marry many wives, and have the right to demand in marriage any

D

girl they may wish. They can therefore select wives from those lineages with powerful leaders. By such affinal ties a king wins the support of such ogo (in-laws) amongst the non-royal groups. Influential members of the royal clan also adopt the same method, so that through the web of kinship ties brought about by these marriages the royal ward can build up support for itself in the non-royal groups. Obi Ossai of Abo is said to have married over a hundred wives[7] and in this way through affinal and cognatic ties he spread his influence among the territories that were connected with him. Oguta and Osomari, whose royal lineages are numerically weak, have made considerable use of marriage connections to strengthen their position.

Umuadaeze (daughters of the royal lineages). Daughters of the royal lineages are also used for diplomatic purposes. Since marriage does not make a woman lose her agnatic tie, royal daughters maintain their royal connections throughout their married life. In any time of crisis they support their agnates, informing them about the attitudes and behaviour of their husbands' relatives, and warning them of any plot against the throne. During the 1958–64 crisis at Oguta, in which twenty-six wards opposed the royal ward, the latter was able to survive the long period of social ostracism on account of the information which was constantly communicated by royal daughters married into these non-royal wards. Oguta people finally insisted that these 'princess' wives should be made to swear on oath not to divulge information to their agnates. Some of the women refused and returned to the royal ward rather than remain in their place of marriage.

Protection of the royal prerogatives. The royal prerogatives define and set apart the king from his subjects. The usurpation of any one of them by a subject is a threat to the security of the office and it is the duty of royal relatives in all these states to defend them and to prevent their erosion. An example of how this may occur can be taken from Oguta. It is forbidden for anyone to wear any dress which is red in colour, for red robes are part of the regalia of kingship and can only be worn by the Obi, the Iyase, the Ezeukwu, the Ndanike and the Ezekoro. On one occasion a certain Okonya Uzoaru from Umunkwocha ward spread red cloths on the veranda of his late father's residence as part of the decorations during the performance of the funeral rites. The members of the royal lineage took objection to this and prosecuted Okonya in the customary court. The court ordered the cloths to be handed over to the royal lineage and burnt by them. Another instance was that of Adigwe

Akpo, of Ngegwu ward. He used the opi drum for the celebration of the funeral ceremony of his late father. By tradition only members of the royal lineage are entitled to perform this dance, so the royal lineage prosecuted Adigwe in the customary court. This happened during the reign of Obi Ohanyere, and it was he who brought the action against Adigwe. The court ordered the drum to be confiscated and destroyed.

A third example was the effort made by the royal lineage to deny one of the kingly officials, the Eze Ukwu, the right to wear his regalia of office and this was brought before a court. The details of this are discussed in Chapter nine, page 194. A fourth example occurred in 1949 when Osere Okereke, a priest of the Ikwa Muo Society, put on a red robe. The royal lineage again brought action in the court against him and obtained judgement in its favour, the court ordering the robe to be burnt.[8]

Membership of title societies. Status in the first three categories was essentially ascribed, depending on the accident of a person's birth and on other factors outside his control. In these two categories superior social status was acquired mainly by the expenditure of wealth, distribution of which in the form of feasts and fees secured for the candidate a superior social position, defined by the award to him of a title which carried with it various prerogatives. In the case of superior titles, these included the performance of specific political or ritual duties. Even in cases where the title was acquired for other than economic reasons (e.g. for military capacity), or was ascribed on the basis of age, as in the case of the Okpala, it was still necessary to distribute wealth to secure public recognition of it. Should the holder of the office be unable to find the money his relatives provided it for him.

In addition to the specific titles awarded to particular persons holding state offices either political or ritual, which are discussed in the succeeding section, there were other titles acquired through membership of an association, a title society. All the full members of the society had the same title and prerogatives and were entitled to an equal share of the fees paid by candidates seeking admission to the society. These fees were normally paid in instalments over a long period. In some title societies there was a division into a number of grades, each with its own title and privileges, and a man who joined the society progressed through them as he completed payment of the fees associated with it to those already in the grade. Other title societies made a distinction between a lesser and a greater title. The former, which cost less, was recognised only within the candidate's own ward or ebo. The latter, which was the full title, was recognised throughout the community. In some states membership of the more important of these title societies was limited to nwadiani (free-born), for example, the Ozo title society in Onitsha, the Igbu society in Oguta, and all title societies at Osomari.

Although the superior status conferred by membership of the society was primarily social, the initiation rituals which accompanied the award of the title, or of the superior grades of the title, sanctified the initiate who was reborn as a new and ritually superior personality. These titles also served as a means test for those seeking the higher political offices of the political elite. A candidate for such offices whether that of Obi, of kingly officials or of Ndichie or Olinzele chiefship must have already achieved membership of the superior title associations of his community. These title societies fall into three main types. The first are those which were associated purely with wealth and with the acquisition of superior social status through its distribution, for example the Ozo title society which has become diffused from the town of Nri (Agu Ukwu) to most of the northern and riverain Ibo. The second, like the Igbu society, originally brought together men who had proved their military capacity by killing an enemy of the state. The third, like the Ikwa Muo society, was concerned with mortuary rituals in which a son performed special obituary rites for his deceased father which made that father a member of a title society in the spirit world, which remained in communication with a counterpart society in the living world. The son became a member of the latter society once he had performed the rites which made his father a member of the spirit world society.

The states of Abo, Oguta and Osomari have developed the Igbu society so that it has now become a wealth society analogous to the Ozo title society at Onitsha. Oguta has also developed the Ikwa Muo society in the same way.[9] Space prevents a study of all these title associations and limits us to the examination of only one, the Igbu society.

The Igbu title society.   In pre-colonial days it was a mark of heroism to acquire the head of an enemy who had been killed or captured in war or as a result of a warlike action such as raiding or ambushing. The head of a slave, that is of someone who had been bought (alive or dead) could not be used for this purpose but only for funeral rituals.

When such killings were abolished a leopard was substituted for a human being in all four states. At Abo and at Osomari this was again modified and all that was required was the leopard's jaw which could be acquired in any manner and which was substituted for the whole leopard. At Oguta a whole leopard was required which had been killed either by the candidate himself or purchased by him from the actual killer. This human head (or leopard substitute) was displayed to the Obi and to members of the society and was eventually buried in a ceremony which culminated in the candidate planting an akpu tree on the grave.

The candidate had to be purified from the shedding of human (or leopard) blood and freed from the ritual danger into which this action had placed him. This ritual was called Igwoju Aka and was accompanied by a period of vigil and seclusion prior to the final ceremony of mmacha (or ipu afia agu). At Abo this seclusion and vigil lasted one night. At Oguta the seclusion lasted twenty-one days and at Osomari from five to seven days.

The insignia of an Igbu title consisted of a sword (mma igbu) which represented the instrument used by the title holder in cutting off the head, a canoe paddle (amala igbu) with a palm frond (omu) tied to it and signifying a safe journey home after the engagement, an eagle's feather, symbol of military superiority and achievement, a human or leopard jaw bone which was tied to the paddle, a red band tied around the head, or worn across the shoulder with a bell attached to it, red being a symbol of bravery.

The cult associated with these rituals was that of Ikenga. Every Igbu man and other men as well had their personal cults of Ikenga, the spirit of good fortune and of a good right arm. All rituals in the ceremonies associated with this title were addressed to the candidate's Ikenga.[10]

The association of this title with the head of the state and with its chiefs emphasised the value attached to war and warlike qualities in these states. The kings and officers of state must all have taken the Igbu title before they could be eligible for the offices.

Apart from Onitsha the Igbu title was developed into a wealth title association, with fees paid to the other members of the society. The highest fees were paid at Oguta and they ranged from £300–£400, excluding the expenses incurred in feasting the members. In Osomari it was linked with a higher title, Agana, for which the candidate paid no fees but had to provide a feast at his own expense. This was after he had been to the Obi who had marked his left and right hands with white clay (nzu) and placed the eagle's feather in the red band around his head. At Abo, the candidate was escorted to the Obi's palace by the members of the Igbu society accompanied by members of the public. The ufie drum was beaten to summon the Obi who appeared in his full regalia and the Igbu title holders of both divisions, Umudei and Ndichie, sat as if in council. The Obi asked the candidate what he had killed and the candidate answered. This was repeated four times.[11] The Obi then took his own sword (mma igbu) and struck the candidate's sword with it four times. The candidate knelt and the Obi put a large cloth (igbo akwa) over the candidate's shoulders and fixed the eagle's feather on his head. For this the Obi received a fee of £6 5s. 0d. and the ufie drummer received 12s.

At Oguta the candidate and his people carried the leopard to the Obi's palace. It was cut up in the palace, the Obi received the claws, teeth and skin, and the meat was shared amongst the members of the state council. At Osomari the title was conferred by state officials, namely the Odogwu of Ugolo, the Ahanza of Isiolu and the Isama of Umuonyiogwu, who were the war chiefs. They tied palm fronds (omu) on the candidate's right arm, and on the second day of the ceremonies they removed them.

At Oguta and Osomari there was a single Igbu title society whose head was called the Okei Igbu (senior man in Igbu) at Oguta and Eze Igbu (head or king of Igbu) at Osomari. At Abo there were separate Igbu societies for each of the four ebo, each with a head known as Odede. These associations combined to form a wider association headed by the Obi which was divided into Umudei and Ndichie as is the state council. In making the Igbu title a candidate had to pay fees to each of the four Ebo associates.

Each Igbu society had its own cult and special rituals associated with it which included an annual sacrifice to it by the members. This was one of the national festivals at which members paraded to the cult, and its centre was called Ekwulu, located in the Umuobi area, and was the place where the omu palm leaves were left after being removed from the candidate's right arm. At Oguta the cult, called Akpuekwensu, was in Umunkwocha ward and an annual sacrifice was made there at the end of the Omelife festival. In Osomari the cult, called Ikenga, was located in the Inwala minor lineage of Isiolu which was the ebo that supplied the Iyase of Osomari. At the annual festival the Odogwu of Osomari, assisted by the Iyase and other superior chiefs, offered sacrifice to the Ikenga of the society.

State officials (the political elite). We can distinguish two categories of people in these states, namely, those involved in the government of the state, and those who submit to this government and are concerned with the protection of their own interests as against the special interests of those entrusted with the government. We can call the second category the commoners and the first the political class or nobility, and we can distinguish a superior category within it, the holders of titled offices of state, as the political elite. The prestige associations referred to in the preceding section are grouped as commoners but they form an intermediate category as most titled offices are restricted to persons who are members of these associations. The titled offices can be further differentiated under the three headings: public, palace and ritual. Public officials are mainly responsible for the performance of legislative, judicial, administrative and military duties. Palace officials are in close and personal contact with the head of the state by reason of the duties which they perform in his palace. Ritual officials are concerned with the ritual well-being of the state and fall into two categories, the Ndi Okpala, who minster to the cult of their lineage ancestors and who because of this preside at lineage council meetings, and the Ndi Nze who are the priests of the tutelary deities of the community. In each of these states law, morality and religion provide sanctions for controlling human conduct which supplement one another and are combined in different ways. Similarly political and ritual functions, though separate, may in some cases be performed by the same official. In any case the gap between them is bridged at the state level by the office of Obi and at the level of the lineage and the ogbe by the office of Okpala. The Obi's person and office is sacred but he is also the political head of the state and the officials associated with his person and his palace have both ritual and secular duties to perform, while the Okpala, the ritual head of the lineage, is also its political head by virtue of the authority of its founder which is vested in his office. The details for each state are summarised in Table A on this page. Some of the palace officials with more menial duties do not rank as political elite and those offices formerly reserved for slaves and eunuchs have been obsolete since the end of the nineteenth century.

TABLE A
STATE OFFICIALS

PUBLIC OFFICIALS	PALACE OFFICIALS	RITUAL OFFICIALS
	ONITSHA	
The six Ndichie Ume chiefs. The Ndichie Okwa chiefs. The Ndichie Okwareze chiefs.	1. The Owelle, a member of the Ndichie Ume, is the head of the royal household. 2. The Okwuba performs domestic duties, and acts as a link between the Obi and the Ndichie.	1. The Ndi Okpala, who are ritual heads of the Ogbe and Ebo. 2. The Eze Udo, the priest of Udo shrine, who officiates during the royal crowning. 3 The Ada, Udo, priestess of Udo, who also officiates with the

PUBLIC OFFICIALS	PALACE OFFICIALS	RITUAL OFFICIALS
	3. The Onyeufie: the servant who plays the royal drum. 4. The Ndi Ugoloma-eunuchs who are in charge of the royal harem and Obi's private apartments. 5. The Ulogo eze—the Obi's closest agnates. 6. The slaves of the palace.	Eze Udo on the occasion of coronation rituals at Udo. 4. The Omodi, the head of Umuase lineage, who is the priest of Ofo Eze and bestows the Ofo on the Obi. 5. The Ezeani, the priest of Ani Deity and head of Mgbelekeke lineage. 6. The priests of the various alushi cults who administer oaths to members of the public.

ABO

PUBLIC OFFICIALS	PALACE OFFICIALS	RITUAL OFFICIALS
1. The Olinzele of all grades of the Umudei and Ndichie divisions. 2. The Odua—he is the regent and can hold courts at his palace. 3. The Akpulosu, the Obi's eldest son.	1. The Owelle, the head of the order. 2. The Olinzele of the Ndichie divisions have special palace duties. 3. The Idibo—ten offices created by the Obi for his wives. They perform the palace duties of the Olinzele if they should refuse to do so. 4. The Ngbalaoto Eze—the eunuchs. 5. The slaves from whom the Obi selects his chief servants. Most of them work for him on the farms and serve as military guards.	1. The Odua, the oldest man of Umudei who acts as the regent and also crowns the Obi. 2. The Otu Ime Ese—the priests who offer sacrifices to the Niger shrine, 'Isu Osimili'. Their head is the Ikogwe who is called Eze Osimili (king of Osimili). 3. The priests of the Alushi who administer oaths to members of the state. Iwele, an autochthonous lineage in Umuossai provide most of these priests of the alushi.

OGUTA

PUBLIC OFFICIALS	PALACE OFFICIALS	RITUAL OFFICIALS
1. The Iyase—head of the military. The Ndanike and the Ezekoro who are also military officials. The Ezeukwu, who crowns the King. 2. The college of	1. The Ogana who is the head of the Olilinzele is an important official of the palace. The Obi can also make use of the services of any of the Olilinzele.	1. The Ndichie, the heads of the wards. They have also ritual functions. 2. The three Osere—heads of the Ndi Ikwa Muo or Agbanta society.

PUBLIC OFFICIALS	PALACE OFFICIALS	RITUAL OFFICIALS
Olilinzele, the officials appointed by the Obi. 3. The college of Ndichie, the heads of the Ogbe.	2. The Odoba Nwanya, the Obi's senior wife who supervises the household and cooks for him. 3. The palace slaves. Three of these, the Nde-Ogbunwonwa Eze, act as Executioners and carry the Royal regalia and the Obi's bell. They also provide his body guard and one acts as chief messenger and announcer of public proclamations. 4. The senior agnates of the lineage whom he consults. They help to run the affairs of the palace.	3. The Ezechioha, the priest of the Chi shrine. 4. The Ndichie Nwanya, senior women, equivalent to Ndichie who assist in offering sacrifices on behalf of the community. 5. The priests of the Alushi who administer oaths to members of the state; these are often the heads of the lineage that own the Alushi cults.

OSOMARI

1. The Oniniogwu (Odobo) and the Iyase, the chief war leaders. 2. The Olinzele made up of the Ndichie Ume and Isugbe of the three political divisions of the state.	1. The Odaje (Asi). He serves the Atamanya daily, speaks on his behalf and organises matters for the king. He offers sacrifice on behalf of the king. 2. The Owelle is the principal household official. He directs the affairs of the household. He mourns on behalf of the king (the king is chief mourner). 3. The slaves—who do most domestic duties for the king. 4. The Asimoha (Akwue) and the Nzenabi (Okia) who serve as advisers at the royal palace.	1. The Ndichie Ume, the heads of the lineages (Ebo). 2. The Eze Ani, the Okpala of Umuchi who is the priest of the Ani shrine. 3. The Odaje Asi performs any priestly function required of the king. 4. The priests of the alushi cults who administer oaths to members of the state. Most of these are owned by the autochthonous lineage of Ndam. 5. The Odobo, who is the Omu of Ugolo. She is the head of the women and acts as priestess to the cult of Ndiem Ohai.

NOTES

1 Allen and Thomson, London, 1848, Vol. I, p. 251.
2 Ernest Baker, 1952, p. 9–11.
3 Allen and Thomson, London, 1848, Vol. I, p. 251.
4 Charles Obi, *A Short History of Abo* (unpublished).
5 *A Selection from the Speeches of Nnamdi Azikiwe*. Cambridge University Press, 1961, pp. 91–94. Speaking on the Second Reading of the Abolition of the Osu System Bill, Dr Azikiwe said that "this Bill seeks to do three things: to abolish the osu system and its allied practices including oru and ohu system, to prescribe punishment for their continued practice, and to remove certain social disabilities caused by the enforcement of the Osu and, its allied system". The Bill defines osu system to "include any social way of living which implies that any person who is deemed to be an osu or oru or ohu is subject to certain prescribed social disability and social stigma". An osu is a slave who is dedicated to a shrine, or deity, of the descendants of such a person. This class of people is not found in the Niger states we are studying.
6 A. I. Richards, 1961, p. 135, Dr Richards' summary review of the position in Africa applies in some respects to our Niger kingdoms.
7 Allen and Thomson, London, 1848, Vol. I, p. 231.
8 H. N. Harcourt, *Report*, p. 48. These examples were cited by Umudei royal ward to impress on the Commissioner that they are the royal lineage and have the exclusive right to defend royalty.
9 Titles in Ibo land are discussed in C. K. Meek, 1937, p. 165; G. I. Jones, *Report*, p. 16. G. T. Basden, 1938, pp. 135–9, discusses titles in Onitsha division.
10 Ikenga is found in almost all Ibo cultural groups. The form in which this is represented differs from place to place. The installation of an Ikenga is an important rite of transition in the life of a man. It marks a new era in his life, the beginning of adulthood, for at this stage of manhood he is considered to be a responsible person in society. He can now own his own portion of land for farming, and undertake other economic activities like fishing and trading. He is 'ripe' to have an Ikenga which is the god of fortune. Ikenga in these areas is a piece of carved wood. The spirit of the cult helps its owner in his undertakings and his success in life pursuits is generally attributed to the action of the Ikenga. When he fails to reward the spirit of this cult object for the good fortune he has received, he is courting trouble, and must therefore sacrifice to his Ikenga.
11 Cf. J. Egharevba, 1947, p. 23. The Oba of Benin represents a house (i.e. domesticated) leopard. If therefore any one kills a leopard, an inquest is held and he is brought before the Oba who asks him the type of leopard he has killed. The person should reply that he has killed a bush (wild) leopard and then he would be honoured by the Oba.

Chapter 3   The Framework
of Government I

ONITSHA

SOCIAL STRUCTURE

Traditionally Onitsha was divided into nine ebo (quarters) which were also maximal lineages. Three of these (Agba, Ute, and Ulutu) have become extinct with any surviving members being absorbed into the remaining six.

The present structure is shown in Table B at the end of the book and consists of twenty-two ogbe (wards). These are grouped for kinship and ritual purposes into six ebo, and these into the two primary divisions, the royal division of Umuezechima and the commoner division of Ugwunaobamkpa. Originally those ogbe which were defined in the structure as belonging to Umuezechima resided in the territory of this division, but expansion of population has led to three of them (numbered 5, 13 and 14 in the diagram) residing in the Ugwunaobamkpa area. This redistribution has led to a reorganisation for administrative purposes into six administrative ebo, each under the administration of one of the six senior chiefs (Ndichie Ume). The arrangement can be tabulated as overleaf. It will be seen that there is no change in the three ebo of Umudei, Umuase and Odoje, that the ritual ebo of Oreze has expanded into two administrative ebo, and that the royal ogbe of Isiokwe (5) to which the three later immigrant ogbe of Ogbeolu (6, 7, 8) were originally attached, has removed to the non-royal division of Ugwunaobamkpa, where it has been joined by the royal ritual ebo of Olosi, and these have combined with the non-royal ebo of Eke na Ube to form a single administrative ebo.

KINSHIP AND DESCENT

All the people of Onitsha are of immigrant descent. The dominant majority claim to be of Benin origin, the children (umu) of King (Eze) Chima and of his son Oreze, and they form the royal clan of Umuezechima. Most of the others claim descent from ancestors who accompanied Eze Chima and Oreze. These Bini migrants were not the first to settle in Onitsha; they were preceded by a small settlement of Igala fishermen whose descendants form the minor lineage of Mgbeleke and who claim that their ancestors ferried the Onitsha people across the Niger to their present home. Their claim to be the first occupants of the place is accepted by the other Onitsha people and for this reason their lineage head (Okpala) is the Eze Ani, the priest of the ani of Onitsha, the deity of the land. Their claim to have brought the Umuezechima people across the Niger is not unanimously believed. There are also the three ogbe (6, 7, 8) from the administrative ebo of Ogbeolu which claim to have come from Igala and who were absorbed into the ritual ebo of Oreze and the two ogbe of Ogboli eke and Ubene which came from Egbema (a riverain Ibo group) and which are now grouped with the three Umuezechima ogbe resident in Ugwunaobamkpa.

Ndichie Ume	Administra- tive ebo	ogbe	Ritual ebo	Primary division
The Onya heads	Umuezearoli	comprising Nos. 1, 2, 3, 4	of Oreze	of the royal division
The Owelle heads	Ogbeolu	comprising Nos. 6, 7, 8	of Oreze	of the royal division
The Ogene heads	Umudei	comprising Nos. 9, 10, 11, 12	of Umudei	of the royal division
The Iyase heads	Umuase	comprising Nos. 19, 20	of Isele	of the non- royal division (or Umuase)
The Odu heads	Odoje	comprising Nos. 15, 16, 17, 18	of Odoje	of the non- royal division
The Ajie heads	Ogboli and Olosi	comprising Nos. 5	of Oreze	of the royal division but residing in non- royal division
		13, 14	of Olosi	of the royal division but residing in non- royal division
		21, 22	of Eke na Ube	of the non- royal division

Most of the twenty-two ogbe are exogamous units and can be called maximal lineages but some ebo containing two or more ogbe are exogamous, they consider themselves a single maximal lineage and look to a single Okpala as their maximal lineage head, for example the Isele (or Umuase) ebo of Ugwunaobamkpa and the Umuezearoli administrative ebo of Umuezechima. The Umudei administrative ebo was an exogamous unit until 1901 then it divided into two exogamous divisions. The first remained a single exogamous unit though divided into two ogbe (9, 10), the second has relaxed its exogamic rule and each of its component ogbe (11, 12) is a separate maximal lineage with its own Okpala. The ebo of Odoje in Ugwunaobamkpa divides into two exogamous units each composed of two ogbe.

RITUAL ORGANISATION

The ritual head of an ebo is the Okpala of its senior ogbe, for example in the Umudei (or Okebunabo) ebo, the Okpala of the Umudei ogbe (9) is the ritual head of the ebo, and in the Odoje ebo the ritual head is the Okpala of the Umuasele ogbe (15).

The ritual head of Oreze, which contains two administrative ebo, is the head of its senior ogbe, namely, Isiokwe (5), which resides in Ugwunaobamkpa. When a meeting of the whole town is convened for ritual purposes, it is referred to as a meeting of the nine ebo (ebo itenani) and the ritual head of the senior ebo (Oreze), that is, the Okpala of Isiokwe ogbe, presides. When a general assembly of Onitsha meets for political or judicial purposes it is convened as a meeting of the six administrative ebo under the presidency of the Obi.

THE POLITICAL DIVISIONS AND CLASSES

The political system of Onitsha, following that of Benin, seeks to emphasise the balanced opposition of the two territorial divisions, the royal Umuezechima and the non-royal Ugwunaobamkpa. The royal division supplies the king (Obi) who is the head of the state and its highest official. His person is regarded as sacred and he is held to be a symbol uniting both divisions. The ritual head of Onitsha also comes from this division. The non-royal division should supply the next highest official, the Iyase (praise name Onowu). This division also supplies the priest and priestess of the Udo cult (the Eze Udo and Ada Udo) whose roles are described in Chapter 9.

Although these two divisions were originally confined to separate residential areas, increase of population has caused part of the royal division to reside in the non-royal division where for administrative purposes it forms one of its subdivisions (ebo).

This dual organisation is made use of in sharing rewards and duties. For example when funds are levied for political and ritual purposes or when tribute is being paid to the Obi, each division has to contribute an equal amount. When title fees are shared between the Ndichie (chiefs), they are divided first into two equal parts, one for the Ndichie of each division. The same is done with the meat of cows and other sacrificial animals when they are being slaughtered in an Obi's funeral ceremony or in other similar rituals.

Onitsha society also divides into the two 'classes' of Ndichie and Agbalanairegwu. The former are the political elite and responsible for the government of the state, the latter are the commoners, the ordinary folk who in addition to being grouped into residential and patrilineal ogbe and ebo are organised into various associations and societies which cut across this segmentary organisation.

THE POLITICAL ELITE (NDICHIE)

There are three grades of these officials, namely, Ndichie Ume, Ndichie Okwa (which has two sub-grades, the five senior chiefs being distinguished as Ndichie Ukpo), and Ndichie Okwareze. Every Ndichie has a title and a praise name, those in the senior grade (Ndichie Ume) having a number of these praise names, those in the Ndichie Ukpo having two and the rest of the Ndichie Okwa and the Ndichie Okwareze having only one such name. The titles and praise names of fifty-one Ndichie are given below:

Ranking Order	Title Name	Praise Name
First Grade: Ndichie Ume		
1st and head of the grade	Iyase	Onowu, Onuiyi, Ngadaba, Orimili
2nd	Ajie	Ukadiugwu, Isagba
3rd	Odu	Osodi, Nkataukwu
4th	Onya	Ozoma, Ukpanaboji
5th	Ogene	Onira, Ukpaka
6th	Owelle	Osowa, Anya
Second Grade: Ndichie Okwa		
1st and head	Osuma	Afa, Akamkposi
2nd	Adazie	Ugulani, Alibo
3rd	Ozi	Odamagwe, Ogwuya
4th	Omodi	Daike, Alumaga
5th	Odua	Ngu, Alamuzo
Other Ndichie Okwa		
6th	Akpe	Olidi, Jebagwu
7th	Ojiba	Imagwe
8th	Ojizani	Obi
9th	Ogbuoba	Aghalogbom
10th	Gboza	Obieze
11th	Ede	Ogbogbogaga
12th	Oside	Eze
13th	Ike	Akatakwumanya

Ranking Order	Title Name	Praise Name
14th	Ojiude	Emena
15th	Oboli	Boja
16th	Ojiadu	Ugbalobi
17th	Ojogwu	Eze
18th	Osuma	Ogwa
19th	Igedu	
20th	Ojiabu	Ujala
21st	Omodi	Eze
22nd	Odua	Balaba

Third Grade: Ndichie Okwareze

1st and head	Onoli	Ogwuda
2nd	Akwe	Isama
3rd	Agba	Oriogu
4th	Igwuoba	Akalamu
5th	Asagwali	Omeikpo
6th	Eseagba	Agbala Udobi
7th	Ijiba	Ogbuogada
8th	Ijagwe	Obi
9th	Ajako	Obi
10th	Ubo	Negbasele
11th	Asagba	Obi
12th	Anuka	
13th	Abi	
14th	Ike	
15th	Okwuagua	
16th	Omobu	
17th	Oza	
18th	Ojugani	
19th	Obiazo	
20th	Obiabo	
21st	Agba	
22nd	Agba (jnr)	
23rd	Okwuagba	Uko-Dei

Those praise names left blank have been forgotten. The offices have not been filled for a long time.

Tradition relates that most of these titles were created by former Obis. Not all of them are filled today. Modern conditions have caused many to be no longer worth the expense involved and prestige is now attached only to those of the first grade (Ndichie Ume) and to a few of the second grade. The Obi of Onitsha is the head of the state and all state officials (Ndichie) are appointed by him and receive the insignia of their office from him. The recipient must be a citizen of Onitsha who can trace his descent either directly from the founder of one of the lineages of Onitsha or from a person adopted into it. He must also be a member of the Agbalanze society (Ozo). The title cannot be awarded to a person who is a member of another community or to an ohu (a member of the servile class). All candidates who become Ndichie have already achieved the Ozo title (are Agbalanze), and have passed through an initiation ritual which makes their persons 'sacred'. The elevation to a higher title brings with it the need for further initiation rituals to mark the change to a higher social and political status.

The offices are not vested either in a specific lineage or in a political unit. Recruitment is open and competition for them is unrestricted apart from the qualifications already stated. Once an Onyeichie (singular of Ndichie) dies, his office automatically becomes vacant. A title is normally held for life unless the holder is promoted to a higher title. No two persons can hold the same title and an Obi cannot revoke a title and confer it on another person. An Obi recruits an Onyeichie on his own initiative, though he may consult the elders of his (the Obi's) lineage (the Ulogo Eze). When an Obi wishes to invite a suitable candidate to take the title, he sends a palace servant to play the egwuota, an exclusive royal drum, at the candidate's house, indicating that the Obi wants him to come to the palace. The Obi has the right to promote any Onyeichie to a title of a higher grade should he consider this necessary. He is expected to recruit into the Ndichie 'class' powerful men who are influential and popular, but some Obis have sought to use this system of appointment for their own and for their dynasty's advantage. This has been the cause of considerable friction between the Obi and members of the various divisions and ebo, particularly when Ndichie Ume who are members of an Umuezechima ebo are appointed to titles which carry with them the headship of ebo in Ugwunaobamkpa division.

The signatories of the 1884 treaty referred to in Chapter 1 consisted of the six Ndichie Ume, four of whom came from Umuezechima (e.g. the Iyase (Umudei) the Odu (Umuikem in Ogbeolu) the Ajie (Ogbeoza in Umuezealori) the Onya (Ogbeoza in Umuezealori) and two from Ugwuna Obamkpa, namely the Ogene (Ogboli Olosi) and the Owelli (Odoje). These Ndichie were created by Obi Anazonwu (who was also of Umuezealori).

Installation Rituals

These are arranged in nine successive ceremonials:

(i)   Iyo Okwa.   These ceremonials in which the candidate has to solicit the support of the Obi and the Ndichie, make it clear that he must 'beg for the office', visiting the Obi and each Ndichie Ume separately and privately. The candidate has to make a private visit to the Obi, stating his desire to take the vacant title. There will be several such candidates going to the Obi and they will each make

a monetary offer. The Obi will eventually select the candidate he considers most suitable but he may well be influenced by the amount he has offered him. Onitsha people say "Ada agba aka eje be eze" ("you do not go to the king empty handed").

To show that he is also soliciting the support of the Ndichie, the candidate goes to the Iyase, the head of the Ndichie, and to the other five Ndichie Ume in their ranking order. During these visits he makes gifts to each of them, but the group as a whole must approve of his being admitted into the ranks of the Ndichie. They cannot over-rule the decision of the Obi in regard to the appointment, but the Obi should listen to their advice.

(ii)   *Igbunye Ewu*.   If the candidate is successful he proceeds to these rituals which mark his official recognition. The Iyase (Onowu) introduces the candidate to the Obi; the candidate kneels before him, greeting him four times, after which the Obi calls him by his title name and declares him a worthy man for the post, and the candidate responds "Ibi Ugoli". A goat (ewu) is then slaughtered and offered as a sacrifice on the Obi's altar to mark the acceptance. The candidate then goes to the Iyase for the same ceremony of Igbunye Ewu and there he pays a fee. This ceremony of recognition is followed by those of

(iii)   *Igo Muo,* in which the ancestors are invoked, and of

(iv)   *Ibu Ego*, in which the title fees are paid to the Obi and to each Ndichie Ume. The Igo Muo first takes place at the Obi's palace and then in the residence of each of the six Ndichie Ume. They all offer sacrifice on behalf of the candidate as do the other grades of Ndichie. Then comes

(v)   *Inyeokwa*—the investiture. The Iyase (Onowu) once again introduces the candidate before the Obi who is seated this time with the other Ndichie Ume in their official order of seating. The candidate kneels before the Obi who repeats the duties of the office, after which the candidate swears to be loyal to the Obi and the Ndichie. The Obi then places the red cap on the candidate's head and gives him a bell, an iron staff (alo) and a fan (azuzu). If he is in the Ndichie Ume grade, the egwuota (the royal drum) is played to welcome him home, and this is done from the palace to his home.

So far the ceremonies have involved only the candidate, the Obi and the six Ndichie Ume. Now that he has been invested with the title he has to be associated with the Ndichie collectively and this is done in the

(vi)   *Imacha and (viii)   Ikpoko Ofo* ceremonials. At the Imacha the candidate pays the title fees due to the Ndichie Okwa and Ndichie Okwareze and provides a feast for all the Ndichie. The

E

Iyase (Onowu) presides at this banquet and the other Ndichie are seated in order of their rank. The senior Ndichie Ume leave after the banquet and the Osuma, who is the head of the Okwa grade, then presides. After Imacha comes the

(vii)   Igba Ilo.   Ceremonies in which the candidate makes his first public display of his new role as Ndichie, making a succession of calls on each of the Ndichie Ume, beginning with the Iyase (Onowu). He has to enter their residences walking backwards and he is embraced by his host, invited to a banquet and presented with gifts. The most important of these integrative rituals however is the

(viii)   Ikpoko Ofo, in which the ofo (the symbol of their authority) of each Ndichie in the first two grades are tied together into a single bundle. For reasons which will be given later, the Ndichie Okwareze do not take part in this ceremony. The Ndichie Ume and Ndichie Okwa assemble at the residence of the new member and the Iyase sits on the candidate's throne (ukpo). Each of the Ndichie brings his ofo from the leather bag he carries, and places it on the 'altar', which is a raised mud construction containing the ancestral shrines of the Ndichie.

A goat, if the candidate is an Ndichie Ume, or a fowl, if he is an Ndichie Okwa, is slaughtered and the blood offered to the shrines on the 'altar'. The Ofo are then placed on this 'altar', a libation is poured, and kola nuts are offered, while the Iyase prays to the ancestors and the spirits of the land to bring the new member into the fold and to unite him with the rest of the Ndichie. All the ofo are then gathered and tied into a bundle.

The ceremony reaffirms the collective solidarity of the two grades of Ndiche into which the candidate is now incorporated and defines their ritual authority as deriving from the collectivity of former, now deceased, Ndichie. It provides powerful religious sanctions for the candidate's oath of loyalty to the Ndichie. It also marks his renunciation of any right he may have had to the office of Okpala (ritual head) of his lineage. For his ofo has now become an ofo Ndichie; its power derives from former Ndichie and it can no longer be associated with the power which comes from the founder of the lineage and which supports the office of Okpala. The new Onyeichie is now a semi-sacred person and this consecration is completed in the

(ix)   Izonye ukwa na mili rituals in which the candidate goes to the shrine of the Onitsha land deity, ani Onitsha, and offers a sacrifice to inform the deity that he is an Onyeichie. Then he goes down to the Niger and places his feet in the water.

The prestige which is attached to a Ndichie title-holder is shared by all his agnates, cognates, affines and other supporters. These people accompany him in all public ceremonies, dancing and singing his praises and manifesting their joy at the lavish entertainments that accompany such occasions.

The distribution of wealth which is a critical part of the title-making also serves to demonstrate the power and social standing of the candidate. Differences in the fees paid for the title also define its rank and the status of its holder, higher fees being required for higher ranking titles. In the early nineteenth century these fees were paid in slaves, a candidate paying two slaves to the Obi and one each to the Ndichie Ume. After the abolition of the slave trade, money payments were substituted and at the beginning of the twentieth century the fees paid for a Ndichie Ume title were about £80, those for an Ndichie Okwa title about £50, and those for an Ndichie Okwareze title about £30. They have risen to between £400 and £500 for the senior grades and correspondingly less for the lower grade.

Payment in slaves meant that the Ndichie purchased several slaves or went to war to capture victims for the title, and because such raids could only be made by a person who commanded his own private retainers, the early recipients exercised considerable military power. This military association, though now forgotten, is still emphasised in the ceremonies.

These installation rituals are the same for all grades of Ndichie but minor differences are introduced to distinguish between particular titles and between the different grades.

There are the differences in fees already referred to; the third ceremony of Igo Muo does not apply to the Ndichie Okwareze, but is restricted to the first two grades of Ume and Okwa as is the ceremony of Ikpoko Ofo, the binding of the members together; at the sacrifice made for the ceremony of Ikpoko Ofo, the Ndichie Ume use a goat for the sacrifice, while the Okwa grade use a fowl; finally, the exclusive royal dances played with special drums are not staged for the Okwa and Okwareze grades, but are exclusively for the Ndichie Ume.

Duties

The principal functions of the Ndichie are political (policy-making and political decisions), judicial (the administration of justice), and executive (the enforcement of law and order). They also have military duties which will be discussed in Chapter 6.

All Ndichie of all grades are public officers of the state; they are responsible to the Obi, who appoints them, and they carry out their duties on his behalf. Hence, at the installation of the Ndichie, the Obi says at the Igbunye Ewu ceremony.

"God and my ancestors! This man is about to take the title of Onyeichie . . . Do help him to look after his people well and to rule them in peace. Protect his life and my life and the life of all Ndichie . . ."

At the stage of conferring the staff of office, he says,

"I confer on you the title of . . . take it and go home and rule your people in peace . . ."

The order to govern is implicit in these words, and the senior chiefs of the Ndichie Ume constitute the main channel by which the decisions made by the Obi in council are transmitted to the people. They can delegate this authority to lesser persons. The Ndichie are both the intermediaries of the Obi in his relations with the people and the representatives of the people to the Obi. Their structural position will become clearer in the succeeding chapters but can be summarised here by saying that the two senior grades of Ume and Okwa stand in opposition to the Obi as representatives of the people, while the third grade of Okwareze support the Obi. Their loyalty is owed directly to him, and they are partly disassociated from and in opposition to the Ume and Okwa.

The Ndichie Ume are the heads of the six administrative units of the state, and the Iyase, who is next in rank to the Obi, is traditionally regarded as the Obi's political rival and opponent, as is his counterpart in the Benin system. He is the head of the Ndichie and the unity of the Ndichie Ume and Ndichie Okwa grades is demonstrated by the ceremony of Ikpoko Ofo, which binds them together, and makes them one united group. At the general State Council, the Ndichie Ume and the Ndichie Okwa are controlled by the Iyase and sit with him apart from the Obi, while Ndichie Okwareze sit beside the Obi. The Iyase and his Ume colleagues thus constitute a check on the power of the Obi, and this is indeed recognised by the Obi, who often suspects the Iyase of trying to usurp his authority.

The Iyase (Onowu) is regent when an Obi dies, and controls the affairs of state until a new Obi is appointed. All royal powers are transferred to him during this period of regency. When the successor is chosen, the Iyase plays a vital role in the installation of the new Obi. All candidates for the office of Ndichie go to him to solicit his support and approval. The ceremonies of Igbunye Ewu, Igo Muo, and Igba Ilo are performed at his house after they have been performed at the Obi's. He presides at all the ceremonies of installation involving Ndichie. He is the official who presents the candidate to the Obi for investiture. He can confer a Ndichie title during the regency, but must retain the fees which do not go to him but must be given to the new Obi.

The Owelle is the official sharer (Oga) of any property to be divided between the Ndichie Ume. He is also the link between the Ndichie Ume and the Obi, and therefore has special access to the Obi for this purpose. He is thus the principal palace official, and takes charge of the royal household. All wives of the Obi must complain through him to the Obi.

The Ndichie Okwa officials have civil and military functions in the subdivisions (ogbe) of their administrative units (ebo) and they assist the Onyeichie Ume of an ebo to carry out his duties, and in his absence may act for him. Their ritual duties include the performance with the Ndichie Okwareze of the Ituogene mortuary dance at the funeral of any titled person (Agbalanze and Ndichie). The Obi may delegate an Onyeichie Okwa to carry out specific duties and there are specific duties attached to the following title holders: the Osuma is the head of the whole Okwa grade and presides over their meetings and he alone can possess an Abani war shield which is otherwise exclusive to the Ndichie Ume; the Akpe is the head of the subordinate grade of Ndichie Okwa and presides over their meetings in the absence of any Ndichie Ukpo official; the Oside is the oga—the sharer for the Ndichie Okwa.

The Ndichie Okwareze are primarily associated with the royal palace and they are the Obi's principal officials, attendants and emissaries of state. As the Obi's personal servants they decorate the palace on all festival occasions, and they help the Obi to put on his state robes and other regalia, making certain that he is splendidly dressed. They supervise all sacrifices for the welfare of the Obi and, through him, of the state. They recruit magicians, herbalists, doctors, and other ritual specialists to safeguard the health of the Obi and on every Nkwo day they assemble with these persons to perform their rituals and offer these sacrifices. At the council of state and at the general assembly they support the Obi and sit behind him and not with the two senior grades of Ndichie. Hence in the ceremony of Ikpoko Ofo, which binds all Ndichie together, the Ndichie Okwareze are excluded. They also serve and assist the Ndichie Ume in the maintenance of law and order in their respective administrative units (ebo), and they join the Ndichie Okwa in the mkpala mortuary dance (known as Otuogene) at the funeral of every titled person.

The head of the Ndichie Okwareze is the Onoli and he presides at all meetings of this grade; the duties of oga (sharer and messenger) belong to the Ijagwe, and the Asagba has special duties relating to the women's organisation of the town. He is associated with the women's council, the Otu Omu, and works with its female titled head, the Omu. He is their spokesman at the palace and keeps them informed of all palace and government matters, holding regular meetings with them, and they give him a share of any food or property they receive on state occasions.

Privileges
The privileges and distinctions attached to the persons and offices of Ndichie are:

Installation rituals, the elaborate religious and secular ceremonials of their initiation and appointment which are exclusive to them.

Distinguishing regalia, namely, a straw hat with a red band and brass ornaments and carrying an eagle's feather; a white robe which is a symbol of purity and sacredness; a leather fan (azuzu); a brass staff of office (ogbonachi); a leather bag in which they keep their ofo; a red cap, a fashion introduced by Obi Okosi which gives them their title of "Red Cap Chiefs"; a special pillow (olosi); a special seat (okpochi); a warning bell (iduma), which is sounded ahead of an Onyeichie when he leaves his residence so that those bearing dead bodies or other objects which Ndichie are forbidden to see may keep out of the way.

Mortuary rituals, which have the following distinguishing features. The death of an Onyeichie, like that of the Obi, is at first kept secret and only referred to euphemistically (e.g. Ogwedachili osimili, meaning "the big tree has fallen across the Niger"). The eldest son (diokpa) has first to inform the Obi and then each of the Ndichie Ume. Each of the persons so informed will send a messenger back with an eagle's feather (nkpo ugo) in acknowledgement. If the deceased was of the Ndichie Ume grade, each Ndichie Ume has to sacrifice a goat to his ofo in a ritual called "Ewu nti anu", which indicates that a tragedy has occurred which must be kept secret. The ceremony of Ije Ani (a visit to the shrine of the deity of the land), which was first performed by the Onyeichie at his installation (in the Izonye ukwa na mili rituals), is performed for the last time with the eldest son impersonating his dead father and wearing his full regalia. All the Ndichie must attend his public funeral when this is performed. If the deceased is of the Ndichie Ume grade, the egwuota (royal dance) is played for him for a month. The grave is made in the deceased's residence and it becomes a ritual spot at which sacrifices are offered to the deceased. Two or more white banners (okonoko) are raised on poles in the deceased's compound.

If the deceased is of the Ndichie Ume grade no funeral ceremonies for any other people in the town may be performed until his own ceremonies have been completed.

Special taboos. They may not travel (leave the town) and, should they break this prohibition, they must sacrifice a goat to their ofo. They may not shake hands, but if they have to do so (e.g. with a person of higher rank) they proffer their fan (azuzu) in place of their hand. They may not invoke any deity or take any other kind of oath. They have a special place (ukoni) in their residence where they eat their meals and these must be prepared by a young girl under the age of puberty. They may not mourn or take part in any funeral ceremonies but must delegate these duties to other person.

Special residences which must contain three special rooms: the innermost (agbaleze) is where the Onyeichie meets with other Ndichie; the second room contains the Onyeichie's throne (ukpo); and the third and outer room is used for ceremonial occasions.

Ritual privileges and duties. The Ndichie share with the Obi the right to perform the Ite Umuato and Ofala celebrations. These festivals mark the beginning and end of first fruit and harvest rituals. The Umuato which precedes the harvest of maize is celebrated first by the Obi and then by each of the Ndichie Ume in their ranking order and then by the Ndichie Okwa and then by the Ndichie Okwareze. The Ofala, the festival of eating new yams, is first celebrated by the Obi, and the Ndichie Ume have the right to dance at this celebration in their full regalia accompanied by their wives and relatives, and other supporters. The Ogbalido festival is celebrated by the Ndichie and the hunters to commemorate their achievements in war and hunting. It provides an occasion for the Ndichie to parade through the town in their impressive military uniforms. Dogs are sacrificed and eaten at this festival except by the Ndichie Ume who each have to provide a goat. Each Onyeichie has to send the leg of the dog or goat to the Obi. In addition to these ceremonial privileges the Ndichie Ume have the sole right to possess and to play the royal egwuota drum music on the ceremonial occasions which demand it.

COMMONER ORGANISATIONS (AGBALA NA IREGWU)

The commoners are grouped into five principal associations each with their own special roles.

The Agbala Nze. This is the Onitsha name for the Ozo title society. It occupies a transitional position between commoners and Ndichie. It is an association of men who are sufficiently wealthy to take the Ozo (Nze) title. This elevates the holder to a superior social, ritual, and political status, and also serves as a means test for aspirants to the Ndichie titles, as none but Ozo titled men can take an Ndichie title.

The principal stages in achieving this Ozo (Nze) title are : Inyedo Muo—the erection of a shrine for the candidate's father; Igo Muo—the sacrifice by the Okpala of the candidate's lineage to the principal ancestral shrines of the lineage; Iwalu Ozo—the introduction of the candidate to the Ozo (Nze) shrine where the title is conferred; Imanzu—the rituals concerned with the administration of the Agbala Nze oath in which the candidate is rubbed with chalk (Nzu Imanzu) by the priest of Ozo and finally is crowned with a white cloth tied around his head into which an eagle's feather has been stuck. These ceremonials transform the ritual status of the candidate and make his person semi sacred. The elaborate and lavish entertainment which follows the procedure indicates the social status. This is a title of the wealthy and used to be paid in kind with yams, goats, and corn. Today, it is paid in cash to the value of between £700 and £900. These fees are shared by the Ozo title holders.

In pre-government days, a non-titled man could not speak in public if the Obi or a higher Ndichie was present. He could only speak with the permission of the Obi or of the Ndichie. As an individual he was considered politically to be of no consequence. In practically everything a titled person takes precedence over a non-titled person. In any event or religious gathering, a titled person is served before a non-titled one. In the mortuary rites of a titled man, a cow is offered as a sacrifice, but this is not necessary with a non-Agbala Nze member.

The Ndi Okpala. These are heads of the lineages whom we have referred to as ritual heads. They are the custodians of the cults of the lineage ancestors, and they are the intermediaries between the dead members of the lineages and their living descendants. Their offices are sacred and they hold the ofo Okpala, the symbol of ancestral authority in the lineage.

At Onitsha, the Okpala are not necessarily the oldest members of their lineages, and the Ibo system of succession to the headship of a lineage by the oldest male does not apply. In Onitsha the succession can only pass to the sons of a man who has not predeceased his father. For example in this diagram :

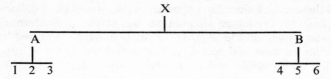

X has two sons, A and B and six grandsons (1–6). If A dies before his father X the line of succession to the headship of the lineage passes to B and his descendants. Again, if 5 predeceases his father B, the headship passes only to the sons of 4 and 6.

The Women's Organisation (Otu Omu).   The women of Onitsha had their own organisation separate from and parallel to that of the men. The chief of the women, referred to in British treaties as the Queen, was the Omu. She was a member of the Ndichie Ume and was selected by the Obi. After her installation she had the right to wear the Ndichie red cap (okpu ododo) and to possess a special type of royal egwuota drum and its associated dance (izabu). Like the male Ndichie Ume, she had the right to perform the Ite Umuato, Agachi and Ofala ceremonials. The Omu appointed the female titled officials, each of whom had duties corresponding to the equivalent male Ndichie Ume. These were known as Ndi Otu Ogene and they acted as the Omu's advisory and executive council; they were the rulers of the women and mediated between them and the Obi and Ndichie.

These female titled officials no longer function, and the last Omu was Omu Nwagbolia who died in the late nineteenth century.

The Age Organisation (Otu na achi ani).   There are twenty-three age sets at Onitsha and these cut across residential and lineage ties, and bring members of every ward into a single organisation based on the criterion of age. It has been the practice of the Obi and Ndichie to make use of some of these age sets, or, at times, of an age class (group of sets), for carrying out particular functions.

The Ora Okwute.   Each quarter has its own Egungu, a secret society of the Muo (ghost) type, and the heads of these societies are combined together into a single association called the Ora Okwute. The masquerades (egungu) performed by these societies are used on specific state occasions.

The Umuilo.   These, the young unmarried men, have no political authority. They are organised as part of the Otu na achi ani, where they form the junior age sets.

All these associations have their separate interests and collectively they help to crystallize opinion in the state. In modern times, the young men of the Agbala na iregwu have organised themselves into a new and cohesive elite called the Onitsha Improvement Union, which seeks to advise and guide the Obi and Ndichie.

ABO

SOCIAL STRUCTURE

The structure of Abo is shown in Table C at the end of the book. It consists of sixteen ogbe which are grouped into four ebo. Abo also divides into two primary political divisions, Umudei, the royal clan, whose members claim to be migrants from Benin and the descendants of their leader and founder Ogwezi, and Ndichie, the non-royal division, consisting of stranger and autochthonous elements. Unlike the other three states these primary divisions are not residential units but live together, each ogbe being made up of Umudei and Ndichie members.

In Abo the term "umunna" (patrilineage) is reserved for minimal lineages and is not applied to any higher grouping. A number of umunna combine to form an ogbe (major lineage) and a number of ogbe form an ebo (maximal lineage) and the four ebo of Abo form the Umudei clan. The lineage organisation of the Ndichie does not extend higher than the idumu and an Umudei ogbe will contain, in addition to its own component minor lineages (idumu) the various Ndichie idumu which are attached to it and which live with it.

The Abo genealogical charter which validates this structure refers only to Ogwezi and his four descendants who were the founders of these four ebo, and all citizens of Abo will tell an outsider that they belong to (i.e. descend from) these founders. But when the internal structure of an ebo and of its component ogbe and idumu are examined, we find that the Ndichie members have their own separate genealogies and traditions of origin relating to their own particular lineages. For example the Iwele Idumu (in Umuossai ogbe) claim that they were part of the Akiri people who originally lived in the Abo area and who were driven out by the Umudei. A daughter of Iwele was married to Obi Ojigbali and the Iwele people accepted his protection and submitted to his government. Another Iwele tradition claims that they, like the Umudei, migrated from Benin and that their lineage founder was the brother of the founder of the Jekri kingdom and that both these brothers left at the same time. The other Akiri villages do not accept the Isele group as belonging to Akiri.

In Abo the four ebo are exogamous units and this rule of exogamy applies not only to the Umudei members but to its Ndichie members as well.

RITUAL ORGANISATION

The acceptance of Ndichie as full members of an ogbe and an ebo is exemplified in the office of Okpala (or Onyeikei) which in Abo is filled by the oldest Umudei or Ndichie male in the ogbe. In the case of the Okpala of an ebo the office is not as in Onitsha, restricted to the senior ogbe but is extended to the oldest male in the whole ebo. The elders of an ebo are collectively referred to as Ndikei. When the Okpala of the four ebo meet for ritual purposes they are subordinate to the supreme Okpala of Abo known as the Odua who is the oldest man in the Umudei clan. Ndichie are excluded from holding this office which has political as well as ritual duties attached to it.

SATELLITE VILLAGES

The Abo state, like the other kingdoms, began as a single compact community. In course of time it expanded into six village settlements. These were founded by titled chiefs (called Olinzele) who moved there with members of their ogbe and other dependants and slaves to establish what were in effect military outposts from which they were able to raid and plunder neighbouring communities. Slaves and other booty from these raids were sent as tribute to the Obi (praise name Obonwe) of Abo who rewarded them with titles and honours.

These outposts grew in strategic importance, and eventually enabled the Obi and his council to control the territorial waters of the Niger against outsiders, and the heroic deeds of these Abo war chiefs earned the state the name of Abo Obuchili Osimili, meaning "Abo, the guard and defender of the Niger". The prosperity of the Abo kings and their officials was derived from their control of the slave trade in this part of the lower Niger. Although these settlements had their own special names, their members remained part of the original Abo ogbe from which they were derived. They attended and took part in religious festivals at Abo and their chiefs were summoned by the Obi (Obonwe) to attend the state council.

There are seven of these settlements and they are off-shoots of the following eight ogbe :

Settlement	*Ogbe or Ebo of Origin*
Udagba	Ogene
Ugbaja	Ndanike
Odugiri and Ukwu Ugboma	Ogbe Ukwu of Ossai
Aseomuku	Agidigbo
Abalagada	Isamale
Iseokpo	Ogweze Ogbe Ukwu and Ossai

This last settlement derives from three wards and each resident in the settlement knows the ward to which he belongs at the capital. These settlements are on average about two and a half nautical miles away from the capital but some are as far as eight nautical miles away. They have developed into permanent modern communities with populations ranging between eight hundred and a thousand, and have schools, dispensaries and modern amenities. However they always regard the capital city as their political centre.

POLITICAL ORGANISATION

Although Abo bases its political structure on a dual division of Umudei and Ndichie and has officials with Benin titles, the roles of these divisions and of the superior title holders are reversed. Instead of grouping the royal division with the Obi and placing the non-royal division with its head, the Iyase, in opposition to it, as in Benin and Onitsha, the two divisions live together combined into the four ebo of Ojigbali, Ogwezi, Ossai, and Ozegbe. They remain however politically distinct and at the level of the state council they are opposed to each other and have their own separate hierarchies of chiefs. When they meet in council with the Obi, chiefs of the non-royal division headed by the Iyase support the Obi, while his royal relatives and chiefs headed by the Ndanike are in opposition to him. The title Ndanike is the local Ibo variant of Edaikan, the title of the Oba of Benin's eldest son and his heir. The Abo Ndanike is an elected Umudei chiefly office while the eldest son of the Obi who holds the titled office of Akpulosu has the role of supporting his father the Obi against the other Umudei chiefs.

THE POLITICAL ELITE

The chiefly officials who in Onitsha are known as Ndichie are referred to in Abo as Olinzele. They are organised into two opposed hierarchies of Umudei and Ndichie chiefs and the offices in these hierarchies are restricted to persons who belong to these specific divisions. In addition there are two intermediate offices, the Odua and the Akpulosu, already referred to, who although belonging to the Umudei division do not belong to either hierarchy. Apart from the Odua all Olinzele are appointed by the Obi.

The Odua. This office is held by the oldest male in the Umudei clan. In addition to being the ritual head of Abo he takes over the political duties of the Obi when the latter dies and acts as regent until a new Obi has been installed, a ceremony which he performs with the Iyase. He is a member of the ruling council which is the inner council (or cabinet) of the state. Since he holds his office independently of the Obi he can rally the Olinzele to his side against a recalcitrant Obi and can hold his own council meetings with them at his residence. He has also the right to hold his own court, appeals from which go to the Obi's court.

The Akpulosu. This office is the only one which is hereditary and held by the eldest son of the Obi. Although graded as an Umudei Olinzele his office differs from those of the other Umudei Olinzele in that he sides with the Iyase and the Ndichie Olinzele in supporting his father against them.

The Olinzele. The Umudei Olinzele, who slightly outnumber the Ndichie Olinzele, are by reason of their birth potential rivals of the Obi and thus of superior status to the Ndichie Olinzele. Only a free-born Umudei who can trace his descent to Ogwezi is eligible for a title. A Ndichie Olinzele title can be conferred on any Ndichie including not only free-born but also slave-born, and strangers who have become assimilated into Ndichie lineages.

The Ndichie Olinzele, in contrast to the Umudei officials, are associated with the Obi and his palace, many of them being responsible for palace duties of a domestic kind, and because of this the female title of Idibo, which is awarded to particular wives of the Obi, is equated with an Ndichie Olinzele title. Thus on any occasion when Ndichie Olinzele are unable or, for various reasons, refuse to perform important palace ritual duties these can be performed for them by the Idibo title holders.

It is difficult to estimate the actual number of Umudei and Ndichie people for not only do they live together in the same ogbe but they also intermarry (subject to the rule of ebo exogamy). As a result of this intermarriage chiefly officials though holding their office in the hierarchy of one division by right of patrilineal descent are often related by matrifiliation to the other division. Indeed this cross relationship is obligatory in the case of the Iyase the head of the Ndichie division for this office can only be held by a man from the Ndichie division whose mother is a Nwa Akpe, that is, a daughter of an Umudei.

The Olinzele hierarchies are detailed below

Grade	Umudei Hierarchy	Ndichie Hierarchy
1st Grade	Ndanike Ozea Akpanuka Ajie Otafulu Ojo Osa Ochia	Iyase (Okwue) Isagba (Ajie) Igboba (Ajie) Ajuma Isama (Okwue)
2nd Grade	Nzanabi Ochiya Ikogwe Ajie Onukpala Asa (oga = sharer)	Onise Ogene Osingwa Ogini Ozoma Onya Ube Akosi
3rd Grade	(Okwa Ossai Ukwu sub grade) = 3 Omodi (Okwa Uno sub grade) = 4 Omodi (Okwa Okolobia Omodi sub grade) = 16 Omodi	Odogwu Abi Akalamu Sanza Asagwali Okpeigbe Agba Ubo Onolio Uti Agwaba (oga = sharer)
4th Grade		8 officials (namely, Damanza, Gbada, Ose, Okulade, Owele, Abi, Ayapata, Ukodei, Ajie and Ojeba

The third grade of the Umudei heirarchy is also known as the Omodi grade as all its officials have the same title, Omodi. It divides into three sub grades. Most of these titles and grades have been created by different Obis in the course of Abo history, although the people cannot recall the particular periods when they were created, nor the ways in which they were ranked. They state that the Olinzele titles were created by their ancestor, Esumai Ukwu, but they cannot say whether the subsequent kings added or modified the grades.

The Obi's choice is guided primarily by the wealth and war-like ability of the aspirant, by his possession of many slaves, wives and dependants, and by other indices of power and influence. A war leader could be expected to supply the Obi with a steady supply of slaves and other booty, and heroism in war could be a means of attaining an Olinzele title provided the aspirant distributed sufficient wealth to the community as a whole to win their support and particularly the support of other titled men.

The Abo constitution does not insist on the Obi distributing the principle offices between the four ebo. Officials may be openly recruited irrespective of their residence but an Obi who wishes to have the full support of the community makes sure that all sections of the state are equally represented. Obis do, however, use their prerogative of awarding titles to win the support of the powerful groups in the state, as well as to attract capable, powerful and potentially dangerous persons into the Council, and to counterbalance the power of the existing officials.

The present four senior Umudei Olinzele come respectively from the following ebo: the Ndanike from Umuojigbali (the ebo to which the present Obi belongs), the Akpanuka from Umuogwezi, the Otafulo-Oji-Osa from Umu Ossai, and the Ochia from Umunobi.

The present Iyase, who is from the Iwele lineage (idumu) was able to remember the following Ndichie titles which had been held by members of the idumu, namely:

Iyase (four)	Ayapata (two)
Ogene (two)	Sanza Asagwali (one)
Odogwu Abi (one)	Osingwa (one)
Agwa (four)	Ggbada (one)

A vacant office is open to competition, the aspirants having to canvass the support of the Iyase and Olinzele particularly those of the hierarchy to which the title belongs. The successful aspirant before his installation has to pay over to the Iyase the fees due to the Obi and to the Olinzele. The higher the grade within the hierarchy, the higher the fee the candidate has to pay. When this has been done the Iyase informs the Obi who arranges the date for the installation, and the Iyase informs the candidate. All Olinzele are present at the ceremony which takes place in the Obi's palace. The Obi is seated on his throne (ukpo) with the Umudei Olinzele seated together on his right side and those of the Ndichie seated on his left side with their leader, the Iyase, seated beside the Obi on his left. The candidate stands facing them finely dressed and carrying his regalia: akansi (staff), azuzu (fan), nkpo ugo (eagle's feather) and okpu ododo (red cap). He carries but does not wear the cap. The Iyase summons the candidate, who steps forward, places the cap and the azuzu (fan) on the floor, and, sitting on the bare floor in front of the Obi, begins to crawl towards him and to raise his two hands in a begging manner, asking the Obi to award him the title. His manner must portray extreme subservience to the Obi, failing which he could be refused the title.

While in this position, the Iyase steps forward and asks the candidate which title he seeks. The candidate replies and the Iyase tells the Obi. The Iyase tells the candidate openly the fees he must pay, even though these have already been paid. When this is done, the candidate crawls nearer to the Obi who tells him to stand. Then the Obi takes white clay (nzu) and rubs it on the candidate's hands.[1] The candidate then lifts the cap and gives it to the Obi, who places it on the candidate's head. This is the completion of the ceremony. The candidate then rises and salutes the Obi and his Olinzele. This is greeted by dancing and singing (igba ogene) by the women who had escorted the candidate to the palace. A series of lavish entertainments follow, and are provided by the candidate who is now addressed only by his title or praise name.

The duties of these chiefs are variously concerned with legislative, administrative, judicial, military and naval duties, sometimes involving the Olinzele collectively, sometimes particular officials or groups of officials. Power lies mainly with officials in the senior Umudei and Ndichie grades who are in constant consultation with the Obi. The duties of some of these officials are given below.

Amongst the Umudei Olinzele the Ndanike, their head, performs on behalf of the Obi the rituals involving sacrificing to the ofo of past Obi, and to the Ikenga and other shrines on ceremonial days. The Onukpala Asa in the second grade is the oga (sharer) for the Umudei chiefs. He decides what things should be presented to the Umudei chiefs and where these should be dealt with. The Omodi chiefs of the third grade are all military chiefs and subordinate directly to the Ochia (of the first grade) who is their head and who with the Odogwu Abi of the Ndichie Olinzele are joint commanders of the Abo fleet.

Amongst the Ndichie Olinzele the Iyase is the head of these chiefs and the chief officer of the Obi. He is known as Iyase Obonwe, the Iyase of the Obonwe (the Obi's praise name) and is also the senior war chief. He shares with the Odua the duty of crowning the Obi. It is in fact he who actually puts the crown on his head. He is the chief speaker at the assembly and defends the Obi against any charges that might be brought against him. The Isagba Ajie is the spokesman of the Ndichie and next in rank to the Iyase. The Onise Ogene is the head of the second grade and enjoys the exclusive privilege of standing when greeting the Obi. The Ozoma Onya, like the Odogwu Abi and the Akalamu, is a war chief, whilst the Agwaba is the oga (sharer) for the Ndichie Olinzele. The Ose in the fourth grade has to carry the Obi whenever he wishes to perambulate the town or to visit an Olinzele. He also washes and anoints the body of the Obi whenever he is being robed for a royal occasion doing this in the presence of the public. The Owele mourns on behalf of the Obi, since it is forbidden for a king to mourn: the Obi must not weep. The Abi is in charge of cleansing the dishes used by the Olinzele after they have dined at the Obi's palace or on other state occasions while the Ukodei is in charge of the riverside market (ose afia). He sees that it is kept clean and that it is conducted in an orderly way.

The Olinzele title holders enjoy political as well as social privileges. Their insignia of office are exclusive to them; if anyone else wears them they are severely punished. Their mortuary rituals are intended to continue in the spirit world the rights and status which they enjoyed in this world. Their death has to be notified to the Obi, accompanied by a gift to him. Their bodies are laid in state and slaves were formerly killed to accompany them into the next world. Today, bullocks are substituted for slaves and in the case of the lesser Olinzele, goats replace bullocks. Their judicial privileges include heavier punishments for offences committed against an Olinzele and the right to stand before the court when giving evidence instead of kneeling. Adultery with the wife of an Olinzele carries heavier damages and the offence has to be purged by the sacrifice of a cow instead of a goat. They enjoy the privilege of attending the king's annual Uje festival at Uge. It is an occasion for the display of their social and political position in the state as national festivals are occasions when the values of kingship are reaffirmed. They have the right to build a residence with three special chambers and with a throne in one of them.

COMMONER ORGANISATIONS

As in Onitsha the government of the Abo state is considered to be the function of the Obi and his chiefly officials. The rest of the community, though closely involved in the administration and organisation of their respective lineages and wards, are not directly concerned with the government of the state, being represented at this organisational level by the Olinzele of these quarters and wards. There are however holders of lineage offices and members of particular ritual and other associations whose influence upon state decisions can be important, or who may be called upon to act as its executive agents or to carry out public works and other duties. The most prominent of these are:

The Ndi Okpala who are the ritual heads of their respective lineages and who through their possession of the lineage ofo (the symbol

F

of the authority of its founder) have behind them the collective authority of all the lineage ancestors.

The Igbu society. This is an association (described in Chapter 2) of men who have achieved sufficient distinction in war to be awarded the title of Igbu (killer). It was formerly given only to those who could produce the head of an enemy killed by them in support of their claim. The Obi is the head of this society and has to be a member of the society before he can become an Obi. Women as well as men are eligible for this title.

The Age Organisation. As in other Ibo communities men (and women) are graded into elders (otu uku), men (otu agbabo), and boys (otu uwai). Age sets are organised in each ebo as boys pass into the otu agbabo grade, and, as in Onitsha the junior age sets in this grade (referred to collectively as umu okolobia) are called upon to perform various public duties.

The Ndiom or Ndi Igosi (the women's organisation). As in Onitsha, women have their separate organisation but in Abo there are no female chiefly titles except the Idibo titles reserved for the wives of the Obi.

NOTES

1   Among the Ada kings (Obi) of the mid-west, who still come under Benin influence, the Oba of Benin performs this function for each new Obi who thus derives his kingly authority from the Oba himself.

Chapter 4   The Framework of Government II

OGUTA

SOCIAL STRUCTURE

Oguta consists of twenty-seven ogbe (wards) which are grouped into the two primary divisions of Ugwunta and Ugwuuku. These are territorial and ritual divisions but have no real political functions. The structure is shown in Table D at the end of the book.

There are three ogbe which claim to be autochthonous, Obutu (number 6 in the diagram), Obeagwa (8) in the Ugwunta division and Amozua (25) in the Ugwuuku. Amozua and Obutu claim that they and Obeagwa originally formed a village group before the arrival of the Oguta people with Amozua providing the village head (king) and Obeagwa the ritual head (Osere), and that three of these kings reigned before the arrival of the Oguta people. Obutu lived at the southern side of the Oguta town and its head, called the Ogini, made a pact of friendship with Eneke, the Oguta leader, when he brought his people to this site.

Most of the Oguta ogbe are exogamous units and maximal lineages. The Ngegwu ogbe has now relaxed the exogamy rule and today exogamy is limited to its five sub-divisions (major lineages) which can intermarry with each other. There are also the three original wards and maximal lineages of Adu, Eke and Alibo which today have segmented each into three ogbe. In the case of Adu and Alibo they have remained exogamous and their component ogbe cannot intermarry; in the case of Eke, the ogbe of Umuayata (13) can intermarry, while Umunsoha (14) can intermarry only with a particular segment of Umuigbo (12), which is considered to be an attached and not a truly agnatic lineage of Umuigbo.

RITUAL ORGANISATION

The ritual head of an ogbe is its Okpala who is the oldest male in the ogbe. In the case of those ogbe whose heads hold particular ritual offices the head who is still the oldest male in the ogbe is known by the name of the office, namely, Osere, Eze Ani (the priest of the earth cult) Eze Chi Oha (priest of the Chi Oha cult) and the Igweuta. In the case of the Ngegwu ogbe there are five Okpala, one for each of its exogamous major lineages; in the case of the Adu maximal lineage, the Umuamam (3) ogbe has its own Okpala while Umuosu (5) and Umudei (4) share a single Okpala; in the case of the Eke and Alibo maximal lineages each of their component ogbe has its own Okpala. The senior Okpala of the whole town is called the Ogene. He is the oldest male in Oguta and is also the Okpala of his own ogbe.

The Ikwa Muo Society (Agbanta).   This ritual association which in Oguta is also called agbanta has been briefly referred to in Chapter 2. It enables members of the society to commune with their deceased fathers, who are members of an extension of the society in the spirit world. In Oguta it is developed as three separate societies, one for each primary division and one for the autochthonous ogbe of Obeagwa and Obutu. The third autochthonous ogbe prefers to belong to the Ugwuukwu Agbanta. Each of these societies is believed to have a corresponding agbanta in the spirit world and a son replaces his father in the living agbanta as soon as he has completed the mortuary feasts, fees and rituals which makes his father a member of the ghostly agbanta. The head of each agbanta holds the titled office of Osere. He has a lodge (echina) attached to his residence at which the society holds its meetings. The Osere must come from a particular ogbe, Umuopu (11) in the case of the Ugwunta society, Umunarukwu (20) in the case of Ugwuukwu, and Obeagwa (8) in the case of the autochthonous one. Part of an Osere's installation rituals involve a ceremonial funeral, so that having undergone 'rites of passage' from this world to the next, he is in a position to communicate with the agbanta of the spirit world. This is one of the reasons given for barring people from these three ogbe from becoming chiefly officials. For such chiefly rank carries with it a 'royal' type of funeral and, should such a chief become the oldest man in his ward, he would also become Osere and have to celebrate another kind of funeral.

The festivals associated with Ikwa Muo such as Ikanzu, Agugu and Owu are performed separately by each agbanta.

POLITICAL ORGANISATION

In Oguta the primary political unit is the ward (ogbe). All but three of these derive from the dominant immigrant group that founded Oguta. The exceptions, Obeagwa, Obutu and Amozua, claim to be the descendants of the original inhabitants of the place. No political or other distinctions are made between immigrant and autochthonous people except in ritual matters, where, as already stated, there is a separate agbanta for the autochthonous group, though even here the division is not complete and one autochthonous ogbe is associated with one of the immigrant agbanta. All twenty-seven ogbe are grouped for residential purposes into two territorial divisions but these have no political function.

Each ogbe must be represented on the state council, their representative being either its titled chief, if it has one, or its ritual head, Okpala. All these superior offices, including that of the head of state, the Obi, are vested in particular ogbe, the members of the ogbe having the sole right to select from amongst themselves a person to fill the office.

In the case of the offices of Obi (praise name Ezeigwe), Iyasara and Ndanike, these rights have passed from one ogbe to another. For instance the right to the office of Obi which is now held by Ngegwu (1) and Umudei (4) ogbe was originally vested in the Ogwuma (10) ogbe; the right to the office of Iyasara now held by Umunkwokomoshi (22) and Umuenu (23) was previously held by Umunkwu (21); and the right to the office of Ndanike is now held by the two ogbe of Umuamam (3) and Umosu (5).

Oguta also differs from Onitsha and Abo in the status of its head, the Obi, and in the political roles of its priestly and ritual offices, referred to collectively in Oguta as Ndichie. The Obi, though still regarded as the head of the state and superior to all other chiefs, can only appoint chiefs of an inferior grade called in Oguta Olilinzele, and he shares this right with the Iyasara.

There are two kinds of superior chiefly officials, firstly those I have termed kingly officials as they share with the Obi various prerogatives which set them apart from all other people, namely the Iyasara, the Ndanike, the Ezekoro and the Ezeukwu; secondly a number of ritual heads who also have important political functions, namely, the Ogene, whose office resembles that of the Odua of Abo, the three Osere, and the priests of the more important Oguta cults.

The offices of Obi and of the kingly officials are acquired ones open to any person of wealth and influence with the right qualifications of ward and agbanta membership and the offices of superior ritual heads are ascribed on the basis of age, as are those of the Ndiokpala, the ritual heads of the ogbe. As explained in Chapter 9, page 194, a number of candidates for the offices of Obi and Iyasara can be appointed and crowned at the same time.

The Oririnzere chiefs are appointed by the Obi and by the Iyasara. These offices are open to any person of wealth and influence provided they are not members of an ogbe which is headed by the Obi, by a kingly official or by one of the Osere ritual heads. Thus every ogbe is represented on the state council by one person who is either a chief or a ritual head.

When they assemble for state council meetings, the senior ritual heads and the Ndiokpala form one group or college, headed by the Ogene and in opposition to the Obi, who is supported by the group or college of Olilinzele, headed by the Ogana (the senior Olilinzele). The Iyasara and other kingly officials sit apart from these colleges and from each other.

In addition to these male officials, the women's organisation is represented on the state council by their head, the Ogene Nwanya, the oldest woman in Oguta.

All these persons collectively form the chiefly class or political elite. They are drawn from the more senior section of Oguta society, for in the case of the male officials they must all be members of the Ikwa Muo society, membership of which is restricted to men who have completed the funerary ceremonies of their fathers.

In addition to this chiefly class there are, as in the other states, various other associations associated with them in advisory, executive or other public business. These are, the women's organisation (Otu Ogene), the Age organisation, and the agbanta and Igbu societies.

THE POLITICAL ELITE

The Kingly Officials
In the past there were four of these offices namely those of the Iyasara, the Ezeukwu, the Ndanike and the Ezekoro. Today only the first two of these offices are filled.

All these offices carry exclusive privileges which are either the same or very similar to those enjoyed by the Obi. The most important of these are similar regalia, similar mortuary rituals, for instance his death must be kept secret for a time, and for a period of three years his eldest son becomes an "udom", that is, he impersonates his father, wearing his regalia and performing the duties of his office. At the final funerary ceremony (usually called the second burial), the deceased chief is represented by an effigy (igbudu) carried on a bier, and at the accompanying feast all the chiefly officials and other important members of the public have to be present. They may build the same kind of reception and retiring chambers in their palaces as the Obi has in his palace. They may hold their own courts. They may perform the Ibina and Omelife festivals.

The Iyasara differs from the others in having installation and mortuary ceremonies which are identical with those of the Obi. The others have their own special installation ceremonies though in the case of the Ezeukwu some of the rituals are similar to those for the Obi and Iyasara.

Their inferiority to the Obi is shown in their having to attend the Obi's council; in the superiority of the Obi's court, which is a court of appeal from the kingly officials' courts, and has exclusive jurisdiction in cases of homicide; in the Obi's right to perform the Ibina and Omelife rituals first; and in his exclusive right to play the ufie drum. (The kingly officials can only share with the Obi the right to play the opi drum.) The Obi also has the sole right to use the Ibom drum to summon people to an assembly; the kingly officials can only use a hand bell.

The Iyasara.   The status of the Iyasara is higher in Oguta than in Onitsha and Abo. He is not on a par with the Obi but ranks as a second or subordinate head of the state and on occasions when the Obi has lost the support of most of his chiefs and people, he can act as the head of an alternative state council. Traditionally his office is also that of a war leader, the head of the war organisation, and in this capacity he is addressed as "Iyasara Ojili aha mala obodo".

In addition to having the general right to appoint Olilinzele, the Iyasara can also appoint a particular Olilinzele for the Ugwu Uku division, who is called the Isagba Ajie, and is the personal official of the Iyasara and his legal adviser. In this installation ceremony the Iyasara conducts the candidate into the inner chamber in his palace, where the candidate robes himself and takes his staff of office (otuchi). He then comes out and sits on the ground before the Iyasara who is seated in the second chamber on his ukpo (throne). The Iyasara takes a pot containing water (agunze) and pours some on the head of the candidate as he confers the title on him. The candidate swears an oath of loyalty to the Iyasara who then offers a sacrifice of palm wine and kola nuts to the Agunze and Nde Muo ancestral shrines and prays for the health of the new Isagba Ajie. The Isagba also pays a title fee to the Iyasara, the amount being determined by the Iyasara. He also gives four pence to every Umuishi who is present at the ceremony. (The Umuishi are those men who have buried their fathers and hold their ofo (ancestral symbol).) He also pays title fees to the Olilinzele who are all present at the ceremony so that he may become a member of their college.

The right to the Iyasara title is held by the Alibo maximal lineage which divides into three major lineages each of which is also an ogbe. The right was originally exercised by the Umunkwo-Komoshi (22) and Umuenu (23) ogbe, though the Umunkwu ogbe has recently sought to revive their claim. Because of his ogbe's association with the Iyasara title, the Okpala of Umunkwu wears the okpu omu (red cap) and other regalia exclusive to the Obi, the kingly officials and the Olilinzele; and when he dies his body, like that of a deceased Obi or Iyasara, is laid out in a similar way and the two other ogbe (Umunkwo Komoshi and Umuenu) play the opi drum and dance.

A number of Iyasara are appointed at the same time, since any man in these two wards who can afford to pay the title fees and can win the support of the ward elders, is eligible for the title. The first to complete the installation ceremonies is usually the oldest of the candidates and he performs the duties of the office. When he dies and after his udom has acted in his place for the required three years, the Iyasara who is next in seniority replaces him and this continues until all these Iyasara are dead. As soon as the udom of the last of these has completed his three years in the office a new set of Iyasara are appointed.

The Ezeukwu. This office is peculiar to Oguta and its principal duty is the crowning of the Obi and the Iyasara, and the removing of the crown from them in their funeral ceremonies. The office is claimed to be as old as the kingship and to have been brought by the Oguta people from Benin.

The office is vested in one of the major lineages of the Okichi ogbe (18) and another of these major lineages has the right to appoint the Ezechioha (priest of the Chi cult). Only two persons are remembered as having completed the installation ceremonies required for this title. The first holder of the office was Ezeukwu Osoa, and the last, Ezeukwu Ossai, who was installed in 1940 and died in 1961. At any time when there is no title holder, the functions of crowning or uncrowning an Obi or Iyasara are performed by a senior member of the lineage delegated for this specific duty by the other members.

The Ezeukwu in his own installation ceremonies has to crown himself. He has previously notified the following groups of people : the members of his age set, the members of his maximal lineage, the sons of female members of his lineage, his mother's lineage (and ogbe), his father's mother's lineage (and ogbe), the Obi and council. Each of these groups has to be presented with a goat for them to sacrifice to Ikwe, the Ezeukwu's special cult which relates to the guardian spirits of the locality.

They assemble for the Inona Ukpo (enthronement) ceremony at the candidate's palace and in the first of the three special chambers of the palace. The new Ezeukwu dresses in his full regalia: a red gown and special head gear (his "crown"), and carrying his odu (a horn made of an elephant tusk). Then the people (but not the Obi, or kingly officials) come forward to salute him with the traditional greeting; first the Ezechioha (the priest of the Ezeukwu's lineage), then the Ogene, then the Ogana (the head of the Olilinzele), followed by the other Olilinzele and Nde-Okpala. This is followed by a feast for the people at which a cow is slaughtered and distributed as follows: a portion goes to the Obi, a leg goes to the Iyasara lineages for division amongst them, a leg is divided up between all the ward Okpalas, the Ezeukwu himself gets a leg, the female members of his lineage (umuada) get the loins and the remainder is used for the feast so that all may share in it.

The following day the Ezeukwu sacrifices a sheep (ebunu) and a white cock (oke okpa) at the Egbenuka shrine in the Ngegwu (1) ward, being escorted there by members of his lineage. This sacrifice is to obtain the support and confirmation of his appointment from this spirit. This confirmation is assumed if at the end of a lunar month he is still alive and he then makes another sacrifice to the shrine.

The Ndanike. The name of this office is derived from the Benin title of "Edaikan", a title which in Benin is reserved for the Oba's eldest son. The Abo and Oguta office of Ndanike has no such association but is a war title. The Oguta Ndanike is a war leader with the right to wage war on his own if he so wishes, and candidates for the office must satisfy the members of their ogbe that they are wealthy and powerful enough to lead the people in time of war. Unlike the Iyasara, only one Ndanike is appointed at a time and if there is more than one candidate seeking the title, the right one is discovered by divination.

The office is vested in the two wards of Umnamam (3) and Umuosu (5) which are major lineages of the Adu maximal lineage. On the night before his installation a new Ndanike has to perform the Ibe ishi (beheading) ritual. A victim is taken to the waterfront of the ward at midnight, the Ndanike beheads him and the blood is sprinkled on the akpu tree which marks the spot where this ritual is performed. This gives to the candidate the power of Ndanike. This is followed by his male and female kinsfolk parading the town singing and rejoicing that he has killed a "leopard", a euphemism for the human victim.

The following morning a gong is sounded summoning people

to the installation and the Olilinzele and Ndichie assemble at his palace. His senior wife washes his body but he robes and crowns himself. They both come out of the inner chamber and the Ndanike seats himself on the throne and his wife steps forward and salutes him saying "Odua, Odua" to which he replies "Omodi, Omodi"; she then sits beside him. The Ogene and then the Ogana come forward and salute him followed by other Olilinzele and Ndichie. This is followed by a feast in which a cow is slaughtered and shared in the same manner as described in the preceding section.

This title has now lapsed since the death of the last Ndanike in 1902. People say that no one is now prepared to make the title as it can only be validated by the killing of a human victim.

The Ezekoro.   This title has not been made for a very long time. It is vested in the Umutogwuma (7) ward and is said to have been a war title and similar to the Ndanike, but no one can now remember much about it except that it carried the same rights and privileges as the other kingly offices.

The Olilinzele
Both the Obi and the Iyasara can appoint these officials who have various title names but the same praise name, Damanze. A candidate for an Olilinzele title has to pay fees to the Obi, Iyasara and to the other Olilinzele. In the case of an appointment by the Obi the fees paid to the Obi (Ego Igba Opi) were formerly paid in cowries (ohu ugbugba) and this has now been converted to £6 10s. 0d. in cash. This gave the candidate the right to play the Opi drum and perform its associated dance. The candidate, if he wished to participate in ceremonies at the Iyasara's palace, had to pay another smaller fee to him (ego iko akpa), and if he wished to participate in the annual Ibina feast provided by the Obi and the four kingly officials, he had to pay them a further fee (ego ubaba) amounting to £3 15s. 0d. He also paid the Olilinzele a fee of £6 10s. 0d. In the case of appointments by the Iyasara, the fees are similar except that a larger fee is paid to the Iyasara and a smaller one to the Obi.

To be eligible a candidate must have already installed his Okwa Chi (the cult of his own personal destiny or personality) and he must have defined himself as an adult male by providing the Ibu Uno feast for his age set; he must also be a member of the Agbanta society (i.e. he must have completed the burial ceremonies of his father and thus defined himself as an 'elder'). Members of wards which supply the Osere (the three heads of the Agbanta society) and the kingly officials are ineligible, as are those of the wards which supply the Obi, except that the Obi can award an Olilinzele title to the oldest male in his ward so that he can enjoy the royal drum music at his funeral.

Originally only an eldest son could become an Olilinzele but this restriction has now been relaxed.

Candidates are allowed to choose their own special title name but this is preceded by the praise name Damanze. There are at present nine Olilinzele, six appointed by the Iyasara and three by the recently elected Obi. They are listed below:

Created by the Obi

Damanze Ogana
Damanze Ogini
Damanze Eneboachi

Created by the Iyasara

Damanze Odini
Damanze Aguenweoyi
Damanze Onye Okwu
Damanze Agundu
Damanze Isagba Ajie
Damanze Oba

Other title names were Akpulosu, Ochia and Ollua.*

The duties of the Olilinzele are associated with the palace of the Obi and the Iyasara. They alone can enter the inner chamber of their palaces. At any assemblies or festivals held in their compounds the Olilinzele have to drink first from anything that is offered to an Obi or Iyasara. They have the right to speak at meetings held in the Obi or Iyasara's palaces and when any salutation is made to the Obi or Iyasara it is their duty to reply in place of the Obi or Iyasara, who are forbidden to reply to any greetings through fear of sorcery.

The head of the Olilinzele is the Ogana. He may come from any ward that can supply an Olilinzele. He acts as the mouthpiece of the Obi, he opens all discussions at the council meetings or courts held at the Obi's palace (Obi Eze), and is the Obi's secret adviser and confident. As already mentioned, the Iyasara has an equivalent Olilinzele official, the Isagba Ajie.

The special privileges enjoyed by the Oririnzere include the following:

Dress.   They wear an eagle feather (nkpo ugo) in their headdress, carry an iron belled staff (okanshi), and a special bead on a string round their neck of a type that can only be worn by the Obi or by them. They wear a cotton cloth over one shoulder and hanging down to their ankles.

Mortuary rituals.   The opi (royal) drum is played at their funerals for three days (in the case of an Obi's funeral it is played for four

* Since the civil war numerous people have taken the Olilinzele title.

days). The Obi is represented at their funeral by an uko (messenger or representative) who comes accompanied by the opi drummers from the royal ward. At the funeral one of the Olilinzele performs a rite of separation in which a sheep is decapitated and its flesh shared between the Olilinzele. In addition two hundred alligator peppers (ihuli ose oji) and two hundred kola nuts (ihuli oji) are sent to the Obi, who distributes them amongst the Olilinzele.

Special prerogatives.   They alone can perform a special royal dance which takes place at the Ibina and Omelife ceremonies; they dance after the Obi and his senior wife (Odoba) have initiated the dancing.

The Ndichie

This college contains the Ogene (the head of the Ndichie), the three Osere who are the heads of the Agbanta society, the Ezechioha (the priest of the community's cult), and the Ndi Okpala, the ritual heads of the wards, who, in the absence of a kingly official or an Olilinzele are also their political heads, together with the Eze Ani (the priest of the ani cult) and the Igweuta.

These are all ritual heads, most of them associated with cults relating to ancestors, and they represent the traditional and conservative element in Oguta. They are responsible for the performance of all public sacrifices and festivals and other religious ceremonials. It is their duty to see that ritual prohibitions and commands are observed by the people of Oguta, particularly those relating to the land (ani) and, like the deities and spirits to whom they minister, they become angry when any of these rules are broken. For example, an attack by a leopard on any townsman is interpreted as the result of a violation of the taboos of the earth deity.

The Ndichie perform four principle roles in Oguta government. Firstly, they serve as ritual heads and representatives of the collective authority of the various ward ancestors. In the administration of justice, and in the deliberations and decisions of the state council, their presence ensures that the interests of the ancestors, the guardians of the law and of the land, are adequately represented. Secondly, as the individual heads of their respective wards, they ensure that the special interests of each ward are represented in the state council, even though it may lack an Olilinzele or other titled head. Thirdly, as the college of Ndichie they stand in the state council in opposition to the college of Olilinzele. Fourthly, by reason of their ritual authority they are able to mediate in political disputes between the Obi and the kingly officials and, in cases where the Obi has lost the support of his people, they are able to provide an alternative government, for state council meetings can still be held in the Ogene's palace with or without the attendance of the kingly officials and the Olilinzele.

The prerogatives of the Ogene and of every Okpala include special dress and regalia—they wear a special head-dress (okpu afuna enupu), which is a cap with red, black and yellow trimmings that every Oguta male should wear on his death bed and without which he cannot be buried. In this, an eagle's feather (nkpo ugo) is stuck. They have a necklace with two leopards teeth (eze agu), an iron belled staff (okanshi), they may rub white clay (nzu) round their eyes, and like the Olilinzele, they wear a cotton cloth draped over their shoulder and hanging down to their ankles. Each of them has a special ofo, which in the case of the Ogene is the ofo Ugwuta; in the case of the other Okpalas it is the ofo of his particular lineage. They are not entitled to the mortuary rites of kingly officials or of Olilinzele, nor may they perform the Ibina or Omelife ceremonies. They have however the right to attend and to be entertained at such ceremonies.

The Ogene

The Ogene is the oldest male in Oguta. Should two men dispute seniority of age, the issue is decided by divination. He acts as the head of the Ndichie and he holds the ofo Ugwuta the supreme ofo (symbol of ancestral authority) in Oguta.

As soon as the funeral rites of the last Ogene have been completed the Ndichie, who have already ascertained the next most senior man in Oguta, call upon him to accompany them to the house of the deceased Ogene to take over this ofo. This ceremony is called the "Iwe Ofo". The new Ogene goes with the Ndichie and the members of his lineage (and ward), the ofo is placed before him, and a cock (nekwu) is killed and offered as a sacrifice to the ofo for it to accept the transfer from the house of the deceased Ogene to that of the new one. All present eat of the food prepared from this cock. Formal prayers are offered with kola nuts, white clay and palm wine, which is also distributed to all the Okpalas and to the other people present in order of their seniority.

This is followed by Iba Ogene—the ceremony of installation which takes place on a day appointed by the new Ogene. The Ndichie and the corresponding senior members of the women's senior age grade (Otu Ogene) whose head is the Ogene Nwanya, are present, as are the Olilinzele in their full regalia. The Ogene sits on his throne, produces the ofo Ugwatu and sacrifices a goat to it, sprinkling the blood of the goat on the ofo, and on the offering of kola nuts, white clay and palm wine. Then the Ndichie come forward in turn and greet him by his praise name, Ogene, which is also his title name. The goat is cooked and all those present partake of the meal.

COMMONER ORGANISATIONS

In addition to the chiefly and ritual officials there are other associations which, in addition to their other functions, are able to influence the decisions of these officials, or may be called upon to advise the Obi and his officials, or to carry out various duties for them. The most important of these are:

The Ndi Igbu. This is a society which was originally a warriors' society as in Abo, but which is today primarily an association of men who have the wealth to acquire an Igbu title, and with it membership of the association.

The Agbanta society already referred to. No person can become a kingly or chiefly official unless he is already a member of an Agbanta society.

The Age Organisation. As elsewhere, Oguta males (and females) are organised into age sets (there were fifty-three sets at the time of writing) and these sets may be called upon to perform public duties.

The Woman's Organisation (Otu Ogene). As elsewhere, the women of Oguta have their own organisation which parallels that of the men. The most senior woman is the Ogene Nwanye and the other senior women form with her a council of female elders equivalent to that of the Ndichie college of the men's organisation.

OSOMARI

SOCIAL STRUCTURE

Osomari is organised into three primary divisions based on a tripartite segmentation of the dominant immigrant clan of the same name into the three ebo of Isiolu, Ugolo and Umuonyiogwu and these ebo give their names to the three primary divisions. To each of these dominant ebo is attached an ebo of autochthonous or other immigrant people, and an ebo made up of the descendants of former slaves whose masters lived in the dominant or autochthonous ebos. This structure is shown in Table E at the end of the book.

An Osomari ebo is not necessarily an exogamous unit even in the case of the dominant clan. In the Isiolo ebo the true agnates remain exogamous but the attached lineages in this ebo are not. The Ugolo ebo has relaxed the rule of exogamy very recently but still remains under a single Okpala. The reason for this relaxation was that over the years their daughters had married into other ebo and had been the proud mothers of eminent Osomari men. Since these men, their sons, belonged to other divisions, some of them tried to challenge the royal status of the Ugolo ward and supported the aspirations of their father's ebo as against their mother's. This had caused some embarrassment, for a daughter's son should not be in conflict with his mother's brothers. They therefore decided to strengthen the unity of the Ugolo ward by abolishing the rule of exogamy so that its major lineages could intermarry. This was done during the reign of the last Atamanya of Osomari when the heads of the major lineages came together and offered sacrifices to the ancestors, informing them that they intended to remain more united by marrying among themselves. Marriage within each of the three major lineages is still prohibited.

In the ebo of Umuonyiogwu the two major lineages of Animali and Idiofi form a single exogamous group but they can intermarry with members of the Umuonwu major lineage, their "half brother". According to their tradition, Onwu, the founder of this major lineage, committed adultery with the wife of their grandfather Ikala, and Onwu was therefore denied the right to inherit the ofo (ancestral symbol) of the ebo and he was told to make his own ofo. Thus he and his descendants were regarded as a separate maximal lineage with its own ancestral emblem. The children of Onwu were therefore allowed to marry with the major lineages of Animali and Idiofo but all three continued as one political unit.

The three autochthonous ebo observe the rule of exogamy and members of the servile ebo follow the rule of exogamy of the particular ebo to which their fathers belonged. Thus, descendants of a slave belonging to a particular dominant or autochthonous ebo cannot marry the descendants of any other slave who belonged to this lineage.

RITUAL ORGANISATION

The people of Osomari confer political titles on their Okpala and they, like those of Oguta, play important political roles in the state. Every ebo has an Okpala as its ritual head and the most senior of them is the Okpala of the Isiolu ebo, whose title is the Asanya (Uzi). He is the ritual head of Osomari. The Okpala of Ugolo is the ritual head only of his political division, as is the Okpala of the Umuonyiogwu ebo.

POLITICAL ORGANISATION

In the traditional political system of Osomari, the three servile ebo are responsible for the internal government of their respective ebo but have no political representation outside it at the divisional or state levels.

Osomari is to a very much greater degree than the other three systems a segmentary state consisting of three separate political units each with its own kingly head and hierarchy of titled officials (olinzele), to which are attached three subordinate political units (the autochthonous ebo). Each division could break away and develop as an independent political unit but in the course of their history the people of Osomari have accepted the notion of a central authority based on the Ugolo ebo, and the heads of the other two divisions and the olinzele of all grades from all three divisions come together under the Atamanya of Ugolo and form the council of the Osomari state.

Matters which concern the ebo alone are settled by its head and its Olinzele (chiefly officials). Those which involve a primary division are settled by the head of its dominant ward (who is respectively the Atamanya in the case of Ugolo, the Iyase in the case of Isiolu and the Oninowu in the case of Umuonyiogwu) assisted by the Olinzele of the division.

In matters which concern the whole of Osomari, the state council of the kingly and chiefly officials assembles at the palace of the Atamanya. The Atamanya presides with the Oniniogwu on his right and the Iyase on his left.

When anything is shared at the Atamanya's assembly it is divided into three and not into six shares, Ugolo, Isiolu and Umuonyiogwu each take one share and then divide it with their subordinate attached ebo of Ndam, Umuoga and Umuchi. Each division has its own court but appeals can be made from those of Isiolu and Umuonyeogu to the court of the Atamanya.

THE POLITICAL ELITE

Kingly and chiefly offices are not open to large groups of people as at Onitsha but as in Oguta are vested in particular ebo or lineages, and a distinction is made between the political and ritual headship of the state, the ritual headship being vested in the senior ebo of Isiolu, the political in the junior ebo of Ugolo.

There are two grades, a senior called Ndichie Ume (also called Ndichie Ukwu) and a junior known as Isugbe (or Ndichie Nta). The title names vary, and titles with the same name may have the same or different duties attached to the office in the different ebo. Kingly and chiefly officials are recruited from within their individual ebo and no person can take a title outside his own ebo. This means that competition for office is limited to the members of the ebo, and outside intervention becomes minimised, except in the case of the kingly officials when the candidate, after selection by his ebo, must receive the approval of a majority of the chiefly officials of the state.

Each of the dominant sub-clans Ugolo, Isiolu and Umuonyiogwu has the sole right to hold the kingly office of its particular division. These offices are the Atamanya (king) of Ugolo, the Iyase of Isiolu and the Oniniogwu of Umuonyiogwu. Candidates for the office must be free-born men of the particular lineage and a member of the five title societies of Osomari, namely Amanwulu, Igbu, Agana, Inya Akpa and Isa Aka. Their installation and mortuary rituals are the same, they have the same regalia, palace organisation and rituals associated with it, they perform the same annual festivals, their persons are sacred, and they are regarded as supreme in their respective divisions. The Atamanya however is regarded as supreme in matters affecting the whole of Osomari. These kingly and chiefly offices are ascribed on the basis of age in the case of the Iyase and of the Ndichie Ume Olinzele going to the oldest male of a particular lineage or sub-clan. In the case of the Atamanya, the Oniniogwu, and the Isugbe Olinzele chiefs, they are acquired through wealth and personality.

The hierarchy in each ebo consists of the head of the ebo, who, in the case of the dominant ogbe, is also the head of the primary division; below him are the Ndichie Ume, whose head is the oldest man (and therefore the Okpala of the ebo) who acts as its ritual head, and also, when the office of ebo head is vacant, as the political head as well. As in Abo and Oguta, it is possible (except in the case of the Iyase of Isiolu ward) for the political head to combine the two offices of political and ritual head should he happen to become the oldest man in his ebo.

Below the Ndichie Ume are the Ndichie Nta or Isugbe. This grade of chiefs divides into a senior and a junior subdivision. The senior contains the military officials and the Oga (whose duties are to apportion any reward or duty that has to be shared by the Isugbe chiefs). The junior subdivision has military duties and forms a panel from which the senior sub-grades are recruited. The political hierarchies are set out in Table F overleaf.

G

TABLE F
OSOMARI POLITICAL HIERARCHIES

	(Division) UMUONYIOGWU	(Division) UGOLO	(Division) ISIOLU
Ebo Head	Oniniogwu (Odobo) *(Right hand chief)*	Atamanya (Okakwu) *(Head of state)*	Iyase (Onowu) *(Left hand chief)*
Ndichie Ume grade	Isagba (Ajie) Ako (Ebija) Gboba (Inoba) Odaje (Asi) Ike (Ike) Afa (Afa) Asimaha (Akwue) Udor (Ato)	Oniha (Ogene) Alanza (Odua) Ozoma (Onya) Alika (Igbobo) Alo (Uda) Oso (Owelle) Daike (Omodi) Olodu (Akpe) Odaje (Asi)	Asanya (Uzi) Alanza (Odua) Oni (Idoma) Uda (Kolokozo) Asama (Odua) Akpashi (Onokwu) Olodu (Akpe) Iko Obim (Ojolo) Osodi (Inolo)
Isugbe grade Military (Onu Otu)	Isama (Akwue) Oza (Okuta)	Odogwu (Abi) Okwula-gwu (Alum) Akpo (Ezeogu)	Ahanza (Onoli) Idoga Omedem
Sharers (Oga)	Asimaha (Akwue)	Asimaha (Akwue) Nzanabi (Okia)	Igeledu (Odugbani) Asimaha (Akwue) Ominaga (Asagwali)
Junior Section	Aguza (Ojubo) Ominaga (Asagwali) Alino (Adazi)	Uda (Kolokolo Atamabo) Alu (Okwulagwu) Osuma (Uti) Damanze (Gbada) Akogwu (Okpa) Igwoba (Akalamu) Onwulu (Akpashi) Azuga (Ojiabo) Akpo (Ezeogu)	Osuala (Nnoli) Olo (Onika) Ojoko (Onokpo) Dalago (Okwu) Ojuka (Okonwere) Asama

Ebo	UMUCHI	NDAM	UMUOGA
Ndichie Ume grade	Okpala (Eze Ani) Agwuba Nwola (Ahanza)	Oniha (Ogene) Odua (Alanza) Isagba (Ajie) Ojiaka (Oluta) Daike (Omodi) Owelli	Owing to internal disputes people in this ebo were not prepared to give the names of their officials.
Isugbe grade Onu Otu	Ahanza (Onoli)	Odogwu (Abi) Isama (Akwue)	
Sharers (Oga)	Aguza (Ojiabo)	Damanze (Akwue) Odogwu (Abi) Oniniogwu (Asagwali)	
Junior	Osuma (Uti)	(Not given)	

(Praise names where known are shown in brackets)

The organisation of the three subordinate ebo follows the same pattern, though the status of their officials is considered inferior to that of their opposite numbers in the dominant ebo. Umunchi and Ndam each claim that they originally had a kingly official, the Eze Igwe, a title which they claim to have brought from Nri; but this office has lapsed for a considerable time and their senior Ndichie Ume chief acts as the political and ritual head of his ebo.

THE COMMONER ORGANISATIONS

Below these chiefly officials are the non-chiefly sections of the community collectively referred to as Idiagwali and organised into various associations, the most important of which are the three title associations of Agana, Igbu and Inya Akpa; the women's association (Otu Omu); the age organisation (Onuotu); and the Egungu secret society. These have no formal roles in the councils or courts of the ebo or state but can be called upon to carry out various public works and other duties under the direction of the chiefly officials.

THE ATAMANYA (OKAKWU)

The Atamanya (Okakwu) is regarded as the symbol of unity, the father of the people. His power is symbolised in the people's mind as a great wind that sweeps across a forest and he is greeted with the salutation "Okakwu" (tornado). He is the king of the Igili, for Osomari people are known as Igili, meaning warlike and brave people. This bravery is epitomised in the warlike power of their Atamanya who, they believe, possesses all the might to defend the state. He declares wars, makes peace and sends ambassadors to distant land. As the head of the state, people look upon him for good government and the maintenance of peace among the subjects. The prerogative of summoning the Ndichie to a political meeting belongs to him. He takes precedence in the performance of the national festivals of the state such as the Ulo Ufejioku, Okposi, Ojo and Igba Ekwensu. The Iyase and Oniniogwu, even though they do not receive their titles directly through him, recognise that they are subordinate to him. The Ndichie in all the political divisions notify the Atamanya when they wish to take the title.

At a political assembly the two kingly officials, the Iyase and Oniniogwu, sit on each side of Atamanya. The Oniniogwu sits on the right, indicating a closer rank to the Atamanya, and the Iyase sits on the left. Both officials perform their state duties as representatives of the Atamanya. For example, during a period of war, the

Iyase goes to the battle front while the Oniniogwu stays at home to pass information from the Iyase to the Atamanya. The Oniniogwu also arranges with the ndedibia (medicine men) for the preparation of war medicines and protective amulets for the soldiers. When an occasion arises for the Atamanya to pay an official visit or make a procession on a ceremonial occasion, he is accompanied by officials of the state and by his court attendants. The Iyase stands on his left, the Oniniogwu on his right, and the senior Olinzele, including those from Ugolo, accompany them in special order.

In Abo state we noted that Abo without an Obi is inconceivable. The same applies to Oguta and Onitsha. With Osomari the position is different because, as will be shown, a deputy head is available and the Atamanya's office can be vacant over a long period before another candidate is installed.

The duties of the office are performed by the Oniha Ogene of Ugolo who acts as the political head of the state in the long period of interregnum. It is almost ten years since the last Atamanya died but Osomari people are just beginning to consider the selection of a candidate, a situation which could not be tolerated in the other states in our survey.

The position of the Atamanya and the Ndichie of his ward in relation to the Ndichie of the whole community is defined by tradition, which specifies that all officials of the other two divisions are subordinate to the officials of the Atamanya who come from the Ugolo ward. For example, in summoning a political meeting at the palace, two officials from Ugolo, the Asimaha (Akwue) and Nzanabi (Okia), have the duty of summoning the other Ndichie. Unless one of them does this, the Ndichie of the town will not regard such a meeting as official.

Similarly, at an assembly, the Odaje (Asi) of Ugolo who is the Onu Eze (mouth of the king), the king's spokesman, takes precedence over the corresponding officials in the other two divisions.

In the succeeding sections we examine the organisation of each division in more detail.

UGOLO DIVISION

Ugolo Ebo
This royal ward is made up of three major lineages—Ada, Olo, and Ulasi. Its royal origin, according to them, arose from the transfer of political headship to Afeke, the founder of the ward, by his father for services rendered to him during his lifetime. Ugolo is the most junior of the three brother lineages, but the other wards, Isiolu and Umuonyiogwu, acknowledge and accept the political head-

ship of the Atamanya of Ugolo. This political headship is expressed in a number of different ways.

The Atamanya of Ugolo is the head of the state and the heads of the two other divisions—the Oniniogwu (Odobo) of Umuonyiogwu, and the Iyase (Onowu) of Isiolu—are defined as subordinate to him, while the title holders of Ugolo at every level precede title holders of equivalent levels in the two other divisions.

The ofo eze of Osomari, the symbol of the political authority of the state, is held by the Oniha (Ogene) of Ugolo, who hands over this ofo to the Atamanya during the rituals of coronation. The Oniha Ogene, who is the eldest male of Ugolo, is the king-maker and takes precedence over the officials holding the equivalent office in Isiolu and Umuonyiogwu divisions even though they may be senior to him in age. In the period of interregnum, he officiates as an Atamanya and his office becomes not only ritual but also political. He alone can officiate in this role, as he is the deputy of an Atamanya. When sacrifice is offered to the ofo of Osomari, he officiates and the two equivalent officials—the Asanya (Uzi) of Isiolu and the Isagba (Ajie) of Umuonyiogwu—sit beside him. Should he be unable to officiate, his deputy must be the official next in rank within the Ugolo Ndichie Ume grade, and not the Asanya (Uzi) of Isiolu nor the Isagba (Ajie) of Umuonyiogwu.

The female offices of Omu (queen) and Ada Osomari are vested in Ugolo lineage. An Ada (female agnate) of Ugolo and no other person may take the title of Omu (queen) and when this titular office is vacant the Ada Osomari who is the oldest woman of the Ugolo lineage and is the ritual head of all the women of Osomari performs the functions associated with it, being referred to as Omu Odobo. As ritual head of Osomari women the Omu or Omu Odobo ministers to the Ndiem Ohai. This is a cult associated with the three medicines of Utita zua ona, which prevents disputes and strife within the state, Ikwe sua nni osuru osi, which brings peace instead of war, and Ebube Igili, the women's shrine for peace. The magical power of Ndiem Ohai promotes the unity and cohesion of Osomari people. Its counterpart is another medicine called Onunu which transfers and projects on to their enemies the strife and evil desires which Ndiem Ohai has removed from the people of Osomari. The Osomari cult of Onunu is shared by the women of the other two divisions. When sacrifice is offered to it, the Ada Isiolu (the oldest woman of Isiolu), officiates, and at another period the Ada Umuonyiogwu will do so. Onunu is subordinate to Ndiem Ohai, and only the Omu or Ada of Ugolo can act as its priestess.

The right to officiate in sacrifices to Ikenga Osomari is reserved to the Odogwu Abi, the senior military official of Ugolo. Ikenga

Osomari is a cult of good luck and it watches over the fortune of the Osomari in war. It is located in the Isiolu ward and is maintained by the Iyase, the head of this division and the senior war chief of Osomari. But he has no right to officiate at sacrifices to it on behalf of the Osomari state, or even to take its carved "image" down from where it is kept in the roof of his palace.

The Oniha (Ogene). The most important office after that of the Atamanya who is the head of the state, is that of the Oniha (Ogene). As already stated he is the oldest man and ritual head of Ugolo but assumes the political functions of the Atamanya when the office is vacant, in which case he holds the ofo eze, the symbol of political office in the state, as well as the ofo okpara of his lineage. The Ogene's correct title is Oniha, Ogene being his praise name, but the people of Osomari prefer to refer to him by his praise name. In Benin the Oniha is the head of the Uzama group of hereditary title holders who are the kingmakers. Among the Ada kingdoms the Oniha is referred to as the Oniha Aka Eze, the right hand of the king.

Ugolo has produced, in living memory, seven Atamanyas, but the number of the Oniha so far remembered are eleven.[1] One must not infer, however, that a major lineage which has supplied a succession of Onihas is the wealthiest or the strongest. It is a matter of chance as the office is based solely on age. The Atamanya, which is a title based on wealth and influence, has come from Ulasi and Olo lineages. The Ada lineage has not been able to supply an Atamanya, but has tasted political office by providing within living memory four Oniha (Ogene).

The rituals of office of the Oniha (Ogene), as well as those of the equivalent offices in Isiolu and Umuonyeogu, connect the recipient with the powers of the ancestors by means of the ofo of the lineage which he assumes immediately after he has been installed. By inheriting this symbol, he becomes the link between his people and the ancestors. Thus his ceremonies of installation are exclusive to his agnates whose ancestors are concerned with their welfare. This also applies in Oguta. In order to be accepted as a chiefly official, he has to pay fees to the Ndichie. This payment makes him an Olinzele, a member of the chiefly class which administers the state. He does this by visiting first the Atamanya, then the Oniniogwu of Umuonyiogwu, then the Iyase of Isiolu and then the other Ndichie in order of their seniority. He pays to each whatever fees he has previously arranged. It is possible that an Onyeiche may waive the payment of the fee if he and Oniha are close relations.

The ofo is taken from the residence of the deceased Oniha as soon as his mortuary rites are completed, for it is only then that the rites of separation have effectively released the dead man from the responsibility of his office and freed the ofo for use by his successor. But he cannot take it until he has paid these fees. A day after he has done this the new Oniha goes to the residence of the last Oniha and takes the ofo back to his residence. This ceremony is called Ikpoko Ofo and is followed by Igonachi, when all Ugolo Olinzele of both grades, together with the Idiagwali (commoners), and the Ada (the daughters of the lineage), assemble at his residence. He sits on his throne (ukpo) on a dais, and the senior Ada, of the ebo "washes" the ofo with a chicken. That is, she takes a chicken, slaughters it by cutting its throat, and sprinkles the blood on the ofo, "cleansing" it with her hands by rubbing the blood into the ofo. This is known as Igoya na chi. A white goat (ewu ocha) is offered by the Oniha as a sacrifice and the blood is sprinkled on the ofo. He prays for the peace, longevity and prosperity of the members and implores the ancestors to support him during his tenure of office. They all partake of the meal prepared from the meat of the goat and the chicken.

It is an occasion for communal joy, and on festival occasions like the Ulo and the Okposi, he is in duty bound to offer a goat as sacrifice to the ofo, and all agnates partake of the communal meal in a ceremony of reintegration.

Other Ugolo Olinzele. In the chiefly hierarchy of Ugolo ebo there are nine Ndichie Ume chiefs namely: Oniha (Ogene), Alanza (Odua), Ozoma (Onya), Alika (Igbobo), Alo (Uda), Oso (Owelle), Daike (Omodi), Olodu (Akpe), Odaje (Asi). These titles are conferred on the nine oldest men of the Ugolo lineage. As we have shown already, the oldest of them takes the title of Oniha with the praise name of Ogene, the eight other titles being filled by the next eight in the order of their age. On the death of an Ogene or other Ndichie Ume titled official the office passes to the next oldest male who, if he is already holding an Ume title, will vacate this title on assumption of the higher office.

There are fourteen Isugbe titles. These titles are open to competition amongst the men of wealth and influence in the Ugolo ebo. The Atamanya has a free hand in their appointment and as soon as he accepts a candidate's fees the office is reserved for him (Okudo). The senior titles in their ranking order are Odogwu (Abi), Okwulagwu (Alum), Akpo (Ezeogu) the leader of the Okolobia (young men). These are war chiefs. Asimaha (Akwue) and Nzanabi (Okia) are Oga (sharers). The junior Isugbe titles are Uda (Kolo

Kolo Atamabo), Alu (Okwulagwu), Osuma (Uti), Damanze (Gbada), Akogwu (Okpa), Igwoba (Akalamu), Onwulu (Akpashi), Azuga (Ojiabo), and Akpo (Ezeogu). Isugbe titles become vacant either through the death of the holder or by his assumption of an Ndichie Ume title. The taking of these titles does not involve much ceremony and the candidate only distributes title fees to the Olinzele of his ebo and to the Atamanya.

Ndam Ebo

This ebo has its own pattern of titles which they claim were their original titles before the arrival of the Osomari people. They also claim Igala origin. According to them, they and Umuchi, both original inhabitants, had their own kings and did not originally attend the political assembly of the three dominant lineages, though they could delegate persons to this assembly. Later the three dominant Osomari groups absorbed each of the three original groups—Ndam, Umuchi and Umuoga—as has already been explained. When Ndam became incorporated into their system, it was attached to Ugolo and shared in political activities with it as Umuchi did with Umuonyiogwu and Umuoga with Isiolu.

Ndam chiefly offices follow the general pattern. There are two colleges of Olinzele, namely, the Ndichie Ukwu (Ume), made up of six titles—Oniha (Ogene), Odua (Alanza), Isagba (Ajie), Ojiaka (Obuta), Daike (Omodi), and Owelli—and the Isugbe titles which are eight in number and are graded as in Ugolo ebo into two military titles—Odogwu (Abi) and Isama (Akwue), three Oga—Damanze (Gbada), Odogwu (Abi) and Oniniogwu (Asagwali), and three junior titles.

Ndam say that they originally had an Eze Igwe (king) as head of their ward and the first Eze Igwe was Eze Igwe Ikewuazor. The number of other Eze Igwes was not revealed nor did they explain the origin of this kingly office.

UMUONYIOGWU DIVISION

The Oniniogwu (Odobo).   The head of this ebo and division is the Oniniogwu (Odobo). His office, like that of the Atamanya, is open to any male of wealth and influence in this ebo.

This office, like that of the Iyase of Isiolu, is a kingly one and the installation ceremonies and rituals follow closely those of the Atamanya. They include payment of fees after selection; presentation to the Atamanya and Ndichie; assembly at the residence of the Isagba Ajie in the case of the Odobo, and of the Asanya Uzi in the case of Iyase; the carrying of the candidate; crowning by the ritual head of the ward, the Asanya Uzi for the Iyase and the Isagba Ajie for the Oninogwu; making offerings to the town deities; and feasting the general public. Their subordination to the Atamanya is shown, however, in certain details of these ceremonies. For example, the Oniniogwu and the Iyase pay fees to the Atamanya and to the Olinzele of all three divisions. They have to be presented to the Atamanya before they are crowned and the Atamanya is represented at their coronation ceremonies by the Odaje (Asi) of Ugolo.

The Oniniogwu and the Iyase are represented respectively as the right hand and left hand man of the Atamanya and in state councils they sit on his right and on his left. The importance of their offices is demonstrated by the participation of the entire town in their coronation rituals. The Oniniogwu, like the Atamanya, has an Ndichie Ume chief who speaks for him at public gatherings and council meetings, and who has the same titular name, Odaje (Asi).

The Umuonyiogwu people have forgotten the names of most of their Oniniogwu; the only one remembered, apart from Oniniogwu Ogbonna who was crowned in 1937, is that of Oniniogwu Oguike who was in office in 1840 during the period of the Royal Africa Company.

The Isagba (Ajie). The ritual head of this ward is the Isagba (Ajie). Like the Ogene of Ugolo he is the oldest man and Okpala of his ward who, when there is no Oniniogwu (Odobo), acts as the head of the ward and of the division.

The rituals of installation are the same as those of the Ogene of Ugolo and the Asanya (Uzi) of Isiolu. Like these officials, the Isagba Ajie in addition to being the ritual head also acts as political head of his ward and division when there is no Odobo. It is also possible for an Odobo to become the oldest man in his ward, in which case he will hold the office of Isagba (Ajie) as well as his own kingly office. The fact that the Isagba (Ajie) can officiate as political head of his ward has meant that there is little urgency to fill the office of Oniniogwu as the functions of head of the ward can be carried out by the Ajie.[2]

Other Umuonyiogwu Olinzele. The other Ndichie Ume titles are the Ako (Ebija), Gboba (Inoba), Odaje (Asi), Ike (Ike), Afa (Afa), Asimaha (Akwue). As in the other wards, they are held by the next oldest men in the ward after the Isagbe Ajie in order of their age. In the Isugbe titles there are two senior military officials, namely, the Isama (Akwue) and the Oza (Okuta), one Oga (sharer), namely the Asimaha (Akwue), and three junior titles, Aguza (Ojubo), Ominaga (Asagwali) and Alibo (Adazi).

The titles are open to competition amongst the men of the ward. The Oniniogwu has the sole right to appoint to these titles. The candidate has, as in other wards, to pay fees to the Oniniogwu and to the Olinzele of his ward, and if he wishes to rank as an Olinzele of Osomari he must also pay fees to the Atamanya. This also applies to the Ndichie of the Ume grade.

Umuchi Ebo.   This ward has the same political hierarchy of chiefs as Umuonyiogwu. Its people claim that they originally had a kingly title, Eze Igwe, which they brought with them from Nri, their original home. The first Eze was their founding ancestor, but after he died the office lapsed. They claim that they also brought an Iyase title with them from Nri. This is unlikely as the political system of the Nri type is not associated with any hierarchy of titled chiefs.

The Eze Ani.   In default of a kingly official the political head of Umuchi, like the heads of the other original wards, is the Okpala, who is the oldest man in the ward. He is also the Eze Ani, the priest of ani Osomari, the local earth deity, a cult in which the whole of this community participates. The cult of ani, the local land deity, is always held by the first group to settle in an area. The original settlers in the Osomari area were the Ndam people who were later joined by Umuchi. When the dominant Igala group arrived Ndam moved away, settling eventually in the Ugolo area. The Igala group therefore asked Umuchi to take over the cult of ani and since then this ward has supplied the Eze Ani who officiates at all ceremonies in which offerings are made to the deity and who receives all fees paid for this purpose. These fees, which are graded according to the importance of the sacrifice, are fixed by the Eze Ani and he can vary them as he pleases. He normally charges 3d. for rituals in which a fowl is sacrificed, 6d. where it is a goat, and 1s. when it is a cow.

In the coronation ritual of the three kingly officials, each has to offer a cow to Ani Osomari at a ceremony in which the Eze Ani officiates. When the sacrifice is made by a new Atamanya, the carcass of the beast is divided into two parts, one of which goes to the Umuchi ebo, the other to the rest of Osomari. These and other public sacrifices to Ani Osomari are great occasions in the ritual and political life of the community. All Ndichie Ume who are Okpalas of their wards and lineages attend with their ofo okpala. These ofos are all placed before the Ani shrine together with the ofo

Osomari (the ofo okpala of the whole community which is held by the Asanya Uzi of the Isiolu ward).

The Eze Ani wears his traditional regalia which includes a red cap (okpu ododo) into which eagle feathers (nkpo ugo) are inserted. This head-dress is part of the distinguishing regalia of those who have made the Igbu and Agana titles. But the Eze Ani has the right to wear it irrespective of whether he has made these titles or not.

Other Umuchi Olinzele. The Eze Ani is the senior of the three Ndichie Ume titles in this ward, the other two titled officials being the Agwuba and the Nwola (Ahanza). In the Isugbe grade the senior war chief (Onuotu) is Ahanza (Onoli), the Oga (sharer) is Aguza (Ojiabo) and the two junior titles are Osuma (Uti).

ISIOLU DIVISION

Isiolu Ebo
This is the senior of the three ebo or sub-clans of Osomari. Its founder, however, did not inherit the ofo eze, the political staff of office of their father, but instead inherited the ancestral ofo okpala which carries ritual rather than political authority. The significance of this ritual authority is shown by other cultural indices found in this ward. The oji tree, an important shrine which, according to them, they brought along from Idah, is located at Isiolu because of their father being the eldest male of the three sons of their father. Onojo oboli, the cult of the earth deity of their ancestor, is also located at Isiolu.

The Asanya (Uzi). These three ritual symbols of authority and unity (ofo okpala, oji, onojo oboli) belong to the Isiolu sub-clan and ebo and are ministered to by its ritual head, the Okpala of this ward, who takes the title of Asanya (Uzi), and is the principal officiator on occasions when sacrifices are offered to any of the cults.

The Asanya (Uzi), like his counterparts, the Ogene of Ugolo and the Isagba (Ajie) of Umuonyiogwu, has to pay title fees to the Atamanya and Olinzele before he can rank as an Ndichie Ume. His installation ceremonies take the following sequence. The first stage of installation is known as the Ikpa aka or "notification". This notification involves his going to the Atamanya, to the Oniniogwu (Odobo), and to the Ndichie Ume in the following order: The Oniha (Ogene) of Ugolo, the Isagba (Ajie) of Umuonyiogwu, the

Oniha (Ogene) of Ndam,[3] the Oniha (Ogene) of Umuoga, the Alanza (Odua) of Ugolo, the Alanza (Odua) of Isiolu, the Ako (Ebija) of Umuonyiogwu, the Oni (Idoma) of Isiolu, the Uda (Kolokozo) of Isiolu, the Ozoma (Onya) of Ugolo, the Gboba (Inoba) of Umuonyiogwu and the Ozoma (Onya) of Umuoga. These are the Ndichie Ukwu who accept the title fees. This is followed by the ritual Ijucha Uno. On the morning before the ceremony, the Ada (eldest daughter) of Isiolu takes a chicken and cleanses the residence of the Uzi (Ijucha Uno) to make it holy. This is done by tying the chicken on a palm leaf and dragging it along the whole yard. All the Ndichie of the ward assemble and act according to the order of their office. The Asanya Uzi brings the ofo, sprinkles water on it, and asks the ancestors to cleanse their hands. He then takes kola nuts and prays, offering them to the ofo. The Oga divides the pieces of the nuts and distributes them according to the seating arrangement.

After this, a goat is offered to the Ndi Muo, the big ancestral shrine. The meat is cooked as soup and ten sets of pounded yam (nsupu nni ili) are prepared. The people eat communally. Drinks are served after being offered to the ofo and Nde Muo.

After the first stages are complete, another ritual offering takes place on the day when he collects the ofo Ndi Muo from the residence of the deceased Uzi to take to his place. A pot of fish is prepared and a goat is offered as a sacrifice to the ofo. The head and two of the legs are cooked and other parts of the goat—the liver and stomach, known collectively as "nyenye anu"—are cooked separately.

The Okpala takes the obu anu (heart), and one leg is given to his supporters who sit beside the ukpo. The head of the goat, the two hind feet, and the head and tail of the fish are all put on one plate and he places them on the shrines. He gives one leg to his senior wife. The rest of the meat and fish are then eaten, the fish being distributed among those present. All his agnatic and cognatic kinsmen each bring a bottle of gin, some palm wine and one kola nut. These are offered to the shrines and are shared among all present. After drinking, the pot of meat, which has been put aside, is then shared. He takes the part called ofu aka anu, and the Asanya Uzi takes the ose anu (the ribs), while the rest is cut into pieces and distributed to all present. The Ada, the senior daughter, takes the ukwu anu (loins).

These are not the only rituals in which the Asanya (Uzi) has to sacrifice on behalf of his ebo to their ancestors. There are the annual Ulo and Okposi festivals attended by all members of the ebo when he has to make similar sacrifices and provide a similar feast.

The Iyase (Onowu). The political head of the ward is the Iyase Onowu. This title is vested in the Inwala lineage, a migrant group from Awka that became incorporated in the Isiolu sub-clan. There are two versions of the origin of this title. The first version, which is popular, and not disputed, is that the title originated when the founder of the Inwala ward saved the people of Osomari from the dangers of two man-eating animals.

According to the story, a leopard appeared one night and made life intolerable in the town, to the extent that the people could no longer go out at nights. The Inwala migrant, who was called Alaguda, assured the people that he would kill the leopard and he eventually caught the animal with a special trap and killed it. The second animal was a crocodile (aguiyi) which appeared at the waterside at dusk. Farmers were afraid of unloading their farm produce and of coming ashore after dark because of it. Alaguda was able to catch and to kill this beast by means of a special type of spear (onya).

In return for these heroic activities, the whole town offered him two gifts and asked him to choose the one he preferred. One was to take a wife from any of the families, so that by marriage he would be fully incorporated into the society and could take Osomari titles reserved for persons who can trace their descent to the founder of the ward. The other was to accept a title. He chose this latter offer and the people of Osomari—the Atamanya and Ndichie—decided to confer on him a title that symbolised a heroic act of bravery, and which also signified the defender of the realm and war leader. They conferred the title of Iyase (Onowu) on Alaguda. Each of the sub-clans carved an Ikenga, and collectively they also carved a larger Ikenga for the whole community. The big Ikenga and the other three small Ikenga were tied together and given to Alaguda and his family. He thus became the defender of the people and their leader in time of war.

The Ikenga became the war shrine of the whole community, and was kept at his residence. On every yearly feast of Ogba Ekwensu, all the Osomari Igbu title holders go to the Inwala lineage to offer sacrifices to the Ikenga. According to this tradition there was no Iyase title before then and Alaguda was the first to hold this title, and it became vested in the Inwala lineage.

Another version is that the title originally belonged to the Umuchi ward of Umuonyiogwu, and that it was this group which surrendered the title to the town when it decided to confer the title on Alaguda. Umuchi, as stated in the previous section, claimed that they could not give the names of the early Iyase or of the one that held the office at the time it was surrendered.

After the death of Alaguda, the Inwala people decided that its inheritance should be based on age. The title thus then went to the eldest agnatic male, who was also the Okpala of the lineage. But as this is a kingly title a candidate for this office must have taken the Igbu, Agana and Inya Akpa titles. The installation ceremonies for the Iyase (Onowu) are the same as those for the Oniniogwu.

Seven Iyase are remembered. The first five in order of their succession are: Alaguda, Odunwu, Onwali, Nwadialo, Akubeze. After Akubeze a dispute arose in which two candidates contested the office, namely Onwodi and Egonu. The Inwala lineage became divided over the issue and appealed for support to the lineages of the mothers of the candidates. This brought the Ugolo ward into the conflict, for Onwodi's mother's lineage was the Odogwunape major lineage of Ugolo and Egonu's mother's lineage was the Alabo major lineage.

Egonu was younger than Onwodi and therefore not entitled to the office but he had wealth and he and his supporters sought to alter the principle of succession and make it open to men of wealth bringing it into line with the principle which applied to the other kingly offices of Atamanya and Oniniogwu. Egonu received the support of the Alabo major lineage of Ugolo and the majority of the Isiolu division and they met together and crowned him as Iyase. Onwodi's supporters in Ugolo rallied, met at the palace (Obieze) and crowned him Iyase. This occurred in 1932. As there was no provision for the deposition of an Iyase, Osomari had two Iyase holding office at the same time, and people waited for both to die before deciding which principle of succession they ought to follow. Egonu died first (in 1937) and this early death was taken as an indication that he had gone against the traditional custom, and after the death of Onwodi the Inwala people reverted to the ancient practice and chose Onwuora the oldest man of their lineage.

The fact that Inwala is a stranger lineage incorporated into Isiolu sub-clan makes the role of the Iyase, the political head of this ebo, significantly different from his counterparts in the other two divisions. As far as the internal political organisation of Isiolu ward is concerned the Iyase is subordinate to the Asanya (Uzi), but his status as war leader and left hand man of the Atamanya gives the Iyase superior status in divisional and state councils and assemblies.

Other Isiolu Olinzele. The political hierarchy follows the same model as in Ugolo and Umuonyiogwu.

The Ndichie Ume consists of ten offices: Asanya (Uzi), Alanza (Odua), Oni (Idoma), Uda (Kolokozo), Asama (Odua), Akpashi (Onokwu), Olodu (Akpe), Iko, Gbim (Ojuio), and Osodi (Inolo).

These titles are filled by the ten oldest men of this sub-clan and ward. The senior military titles in the Isugbe grade are three, namely the Ahanza (Onoli), the Idoga and the Omedem. There are three Oga (sharers), namely, Igeledu (Odugbani), Asimaha (Akwue), Ominaga (Asagwali)—which last is reserved for the Inwala lineage only. The junior Isugbe titles are six, namely, Osuala (Nnoli), Olo (Onika), Ojoko (Onokpo), Dalago (Okwu), Ojuka (Okonwere), and Asama, who is the attendant of the Iyase. These six titles, as in other wards, are open to competition, and title holders in the junior grade move to the higher Isugbe grade when an office falls vacant and to an Ndichie Ume should their age entitle them to hold the office.

NOTES

1   The Oniha, according to their chronological order, are: Ossai, Nwagbua, Atokwu, all from Ada; Chukwuofo, Nwagbue, Ugliogwu, and Chukwuma, all from Olo; Obiora from Ada; and Agudusi, Anyesom, and Okapu, all from Ulasi.
2   The people remember the names of twelve Isagba Ajie namely, 1st Ite, 2nd Nwagali, 3rd Odobo Agun, 4th Mgbomere, 5th Osaji, 6th Iwuchukwu, 7th Oholo, 8th Adione, 9th Etele, 10th Nwokochu, 11th Okweso, and 12th Ogbonne (who is also the Oninowu Odobo).
3   This is a recent development since Ndam people began to pay title fees in Osomari.

Chapter 5 The Functions of Government I

POLICY MAKING AND THE LEGISLATIVE PROCESS

In this and in the succeeding chapter we seek to show how policies are made in each state, how decisions are implemented, disputes settled and law and order maintained and finally how the state is organised for war.

Decision making in each state whether in political, judicial, executive or ritual matters is concentrated in a state council whose members hold their positions either by virtue of an acquired titular office or by one that is ascribed on the basis of age and descent. But these councillors are expected to represent the interests of all segments of the community organised in a hierarchy of councils with the state council at the apex. This hierarchy corresponds to the segmentary structure of the community, each political segment at every level of the structure having its council which deals with its own internal affairs, and which is represented on the councils formed at the levels above it. We can in most of these states distinguish three principal levels which we can call the local, intermediate and state levels.

These various councils particularly at the higher levels are dominated by a class of people who perform important functions in carrying out governmental activities. They are the politicians who seek power and authority within the structural political units in each kingdom. For convenience's sake, I use Bottomore's terms of "political class" and "political elite"; by "political class" I mean all those people who seek political power and influence, and who are directly engaged in the struggle for political leadership. Within this political class Bottomore distinguishes a small group, the "political elite", which comprises those individuals who actually exercise political power in the society.[1]

In these states the political elite is relatively easy to determine. It is, as Lloyd has rightly stated, "those who have the ear of the king".[2] In these kingdoms, as we have shown in Chapters 3 and 4, there are titled officials who are recruited in various ways in each state and who are the members of the political class and the political elite. Most of the political offices are only open to those who are already members of particular title associations (e.g. Igbu and Ozo

at Onitsha; Igbu at Abo; Ikwa Muo and Igbu at Oguta; and
Inyakpa, Agana and Igbu at Osomari). Entrance to these societies
involves considerable expenditure on entrance fees and feasting
and they thus impose an effective 'means test' on those seeking
political recognition.

From this class are recruited the heads of each state and their
principle officials, whether kingly officials as at Oguta and Osomari,
or colleges of titled chiefs (called Ndichie at Onitsha, Olinzele at
Abo and Osomari, Olilinzele at Oguta).

In addition to these political offices acquired through wealth and
influence there are other traditional Ibo offices which are ascribed
on a basis of age and descent and which are primarily associated
with the ritual headship (Okpala) of a lineage or clan. Some of
these are incorporated into the political system of all the states
except Onitsha and form part of the state council. Such officials
are the Odua at Abo, the Ogene, the Ezechioha and the three Osere
at Oguta, and the Ogene, Uzi and Ajie at Osomari. In addition
the ritual heads form the Ndichie college of chiefs at Oguta and the
senior grade of Ndichie Ume chiefs at Osomari. There is also at
Abo the special office of Akpulosu which is held by the Obi's
eldest son.

These two categories of officials based respectively on acquired
titles and on age and descent are not exclusive. Okpala and other
ritual heads are usually members of title associations, and any
Olinzele chief or kingly official or even the head of the state himself
should he become the oldest man in his lineage can also become
its Okpala. The tendency in Oguta and Osomari, as we shall show,
is to use one category to counterbalance or support the other.

The political class thus comprises the titled chiefs and ritual heads
and the title association members from amongst whom members of
the political elite may be recruited. The political elite consist of
two grades, a senior grade whose officials have direct access to the
king and a junior grade whose members do not. Their composition
differs in each state.

At Onitsha there are the six officials of the senior grade of Ndichie
Ume who have direct access to the Obi and are each in charge of
one of the six administrative Ebo (political subdivisions) of the state.
They are assisted by the two lower grades of Ndichie chiefs, and in
the Ebo councils by the Agbalanze and the heads of the lineages
contained in the Ebo.

At Abo the elite comprises the eleven first grade Olinzele (six
from Umudei and five from Ndichie) who have regular access to
the Obi, being regularly summoned by him for consultation at the
palace. Like Onitsha, they have subordinate officials under them

H

who attend state councils and assist in the administration of the state.

At Oguta the political elite are the four kingly officials and the Ndi Okpala who form the Ndichie college of chiefs. They have the right to see the Obi in person but do not usually approach him unless summoned to a council meeting. There are also the Olinzele chiefs who, though ranking below the kingly officials, are in constant contact with the Obi and his palace and who in state council meetings range themselves with the Obi and in opposition to the Ndichie chiefs and the kingly officials.

At Osomari the elite are the Ndichie Ume chiefs who with the heads of the three political divisions form the governing body of the state assisted by the Olinzele titled chiefs.

The making of law is the concern of the political class who operate within the hierarchy of councils already outlined, through which the opinion of the people is crystallised into a national policy.

In each of the kingdoms, there are various interest groups, corporate descent and quasi-descent groups within an Ogbe, age organisations, title associations, and women's associations. Each group has an interest in its welfare and in the defence of these interests within the framework of the law of the state. They express their opinion through their own members in the political class who are in constant communication with other members of this class.

The political class has to operate through the recognised institutions of government in order to reconcile the interests of the various groups and to carry out the activities of administering the state. The ways in which the opinions of the various groups are channelled will be shown as we describe the process of decision making at each level of the political segment, and how ultimately at the state level, the opinions collected from below or derived from above become the laws of the land.

THE LOCAL COUNCIL (IZU OGBE)

Matters generally discussed at this level are those which affect the members of a corporate descent group (ogbe) such as:

Ritual matters. These include decisions to offer communal sacrifices to the ancestors or other cults of the group; the performance of the mortuary rites of deceased members; the consultation of the native doctors (dibia) to find out the cause of a particular mishap within the group; planning the proper performance of the festivals of the year.

Economic matters. The discussion of land allocation, of rents or leases, and the collection of rents from tenants. This can be done also at a lower or major lineage level, but where land is not divided up into fragments but is held by the Okpala on behalf of the whole group, land matters often occur at this level. Again, they resolve land disputes between the different lineage segments within the larger corporate group. Accounts are rendered about properties owned corporately by the group and held in trust by the head of the lineage.

Marriage regulations. The members see that the rules governing the institution of marriage are maintained. They take part in the marriage ceremonies, and also the negotiation for marriage between any of their members and a member of another Ogbe. They assist members to enforce the rule of divorce, particularly in ensuring that the bride price is refunded to any of their agnates whose wife has deserted her husband. They discuss all matters that will strengthen the institution of marriage among their members.

Titles. They assist their members who desire to take titles by directly participating in the ceremonies and by turning out on ceremonial days in full numbers to support their king. They may assist by helping the recipient to pay the title fees or to defray the cost of the other expenses involved. They discuss all matters which affect the taking of titles. If a particular title association is headed by any of their members, they ensure that the rules of the title society are preserved so that they do not lose the right to the headship.

All these activities are still carried out today at this level in each of the states.

INTERMEDIATE COUNCILS

This level of Council applies to the six administrative ebo of Onitsha, the four administrative ebo of Abo, and the three political divisions (Ugolo, Isiolu and Umuonyiogwu) of Osomari. Such councils discuss the following: matters brought from the local councils within the ebo or division arising from the four subjects already outlined; matters affecting law and order, like the settlement of internal disputes within the ebo; the recruitment of an army in the time of war; the mobilization of labour for public duties; the collection of obligatory gifts for the higher officials and for the king at festivals. The elite members of these councils also explain and obtain support for state policies and help to enforce the laws passed by the state council.

THE STATE COUNCIL AND THE GENERAL ASSEMBLY

At this level the political elite are involved in activities which affect all members of the state and, to enable them to carry out these functions more effectively they are organised into three different types of council namely:

The privy or executive council which is a regular standing committee of the full council which makes routine decisions and carries them out either collectively or through the appropriate officials charged with these specific duties.

The full council (Izu Ndichie or Izu Olinzele) which provides for the representation of all major political segments of the state through their titled officials, and determines by a concensus decision matters which are too important to be left to the Privy Council.

The general assembly (Izu Obodo) is one which all members of the state are entitled to attend or to be represented, either as members of their respective lineages (ogbe) or of the various age and other associations (including women's associations) and which must be convened to accept and approve all major state decisions.

The use made of these types of council varies in the different states. In Onitsha and Abo where there is a greater concentration of power at the centre, greater use is made of the privy council which in Onitsha consists of the Obi and the six Ndichie Ume, and at Abo of the Obi and the eleven Olinzele chiefs. The general assembly is used principally to collect opinions and to promote discussion of controversial topics but the decisions are made in the privy council and ratified, should the subject be of sufficient importance, at the full council.

In Oguta and Osomari where power is more broadly based and distributed between component ogbe, there is no standing committee or executive council of this sort. Decisions which concern the state as a whole are made at the full council and ratified by the general assembly.

The activities of the political elite in the State Council and the General Assembly include such matters as:

International affairs. For example, the decision to wage war or make peace. The formulation and approval of treaties. All treaties ith the British Crown in 1863, 1874, and 1885 were signed in each ate by the then Obis and the senior titled officials of the state.

itual matters. They fix the dates of national festivals, and they irect ritual affairs, such as the offering of communal sacrifices to ppease the gods. The Obi and officials are responsible for the rganisation and conduct of all sacrifices which are offered for the llective welfare of the community. Together with the priests and diokpala they are the moral guardians of the community, and e symbols of the spiritual unity of the state. On such occasions ey pray to any deities who might be offended, asking them not turn their faces away from their children, not to inflict punish- ent on any of them.

conomic matters. They legislate on issues dealing with land ghts if they involve conflicts in the community, or issues which re referred to them from any of the lower levels of the system, or om individuals.

itle taking. They legislate on rules governing title associations y fixing fees, altering rules that are considered no longer applicable, d enforcing new rules that are approved.

larriage and public morality. They legislate against any abuse f the institutions of marriage and family life. They regulate the nduct and morals of younger members of the community. In ch cases, the council reviews any matter or matters brought from low.

LITE AND ARENA COUNCILS

he behaviour and attitudes of the political elite are often a reflec- on of how they assert their power and authority. At every level the political structure they play an important role, and help in e making of policies and the enforcement of the authority of the vernment. Where, for example, as at Abo or Onitsha, power is ncentrated in the hands of a small group (the elite), their tendency ill be, as is often the case with politicians, to retain this concentra- on of power and to be reluctant to surrender any part of it by nceding some form of 'sovereignty' to the people.

In both states, the elite have won their position not by majority te, but by appointment by the Obi; once appointed, they retain eir office for life and cannot therefore be challenged by the people, though the latter may rebel against one of them in which case they would ask for a new leader from within the political class to replace him. The tendency is for the elite to defend their collective position against the standpoint of the people.

The privy (standing committee) council at Abo and Onitsha is similar to Bailey's "Elite Council". By this term he means "those who are or consider themselves to be (whether they admit it or not) a ruling oligarchy". The dominant cleavage in such a group, he argues, is between the elite council (including, where appropriate, the minority from which it is recruited) and the public; thus the dominant cleavage is horizontal.[3]

Onitsha and Abo state councils are typical elite councils. Their elitist attitude is based on the belief in their common interest. At Onitsha the Ndichie Ume are bound together by the rituals of the 'rites de passage' during the installation of each of them. This is the Ikpoko ofo, a ceremony described in Chapter 3. In the chapter on succession we shall show further how they hold together when they defend their actions in the installation rituals in support of an Obi as opposed to the wishes of the people. Whenever, in either state, they have to take unpopular action, they defend and try to justify it by citing traditional precedents.

The opposite to an elite council is defined by Bailey as an arena council, here the dominant cleavages are vertical rather than horizontal. Such councils are the state councils of Oguta and Osomari which provide for the representation of each political segment (ogbe or ebo) in the community. Here although the representatives of the segment may be drawn from the political elite, they primarily represent the interests of their segment as against those of other segments, and thus differentiation of interest between elite and the people who they represent is minimised. At the local level the councils tend to be Arena Councils. They represent the various lineage segments within each ogbe except when the common interest of the group is to be considered and a common policy is involved which is in opposition to that of other similar groups.

ONITSHA

At Onitsha there are at the lowest political level twenty-two ogbe, each of which has its own ogbe council consisting of the head (Okpala) of the ogbe, the Ndiokpala of its component lineages together with any Onyeichie or Ndichie or Ozo titled persons in the ogbe and any influential Agbalanze members or igiro (young men).

The twenty-two ogbe are organised into six administrative political units, ebo, each of which has its council headed by one of the six Ndichie Ume, the first grade of title holders of the state council. At the highest level is the state council and the general assembly discussed in greater detail in a later section.

The state council is the focus of the unity of the state, although the groups within this council reflect the segmentary structure of the state, particularly the opposition between the royal and non-royal divisions. Each political division can also, should the need arise, hold a council meeting consisting of Ndichie and elders for each of the Ebo in the division.

We can also distinguish a further type of council which comes into being when there is conflict between the Obi and the non-royal division of Onitsha (Ugwuna Obankpa). On such occasions this division withdraws from the state council and forms its own divisional council which is headed by the senior ranking Ndichie Ume chief in Ugwunaobamkpa.

THE LOCAL COUNCIL (IZU OGBE)

The head of the Ogbe council is usually its Okpala (ritual head) unless he has failed to make the Ozo title, in which case he appoints one of these titled men (Agbalanze) to act for him, or unless one of the Ndichie chiefs is a member of the ogbe in which case he takes precedence over the Okpala and is recognised as its political head. All adult free-born males of the ogbe have a right to attend and speak at the meeting and the young men (igiro) may also attend if invited by the council.

The meeting is opened in every case by the Okpala of the ogbe who makes an offering of kola nuts to the ancestors. These are then shared by the members in order of their rank: the head of the ogbe, the Agbalanze (Ozo titled men), the Ndi Okpala (lineage heads), ordinary men and igiro (young men).

Any person can initiate a discussion by informing the head of the ogbe if it is a matter that concerns the whole ogbe, and if he does not want it to be discussed within his own major lineage. The head can either inform the council of the agenda for discussion before the meeting takes place, or he can reserve this until they have assembled. He can also confer first with the senior members of the ogbe before the meeting begins.

After the agenda for the meeting has been announced, the head of the ogbe opens the discussion. He speaks first, then the Agbalanze according to their seniority in the Agbalanze society, and the non-Agbalanze (the ordinary men) speak last. If the Okpala of an ogbe is not an Agbalanze, he speaks as an ordinary man.

The aim of the council is to reach a collective decision. To this end all who wish to are encouraged to express their opinions and when they seem to be approaching a consensus the head of the Ogbe, if he is able, sums up the decision of the meeting. When no concensus is achieved, the meeting can be adjourned or terminated, or the matter can be referred to the council at the higher level. For example, should the Agbalanze titled members behave as a political elite and seek to try and dominate the meeting and impose their will upon the rest, the non-Agbalanze can refuse to agree and insist on the matter being referred to the ebo council which can over-rule a decision of an ogbe council.

THE INTERMEDIATE COUNCIL (IZU EBO)

There are six ebo councils each of which is headed by a particular Ndichie Ume chief appointed for this purpose by the Obi and who is not necessarily or usually a member of the ebo. Other members are Ndichie of the second and third grades who are members of the ebo, the Agbalanze, the Ndi Okpala of all the lesser lineages within these ogbe and all adult males of the ebo. The Ndichie in each ebo constitute a standing committee (privy council), and they discuss day-to-day affairs of the ebo with the chairman; but full council meetings are convened for more important matters and for explaining and discussing policies and decisions of the state council.

In their efforts to advance a point to which they feel committed by virtue of their position, they behave in an elitist way.

At a full council meeting, the chairman, the Onyeichie Ume, presides and the most senior Okpala of the ebo performs the ritual offering of sacrifice before the assembly opens. He cannot sit on the ukpo (throne) of the Onyeichie Ume who is an important person, unless he too is an Onyeichie Ume as well as Okpala. The matter to be discussed is thrown open to the assembly, and as at the ogbe council, the Ndichie speak first followed by the Agbalanze and then by the non-Agbalanze, speaking according to the order of their authority.

Representatives of an ogbe have the right to express the views of their local council (izu ogbe) and by doing so they bring them to the notice of the Ndichie and of the Onyeichie Ume who is the head of the ebo, and thus bring the matter to the notice of the Obi. State policy is very largely based on the collective opinion of the people obtained at the ogbe and ebo council levels. Discussions are directed by the Onyeichie Ume and decisions are reached by the chairman weighing the opinions of the various speakers or interest groups, and accepting as the decision what he and his privy council feel is the general consensus.

There is, as in the ogbe council, the right of appeal, and dissentient groups are free to appeal, through the Onyeichie Ume, to the Obi's council because the people believe that it is the duty of the Obi to protect them even against their own relatives.

THE PRIVY COUNCIL (IZU NDICHIE UME)

This is a standing committee of the Obi and Ndichie Ume who throughout the year are in regular consultation. They are all involved in the affairs of the state, and at the local and ebo levels they are busy enforcing state policies, regulating the affairs of their administrative unit and seeing that the government functions in accordance with what they consider to be standards for the public good. They are the chief administrative officers of the state to whom the subordinate officials and interest groups report all matters; they can co-ordinate and supervise such matters, and ensure that these subordinate officials present to the people the official state policies and see that these are carried out. We have shown how, in the period of recruitment, the Obi admonishes each recipient of the title, particularly those of the elite group, "to rule his people well". We have also shown that they are acting on behalf of the Obi who, although he is the head of the society and therefore of all assemblies, cannot come out of the palace, and therefore has to delegate his authority to these officials.

The status of the Ndichie Ume corresponds to the nature of the roles they play in the affairs of the state. They confer regularly with the Obi, reporting the affairs of their territorial units (ebo) to the Obi, and acting as a standing committee of the state council. It is because they confer regularly with the Obi that they are known as Ndichie Ume (Ume in Ibo means consultation in private). The meeting is exclusive to the members of this grade and the Obi is the person who has the right to convene it. The Iyase may, however, after consulting the Obi, also convene a privy council meeting.

THE STATE COUNCIL (IZU NDICHIE)

This council embraces the three grades of Ndichie and the Obi is the chairman. At this meeting, which is held at the Obi's special chamber, they sit according to their rank and the manner in which they greet the Obi as they arrive indicates the grades of their title. The first grade of Ndichie stand as they greet him, while the others remove their head gear and prostrate themselves, bowing their heads to the floor in front of the Obi. They occupy the seats according to their order of seniority, each grade sitting separately from the other.

State councils are summoned on the initiative of the Obi, or on the collective initiative of the privy council. The Obi summons the council through his official the Okwugba, who is the link between the Obi and the Ndichie.

THE GENERAL ASSEMBLY (IZU OBODO)

Occasionally, when the Obi and Ndichie Ume desire, or the public demands, and the Obi and the Ndichie Ume accept, a general assembly of the state is held at the Obi's palace or at Ilo Oreze— the original home of Oreze, who was the founder of Onitsha. These two places are the only legitimate places for the holding of the general assembly. Originally there was only one place, the Obi's palace which was at Ilo Oreze. When the Umuezealori lineages which had previously held the kingship lost the position to the Okebunabo lineage in 1900 they refused to allow the new Obi (Okosi I) to occupy this palace. Okosi I therefore built his own palace and from 1900 to 1963 state council meetings (including the general assembly) have been held at his palace. Umuezealori has now recovered the kingship and the general assembly is now held at the Ilo Oreze.[4]

The general assembly is attended by the political and non-political classes. At this level the interest groups constitute lobbying groups. Legislation may affect different groups and each interest group therefore endeavours to advance its views. Such lobbying is undertaken even before the assembly is called, and the interest groups by their lobbying and pressuring often do initiate indirectly the summoning of the assembly and the agenda put before it.

The seating arrangement reflects the distinction between the various classes in the state, the functional differentiation within the state council, and the relationship between the Obi and the grades of Ndichie. The Obi occupies the throne as the president of the assembly. Chiefs of the highest rank, the Ndichie Ume, sit relatively far away from him, and behind them sit the second grade, the Ndichie Okwa. The Iyase, who is the head of the Ndichie Ume, sits in front of these two grades and at a distance from the Obi. The reason for this position is that the Iyase and his supporters are the potential rivals of the Obi and thus he keeps them at a distance. The Ndi Okpala, the ritual heads of the various Ebo and Ogbe, sit on the Obi's right and give him advice to ensure that he is not misled by the Iyase, who actually directs the meeting, and his followers. The Ndi Okpala are thus in a position to advise the Obi not only on ritual matters but also on the general views and opinions of their lineage members. Beside them sit the Ulogo Eze, the trusted relatives (agnates) of the Obi who keep him informed of what people are privately saying about his government.

The Ndichie Okwareze, the most junior officials, sit on the Obi's left. The Obi thus sits between the Ndi Okpala and the Ndichie Okwareze. The Ndichie Okwareze are the personal officials of the Obi and are directly attached to the palace. They are the defenders of the Obi and they look after his security. The Obi can promote any of them to the higher grade of Ndichie if a vacancy occurs. Most members of this grade are elderly men who are versed in the tradition of the land and are the Obi's trusted advisers.

The Obi thus keeps close to his person two important groups of ritual and political officers, whom he relies upon to ward off the 'misguidance' of the Iyase and his group, whom he distrusts. This opposition between Obi and Iyase is the same at Benin.

The rest of the people, the Agbala na Iregwu, stand apart and on the left. Everybody except the Obi has to be bareheaded including the women who can attend on special occasions when they sit facing the Obi. They are headed by the Omu—the head of Otu Omu, the women's association. The Iyase opens the assembly by stepping forward and greeting the Obi in the following manner: he stretches his right hand forward towards the Obi and then recites one praise name, Igwe. He then withdraws his hand, stretches it forward again and recites another praise name, and repeats this procedure until all the Obi's praise names have been called. He then withdraws to his seat. The next official in rank, the Ajie, repeats the Iyase's actions, and the others follow—Odu, Ogene, Onya and Owelle in order of their seniority. The first subgrade of Ndichie Okwa, the Ndichie Ukpo, greet in the same fashion as the Ndichie Ume officials. The other Ndichie Okwa sub-grade greet the Obi by kneeling on the ground and as they bury their heads in the ground, they exclaim "Igwe" three times. The Ndichie Okwareze come forward and greet in the same way. After these three grades have all greeted the Obi, the Agbala na Iregwu and the Ndi Okpala come forward; the Agbalanze greet first, the Okpala follows, and then the rest.

The Iyase then declares the assembly open, announcing the agenda or asking those who have any order to raise to do so. The Okwugba has freedom of speech at the assembly and can challenge the Ndichie and put forward the point of view of the public. The Ogbo na achi ani, the age class delegated by the Obi and Ndichie to supervise the affairs of the state, can initiate a proposal, and with the support of the Obi and Ndichie, the proposal, if adopted, becomes law.

As at the two other councils, the discussions are dominated by the Ndichie and the Agbalanze, and the usual rules of political seniority and order are followed. The political elite are given preference, and their subordinate ranks speak before the Agbalanze and the Ndi Okpala, who have first right of speech before the rest of the igiro can speak. Thus members of the last class scarcely speak, and are usually onlookers.

The Obi can make a decision which runs counter to opinions expressed in the assembly if he feels that these are not in the best interest of the state. At times, the assembly is only called to enable the Obi and Ndichie to collect opinions of the members on specific issues which have been presented to the assembly by the Obi and his privy council, or by the Obi and the state council. The Iyase, too, speaking on behalf of the Obi, can sum up the decision and this if approved becomes the law of the state.

Records of the case laws and other laws made by the Obi and privy council or state council and at the assembly are memorised by the Ulogo Eze, as is the case with many royal agnates. Today an attempt has been made by the Improvement Union to secure a more permanent record by recording in writing any laws now being promulgated by the council.

EXAMPLES OF RECENT LEGISLATION

As pointed out earlier, Onitsha has been exposed to western influences since 1857, and by the end of the last century, missionaries, trading and governmental activities had all combined to make the town an urban centre. The increase in population and the cultural affects of these changes are reflected in the examples of laws made in regard to the following subjects:

Marriage Laws. Some of the most acute problems involved the institution of marriage. The Protestant Mission was established in 1857, the Catholics arrived in 1885, and both have endeavoured to introduce their own notions of marriage and family life. The rise in the amount paid in bride price, the rate of divorce, and the abolition of certain rules connected with marriage since 1900 have been the subject of legislation by the Obi and Ndichie, and in the early 1930s the new educated elite, who have since then organised themselves into the Onitsha Improvement Union, have been actively involved in these changes. People looked to the Obi and council to determine what changes should be accepted, and which traditional conventions should still be enforced.

The bride price, which was formerly paid in cowrie currency, rose to seven pounds sterling at the beginning of this century. By 1910 it rose to seventeen pounds and five years later, in 1915, it soared to between sixty and seventy pounds. This alarming increase in bride price appeared to some as the commercialization of marriage by parents, and a pressure group, initiated by the age class Ogbo na chi ani, asked the late Obi Okosi I and the Ndichie to give a lead as to the policy to be followed in checking this inflation. The Obi and the council considered the whole matter and legislated that thirty-two pounds be fixed as the price to be paid, and that this should be the sum refundable to a man who had divorced his wife or whose wife had divorced him. The Obi and council introduced this law in the Native Authority Council. It was approved by the Colonial Government and became enforced in the Native Court. After 1938, however, the bride price soared again to eighty pounds and then up to a hundred pounds. Public opinion, therefore, as expressed by the young men and organised through the Onitsha Improvement Union, brought pressure again upon the Obi and council. They reviewed the matter and fixed the legal bride price at seventeen pounds, and three pounds was to be the sum to cover the extra expenses that might be incurred in other matrimonial ceremonies. As the legal amount of the bride price was only seventeen pounds, it was thought that husbands would be deterred from paying a higher bride price as the amount recoverable in case of a divorce was only seventeen. To enforce this law, the Ekwueme age set was appointed "to keep a watching brief on its workings".[5]

Divorce problems at Onitsha were and still continue to be a source of anxiety among parents. The rate is high and from 1937, the young men have urged the Obi and Ndichie to investigate the matter. People considered that the price being paid for the changes which were sweeping their new urban town was "the disruption of our good social order". Two issues demanded legislation. One was whether a child born to a divorced woman belonged to the 'lover' or to the man who paid the bride price but who had not obtained a refund from the woman's lover. The second was how to stop men enticing away other men's wives and laying claim to their children. A child, people insisted, was a kind of premium on the payment of bride wealth and paternity should be socially and not biologically determined.

The Obi and council legislated that no one except the original husband should have a claim to any child born to a woman who had separated from her husband but had not fulfilled the fundamental law of divorce—the refund of the bride price. The law further stressed that should a woman divorce her husband and remarry, and the bride price be refunded, that a period of six months should elapse before the new husband's rights over her issue should take effect. They considered that a woman who had left her husband to remarry immediately might have been committing adultery with the new husband while she was at the former husband's house. This adultery might result in pregnancy even before the departure to the new husband, and before the refund of the bride price and therefore a child born within the first six months of her marriage should belong to the former husband. Evidence of litigation in the Native Court on issues arising out of these laws is abundant.

Ije Ilo. In 1915, pressure from the missionaries caused the Obi and Ndichie to make a law prohibiting that part of the marriage rule of Ije Ilo, which involved periodical visits by the betrothed girl to her suitor's family group. The aim was to give his family the opportunity of studying the character and behaviour of the girl. The church authorities urged the Obi and council to prohibit this custom, because they thought it was 'immoral' by encouraging sexual intercourse before wedlock. Thirty years later in 1945, the Obi and council made another law prohibiting another part of Ije Ilo. This custom was the regular visits of the groom's young kinsmen to the bride's family. Reports coming to the Obi and Ndichie from several sources claimed that these visits were no longer necessary since the custom was being abused by some young men. The Obi and council legislated against this practice and the custom was abolished.

Idu Uno. In 1962, the Ndichie in the house of the Iyase again made a law prohibiting another marriage custom, idu uno, in which the bride was escorted at night to the bridegroom's house by young boys and girls of her ward, her agnates. There was need, they argued, to "halt the practice which lent colour to most undesirable moral laxity". They therefore prohibited idu uno taking place at night and ruled that it should "be made between the hours of 4 p.m. and 6 p.m.".[6]

Succession to the Kingship. Onitsha, as we shall show later, is often beset by the problem of succession, and in 1931–35, after a prolonged political contest for the throne between two dynasties of the royal clan, an age class (ogbo na achi ani) worked out a rule of succession which obtained public support and caused the Obi and council to legislate that the succession should rotate between these two dynasties.[7]

Public Morality. In 1949–50, a new kind of association of young men and women was formed. Most of the women were divorcees, or were women of marriageable age. This association was not a formal age set or organised on age set lines, its aims were not defined, and such an association which brought males and females together conflicted with conventional attitudes. The association became branded as "otualu" (immoral or abominable). Pressure from other societies, particularly from the Otu Omu, the women's association, mounted, and the Obi and council eventually legislated against the society and banned it.

The legislative powers of the Obi and council can be brought to bear on various aspects of people's life. The state council, however, tends to be reluctant to intervene unless it is assured of public support for its action, and in many cases only after action has been initiated by bodies representing various strata of the society.

ABO

At Abo there are at the lowest level sixteen ogbe each with its own council, comprising the head of the ogbe (Okpala) and the heads (Ndiokpala) of the various minimal, minor and major lineages (whether immigrants or autochthonous) together with any other important men in the ogbe.

At the second level are the councils for each of the four ebo. An ebo council consists of the heads (Ndiokpala) of each of the component ogbe, together with the Olinzele titled members of the ebo and any other influential persons in the ebo.

At the highest level is the council of the state and the general assembly council, made up of the Olinzele drawn from the two political groups within the state—Umudei and Ndichie. Membership of these groups cuts across lineage segmentation, as there is no residential or territorial dichotomy between the Umudei and Ndichie political groups. At this level, there is another important title-holder, the Odua, the eldest male of Umudei, who has the right to convene meetings of the council at his residence.

The pattern of council meetings at the ogbe and ebo levels is almost identical to that of Onitsha. At every stage, the Olinzele, who are members of the political class, are the chief legislators. They preside over the meetings, and ensure that the policies of the council are carried out.

As in Onitsha, the privy council is a standing committee which confers regularly.

The seating arrangement at the state council reflects its internal political structure and the role assignments of the officials of the state divisions. The Obi sits on his throne facing the entrance. On his left sit the Olinzele of the Ndichie division. The Iyase sits at the head of these Ndichie, and near to the Obi. He is the chief speaker and the official defender of the Obi. His Ndichie members support him. The Akpulosu sits next to the Iyase. The Umudei Olinzele sit on the Obi's right and the Ndanike, who is their head, sits at their front near the right of the throne and heads the opposition of the Umudei Olinzele.

Discussions are opened by the Iyase in the name of the Obi and he tells the Obi what each member says. The deliberations are conducted within strict rules of decorum and the two Olinzele groups debate issues until the policy to be adopted has been adequately discussed. The Obi scarcely speaks at meetings, but the laws are made in his name. This is because the issue has been discussed beforehand at the privy council and a decision has been reached, so that the law made at the open state council or at a general assembly has already been accepted by the Obi. The Akpulosu, the Obi's senior son, defends his father's policies and he supports the Iyase at the meeting in answering criticisms directed against his father. At the general assembly, which members of the general public attend, the ritual heads are given a special position, while the rest stand outside the main Uge, the place for the assembly. The general assembly (Izu Obodo) is held in order to bring legislation to the knowledge of the public and to enable all to understand and support the state policy and to accept its enforcement in their respective administrative units.

OGUTA

At Oguta there are twenty-seven ogbe councils each consisting of the head of the ogbe and any titled men (Olilinzele) and elders in the lineage. Four of them are headed by the kingly officials namely the Eze Ukwu, the Iyase, the Ndanike and the Ezekoro, the rest by the eldest male in the lineage (Okpala). There are also three maximal lineages referred to in Chapter 4 which have divided into a number of ogbe. Each of these has a maximal lineage council which meets whenever necessary to decide matters which are the sole concern of the maximal lineage.

At the highest level are the state council and the general assembly.

At Oguta there are only two levels of political importance, the ogbe and the state.

THE LOCAL COUNCIL (IZU OGBE)

Councils at this level can only act on issues within their competence which is limited to the internal government of the ogbe. The procedure is the same as in Onitsha, but at Oguta the Okpala of the ogbe presides as he has both political and ritual power. At Onitsha only the members of the political class of the Agbalanze or of the Ndichie preside.

THE STATE COUNCIL AND GENERAL ASSEMBLY

The state council is more of a consultative and advisory council and decisions can only be reached at the general assembly of the people which can be held at recognised places. The general assembly and state council normally meet at the Obi's palace (obi eze). There are, however, three other sites where it can be convened, namely:

Akpatakwuma. This is the spot where the war shrine is located. Meetings are held here in a period of crisis, such as a war with any outside community, or when there is disagreement with the Obi or the royal lineage.

Agbata Ani. This lies in Ishibe ogbe (17) on the boundary between the two territorial divisions. Political meetings used to be held here, however, whenever there was a dispute between the two divisions.

The Ogene's Residence. As the Ogene is head of the Ndichie, Oguta people can hold the general assembly at his residence and decisions reached here can be referred to the Obi's palace for further confirmation. If, for example, there is a conflict between the Obi and the College of Ndichie, the people can use the Ogene's residence as an alternative meeting place.

The seating arrangements are as follows. The Obi occupies his throne with his senior wife, the Odoba, on his right. The Ogana, the leader of the Olilinzele and the Obi's chief speaker, sits below him on his right. The Ogene, who is the leader of the Ndichie College, sits next to the Ogana and on his right. The rest of the Ndichie sit in a semi-circular row still further to the right and in front of them are the four kingly officials in their seats. The other members of the Olilinzele are seated opposite the Obi and facing the Ndichie on a raised dais. They sit at the entrance to the hall and reply on behalf of the Obi to all greetings made to him. Further away and on the left between the Olilinzele and the commoners are the king's agnates. The commoners stand outside the hall unless they are given seats by members of the royal household.

The procedure here is as elsewhere. The Ogana comes forward, bows and greets the Obi four times, then introduces the subject of the meeting. Only the Ndichie and Olinzele have the right to

speak, but any member of the public may do so with the permission of the Olilinzele. Deliberations are free and open and after
long debates about various issues, the Ogana will rise to sum up
the consensus of opinion. If the matter is of an intricate nature
the Obi and his state councillors retire to consult about their
decision, which is then conveyed to the rest of the assembly by
the Ogana in the name of the Obi and Ndichie. The announcement
of this decision implies that a law has been made which becomes
binding for all members of the state.

Lobbying for a particular issue is carried on outside the council.
The interest group concerned canvasses influential members of the
council, for instance those Ndichie whose techniques of persuasion
are superior, and whose influence over the community is recognised.
Such men are known as "ndi okwu oma" (the men of good words),
"ndi ofu onu" (of truthful mouth), "ndi oka okwu" (of able words).

When effective lobbying goes on, it is not unusual for the Ogana
to mention the issue to the Ndichie, and if it is a matter which
they all feel strongly about, they may endeavour to act as elite
councillors and take a definite position even before public opinion
has been formally ascertained.

The language used at council meetings is an idiomatic and erudite
form of the local Ibo dialect, one which makes great use of proverbs,
parables and references to past history and mythology which can
be used as precedents to support the courses of action advocated
by the speaker. This kind of oratory is one of the great attractions
of the Obieze meetings. People say "ka nje ibe eze egele okwu",
which means "let us go to the king's palace to learn new ideas, to
listen to words of wisdom". Men who possess this skill in oratory
are local spokesmen and are specially invited. If they do not come
from the royal ward, the Obi can confer the title of Olinzele on
them so as to enable them to speak and to be full members of the
council and the Ogana is usually selected from persons who possess
these qualities.

EXAMPLES OF RECENT LEGISLATION

Regulation of Waterways.   In 1962 the Obi and council, in order
to safeguard the lives and properties of the farmers, made a law
prohibiting any Oguta landowners or owners of river ponds from
renting their fishing water fronts to any group of persons who
wished to construct a fishing weir (ano) contrary to the method
adopted by Oguta people. This law was made in order to prevent
Isobo people from constructing their fishing weirs in a way
dangerous to persons who use the public waterways.

Regulation of Age Sets. For several years one of the great concerns of the Obi and Ndichie had been the consistent deterioration of behaviour and morals amongst the younger members of the community. One way in which the Obi and council sought to regulate this was to legislate that male and female age sets should dance separately instead of dancing together. In 1955 and on various occasions before then, the Obi and council have legislated that the age organisation in every ward should organise the keeping of night patrols against thieves, and have compelled all ogbe to do so.

Electoral Reform. The procedure governing the selection of Ogbe representatives at the general assembly and other council meetings was defined by the Obi and council following the advice of the Oguta National Union (the association of educated Oguta men).

Public Health. In 1945, there was an epidemic among the children in the town. A group of students made a survey of the number of infant deaths throughout the whole town and presented the statistics to the chief medical officer. They explained the nature of the disease and the great havoc it caused in the town. From their observation the students suspected that the disease was caused by a poisonous gas which came from the frying of palm kernels by old women who extracted the oil for use as a form of pomade (ude aku). They went to the Obi and council and explained the result of their investigations. The Obi and council at the Obieze then legislated that no woman should fry palm kernels after six o'clock in the morning, and that those who did should go out of the compounds (ngwulu uno) to do so, and then only at midnight when every one was asleep. This law was enforced and the epidemic stopped.

In 1950, as a result of dog bites, two children died in the town and the Obi and council legislated that no dog be allowed into the town. No dog has been brought into Oguta since then.

As at Onitsha, most of these laws were made when the Obi and council knew that they would obtain public support and usually at the instigation of various pressure groups which had initiated the demand for it.

OSOMARI

The three political divisions of Ugolo, Isiolu and Umuonyiogwu are each, as already shown, made up of three groups consisting of the three subdivisions of the dominant migrant group each of which has incorporated two other groups, namely an autochthonous and a servile group. Each of these nine groups is known as an ebo. There are thus the nine ebo councils of Ugolo, Ndam and Okpanam (in the Ugolo division); and of Umuonyiogwu, Umuchi and Ogwashi (in the Umuonyiogwu division); and of Isiolu, Umuoga and Igbuzo (in the Isiolu division). At the next level are the three divisional councils of Ugolo, Isiolu and Umuonyiogwu each consisting of its head (the Atamanya, the Iyase and the Odobo), the Olinzele and elders of the division. The three servile ebo are not represented in this or in the state council. At the highest level is the state council which meets in the Ugolo division consisting of the Atamanya, the Iyase and the Odobo together with the Olinzele of both the Ndichie Ume and Isugbe grades.

The segmentary nature of Osomari gives a much greater measure of autonomy to its three political divisions, and the state council becomes a federation of these semi-autonomous units.

THE LOCAL COUNCIL (IZU EBO)

Within each division the ebo council meets at the residence of the head of the ebo and consists of the Ndichie of all grades and other elders and important men of the ebo. Most of the talking and decision making is done by the Ndichie and elders; to take for example the Ugolo division, the ebo Ugolo will hold its own ebo council, presided over by the Ogene and assisted by the Ndichie Ume and Isugbe chiefs. The ebo of Ndam (of the autochthonous group) has its own ebo meeting presided over by its head and its own Ndichie and Isugbe chiefs. Okpanam (the servile estate) has its own ebo meeting with its own head and titled officials. It is the same in the case of the ebo councils in the other two divisions.

THE DIVISIONAL COUNCIL

Each division will also, if occasion demands, convene a divisional council meeting at the palace of its head (respectively the Atamanya, the Iyase and the Oniniogwu), presided over by this head and assisted by the Ndichie and other chiefs of the immigrant and autochthonous wards.

THE STATE COUNCIL AND GENERAL ASSEMBLY

Both the state council and the general assembly are held at the palace of the king, the Atamanya of Ugolo. The Atamanya occupies his ukpo. The Iyase sits on his left and the Oninowu on his right. Each of these kingly officials has an official called Odaje (Asi) and in the case of the Iyase, Asimaha, who sit at their feet and speak for them. The Ndichie Ume from the three divisions sit as a single group in front of them and on their right. The seating order combines the ranking order of their divisions and their seniority within it. Thus the Oniha of Ugolo sits nearest to the throne, next to him is the Asanya of Isiolu, next the Isagba of Umuonyiogwu, then the Oniha of Ndam, then the Oniha of Umuoga, then the Okpala of Umuchi, then the Alanza of Ugolo, followed by the Alanza of Isiolu and the Ako of Umuonyiogwu and so on in rotation for the lower grades of Ndichie and for the Isugbe chiefs. In the case of the general assembly, other members of the community stand at the entrance to the palace facing the throne.

The Odaje (Asi) of the Atamanya announces the purpose of the gathering on behalf of the Atamanya. The matter is then thrown open to the meeting. The Oniniogwu (Odobo) speaks first, through his Odaje (Asi), after which the Iyase speaks through his Asimaha. After these have spoken, the Ndichie Ume then begin to contribute their opinion to the debate, speaking in the order of their rank and beginning with the Ogene and followed by the chiefs of the other grades.

When all have spoken, the Odaje of the king, who is referred to as "Onu Eze" (the king's mouth), will be told by the king to ask the Ndichie Ume, who in Osomari are the three senior Okpalas, to go and consult privately with the other councillors and determine the opinion of the council. This act is known as "ichi ume", hence they are called Ndichie Ume. When they have concluded their consultation, three of them privately tell the king, the Oniniogwu and the Iyase the decision they have reached. This action is referred to as "ichi isi" (whispering). When the three kingly officials accept the decision, they authorise it to be announced, and the Atamanya gives the order. One of the Ndichie Ume then announces the decision. Once this is announced the decision becomes law and is final and binding on the people.

EXAMPLES OF RECENT LEGISLATION

Title Regulations. Christian opposition to ritual ceremonies connected with Igbu and Agana titles led to agitation among some Osomari Christians. Like Christians in other communities, they wanted the traditional initiation rituals associated with such titles to be reformed so that Christians could take the title without offending against the tenets of their religion. In 1918, the late Chief Jacob Odu Egonu, and other Christians, proposed to the Atamanya and council that Christians should be excused from performing the following rituals in the case of the Agana and Igbu titles: Igwanye Okpa, in which a cotton tree was planted to commemorate the initiation of the recipient of the Igbu title; this was accompanied by rituals of sacrifice such as the burial of the head of a human victim whose death was required for these Igbu ceremonies; Igo Ikenga, in which sacrifice was offered to the Ikenga (god of fortune) of a candidate for the Agana title, and was considered by the Christians as worship of a false god; Ima Nzu, the rubbing of the body of the Agana or Igbu candidate with white clay to cleanse him and transform him from a 'profane' to a 'sacred' person; Iwanye Agana, the robing of the Agana candidate in the regalia of office, in which he is again clothed at his death.

The Atamanya and council considered the proposals, and made a law which freed the Christians from having to perform these rituals. At the same time they increased the entrance fees and expenses in the case of Christians from forty-one pounds sterling to sixty pounds. A non-Christian, in addition to his fees and expenses, had to provide a cow, three goats and other victims for the sacrificial rituals from which Christians were excused and the increase in fees was to compensate for this saving.

Between 1930 and 1950, the Atamanya and council agreed to review these title fees. They accepted the amount proposed by the title associations, and fixed them at sixty pounds for non-Christians and eighty pounds for Christians. In 1950, the council accepted another increase in fees suggested by the title associations, and ruled that non-Christians should pay one hundred pounds and Christians one hundred and twenty.

Bride Price.   In 1954, in an attempt to check the rising bride price, the people of Osomari tried to fix the price and the Atamanya and council decreed that it should be thirty pounds. Bride price, however, continued to rise and since no son-in-law would bring his parents-in-law before the Atamanya's court, nothing could be done about this increase. In 1963, the position was reviewed and the council made the following regulations: that a present to the bride should not exceed five pounds; that expenses paid for leading the bride to her husband should be limited to ten pounds; that the actual bride price be fixed at thirty pounds. The council further decreed that any defaulter should pay a fine of ten pounds and if he failed, that the council should take action in the Native Court to enforce the decision.

Recreational Activities.   The Osomari educated elite, realising that the traditional cultural and recreational activities in the town were dying out, recommended that the council should urge the age sets to learn new dances and to revive the old ones, which could be staged at the national festival and other ceremonial occasions. They also suggested that competitions be organised to encourage the revival of riverain sports such as canoe racing and swimming. They also recommended that wrestling, which could be dangerous if not properly supervised, and egwu onwa (moonlight dancing and singing) which was conducive to immorality amongst the younger age sets should be discouraged. The state council took action on their proposals and made the required regulations.

NOTES

1   T. B. Bottomore, 1964.
2   P. C. Lloyd, 1965.
3   F. C. Bailey, 1965, p. 10.
4   The new Obi comes from Okebunabo (Umudei) and meetings are again held at the former Obi Okosi palace.
5   Report of the Committee on Bride Price: Eastern region: Enugu 1955.
6   Memo submitted by Ndichie Ume, 1963.
7   For details see Chapter 9.

Chapter 6   The Functions of Government II

THE JUDICIAL PROCESS

The system of law which prevails in these states does not differ in any important details from that described for other parts of the Ibo country by Meek and others.[1] In this section we are not concerned with the content of Ibo law but with its adjudication and enforcement. Our study is also limited to the traditional structure and excludes the Native Court system established by the colonial government and the Customary Court system which replaced it after independence.

The judicial structure corresponds to a considerable extent to the political and a council at any level may have judicial as well as legislative functions. But the correspondence is not complete and in addition there are various senior chiefly and kingly officials who in addition to presiding at ogbe, ebo or divisional councils, when these function as courts, have the right to hold courts of their own for the settlement of predominantly civil cases.

At Onitsha there are three grades of courts, for the three administrative levels—the ogbe, the administrative ebo, and the state—presided over by the head of each of these units. Major criminal offences are reserved for the state court of the Obi, which is the supreme court and which can also function as a court of appeal.

At Abo there are again the courts of the ogbe, of the ebo, and of the state and the Odua has the right to hold his own court.

At Oguta there is a court for each ogbe, a state court presided over by the Obi, and each of the four kingly officials has the right to hold his own court, as has the Ogene.

At Osomari the court structure corresponds to the political divisions and a supreme or state court—that of the Atamanya of Osomari. The jurisdiction of the lower courts is limited in the case of ogbe, ebo and divisional courts, to the members of the particular ogbe, ebo or division. Serious criminal cases are reserved for the supreme court.

The aims and methods of traditional African courts have been described at length by Gluckman[2] and what he says about Lozi judges applies equally here. Their task is to right wrongs, to adjust claims, to defend norms, and where permanent relationships are concerned, they have to strive to prevent them from being broken. This principle of using the court to effect a reconciliation of parties can be seen particularly in disputes between groups of kinsmen where the judges order the parties to take an oath to resume and maintain kinship solidarity. For example, there is the ritual called Ikwa Nligba in which the disputants are brought together in the presence of the elders and made to share in eating kola nuts and in drinking liquor which has been sacrificed to the lineage ancestors. There is also the ritual called Ijiaka in which they are made to take an oath on a tutelary deity or on an Alushi never to harm or to use sorcery or witchcraft against one another. Similiar rituals are used in cases of accidental homicide to reconcile the relatives of the victim and his killer. In addition to the normal form of compensation in which a woman from the killer's lineage is married to a man in the deceased's lineage, the ritual of Ikwa Ochu is performed to reconcile the dead man's spirit and those of his ancestors to prevent them avenging themselves upon the killer and his relatives. This is known as Ijiaka or Nligba. The parties are brought before the judges and sacrifice is offered to the shrines at the Obi's court to invoke the local deities and ancestors to bring the two groups together. The parties are then ordered to drink together in the presence of the judges.

If the case is at the ogbe level, the parties are made to drink before the court panel, with the Okpala of the lineage offering sacrifices to the ancestral shrine of the ward and calling upon the ward ancestors to reconcile the parties and to restore the solidarity of the lineage.

The responsibility of a lineage for their members is crucial in each of the states. A man who takes a case to a higher grade court does so with the consent of his kinsmen who give him their full support so as to defend his reputation and with it that of the lineage. They help him to marshal his witnesses and in some cases they assist in explaining the case to the judges even before it comes to court. In the course of the trial members of the public unrelated to the parties may be called to give evidence and thus involve their lineage in the case. Litigation thus imposes considerable strains upon the peaceful co-existence of social groups within the community and makes it imperative for the judges to arrive at a summing-up and judgement which will reduce rather than aggravate the tension.

Throughout the year at Oguta, Osomari and Abo, the Obis sit with their judges to hear cases, administer justice, and collect court fees. At Onitsha, the Obi may hold his own court but most cases are heard in the Customary Court as explained on page 107.

THE SUPREME COURT

We shall now describe the supreme state court, which is the final court of appeal, and also a court of first instance.

Composition. In all the states, the Obi (or, at Osomari, the Atamanya) is the chairman of the court and the officials of the council constitute the judges. The seating arrangements at the court are the same as at political meetings of the state council. The principal speakers are the Iyase at Onitsha and Abo, the Ogana (who is head of the Olilinzele college) at Oguta and the Odaje (Asi) of the Atamanya at Osomari. They are, as it were, the chief prosecutor of the court; they introduce the case before the court and call the plaintiffs and defendants and also their witnesses to come forward and give evidence; they ensure that order is maintained; and they pronounce the verdict on behalf of the Obi and the judges though this duty can be delegated by them to another official.

Court Fees. The fees which are charged vary in each state. At Onitsha, there are notification fees as well as sitting fees. Each Ndichie Ume is paid a notification fee of four shillings. Two shillings are paid to each Ndichie Okwa, the second grade, and one shilling to each of the third grade, the Ndichie Okwareze. The Obi may demand a special notification fee or he may waive it. Sitting fees (ego okwu) are paid to the judges for hearing the case. The amount is determined by the judges. The money paid by both plaintiff and defendant is divided into two parts. The Obi takes one part and the other is again divided into two. The Ndichie Ume takes one part. The remaining part is once again divided into two and the Ndichie Okwa, the second grade, take one part and the other goes to Ndichie Okwareze. When they divide their shares amongst themselves each receives according to his seniority within the group.

At Abo, the only fee paid is the notification fee and this is eight shillings paid to the Obi.

At Oguta, there are three types of fees. The first is a notification fee, called "ego itu ogbo". This is paid to the Obi to summon the court. It is now fixed at two shillings. The second is "ego isha ogbo", which is paid by the defendant. This fee is refundable if the court finds him guiltless. The third is "ego ikpe", the sitting fees. These are paid to the court by both the plaintiff and the defendant. At the end of the case the guilty party forfeits the whole of the sitting fee, while the successful party receives a refund of part of his. These court fees are shared in two equal parts. The Obi takes one and the judges share the other. Their leaders, the Ogana and the Ogene, take larger shares than the other Ndichie and Olinzele. There is a fourth charge known as "ego nde oka okwu", the fee which a client pays separately to special "local barristers" (Nde Oka Okwu) who can be hired in this manner to come to court to plead his case. This is however a private arrangement between the client and the man who pleads for him.

Osomari courts charge only one court fee, the sitting fee. This is four shillings and a bottle of gin,[3] paid by each of the parties. The money is divided into three equal parts, one for each division. Ugolo always takes its share first, Isiolu follows and Umuonyiogwu is last. Each divisional share is then divided into two parts, one for the head of the division and one for the judges (officials). This latter is again subdivided into two for the senior and junior grades of chiefs.

Procedure.   The "official prosecutor" opens the session by greeting the Obi as is the case at council meetings. After this, he briefly announces the case and orders the witnesses to the case to go out. They are taken into a separate chamber or a neighbouring house to make sure that they do not overhear the statements of the plaintiff, defendant and of other witnesses. The plaintiff states his case before the court, making sure that he does not use derogatory words before the Obi. Interruptions are not allowed in the presence of the Obi. The plaintiff is cross-examined after stating his case, and his witnesses give their evidence after him. The court leader calls for questions (ajuju) from the judges, and in some cases from members of the public, in order to obtain and verify relevant facts.

Then the defendant opens his case and he is also rigorously examined. His witnesses are called and cross-examined in the same way. The judges favour the evidence of eye-witnesses, whereas circumstantial and hearsay evidence, though admitted, carries less weight. The judges often ask a witness "Ifulu na anya?" ("Did you see it yourself?") or "Agwalai agwa?" ("Were you told?"). If after cross-examination they discover that the witness is giving hearsay evidence, the judges can insist that he calls the person who told him the story. If he fails to do so, his evidence is weakened. If his evidence is relevant to the case, he may be compelled to produce the person or to disclose the source of his information. The court also probes carefully into the social background of the witnesses of the plaintiff and the defendant, for such information enables the judges to assess the character of their evidence.

Oath Taking. An untruthful witness exposes himself to the threat of being asked to support his statement by swearing an oath. He is upbraided and asked to think carefully (loa ililo) before he makes statements to the court. Unreliable witnesses are rigorously cross-examined and it is here that the Nde Oka Okwu ("barristers") play their role, for their aim is to confuse the witnesses so as to create an impression of doubt in the minds of the judges. The extent to which their activities help their clients to obtain judgement depends on the nature of the offence because the court has the right to ask either party or both to swear by an Alushi or by Agunze (the Obi's special shrine).

Those giving evidence are not called upon to do so upon oath, but in cases where the evidence is in doubt, the court may order one or other of the parties or their witnesses to swear to its truth, that is, to invoke a local deity to prove the truth of his assertion by killing or harming him or his relatives if he has given false evidence. The truth is believed to be demonstrated if, after the oath has been taken, the person suspected or any of his relatives does not die. He then performs the ritual of iwucha alushi, after izu asa (one lunar month).

Oath-taking, as a way of deciding a case, involves the kinsmen of the oath-taker, and before allowing an oath to be taken, they vigorously question their kinsman in private to make sure (iji obu aka) that he is not trying to deceive them and the court. Nevertheless, there are some rash and obstinate men who refuse to admit that they have lied before the court, and by taking the oath falsely they expose themselves to an early death and bring the vengeance of the spirit (alushi) on their kinsmen as well.

This invocation of local deities to determine disputes can be exemplified by a recent case from the Obi of Oguta's Court. Two persons, X and Y, who farmed in one area had for several years maintained a definite farm boundary, each planting his crops on his side of this boundary. Then X brought an action claiming that Y had trespassed into his land. The defendant Y denied this, counter-claiming that the area in dispute was part of his farm land. The case was brought before the Obi's court. The plaintiff X had three witnesses who testified that the defendant Y had actually trespassed into X's land. Y also brought witnesses who stated that Y had allotted them plots of land for farming on the land now in dispute, and that X had not asked them to pay ina egwe, the annual tribute of yams, which is customarily paid to a landowner to show that the land belongs to him. Since X had not demanded this tribute over the years, it was illogical, they argued, for him to now claim that this land belonged to him. The plaintiff X argued that both

he and the defendant Y had neglected to collect this tribute, and
that both of them were therefore guilty of this negligence; hence, the
argument should not be used solely against him.

The case was doubtful, and it was difficult to establish whether
one or both of the parties had failed to collect this tribute. The
plaintiff was ordered to carry the cult objects associated with a
local spirit (alushi) and place them on the land in dispute, and the
defendant was told that if he continued to maintain that the land
was his, he should prove it by removing them within a few days.
The plaintiff did as ordered, and when the defendant failed to
remove them, reported this to the Obi. The Obi recalled the judges
and summoned the community for the hearing of the verdict. The
court gave judgement for the plaintiff and ordered the defendant to
refrain from further trespass.

I witnessed two similar cases at Abo and Osomari involving
disputes over the right of ownership and the use of fishing ponds;
oath-taking was the way in which the judges resolved their dilemma
and established what society regarded as equity and justice.

The Judgement.   Judgement is given after consultation among the
judges. They may appoint a committee of chiefs of the court to
consider the case and inform the judges of their opinion. This is
passed to the leader of the court who whispers it to the Obi, and
if he accepts it the leader rises, makes the customary greeting to
the Obi, comments briefly on the case, and pronounces the verdict.

Relations with Colonial and Regional Government Courts.   In
pre-colonial times the decision of the Obi's court was final, but since
the establishment by the central government of Native and then of
Customary Courts, individuals are free to have their case heard
anew in these courts. In such cases, the judges of the Obi's court
may be called to give evidence, and unless the judgement of the
Obi's court is a bad one, the Customary Court either confirms it
or gives a similar judgement.

As an example of this we can take a case that occurred at Oguta
in 1962. Dances at Oguta are organised by age sets. Each one has
its own age set organisation and for each male set there is a
corresponding female set. It had been the practice for these corresponding sets to perform a combined dance on certain formal
occasions, and this dancing together had offered opportunities for
selecting marriage partners. This was the case in the past but
from the early 1920s this open courtship stopped, though continued
surreptitiously. In more recent time parental authority, particularly
over their daughters, has diminished. A particular male age set

within the age range of 15–17 years, called Ita Amala, organised joint dances with their corresponding female set, Ita Major. These dances did not conform to the traditional pattern and went on late into the night so that mothers complained that their daughters got no sleep and neglected their domestic duties. Most of these and other dancing sets consisted of boys and girls attending school and parents and teachers both felt that they were neglecting their school work for incessant dancing at which they also learnt to drink and smoke. There were also complaints of fighting and unruly behaviour and of singing slanderous songs about their elders.

Eventually in 1962 some parents complained to the Obi. He summoned the Ndichie and the public to a meeting at which several parents described cases of drunkenness and unruly behaviour. The Obi summoned the leaders of the Ita Amala and Ita Major age sets to a council meeting and ordered them to stop this dancing together, and any unruly behaviour or slanderous singing on pain of a collective fine.

In 1963 the two sets disobeyed this order and held another such dance. They were again summoned before the Obi's court and each set was fined £5. They refused to pay the fine and the Obi and Ndichie arranged for some prominent members of the Oguta National Union to prosecute them in the central government's Customary Court at Oguta. They were brought before the court. The Obi and Ndichie gave evidence before it which the leaders of the age sets sought unsuccessfully to refute. The judges of the Customary Court found them guilty, upheld the judgement of the Obi's court and increased the fines to 15s. for each accused person or one month's imprisonment in default, and they had to pay both the fines of the Customary Court and the Obi's court.

INTERMEDIATE COURTS

Onitsha
Each of the six administrative units (ebo) have courts to hear cases which may either come from their component units (ogbe) by way of appeal, or which may be brought before them at first instance. The Ndichie of all grades in the ebo constitute the panel of the court, and the Onyeichie Ume of the ebo is the chairman.

The person who convenes the court pays a fee of two shillings to enable the chairman of the court to summon the judges. When the court assembles, the plaintiff and defendant both pay court fees. The amount is determined by the judges; it is paid before the session begins, and is shared by the judges before the judgement is delivered, so that none of the parties may demand a refund.

The procedure is the same as at the Obi's court, and the verdict is delivered after the judges have consulted privately. It is usually the practice to send the public away and to call them back when the judges have weighed the evidence and have reached a unanimous decision. The chairman delivers the judgement.

A dissatisfied party can appeal to the Obi's court. When such an appeal is made, the Obi invites the Onyeichie of the division to discuss the issue with him. If the Obi is satisfied with the decision of the court, he may tell the appellant to accept the verdict of the court. If not, he may hear the case in his own court.

Abo
The Court of the Ebo.
Abo has four ebo each with its court. The Olinzele of the ebo are the judges and the senior Olinzele is the chairman of the court.

Court fees are paid in bottles of gin. The convener gives the head of the ebo two bottles of gin to summon the court. When the court opens, both plaintiff and defendant pay a fee of four bottles of gin each. The procedure is the same as at Onitsha and the manner of delivering the verdict is also the same.

A successful litigant then visits the Odua and stands before him while he rubs nzu (white clay) on his hands. After doing this, the Odua takes him by the right hand and, raising it, he exclaims "Onye nweo olo!", meaning, "he has won the verdict". The litigant then goes home, rejoicing with his kinsmen, and they parade through the whole quarter singing and shouting "Onye nweo olo!". This ritual is important as a way of removing the stigma of the accusation; for the winner must demonstrate his innocence of the charges publicly in order to restore his social position in the various groups of which he is a member.

A dissatisfied party can appeal to the Obi's court if it is a matter of sufficient importance, or to the court of the Odua.

The Court of the Odua.
The Odua and Olinzele constitute the judges, and the Odua presides at the sittings. The complainant pays a court fee of eight shillings, after which the Odua's servant sounds the gong and all Olinzele assemble. The defendant also pays a fee of eight shillings or four bottles of gin.

The procedure is the same as in the ebo court. The verdict is given by the Odua who selects five or six persons to go out for consultation (izu) on the basis of the evidence before the court. When they return one of them whispers the verdict to the Odua. If he is not satisfied, he may send them to reconsider their decision, and if he agrees with the second verdict, he appoints one of them to announce it. When this is done, he performs the ceremony of rubbing white clay on his hands as has been described.

Oguta

The intermediary courts at Oguta are those held at the residences of the Ogene, and of the kingly officials, the Iyase, the Ndanike, the Eze Ukwu and the Ezekoro. Each is both a court of first instance and an appeal court for any of the ward (ogbe) courts. In the case of the court of a kingly official the court judges consist of the kingly official and any of the Olilinzele and Ndichie whom he may invite to join him. He may restrict the personnel to the Olilinzele and Ndichie of the wards that are adjacent to him. In the case of the Ogene's court, all Ndichie are summoned. The fees paid in the three types of court are the same as those paid at the Obi's court, except that they may be less, depending on the judge's decision. The procedure is the same as at the Obi's court. The verdict is given by consultation of the judges who ask the persons involved to leave the court. They are recalled and the verdict is pronounced by one of the judges. If the Ogene is present in any of the courts, he pronounces the verdict.

A person not satisfied can appeal to the Obi's court, and the Obi can either dismiss the appeal or hear the whole case again. He does not, as in Onitsha, call any of the officials to question them on how they have arrived at their verdict before making his decision on whether or not to allow the appeal.

Osomari

The three divisional courts of Isiolu, Ugolo, and Umuonyiogwu are quasi-independent courts. They hear appeals from the courts of the ebo of the division and are also courts of first instance. In the case of Ugolo the divisional court which is headed by the Atamanya becomes, with the addition of the kingly officials and the Olinzele from the other two divisions, the supreme court.

The judges of these divisional courts consist of the head of the division and the Olinzele of both grades in the division. The person instigating the case pays a summons fee of two shillings and a bottle of gin. When the court assembles both parties pay hearing fees of two shillings and a bottle of gin. The proceedings are the same as in the supreme court in other states and a verdict is given after judges have retired to consult and their whispered verdict has been accepted by the chairman of the court. The chairman as in the other states, has the right to reject their decision and ask them to reconsider it.

1 *Iyasara Uzoka of Oguta performing the ceremony of Ibe Odu (the singing of praises with the horn). Note the regalia of office.*

2 *Mgiligba imi na anya, the bell with human features. Jingling these bells, the bearer precedes the Obi and announces his coming.*

3 *Iyase Onowu Anatogu of Onitsha. Note especially the bell, which he rings as he goes so that those carrying corpses may avoid him, it being taboo for him, as for other Ndichie, to see a corpse.*

4 *Obi Oputa II of Abo. Crowned in 1916; as the oldest male in Abo, he was therefore the Odua as well as the Obi.*

LOWER COURTS

Lineage Conclaves. The maximal lineages which correspond to the ogbe or ward at Oguta and Onitsha and to the ebo at Osomari and Abo, are corporate descent groups, which may also include attached lineages. Each maximal lineage segments into smaller lineages each with a lineage head. At these lower segmentary levels, the members constitute for the purpose of settling a dispute what, following Gulliver,[4] I call a conclave. A conclave "comprises either the members of the same nuclear group to which both disputants belong, or a few other close associates where the disputants are members of different nuclear groups". I accept this definition and regard a minor lineage or a major lineage within an ogbe (or ebo, as at Osomari and Abo) as a conclave.

The elders (ndi ikei) of such a lineage are involved constantly in reconciling members of their lineage by settling disputes, and in trying to restore the unity of the lineage, if necessary, by imposing fines on offenders, but not heavy ones. They try to reconcile the disputants by bringing them together before the ancestral shrine and by making them publicly swear not to quarrel or break the rules of their lineage.

The Maximal Lineage Court. This court serves for members of all the lineages within the ogbe (maximal lineage) including attached lineages as well as true agnates. At Oguta and Osomari the head of the court is the Okpala of the maximal lineage who is assisted by the elders of the various conclaves. At Onitsha any Ndichie or at Abo any Olinzele of both divisions residing in the ogbe are the judges. This becomes a 'joint congress' of their respective supporters in a formal meeting, at which attendance is open to any one who cares to be present.

In all these states, the procedure in the lower courts is the same as in the higher courts. All judges attempt to establish the truth and, in order to do so, they assess all that has happened in terms of both legal and moral norms. They endeavour to find out which of the litigants has conformed to the rule of society and which has broken it. The verdict is again determined by the nature of the evidence, and the court judges consult among themselves, after which one of them is selected to deliver the verdict.

An appeal can be made from this court directly to the Obi's court; it can also go to the court of the ebo at Onitsha; to the court of the Odua at Abo; to the court of one of the kingly officials or of the Ogene at Oguta; and to a divisional court at Osomari.

The judges who try the cases in the lower grade of courts are

K

aware of the fact that the person they are trying may appeal to a higher body. Because they do not want to lose face at the appeal, it behoves them to consider their judgements carefully.

MAINTENANCE OF ORDER

In this section we shall study how social control is maintained, firstly in the field of law enforcement, secondly in that of ritual sanctions and finally in those of other social sanctions.

ENFORCEMENT OF THE LAW

Although the political elite are responsible for the promulgation and enforcement of laws, they make considerable use of wards and lineages and associations of the non-political class for carrying out this enforcement. These are called upon to act as agents of the state government in carrying out decisions of the council, in the execution of court judgements, in the performance of public works and in the enforcement of law and order. They are able to discipline their members through the imposition of fines or by expulsion from the association if such members fail to conform to the accepted standards of morality and good conduct. They are also powerful agencies for the formation and expression of public opinion. The most important of these groupings are:

Kinship and Territorial Groups.   Ogbe and in some cases ebo are maximal lineages and their members are responsible for the maintenance and enforcement of order within their group. They are held responsible for the misbehaviour of any of their members and for the payment of any fine that may be imposed upon him.

The Age Organisation.   The Obi and Council may delegate particular duties to a particular age set, or to a group of age sets (an age class). In all four states, age sets are used not only for the enforcement of judicial decisions, but also for the recruitment of personnel for the defence of the state. They can perform both police and military duties. For example, at Onitsha in 1935 the Ekwu Eme age set was appointed as the supervisors of the law controlling the amount of the bride price. Between 1938 and 1942, the Obi and council instructed the Ogbo Nachi Ani age class to prosecute two Ndichie officials who were charged with abusing the prerogatives of their offices. We shall expand on this in Chapter 10.

At Oguta, the members of an age set act as the agents of the Obi and council in enforcing a judicial decision on any of their

members found guilty of stealing. At Oguta again, three specified
age classes were authorised in the past to equip and man their own
war canoes.

At Abo, specific responsibilities are allocated to sets in each of
the three grades. The heads of the age sets at Osomari are the
deputy military leaders of their political divisions. Since 1927
Osomari have used their sets for keeping watch at night over the
town.

The Ndi Okpala, who are the ritual heads of maximal and other
lineages, and who are also known as Ndi ikei in Abo, Ndichie in
Oguta, and Ndichie Ume in Osomari, are responsible for the cult
of the ancestors in their respective lineages and collectively in the
whole community. The ancestors are considered the guardians of
the moral order and their priests (the Ndi Okpala) give warning of
the consequences of ancestral vengeance should their "laws" be
disregarded, particularly in their injunctions against civil disputes
and disturbances.

The Spirit Societies—Mau or Egungu. These societies at Onitsha
and Osomari are responsible for the performance of a masquerade
in which members of the society appear in masked costumes representing ancestral spirits. Each ebo has its own society and the senior
members, who are called Oraokwute at Onitsha, are believed to
have the power to cause the spirit to enter the costume of the
masquerader. In both Onitsha and Osomari the state government
can call upon the senior members of these societies to collect fines
or other levies imposed upon members of their ebo.

Title Societies. Title associations are used by the state council
for specific duties. At Onitsha for instance a member of the title
association (Agbalanze) in the absence of an Onyeichie takes precedence over the lineage head (Okpala) and acts as the chairman
of an Ogbe council meeting. Members of this association assist in
enforcing decisions of the state council. In all four states, they can
as occasion demands be given executive authority to enforce the
observance of particular laws or to carry out other specific duties.

Women's Organisation. Women in these as in other Ibo communities have their own separate organisation with their own council (a
general assembly of all the women in the community), which is
responsible for disciplining the women of the community. Except
in Abo, their head ranks as a senior official with the title of Omu
in Onitsha and Osomari and of Ogene Nyanya in Oguta. It is a

title, acquired through the expenditure of wealth in Onitsha, equivalent in rank to the male title of Ndichie Ume. The holder has a seat on the Obi's council where she represents the interests of the women of Onitsha. At Osomari the title is held by the oldest woman in the Ugolo ward, at Oguta it goes to the oldest woman in the community.

RITUAL SANCTIONS

The Ndi Okpala, as already explained, are the representatives of the ancestors who are the guardians of morality. Any departure from custom is believed to incur the displeasure and vengeance of the ancestors, a situation which it is the duty of these heads to prevent.

As well as the Ndi Okpala, the offices of head of the state and of the Ndichie, Olinzele and other state officials have a sacred character and people believe that the authority vested in the office derives from the ancestors and from the tutelary deities of the community. Their installation rituals all include ceremonies which make the candidate sacred and which transform him into a person possessed of spiritual as well as temporal power. The passage rituals of the king in all these states transform him into a semi-divine person, while those of Ndichie or Olilinzele chiefs involve sacrifices to shrines of local deities and ancestors. Thus at Onitsha the candidate has to sacrifice to the Ani Onitsha shrine (the earth deity of Onitsha) and to the deity of the River Niger, where he has to dip his feet into the river, thereby bringing himself into close association with these deities and incorporating in his person some of their protective powers. At Oguta and Osomari the offices of Ndichie and Ndichie Ume are restricted to persons who are Ndi Okpala and who thus possess the ofo Okpala, the symbol of ancestral authority.

Alushi Cults. In addition to cults of ancestral spirits there are others associated with nature spirits (alushi) which affect the lives of people living in the vicinity of their shrines. Besides their influence upon the fertility of women and of crops, many of them operate, as has already been mentioned, as powerful instruments for the enforcement of law and the maintenance of order, as the spirit is believed to punish any man (or relative of the man) who forswears himself upon it. A lineage or larger section of the community may enforce the observance of a rule or law by making its members swear upon an alushi to obey it. A court of law may test the veracity of a witness by ordering him to swear upon an alushi, or it can determine a doubtful issue by ordering one of the parties to invoke the spirit to prove the rightness of his claim.

The right to minister to such an alushi is usually vested in a maximal or major lineage and it alone can supply a priest for its shrine. Such priests are usually the Okpala of the lineage.

At Onitsha there are seven alushi cults, namely: Aze, which belongs to Umuezearoli; Aro, which belongs to Umuikem; Ogwugwa, which has two cults, one belonging to Ogbolieke, the other to Obikporo; Okike, which belongs to Ogbolieke; Ojedi, which belongs to Umudei; and Uto, which belongs to Umuasese and Odojele.

Abo has two powerful alushi, namely, those of Iyi Oji and Onye Uku which are known and recognised even by neighbouring peoples who are not members of the community. These cults belong to the autochthonous group of Iwele who supply the priests who officiate for those who come to invoke the deity, or to beg for its assistance in granting fertility or other blessings.

At Oguta, there are nineteen wards with such alushi, and the Okpala of the lineage acts as the priest of the cult in each case. At Osomari the autochthonous group of Ndam ministers to most of the alushi. There are sixty-one such cults, the most important of which are those of Alushi Nwanya Ndam (which aids and protects the women of the community), Iyioji, Ugbelefe, Okwute, Nchala Ubom, Ntapa, and Agbu Ndam. As in the other states, their priests are the Ndi Okpala of various Ndam lineages.

State Cults. As in the Delta states[5] and other kingdoms in Nigeria, there are superior alushi, local deities who are believed to act as the tutelary deities of the community. The moral code of the community, as well as being the law of the ancestors, is believed to be the law of these tutelary deities, and it is the duty of the state to enforce it upon all persons resident in its territory.

At Onitsha there are four important cults regarded as national cults serving the interest of the community. These are: the Ani Onitsha (the earth deity); Otumonye (the river deity); and two other local deities, Omini and Uronye. At Abo there are also four such cults, the Ani Ukwu (the earth deity); Osimili (the river deity); Ngwulu and Nzenwadei. At Oguta, there are four such cults, namely Akpatakwuma (the war deity); Ndukwuokpala (also a war deity), which can be invoked to bring down rain upon the enemy; Anigbala Ute (the promoter of peace in the state); and Akpu Ekwensu (which is associated with the Ndi Igbu society). Osomari has four cults, the Unoje Oboli; the Ani Ulashi (the river deity); Ala Ite; and Ohai Ndiem.

The shrines of all these deities are sacred places, and their priests perform important functions (e.g. at the installation of kings and state officials, which we shall return to in Chapter 8).

These cults also serve the members of the society, and the state councils can invoke them in the same way as the cults of the lesser alushi. Space does not permit a fuller discussion on the use of these cults as a means of enforcing the authority of the state, but their influence continues to dominate the belief of those who have not fully accepted Christian teachings and practices.

SOCIAL SANCTIONS

In addition to ritual procedures use is made of other social sanctions to support the authority of the state and these are also used by other groups within the state to discipline their members. The most common are those of expulsion, ostracism and boycott and they can be enforced against an individual or against a whole lineage or other social group. An association, for example, can discipline one of its members by fining him, or in the case of serious offences, by expelling him, and this will involve the loss of all privileges and benefits which belonged to him as a member of the association. Ostracism or boycott may include the banning of all social intercourse with the offending person or group and involves such essential fields of social interaction as (a) marriage, which is a serious inconvenience when the ostracised group is an exogamous unit that has to obtain its wives from other groups; (b) funeral rituals which cannot be completed without the participation of the entire community and thus result in the deceased entering the spirit world in a state of uya na ifele, that is, of humiliation and spiritual inadequacy; (c) economic co-operation, particularly in the case of certain collective farming activities.

The enforcement of such social sanctions may be accompanied or reinforced by religious sanctions by calling upon all those who are, for example, applying a boycott, to swear upon an alushi that they will adhere to the terms of the boycott.

Colonial rule put an end to the use of force for the settlement of political disputes and following from this increasing use has since been made of such sanctions both by the government of the state and by competing groups within it. We shall be referring to some of these occasions in the case of Onitsha in a later chapter and will conclude this section with an example from Oguta.

After the second world war the Obi and council had accepted the suggestion of the Oguta National Union, an association of all the educated, wealthy and progressive men of the community, that the town should be replanned and organised by the regional government as an urban district with a council of elected members. The number of such councillors (16) was much less than the number of traditional wards (ogbe), and as a consequence many of them had to combine together to form electoral wards. The Oguta National Union, which was accepted as the authority which should decide how the elections should be conducted, decided that in cases where more than one ogbe was included in an electoral ward, each ogbe in the electoral ward should take it in turn to put forward a candidate who should be returned unopposed to the seat on the council. In 1963 this ruling was challenged by the Umunkwocha ogbe which was the numerically dominant ogbe in an electoral ward which they shared with two other ogbe. Instead of accepting the candidate put forward by these two ogbe they put forward their own candidate for re-election despite the fact that a few of their members adhered to the National Union's ruling and voted for the candidate from the other two ogbe. Umunkwocha won the election by 83 votes to 54.

After the election Umunkwocha decided to punish those of their members who had voted against their candidate and ostracised them, making a rule that as those members had offended against the cardinal ancestral precept of lineage solidarity, the rest of the ogbe should not associate with them or assist them in any sacrificial or funeral ceremonies under penalty of a fine of £2. They reinforced this decision by swearing a collective oath upon a tutelary deity, invoking it to punish anyone who might transgress this rule.

This produced an immediate reaction from the heads of the other ogbe in Oguta, that is, from the Ndi Okpala, and they proceeded to ostracise in much the same manner the head of Umunkwocha who was also the Ogene (oldest man) of Oguta and the head of the college of Ndichie. It was held that as Ogene, the holder of the ofo of Oguta, he should have remained neutral in this conflict. Instead he had supported his own lineage and, it was alleged, had used the ofo of Oguta to bind the members of his ward to oppose the will of the rest of Oguta.

The dispute was eventually settled by the senior members of the Oguta National Union on the 16th November 1963. They convened a public meeting at which all parties were present and after hearing the evidence from both sides they ruled that Umunkwocha was in the wrong for having disregarded the accepted electoral procedure and for having taken oath together against those of their lineage who had adhered to this procedure. The ogbe was ordered to revoke the oath which they had sworn against their fellow agnates and then to appear before the Ogene for him to perform the Ikwa Nligba ritual which bound them together once more. The other two

Ogbe were asked to forget the wrong committed against them on the assurance that their candidate would be returned at the next election to the urban district council.

WAR ORGANISATION

Their preoccupation with economic activities associated with the River Niger and its tributaries meant that the states of Abo, Oguta and Osomari were involved in fighting with other kingdoms along the Niger and mostly in engagements on water. Onitsha was concerned with defending her territory against her neighbours who were mostly land dwellers, and she also had to guard her shores against attacks from the Niger States; hence her Iyase is known as Ngadaba Orimili—guard of the Niger. It was the practice of these states to make a declaration of war against an enemy. The enemy had the option of suing for peace or preparing for war. In the course of war, the aim was not only to loot and plunder, but also to bring home captives who could be sold as slaves, or who could be killed in Igbu title ceremonies, or used as domestic slaves. The capture of a war leader implied victory. Osomari maintain that in their last contest with Abo, the Odogwu, the military leader of Abo, was captured, and that this brought not only victory for her, but also lasting peace. Both states became dominant powers along the Niger. Abo traditions do not deny the military strength of Osomari, though they are silent about the capture of their war leader.

In his study of the trading states of the Oil Rivers, G. I. Jones has vividly described the nature of the canoe house, an important military, commercial and domestic grouping which was the basis of social organisation in the Delta States.[6] Most of his remarks apply to these states which adopted such war canoes as their main armaments, though not the canoe-house system responsible for their maintenance in the Delta. Wealthy titled men in the Niger States maintained their own war and trading canoes which were called ugbo ekele. Many of them were manned by their slaves and poorer agnates.

Trotter described the naval fleet of Abo state, an account which has been confirmed by Abo people. According to Trotter,

> Although the Ezzeh has only two large canoes "in commission" he is said to possess, in all, fifteen of different "rates", having from twenty to fifty paddlers, with a small cannon in the bow of each. The first rate war canoes can carry twenty warriors. In the event of hostilities with any other tribe, or when the King proposes to make a "great war", he sends to all the Chiefs who are tributary to him, and they furnish armed canoes according to their means or the

size of the villages under their authority—some four, some only one canoe each. The ten elders at Abòh have each from two to six war canoes. On an extraordinary occasion, it is said the King can muster about three hundred, many of them armed with muskets and cannon in the bows, these last especially, are not however very formidable, as they are lashed to the bow, rendering the aim uncertain. A chief is sent from Abòh to command the expedition . . .'

The original weapons of war were matchets, spears, bows and arrows (uta ogu), basket shields and wooden head gear (okpu ogu). In the late eighteenth century various types of guns, mbachi—short guns, okwalaka—long guns, nwale—medium-sized guns were being used and by the middle of the nineteenth century cannon were introduced from the Delta. These changes revolutionised the strategy of war.

Most of these contests were concluded by a peace in which any shift in the balance of power was defined. An armistice was arranged on a neutral ground, both parties obtaining the mediation of a neutral state. A traditional example of this was the appeal to the Obi of Oguta to mediate between Abo and Igala during one of their long drawn out naval encounters. Another example in the traditions of Osomari was that the Odimegwu of Ihiala was the mediator between Osomari and Ogwu people after years of protracted warfare between both states. The Odimegwu summoned both parties to a neutral ground. He came with his own warriors well armed, and asked both fighting communities to lay down arms and accept his peace offer. Then he ordered his men to shoot in the air and they did so, covering the whole spot with smoke. After this had cleared, he made the leaders both of Osomari and of Ogwu swear an oath together and sent them back as friends.

ONITSHA

The Ndichie chiefs were military as well as administrative officials and the Ndichie Ume under the supreme command of the Iyase were the senior war leaders. The Ndichie Okwa held military posts subordinate to them and the Ndichie Okwareze were primarily concerned with the rituals affecting warfare, though some were also subordinate military officers.

The fighting men of the state were grouped into three army divisions headed respectively by the Iyase, the Ajie and the Odu (the three senior Ndichie Ume), the remaining three Ndichie Ume chiefs forming their deputy or second in command, the Ogene for the Iyase, the Onya for the Ajie, and the Owelle for the Odu.

The six administrative ebo of Onitsha were brought together

in this tripartite military structure in a manner that cut across territorial and political groupings and prevented any expression of territorial or kinship interests, as each military division contained men from both the royal (Umuezechima) and the non-royal (Ugwunaobamkpa) primary territorial divisions.

Each military division was organised into eight regiments under the command of one of the Ndichie Okwa or Ndichie Okwareze chiefs as follows. The first military division was under the command of the Iyase and his second in command the Ogene and consisted of the fighting men from the administrative ebo of Umuase (non-royal) and Umudei (royal), who were organised into eight regiments under the respective commands of five Ndichie Okwa (the Ozi, Omodi, Akpe, Ojiabu, Ozizani), and three Ndichie Okwareze (the Ojole, Akwe and Asagwali). The second division was under the command of the Ajie and the Onya and consisted of fighting men from the Ogboli-Olosi (non-royal), and the Umuezealori (royal) ebo, organised into eight regiments under the respective five Ndichie Okwa (the Osuma, Ike, Gbosa, Ede, Ojiude, and three Ndichie Okwareze (the Eseagba and two others). The third division was under the commands of the Odu and the Owelle and consisted of fighting men from the Odoje (non-royal) and Ogbolu (royal) ebo organised into eight regiments commanded respectively by four Ndichie Okwa (the Adazie, Odua, Ojiba, Oboli) and four Ndichie Okwareze (the Agba, Ojegbe, Onoli and Ijagwe).

The war cabinet was composed of these six Ndichie Ume military chiefs, who conferred with the Obi and planned the war strategy. The Iyase was the supreme commander and maintained a direct link with the Obi and other war chiefs. These summoned public meetings of their military divisions and organised the recruitment of the regiments. On an Nkwo market day, a complete assembly of the regiments was held and the directives for war were finally given.

The three senior commanders, Iyase, Ajie, and Odu remained at home and the army in the field was commanded by their deputies the Ogene, the Onya and the Owelle. These three field commanders kept their respective heads informed of the progress of the war and the Ajie and the Odu passed the information which they received on to the Iyase. The whole chain of communication ran in this hierarchical order, and military efforts and directives were thus centralised and co-ordinated in a systematic way. Other regiment leaders were in constant touch with their military heads—the Owelle, Ogene and Onya, who were at the war front in command of the units. Although the three chiefs' commandants, the Iyase, the Ajie and the Odu normally remained on the home front, when the battle was fierce they could move to the front and take over full direction of activities.

Throughout the whole process, most of the third grade Okwareze, whose special duties were to consult oracles and to prepare charms, carried on their activities and communicated their results to the war chiefs who distributed the charms and explained how they should be used, as well as re-organising the regiments in accordance with the direction of the oracles.

Some regiments were left to guard the town and the Obi's palace and to protect the women, children and old people. Women supplied food to the regiments at home who, under the direction of regimental heads, organised the sending of food and munitions to the field of war.

ABO

Unlike Onitsha, Abo fought mainly on water but its war organisation reflected the same determination to emphasise unity and prevent the expression of divisive sectional interests. Thus the two political divisions of Umudei and Ndichie were combined in a tripartite organisation of fleets each composed of Umudei and Ndichie fighting men under the command of Umudei and Ndichie chiefs. It was the duty of chiefs in all three senior grades to provide, maintain and man the war canoes in these fleets, the only senior chiefs exempted from these duties being the Odua (the oldest man and ritual head of Abo) and the Akpulosu (the eldest son of the Obi). Thus the war organisation of Abo consisted of fleets of war canoes provided by the Olinzele chiefs.

As there were three senior grades of these chiefs so there were three fleets. A first fleet was under the command of the Iyase (head of the Ndichie division) and his deputy the Ndanike (the head of the Umudei division) and consisting of ten or more war canoes provided and captained by the ten chiefs of the senior grade. As Trotter correctly stated, an Olinzele in this grade was able to provide not less than one or more than ten war canoes. A second fleet was provided by the nine Olinzele of the second grade under the command of the Ochia (of Umudei) and his deputy the Odogwu Abi (of Ndichie). The minimal number of war canoes was nine and if some of the Olinzele in the first grade had a surplus of war canoes they could allocate some of them to this second fleet. A third fleet contained the war canoes of the thirty Olinzele of the third grade (twenty-one Omodi chiefs from Umudei and nine chiefs from the Ndichie division) and was under the command of the Ochia of Umudei and his deputy, the Akalamu of Ndichie division.

The fourth grade of Ndichie Olinzele which was assigned to the palace consulted the oracles (Igba afa) and offered sacrifices for the success of the war. Some of these chiefs might have their own war canoes, and they could also be allocated canoes to use in the fleet from the stock held by the wealthy Olinzele in the first fleet.

The owners of war canoes recruited their crew from free-born men of both political divisions of the state and from slaves. The mark of a great chief was shown in his ability to command and by the number of war canoes he owned; at Abo, each senior military chief cut a channel from the Niger to his home, so that during the wet season (oge iju) his canoes could be moored in front of his house. These canals can still be seen today and have distorted the lay-out of Abo town, so that in flood time, people can only cross from one Ebo to the other by canoe.

The Iyase was the supreme commander and the chiefs of the senior grade division constituted the war cabinet. They directed the fleet and planned the strategy of attack. The third or the Omodi fleet made the first attack, endeavouring to land in the town they were attacking. If they met with strong resistance, the first and second fleet supported them.

Having landed, they attacked the enemy and they tried to capture as many prisoners as they could and as much booty as possible. Prisoners of war were made domestic slaves and provided crews for the war canoes of the wealthy Olinzele. If a man was able to obtain the head of any enemy, he went to the Obi who awarded him the Igbu title which made him a member of the Igbu society.

Women also played important roles in warfare. They had their own war fleet and their commanders of these canoes carried special fans (azuzu) which, according to their belief, warded off the bullets of the enemy. They did not engage in fighting, but they accompanied the fleet singing special war songs.

OGUTA

Unlike Onitsha and Abo the war organisation of Oguta was on a ward basis, every ward having the duty of providing and manning at least one war canoe with those wards whose chiefs or heads were superior military chiefs providing many more than this. Some of these chiefs indeed were powerful enough to wage their own private wars against outside enemies. In times of national emergency however these fleets were mobilised on behalf of the state and were under the supreme command of the Iyasara who was the defender of the state and in charge of the Ndanike and the Ezekoro. Each of these three war chiefs provided their own fleets of war canoes,

the crews being recruited from members of their respective wards
and from their domestic slaves. The fleet of the Iyasara was normally the largest of these fleets. In addition the Abatu ward, whose
major lineage of Umueyiche had the right to provide a war leader,
also had its own fleet and during the late nineteenth century three
age sets. Otu Ozumba, Otu Umuamaneme and Otu Oranze were
given the right to equip and man their own fleet. The naval forces of
Oguta were thus comprised of four separate divisions namely:
(*i*) the fleet of the Iyasara, (*ii*) the fleets of the Ndanike, the Ezekoro,
and of the Abatu ward, (*iii*) the fleet of the three age sets, and (*iv*)
the fleet made up of the war canoes provided by the remaining wards
of Oguta.

The Iyasara was the chief commandant of all four divisions, and
he directed the war activities and ensured that all efforts were co-
ordinated.

Oguta brought with them from Benin two war cults, one male,
the other female, each performing a different function. The male
cult, known as Akpatakwuma, is located in Umunsoha ward and
its head is the priest of the cult. Its cult objects consist of a war
paddle, a mortar (ikwe) and a medicine which is buried in the
ground and cannot be seen even by its priest when offering a sacrifice. The chief function of this cult was to give strength to all
Oguta people in the period of war, and according to them to protect
the fighters against bullets and matchet wounds. The paddle was
used to steer a canoe equipped and manned by members from
Umunsoha ward and carrying the mortar, which they believed
attracted the bullets of the enemy.

The female counterpart of Akpatakuma is known as Ndukwu
Okpala. It is located in the Umuigbo ward (a brother lineage to
Umunsoha), and the Okpala of Umuigbo is also the priest of this
cult. Its principal function was to cause rain to fall in any town
to be attacked by the Oguta fleet. The ward members of Umuigbo,
the keepers of the cult, prepared the charm and put part of it into
a calabash (mbubo). They offered sacrifice to the shrine, and in
time of war they blew the medicine, which was in powder form, into
the air. This was to induce rainfall in the town to be attacked.
Throughout the period of attack, the priest continually blew the
powder in the direction of the town.

When war was declared people assembled at the Akpatakwuma
site in Umunsoha ward. The Okpala of this ward offered sacrifice
to the god of the cult. Water was poured on the floor of the small
hut where the medicine was buried. Men and women came forward and rubbed themselves with the clay from the floor as a protection against bullets. Women took their cooking spoons (eku),

rubbed them on the floor, and paraded the town in groups, singing, and invoking the spirit to render the enemy's bullets ineffective.

Before the fleet which had been mobilised for the war set out, Umusoha manned their special war canoe. The war paddle was used to steer it and the adult males of the ward constituted the paddlers. The ikwe (mortar) was put in the stern (onu ugbo) of the canoe. They had a trial run on Oguta lake to make sure that the medicine was effective. People fired at the canoe, and their bullets were supposed to be attracted to the mortar, while the paddle was supposed to cause the canoe to take a zigzag course so that its occupants escaped being hit. If the run was successful, the entire fleet would move off, preceded by this canoe to attract the enemy's fire and so render it innocuous.

The fighting order behind the war medicine canoe consisted of the first fleet commanded by the Iyasara, followed by the fleets of three other war leaders. These were followed by the third fleet provided by the three age sets and this in turn was followed by the fleet provided by the other Oguta wards. They kept in this formation, the Iyase directing the entire convoy under the guidance of the war medicine canoe. Their objective, like that of Abo, was to attack their enemy's town and to land and capture as many of its people as possible, along with any other booty they could find.

Women continued to chant war songs every day and to invoke both war cults to assist their men in winning the war. It was possible in Oguta, as in Abo, for powerful and wealthy individuals with the aid of their kinsmen to equip and maintain their own war canoes and to use them for their own private wars. Two examples of this can be instanced, namely:

Ndanike Obua Ajukwu. This man was the last to hold this office and was a very powerful war chief. He maintained three war camps. The first was at Ubi Oshimili, in the Oguta farm settlements near the Niger. This unit guarded Oguta territory against the kingdoms of Abo, Ogwu, Ndoni and Umuonya. Three hundred slaves lived permanently there with their wives and families. The second was at Iyionumu at Oseanwashi where fifty slaves lived with their families, guarding the arsenal in which he kept his cannon, guns and other weapons. The third was a small detachment of forty slaves and their families stationed at Nnebukwu, a neighbouring village. This was to guard Oguta against attack from the small villages along the Njaba River.

He had six distinguished military captains who directed all his operations, and he himself fought with them. Every war canoe had an ekele, a slit drum, which was played by special signallers while the convoy sailed to its destination. Some of the crew were specialised in firearms, some were experts in shooting with the bow and arrow (uta) and in throwing spears (obo), while all were trained in the use of the matchet (nma). The utita aha, a special basket shield, was used to ward off arrows and spear thrusts.

Ifi Eyiche, of Abatu Ogbe. This ward and its head acquired military status because of its wealth. One of its members, Eyiche Odinibe, to demonstrate this wealth, bought the Iyasara title from an Obi of Umudei ward, even though this was contrary to the constitution. One of his sons, Ifi, assumed the role of a war leader. Ifi had his own war unit and built up his war canoes. His slaves and some of his sons were his soldiers and three of these were the captains of his three war canoes.

He went to war himself and inside the stern of the canoe (onu ugbo) he placed his war charm (mbubo), which acted as a protection against the bullets of the enemy. Ifi waged war against any community he wished to and his two most famous wars were a private war against Akiri people, and a war in which he led Oguta forces against the Royal Niger Company in 1891. Two of these war canoes were used on each occasion and about forty men constituted the crew. Of these, sixteen were paddlers, while others were gunners or drummers assisted when they besieged an enemy camp.

OSOMARI

Each of the three political divisions of Osomari had war leaders and deputies, but the Iyase was the head of the entire naval forces. He was the chief war officer of the state and was assisted by the Odogwu Abi from Ugolo. Each territorial division supplied its fleet of war canoes commanded by its particular head, and when they moved off they formed three fleets with Ugolo in the front, Isiolu following, and Umuonyiogwu in the rear. In addition the Iyase had his own squadron and he was the person who led the entire fleet when they attacked an enemy town.

The crews of the war canoes were recruited from the slaves and age sets in each division. The leaders of the age sets (otu) were also deputy war leaders in their respective divisions.

The period of war was a time of emergency in which the unity of the state around the kingship was emphasised. The Atamanya was kept informed of the activities of the militia in the front. The Oniniogwu did not go to the front but consulted the dibia (diviners and medicine men). His duty was to inquire about the progress of the war through these oracles who informed him about the nature of the sacrifices to be offered in order to promote victory. The Oniniogwu kept the Iyase informed of these oracular directions and instructed the Iyase how to apply the charms prepared by the dibia. He kept the Iyase supplied with a variety of charms.

The Omu, the 'queen', also had war duties: she prepared a war canoe in which she carried a medicinal shield (utita zu ona) which was believed to make the Osomari warriors invisible to their enemies. She also mobilised the women and invoked the charms of the medicinal cult associated with her title so as to make the Igili fighters victorious.

The declaration of war was the affair of the Atamanya and council. Immediately war was declared, the Iyase went on ahead with his squadron and landed at a secret place in the forest near the town to be attacked by the militia. Here he invoked and pleaded with the war spirits and sacred cults of the state to enable it to win the war. All the information from the Oniniogwu was passed to him in here and the Iyase directed the war from the camp until the enemy town was captured. All booty was brought down to this camp, where the Iyase kept it and rendered account of it to the council. The spoils were handed over to the Atamanya and he summoned the council in order to divide them. If there were any casualties, the Iyase had to report this to the council. The booty was shared into three equal shares each division of the state taking one of them. Ugolo took first, Isiolu second, and Umuonyiogwu third. Each division then divided its share among its component units.

CONCLUSION

There are certain common principles in these states.

Firstly, any division of the state into royal and non-royal political divisions disappeared in the period of war. Apart from Oguta they organised their military systems in such a way that no sectional interest could express itself. Secondly, in all of them, the conduct of war was outside the control of the Obi and was in the hands of the Iyase and the senior war chiefs. These officials could, as in the case of Oguta, use their fleets for private warfare provided this did not endanger the peace of the state. Thirdly, the booty and loot enriched not only the war chiefs but also the kings, for all wars were waged in their names and they received a share of the spoils. Fourthly, warfare between these Niger states was governed by various conventions, e.g. in regard to declaring war and submission to arbitration. Fifthly, wars were accompanied by elaborate rituals. Oguta had their medicinal cults, and at Abo, the military chiefs also had their medicinal charms to ward off bullets from the enemy.

5 *Igbudu Ezeukwu: the funeral effigy of the deceased Ezeukwu, guarded by his acolytes. The royal crowns (red caps) are placed on the four corners of the igbudu.*

6 The late Uzoma Ossai II, Ezeukwu of Oguta, the principal king-maker, with his acolytes. Crowned January 18, 1940; died July 19, 1961. He crowned four Obis and two Iyasaras in his lifetime.

7 Udom Ezeukwu of Oguta. Sitting below the throne, he places kola nuts on the Nde Muo ancestral shrines of the lineage.

8 *Obi Mberekpe of Oguta, nineteenth in succession to the throne and fourth in Ngegwu lineage.*

At Onitsha, the Ndichie Okwareze performed the ritual duties and the Oniniogwu did this at Osomari. Sixthly, warfare involved a division of labour which involved not only the various grades of chiefs but all sections of the community, not excluding the women, who played a very important part in the rituals affecting warfare, and were involved in these and other military and naval duties.

NOTES

1   C. K. Meek, 1937; T. O. Elias, 1951.
2   M. Gluckman, 1955.
3   Gin at the end of the nineteenth century was a form of currency on the Lower Niger.
4   P. H. Gulliver, 1963, p. 4.
5   G. I. Jones, 1963, p. 18.
6   G. I. Jones, 1963, pp. 55–56.
7   Allen and Thomson, 1848, Vol. I, p. 236.

L

PART II

Chapter 7 The Notion of Kingship

MYTHS OF ORIGIN

In Chapter 1 we outlined the myths of origin of the kingship in these four states.

The Onitsha kingship is derived from the ancestor Chima who was also the ancestor of the kings of the nine Ada kingdoms of the Umuezechima clan in mid-western Nigeria. The first king of Onitsha is said to have been Chima and all Onitsha kings trace their office to him. The Abo kingship was founded by Ogwezi, the son of Esumai Ukwu who, according to Onitsha legends, was a brother of the Chima Ukwu of the Umu-Ezechima myth. Oguta people maintain that one of the sons of Ugwunta, their ancestor, from Ogwuma, was asked to provide a candidate whom the people crowned as their first Obi. These three communities say that they derived their kingship ultimately from Benin City (Idu na Oba) from where their ancestors migrated to form their present kingdoms. Osomari people tell us that their father Osamene, who originally lived at Idah and later migrated, bequeathed the kingship to Afeke the ancestral father of Ugolo and henceforward the Ugolo ward provided the head of the state.

It can be seen, then, that these four kingdoms attributed the origin of their kings to persons remote in their history, but of the same descent and ancestry.

In the preceding chapters we mentioned the role of these kings as heads of their states, as creators of titles, and in the case of Onitsha, Abo and Osomari as possessing the right to endow their state officials with political power and authority.

The kingship is endowed in myth with special political and ritual powers so that the office becomes the focus of people's political values. Two aspects of kingship are emphasised in their idea of this sacred institution. One is the sacred ritual aspect, and the other is the secular-political aspect. Both are emphasised at various points in the life cycle of a king who is the symbolic representative of the values that support the institution.

PREROGATIVES OF KINGSHIP

The king is the head of all societies. No one can remain with his

147

head covered in his presence.* He is the sole distributor of authority. He transfers ritual and secular authority to the chiefs at their ceremonies of installation. The throne can never be left vacant, hence the notion that the king never dies. This belief in the continuity of the office stems from the belief that there would be chaos if there was no Obi on the throne. Thus when a king dies his death is kept secret and, as at Oguta, it is Odibo (his servant) who is said to have gone to rest. Until his successor is chosen and is ready to be installed, the eldest son of the deceased king takes his place and, as at Onitsha, impersonates his father in the ritual offices at which the Obi should officiate.

The king's political superiority is emphasised in the following ways:

Praise Names. He receives all the great praise names to which no one else is entitled. Onitsha ascribe to him a long list of praise names, like:

"Igwe" (the sky). He whose power is likened to the great one above. The Obi is above all mortals.

"Agu" (leopard). The leopard is the king of the animal kingdom and the Obi is also the ruler of men in their kingdom.

"Akameigbo" (he who vanquished his Ibo neighbours). This implies that he is the defender of the people against their enemies.

"Ogbuonye mbosi Ndu anagua" (lord of life). The Obi is the fountain of justice as well as the person who can take away life or save it.

"Onyenwe Obodo" (he who owns the town). The head of the community.

"Ogbondu ne eji ntu". His power is likened to that of the cannon and to that of gun-powder, which has the force to shatter even a cannon.

"Okwu Ebe". He who has the last word.

"Muo" (a spirit). This means he who has undergone spiritual metamorphosis during the rituals of coronation ceremonies.

"Ogbuefi". He who offers a cow as sacrifice on behalf of the dignitaries of the state. The Obi has this exclusive privilege.

Abo greet their Obi as "Obonwe"—he who is above all, the great ruler, and owner of everyone in this world. Oguta greet their Obi as "Igwe", as at Onitsha, and he is generally called "Nnani", the father of all. Osomari greet their Atamanya as "Okakwu", meaning, the great ruler of his people, whose fame is widely acclaimed.

These praise names, particularly the elaborate ones used at

* Except the Ndichie at Oguta. It is taboo for them to remove their caps in public.

Onitsha, indicate the notion of the king as the head of society, and the most feared, revered and adored leader to whom all powers are attributed.

Royal Insignia. The king's insignia of office, which we shall describe and explain in Chapter 8, reinforce his secular authority. The king has special regalia, part of which he shares with his chiefs as their privilege of office, and part of which he alone holds in order to distinguish between his position and that of his chiefs.[1]

The royal drum, ufie, is exclusive to the kings of these four states, while the Obi of Onitsha shares the egwuota drums with his senior chiefs, the Ndichie Ume.

Gifts and Tribute. The king receives gifts and fees from his subjects. Tribute is paid to him in the form of gifts which come from the chiefs and notables in the state. Those who take office pay him title fees. Court fees are paid at all sittings at his palace. Tributes are paid in various forms. Members of the Igbu association at Oguta take a leopard, which is their symbol, to the king's palace. The king takes the claws, teeth and skin (akpukpo). These are his prerogatives which no one can deny him. Chiefs at Abo and Onitsha help to collect tribute for the Obi from his subjects and retain part of it for themselves.[2]

Abo substitutes for the annual tribute formerly given to the Obi specific property from which he derives his income. They allocate to him seven fishing ponds, called Ofolo, Usha, Iyiosi, Otu, Elili, Ugo, and Mili Ukwu. He holds these, not as private property, but as property attached to the office which is transferred to his successor in office. Annually, after the flood season, the Obi makes a proclamation inviting the public to go and fish in these ponds. The fish are then sold and the proceeds are given to the Obi. The Obi divides this into three, taking two-thirds for himself, and giving one-third to the Olinzele to share between the wards. At present, the fishing rights have been leased to the Isoko fishermen who at this annual occasion again surrender the proceeds to the Obi, who shares them as above. The Akpulosu, the Obi's senior son, administers this property.

RITUAL DUTIES

The sacredness of the office demands that he should abide by certain taboos and avoidances to safeguard his health and spiritual powers. Thus a king must not eat food cooked by a woman who is able to menstruate hence only a virgin, a girl of about ten, may prepare his meals.³ This applies to the kings of Abo, Onitsha and Osomari, whereas at Oguta the senior wife upon whom is conferred the title of Odoba must prepare all his meals. In most cases, she is a woman who has passed the menopause. The king does not weep, for he is above ordinary men, and anger and sorrow belong to mortal men. At Abo and Osomari special officials of the palace weep and mourn on his behalf and represent him at funerals. The same applies to Onitsha and Oguta where one of the king's agnates must weep and mourn on his behalf. The king may not see a corpse, for to do so is to desecrate himself. This applies in all the states.

The daily ritual activities of the kings emphasise their ritual obligations and sacredness. Thus it is obligatory for the Obis of Abo and Oguta and for the Atamanya of Osomari to make daily offerings for their welfare and for that of the members of the state. The Odaje Asi performs this on behalf of the Atamanya of Oso-mari. The kings of Abo and Oguta must offer regular sacrifices to the ancestors on Eke market days⁴ for the welfare of the state. At Abo, the king performs this weekly sacrifice at the Uge Ikenga and the first grade Olinzele of both Umudei and Ndichie must be present at this ceremony. At every national festival, the king offers sacrifices to the ancestors on behalf of the members of the state.

At Abo, the Obi offers annual sacrifices to the cults of Ikenga and Ofo on behalf of the past Obis. This is done at the Uje festival, his annual yam festival when he entertains the Olinzele and members of the Igbu title association. Again, he must offer an annual sacrifice to the shrine of Isu Osimili, the goddess of the Niger. This sacrifice is offered in the presence of the Otu-Imese whose head is the Ikogwe, and who are delighted to officiate at this annual sacrifice. This shrine, located in the middle of the Niger, belongs to the goddess that guards the Abo water frontiers.

At Onitsha, the annual Ofala festival is preceded by an important ritual function carried out by the Obi. This is known as Iyi ukwu na alo, a period of retreat (Ina Obibi) in which the Obi re-enacts the rituals associated with his retirement at Udo during his corona-tion ceremony.⁵ The ceremony starts at noon on Oye market day when the Obi retires into a hut specially erected near the palace for the purpose of this ceremony. He remains in this hut till the following day, Afo, and there celebrates the feast of Ogbalido with the Ndichie. On the third day, Nkwo, he retires to the palace during the day and at night-time he returns to the hut. On the fourth day, Eke, he retires to Iba Ume, one of the consulting chambers in his palace, and spends the day there, returning to the hut at night-time.

Throughout this period the Obi is clad in a white dress and rubs himself with white chalk (nzu). He meditates and no one is allowed to see him. He is spritually in communion with the past Obis of Onitsha, imploring them to guide him in leading the people. At the end, the Ada (the senior daughter) purifies him (ijucha ahu) with a chicken and prepares him for the great annual festival in which his people pay him homage.

The Obi of Oguta and the Atamanya of Osomari make offerings to the ancestors at their annual sacrifices.

NATIONAL FESTIVALS

The values of kingship are reaffirmed and consolidated by periodic ceremonies the most important of which are the national festivals outlined below. They are focussed on the various aspects of their social and economic activities. In all these kingdoms, the royal festivals are occasions when the subjects pay homage to their kings. They are occasions for festivities, dances and merriment when people reaffirm their association with their ancestors and with the different cults which assist them in their day to day economic activities. Some of these festivals determine the periods of seasonal economic activities. All are times when people rededicate their loyalty to their traditional authorities.

The calendar of the year begins with certain feasts and ends with others, so that festivals may be used to determine the chronological sequence in their history. Oguta people sing "Owu bu ife ejili yi agba", meaning "Owu festival is the period that we have set out as our date for such and such an event".

These festivals have specific political connotations which re-emphasise the role and importance of the king and his chiefs in the state. In these states, certain specific festivals exclusive to the king are namely the Ofala at Onitsha, the Uje at Abo, the Ibina at Oguta and the Ulo at Osomari. In those ceremonies which concern all members of the state, the king begins first, and is then followed by his chiefs according to their order in the hierarchy and then by the members of the public. There are also ceremonies which glorify the heroic activities of particular titles associations such as the Ogbalido at Onitsha, which concerns the hunters, and Igbube Ekwensu at Oguta and Osomari, which concerns the Igbu society. The principal festivals will be described below.

ONITSHA

The Ofala. The Obi prepares for this by the spiritual purification to which we have already referred. The Ndichie are informed of the date and a cannon is fired on the morning of that day. The egwuota, the royal dance, is performed, and the ufie talking drum recalls the heroic deeds of past kings. The palace is decorated by the lowest grade of Ndichie (the Okwareze). At noon the people throng to the palace to perform several dances. The Ndichie Ume, dressed in their full regalia of office, begin to arrive each accompanied by his followers, comprising the drummers playing the egwuota, women showering praises on the Obi, and acolytes (ogbu ngwo gwa), standing on his left and right. The drummers stop playing as each arrives at the royal square, and the Onyeichie dances to the egwuota being played at the palace.

The Obi, fully dressed, emerges from iba ume (the inner chamber) amidst great cheers and parades around the square making signs of welcome to the Ndichie and his subjects. He returns to the throne at the iba afa in the square. The Ndichie come forward in order of seniority to pay him homage. A cannon is fired and the Obi emerges a second time into the dancing square, followed by the Ndichie. They chant the traditional song which is sung when the Obi is carried out of the udo in one of the ritual ceremonies of installation. They sing "Ewo! Ewo! Obi Echie oh oh!" meaning "The king is crowned". He dances as far as the square and then returns to the throne.

After an interval, the cannon is fired again for the third time and the Obi comes out for the last dance. He parades round the square so that every spectator will see him. He dances for about fifteen minutes from one end of the square to the other and at the end he retires to the iba ume. The crowd disperses gradually as the Ndichie Ume return to their homes accompanied by their entourages.

ABO

The Uje.   The king's annual Uje, the festival that marks the eating of the new yam by the Obi, is preceded by Ika Uje, the announcing of the Uje festival. On Eke Ukwu, the Obi (Obonwe) indicates that the Uje festival has begun and he offers sacrifice to the ancestral shrine, to ofo Eze (the ofo of the past Obis), to Ikenga, and to other shrines. At the end of this sacrifice, he sends one of the palace servants to inform members of the Igbu title association that the Uje has started. The messenger holds a sword in his right hand and a paddle (amala) in the left and as soon as this message is delivered, all Igbu members cease playing the egume drum.

On Eke Ukwu, nine days after Ika Uje, the Uje is celebrated. In olden days the Igbu and Olinzele members would go to the

Niger on the preceding night on a man hunt for heads for presentation to the Obi the following day.

The Igbu members are invited on Eke day and each arrives in a war canoe, decorated, and with his entourage playing the Egume drum. As each member nears the uge (the royal palace), the king's talking drum (ufie) calls the Igbu member, recounts his great deeds and the Igbu man replies. By this time they have all arrived, each with the insignia of the title, a sword (nma igbu) in the right hand a paddle (amala igbu) in the left, and an eagle feather (nkpo ugo) on the head. The Ndi Igbu of the Umudei sit on the right, and those of the Ndichie on the left of the Obi. As each enters, he dances four times towards the Obi and four times backwards, holding the sword all the time. He kneels and stretches the sword four times towards the Obi. The royal drum plays, and each member as he stands in audience dances and recounts the heroic deeds of his ancestors.

The ritual sacrifice begins when the Obi presents a bowl containing white clay. He first rubs the clay across his eyes; then the bowl is passed round and each member takes a portion of it with his left hand and rubs it across his eyes. It is passed first to the Igbu of Umudei and next to the Igbu of Ndichie. This emphasises the higher rank of Umudei. Kola nuts are then served after the Obi has taken some of the clay and thrown it on the shrines. Then a cock (okwa) is killed, and its blood is sprinkled on the shrines; after this a goat and a cow are offered. These sacrifices of a cock, a goat and a cow are performed by the Akpanuka. He slaughters the animals while the Obi holds the victims.[6] The meat is shared among them while the heads and intestines are cooked and eaten at the Uge. Dances continue till the evening when the Obi retires to the inner chamber and the Igbu return to their homes.

On the following day (called Olie) members of the Obi's council, who are the Olinzele of both Umudei and Ndichie, are invited. Throughout the Eke night, the Ofo Eze and the Ikenga are kept at the Uge Ikenga and young men of the town keep vigil. They play egume and ekele drums and a goat is killed and the meat is used to prepare a meal for all of them. In the morning these shrines are brought to uge anya asa again, which is the open chamber where the Obi received the Igbu and now the Olinzele. At noon the Olinzele arrive, and the senior ones enter first. The Ndichie sit on the left and Umudei on the right. As they enter, they kneel and greet the Obi, using the praise name "Obonwe"; only the Iyase stands up to greet him.

The Akpanuka deputises in the ritual offerings. He slaughters the cock, goat and cow while sitting beside the Obi, and the Obi touches the knife and each animal before the Akpanuka slaughters them. The blood of each animal is poured on the shrines. The kola nuts and drinks are served after they have been offered to the shrines. The Olinzele Umudei are served first and then the Ndichie. The meat is shared into two portions and the heads and intestines are cooked and eaten at the Uge. The Obi can now eat the new yams and his chiefs, the Olinzele and Igbu can follow suit, each making his own new yam feast for his own people and offering sacrifice to both his and their ancestors before eating the new yams.

OGUTA

The Ibina. This is the Obi's annual new yam festival when he invites all the chiefs of the state and the elders and representatives of the wards to an annual banquet at the palace (Obieze). It is the period during which the people pledge their support and loyalty to him, and rededicate the chiefs to the service of the state.

The Obi sends his servant to make a proclamation with the ibom gong (iron gong) inviting the chiefs and people to come to the Ibina feast. This consists of a pot of soup (ofe) made with fish, and two pots of soup made with goat's meat cut into pieces, and portions of yam foo-foo (anya nni) made from old and new season yams. All married male agnates contribute to this foo-foo, sending from two to four plates of it to the Obi. This fish and foo-foo is used for sacrifice, the Obi placing small portions of them on the Agunze shrine, and the rest is shared among those invited for the feast.

The food is distributed to the officials in this order: (a) two plates each to the kingly officials (Iyasara, Ezeukwu, Ndanike and Ezekoro) and to the Olilinzele; (b) one plate to each of the Ndichie; the rest is shared in smaller portions (c) to all ward members present; and (d) to groups who are unable to be present. The ufie drum which is the prerogative of the Obi is played all the while. The Olilinzele who share this prerogative can dance to it as can untitled women who by virtue of their female status have no political rank.[7]

The Iyasara, Ezeukwu, Ndanike and Ezekoro celebrate their own dancing Ibina feast after that of the Obi.

The Omelife. This is a national festival which has both political and ritual significance. It is the people's belief that many of their ancestors return to take part in the celebrations. Because of this, it is compulsory for all holders of the shrines of the ancestors, i.e. the heads of any segment within a maximal lineage (ogbe) to offer sacrifice to the ancestors of his segment. He who fails to do this invites disaster and certainly, as they firmly believe, exposes himself to ritual danger. The festival is in two parts: a preliminary part called Ogene Nkirika, and a main part called Omelife. The manner of celebration is the same except that the dances staged by the various age sets at the Ogene Ndirika are more warlike in character, and the dancers are dressed in warlike attire.

The political aspect of the Omelife festival centres around the Obi and the kingly officials (Iyasara, Ezeukwu, Ndanike and Ezekoro). On Afo Ukwu market day, the ufie talking drum is sounded in the Obi's inner chamber (ime obu). It is played throughout the night till the following morning. It calls on the subjects and reminds them that the Obi will celebrate the Omelife the following day. On the following day, Nkwo, the Obi's dance is staged in the outer chamber (obu ihu). All the members of the council are present, and large numbers of people turn out to watch this annual dance of the Obi and Oririnzere.

The Obi (Eze Igwe), dressed in his royal robes and full regalia of office, comes out, the bell man preceding and jingling the bells (mgbiligba imi na anya) cast in the shape of human heads. He moves around the square with the odu (an ivory tusk horn) in his right hand, and the staff of office (ogbaji-oroji) in his left hand. He goes to the sites of the shrines, salutes them by sounding the horn four times and then returns to the throne. As he moves, he is accompanied by a bevy of women showering praises on him and recounting the historical roles of the ancestors. The ufie is played all the while, and also the opi, another dance, is played for all members of the public. He dances forward towards the drummer and pipers (nde opi) and backwards to the front of the chamber where the Ndichie and Olilinzele are seated. He does this four times, then retires.

The Odoba, the Obi's senior wife, then dances and thirdly the members of Olilinzele dance in order of seniority. The commoners then dance, but a different rhythm is played for them, as that played for the Obi and Olilinzele is exclusive. Towards the close of the day, before the sun sets, the Obi dances once again, followed by the others in the same order.

On the following day (Eke), the Iyasara and other officials celebrate their Omelife, and on the night before this the opi drums are played, but not the ufie, for this drum is exclusive to the Obi. All Olilinzele and Ndichie attend, and the order of dancing is the same as in the Obi's Omelife.

OSOMARI

The Ulo. This is celebrated about the month of April. It begins on an Eke market day when the Atamanya invites members of his political division to the palace. He slaughters a goat and soup is prepared from the meat. Ten plates of yam foo-foo (mbu nni ili) are prepared.

The Olinzele and representatives of the ebo in the Ugolo political division participate in this annual meal. The royal dance elegede is played and as well the war drum (ekele). All the citizens dance and sing the praises of their head of state. Unlike the Obi of Oguta, the Atamanya does not dance, but the Odaje Asi, his personal official, dances on his behalf. He opens the dance and closes it.

On the following day, the Ogene, the head of the Olinzele of Ugolo performs his own Ulo festival and after him, the heads of the other Osomari divisions, namely Isiolu and Umuonyiogwu, follow with their festivals, and then the respective heads of their Olinzele. The other chiefs and householders follow with their celebrations. The feasting continues for more than two weeks.

The Okposi. This is the annual new yam festival (Iwaji). The Atamanya begins it on an Eke day. He roasts five ekpe yams at about 5 a.m. and this is prepared as an olite, which is a mixed yam porridge made up with fish, oil (ofigbo), oil beans (ukpaka), and vegetables (akwukwo). The Olinzele assemble at his palace at noon. The olite (porridge) is served, and after this meal a goat is slaughtered and yam foo-foo is then prepared to provide a second meal. Elegede and ekele masquerades are played, and dances are staged similar to those of the Ulo festival. The order in which the chiefs and people follow with their celebrations is the same as that of the Ulo festival.

RITUALS OF KINGSHIP

The accession ceremonies of the kings are discussed in Chapter 8. Only kings are installed with these elaborate ceremonies, which, like some of the annual royal festivals, emphasise the pre-eminence of the office and provide occasions for the people to reintegrate themselves with the values of the institution. The mortuary rites, considered in Chapter 8, reinforce the notion of the immortality of the spirits of the deceased kings. The saying "Obu ka eze si bia ka osi ana" ("as the king comes so he goes") expresses succinctly their notion of the continuity of the office.

PALACE ORGANISATION

In these states the king's household consists of a limited number of personal servants, slaves and eunuchs, and of specific state officials whose duties are carried out at the palace. The small size of these kingdoms precludes the elaborate number of palace officials which we find in Benin, Igala, Zazzau or other larger African states.

The respective palace organisations are as follows:

ONITSHA

The Palace. This is divided into four chambers. These are: the iba ufufe, a small chamber facing the royal square where the Obi's annual festival is held; the iba afa, where the Obi receives visitors and conducts state council meetings; the iba ume, where the Obi meets with his senior chiefs (Ndichie Ume); the agbalaeze, the private chamber of the Obi. It is exclusive to him and members of his family.

There are also exclusive apartments for the Obi's wives and their children. The royal servants do not live in the palace, but have their residence in a nearby village, except those that help to guard the palace at night.

The royal household consists of:

The Owelle, who in addition to his duties as an Ndichie Ume chief and head of an administrative ebo is the head of the royal household.

The Ndi Ugoloma (eunuchs), three in number, who are chosen from amongst the slaves and servants and play important roles at the palace. Their main duty is to attend the Obi regularly and this involves them in state affairs because they act as the liaison between the Obi and the Ndichie and are responsible for their safe-keeping. One of them, with the assistance of the Ndichie Ume chief, the Owelle, supervises the royal harem (ndi onoju). They fetch water for the Obi and perform all services in the private chamber (Agbalaeze).

The Okwuba. This position, which is no longer filled, was formerly an important palace office. Its holder was known as Anasaeze (the king's beloved first wife) and was intimately linked with the royal household. He was also referred to officially as Odibo Ndichie, the servant of the Ndichie though his role was far from that of a servant in the accepted sense. He was appointed specially by the

Obi and did not belong to any grade of Ndichie, but had the right to wear the Ndichie regalia and the sole right to begin the royal dance called "egwu ota" at any palace ceremony. Because he did not belong to any Ndichie grade, he and he alone could challenge or question any opinion expressed by the Ndichie at the state assembly and it was his duty to draw the attention of the assembly to any act which was considered contrary to the public interest. He was also the link between the Obi and the Ndichie and assisted the latter in carrying out their state duties. He was thus in a position to know the opinions and activities of the Ndichie and could keep the Obi informed of them, and could thus protect him from any plot they might form against him. The last recorded Okwuba was a certain Tagbo Anieka from Ogbeabu, in the Umudei sub-clan of Umuezechima. He was appointed by the Obi Okosi I.[8]

The Palace servants, one of whom has to play the ufie drum every morning and on ceremonial occasions.

The Ulogo Eze. The royal agnates with whom the Obi is in regular consultation.

The Ndi Onoji. The wives of the Obi, who live in their exclusive quarters attended by the Ugoloma and the Owelle. They have their own special status as wives of the king and observe strict regulations. They have their own market at the palace. They cannot be visited without the permission of the Obi or of the Ugoloma responsible for their welfare. The Obi may associate with his wives only in the daytime and they take turns in sleeping with him in the day. The Obi must sleep alone in the night so as to maintain his state of purity. This is peculiar to Onitsha. Adultery with the wife of an Obi used to be punishable by death. There is no divorce of an Obi's wife and on his death she may not remarry.

ABO

The Palace. Abo has an elaborate palace. There are five apartments, namely: the uge chi, the private chamber of the Obi (Obonwe), where he keeps his chi shrine and offers sacrifice to it; the uge agbaku, where all his meals are prepared; the Uge Ikenga, where he keeps the Ikenga Eze and sacrifices to the spirit of this Ikenga; the uge anya asa, the general assembly place where he meets the Olinzele; the uge ndiom, the apartments of his wives.

The Royal Household. As at Onitsha, there are also eunuchs and slaves and they perform similar duties. But the important officials of the palace are the Idibo, the members of the council of Idibo, who are created from among the Obi's wives. These titled officials are ten in number and have the following titles: Owelle, Ajie, Uchi, Ajua, Akpasi, Ugbadu, Ikealea, Ewuije, Ono, Oso. The status and the functions of the office of Idibo correspond with those of the first grade Olinzele Ndichie. The duties of the Idibo are to carry out the ritual and political duties normally performed by the Olinzele when these chiefs are unable or unwilling to perform them, as for example whenever, following a dispute between them and the Obi, they boycott the palace. The Idibo title holders enable the Obi to continue his normal duties and to ensure that the ritual and political continuity of the kingdom is not broken. Some of them are also assigned special duties. The Owelle (Isi Idibo) is their head, and they are under her direction. The Ugbadu cooks for the Obi every Eke Ukwu day. One holds the pillow (idei) when the Obi sits with his Olinezele. She has also to laugh for the Obi when he wishes to do so.

The Obi's wives live in the uge ndiom (their private section of the palace) and they have a special time when they take their bath, and when no one may see them. They may dance throughout the day in the uge ndiom.

Other officials, including the Obi's eldest son, the Akpulosu, have been referred to in Chapter 3.

OGUTA

The Palace at Oguta has three chambers: the obu ime ofe, the inner chamber which is exclusive to the Obi and his family; the ime obu, where he receives visitors and his council; the obu ihu, where the annual festivals and public assemblies are held.

The Royal Household. As at Abo and Onitsha, the Obi has servants and eunuchs (mgbala oto eze). The Ogbunwogwa, his sword bearers, are his most intimate and regular attendants. They usher visitors to the palace and announce all public proclamations made by the Obi and council. They summon people to the Obieze for the state assembly and for the state court. No one dares refuse their summons, for they act on the authority of the Obi. They serve as his bodyguard at night, and sleep at the door leading to the inner chamber; they may not, however, greet him in the morning until the Odoba has done so.

The Odoba is the Ishi Nwanya (the most senior wife) of the Obi and ascends the throne with him. Her praise name is Omodi which is also the title name of the senior wife of the Iyase and also

M

the praise name of the Ndanike, one of the kingly officials. She performs important functions in the state. She sits on the throne at the right hand of the Obi and her duty is to control him. She does so by pinching him (ndubu) secretly and this regulates his conduct at the council meeting. In this way she ensures that the Obi does not talk too much or go beyond etiquette at such public meetings. She sits with him at periods of sacrifice, and we have described elsewhere her role at the annual festivals. She is also the official cook of the Obi.

Other wives live separately but have access to the Obi, though this is controlled by the Odoba.

OSOMARI

The Palace, as at Oguta, has three royal chambers: the iba ime, the inner chamber; a second iba, where the council of the state are received and where also the Atamanya can entertain his visitors, and a third iba, where the annual festivals and public assemblies are held.

The Royal Household. This comprises servants and slaves who carry out all the duties at the palace. The Atamanya's food is prepared by a young girl of between ten and thirteen years, living at the palace, and she is usually one of his daughters. The senior wife is given an Olinzele title and, as at Oguta, she is known as the Odoba. The wives have their own chamber at the palace, and the senior wife supervises the junior wives. Royal wives are buried at the palace and their bodies are not returned to their lineage for burial.

Slaves perform all the work connected with farming and fishing. In conformity with the characteristic Osomari attitude towards slaves they must always remain at a distance from the Atamanya.

The four important officials of the king, the Odaje (Asi), the Oso (Owelle), the Asimaha (Akwue), and the Nzanabi (Okia), in addition to their particular functions as officials of the state, have special functions which are carried out at the palace. We have referred to them in Chapter 4.

CONCLUSION

We have thus listed several points to show that the king's office is sacred or quasi-divine, and that he could be described as a "divine king", though not in the orthodox Frazerian sense, for the health of the king of a Niger state was not identified with the health and prosperity of his people,[9] nor was he ever killed when his powers were thought to have declined.[10]

In the following chapters, we shall discuss the life cycle of each king and this will enable us to understand the deeper notions of kingship as an institution, and of the king as the embodiment of the political and institutional norms and policies of society.

NOTES

1 Cp. J. E. Beattie, 1964, p. 30.
2 Cp. J. E. Beattie, 1960, Chapter 3. This was a general pattern in Benin until recently. Cp. R. E. Bradbury, 1968.
3 Cp. Lucy Mair, 1962, p. 225. Mair has examined similar taboos in the interlacustrine kingdoms in Africa.
4 There for four Ibo week and market days: Eke, Olie, Afor and Nkwo. The first day, Eke, is known as the king's market day.
5 Discussed in Chapter 8.
6 Cp. J. Boston, 1964, p. 236. Boston points out that this sort of practice obtains at Igala and the Ata is assisted by one of his chiefs when he offers a sacrifice.
7 But not the Ndichie Nwanya—the women equivalent to the male Ndichie. Their head is Ogene Nwanya and she and her council exercise political functions in the state.
8 S. Ifeka, 1962; J. Orakwue, 1955.
9 J. G. Frazer, 1960, Chapter XXIV, p. 348; E. E. Evans-Pritchard, 1962 (Professor Evans-Pritchard has refuted in this paper the notion that the king was killed); J. Boston, 1964. Boston has also shown that Frazer's citation of Igala as falling within the category of these kingdoms where the king was put to death was not correct and that the king of Igala was never put to death as claimed by Frazer's explanation.
10 Cp. Tor Irstam, *The King of Ganda*, Stockholm, 1944, p. 56.

Chapter 8   **Rituals of Kingship**

INSTALLATION RITUALS

The installation rituals in these four states are very similar. Those of Onitsha are the most elaborate and can be divided into four stages, namely, the initial rituals and those of seclusion, investiture and integration. We shall use this classification for all four states with the proviso that Abo and Oguta have no initial rituals and that Abo and Osomari have no rituals of seclusion. The investiture rituals at Abo and Oguta are brief and can be completed in a single day while those of Onitsha and Osomari are more elaborate and protracted. The final integrative rituals involve the provision of banquets and feasting by the new king for his chiefs and people and the celebration by him for the first time of public festivals which are repeated thereafter annually for the rest of his reign. The table below summarises the main ceremonies in the four states.

TABLE G

STAGES IN INSTALLATION RITUALS

	ONITSHA	ABO	OGUTA	OSOMARI
INITIAL RITUALS	1. Igo Muo = sacrifice to the shrines.	—	—	Ika Oge = fixing of date for the coronation. Igo Ife = sacrifice to the ancestral shrines by the Ogene on behalf of the elect.
	2. Igba Okonti = ceremony of information of the intention to be crowned.	—	—	—

	ONITSHA	ABO	OGUTA	OSOMARI
	3. Igwasi na Ilo Oreze = presentation to the people by the Ndichie.	—	—	—
SECLUSION RITUALS	4. Imanzu = rituals of cleansing.	—	—	—
	5. Ichendo = seclusion and rituals of meditation.	—	Ikwo Omu = seclusion and period of purification and preparation.	—
INVESTITURE RITUALS	6. Iwe Ofo = receiving the Ofo and the emblem of office.	—	—	Iwe Ofo = taking of the Ofo, the emblem of office from the house of the regent, the Ogene. This takes place after Igbu Efi (No. 10).
	7. Ijeudo = going to the Udo shrines for integration with the ancestral kings.	Ibu Eze = carrying the elect to Ani shrine. Igo Ani = sacrifice Ani (Earth deity) shrine.	—	—
	8. Ibu Eze = carrying the king elect.	Ibu Eze = carrying of the elect from Ani shrine to palace.	—	Ibu Eze = carrying the Atamanya to the throne.

	ONITSHA	ABO	OGUTA	OSOMARI
	9. Ijeozi Obodo = performance of domestic services at the residence of the Iyase. (a) Administering of the oath of office. (b) Ikpube Okpu = crowning by Iyase.	Igo Nze = sacrifice at the palace when the elect receives the emblem of office. Ikpube Okpu = crowning by the Iyase.	(a) Invocation of his Ofo by the Eze Uku. (b) Ikpuya Aboshi = placing of Aboshi plant in Obi's mouth. (c) Ewu Ikwe = sacrifice of goat and collection of its blood in a mortar.	(a) Sacrifices by Ogene. (b) Ikpube Okpu Eze crowning by Ogene. (c) Nnoko Olinzele assembly of chiefs at the palace.
	10. Ewu Onu Egbo = sacrifice of a goat at the entrance of the royal palace.	—	—	Igbu Efi = sacrifice of cows to state deities.
	11. Idoba na Ukpo = placing on the throne.	—	Ibu Eze = carrying the elect to the throne.	—
INTEGRATIVE RITUALS	12. Ofala = Royal festival for the people.	Olili = feasting the community.	Nni Eze = feasting the community.	Isi Nni Obodo = feasting the community.

ONITSHA

Initial Rituals

There are three main ceremonies in this preliminary stage. The first is igomuo. The candidate aspiring to selection goes to the Okpala of his lineage and declares his intention. The Okpala offers sacrifice to the ancestral shrines and informs the ancestors of the intention of their son and also requests them to assist the candidate in the spiritual world by interceding so that nothing will stand in his way in this endeavour.

The second is Igbaokonti. The candidate having notified the Okpala of his ward and his agnates of this intention, presents himself to the Ndichie and indicates his intention to be selected. The Okpala and his kinsmen lead him to the Ndichie.

Many candidates perform these two initial ceremonies and these preliminaries are periods of distribution of gifts, of lobbying and canvassing for support from the royal and non-royal divisions. A cow is given to each of the nine ebo and acceptance means that the candidate is adopted by them.

The third is Igwasi na Ilo Oreze, or Presentation. The candidate selected is presented to the Ndichie and the Iyase (Onowu) and he in turn presents the candidate to the Agbala na Iregwu at Ilo Oreze. The people will then acclaim him as the Obi elect, and the other ceremonies will then commence.

Seclusion Rituals

The second group of ceremonies involves a period of retirement from the public and intense meditation in preparation for the third series that bestows the office of kingship. The two ceremonies of seclusion are the Imanzu and Ichendo.

Imanzu is a ritual of purification in which the candidate is cleansed for the other greater rituals ahead. Again, this is held at the residence of the Okpala who officiates on this occasion. The Obi elect brings kola nuts (oji), tobacco (otaba), ten yams (iji ili), two gallons of palm wine (nmanya) and white clay (nzu) in a calabash container (oba).

The Okpala offers kola nuts and palm wine to the ancestral shrines and prays for the success of the ceremonies, and for the guidance of the ancestors and their protection of the Obi elect. The Okpala then rubs the white clay on the body of the candidate who ties at this stage only a piece of white cloth around his waist. This whitening of the body has its root in the idea of resurrection from the dead. To become a member of a title society, a man passes through sacrificial ceremonies whereby he enters into "muo", that is, into the realm of the spirit world. Thus he metaphorically dies. After the purification is completed, he emerges as a resurrected being, hence the white body. From this time, he is respected as a semi-spiritual being and, as such, sacrosanct.[1]

The next ceremony is Ichendo. The candidate having undergone the Imanzu ceremony retires for twenty-eight days and remains incommunicado throughout this period. He continues to rub his body with nzu to keep himself in this state of purity and remains in this state awaiting the next important ceremonies.

Investiture Rituals

The third group of ceremonies are those which involve the bestowing of the emblems and insignia of office, and other ritual ceremonies which bring the elect closer to the ancestral kings of the past. The personnel who are the kingmakers are divided between those who perform the ritual ceremonies, and those who perform the secular ones. The ritual consists of the following successive ceremonies:

Iweofo.[2] The giving of the ofo, the emblem of political authority. The ofo is supposed to be that of the first king which is handed from one Obi to the other to symbolise the continuity of the office and the power and authority attached thereto.

The head of the Umuase lineage, known as the Omodi, is the principal official and hands this emblem of office to the Obi. The Okpala of the Obi elect goes to the Omodi of Umuase in Ugwu na Obamkpa and asks him to come to the imeobi (palace) for the ceremony. The Omodi and his agnates go to the Obi. They are all clad in white clothes. The ofo is put in a bag and wrapped with a white cloth. At the imeobi, the Omodi offers a sacrifice to the ofo, blesses it, and then hands it to the Obi elect.

The ofo having been given to him, he then proceeds to the Udo shrine, where the spirits of the past kings dwell, for the important ceremonies that eventually confirm him as the Obi.

Ije Udo. The Udo shrine is shrouded in thick bush beside an ant-hill (ikwube). This is supposed to be the place where the first Obi was buried and the new Obi goes there to commune with the dead Obis and to be, according to Meek, "dynamised" by the spirits which haunt ant-hills (an ant-hill being regarded as a porch to the underworld).[3]

At the Udo, the priest of Udo (Eze Udo), who comes from the Obio lineage of Ugwunaobamkpa, officiates. The Obi elect, who is clad in a white robe and wearing a white cap, sits on a mat. The Eze Udo then prays and invokes the spirits of his fathers who had performed this office for previous Obis, imploring them to assist him in carrying out the ceremonies in accordance with tradition. Then he recounts all the previous Obis of the land whose vigil and dedication had taken place at the Udo.

He slaughters a white goat and spreads the blood on the shrine. He also places on it white chalk and kola nuts (oji) which are also offered on the shrine. A white cloth is also placed on it. Then he releases a white cock into the Udo bush, to stray away and to carry away the impurities and objects that desecrate the Obi.

He slaughters another white cock and spreads the blood on the ufie, the royal drum, and pours a libation with palm wine and offers kola nuts on the ufie drum.

The Onye Ufie, the Obi's servant in charge of the drum, gives the drumsticks to the Eze Udo who then returns them to him, thus granting the authority to play the ufie to the Obi's servant. This completed, a cow is slaughtered and the meat is shared into two. The priest takes one part and the other part is shared between the two political divisions of Umuezechima and Ugwumaobampka. The Obi and the priest pass the night at the Udo and at dawn they leave this spot and move to an area where a small Ogwugwu shrine is located. It is part of the Udo shrine.

The Ada of Obio from the Udo priestly lineage comes forward and shaves the hair of the Obi and hands the hair to the Udo priest who deposits it on the okwu Udo. This ceremony is to commit the life of the Obi to the guidance of the Udo spirit. At this stage, he removes the white cap from the head of the Obi and rubs his head and body with white clay. He ties a white band on the Obi's head and puts an eagle feather in it and then calls the names of his own ancestors informing them that he has completed his duty. Immediately the ufie is played, re-enacting the playing of the ufie by Oreze.

Ibueze. The carrying of the king. Having completed the rituals of Udo and thus reinforced by the ancestral powers, the candidate has become an Obi and as he comes out, he is carried shoulder high (ibueze) by the surging crowd, and they move to the Iyase, the people chanting "Obulu Eze Ayo! Obulu Eze Ayo!" ("He is the king, oh yes! He is the king, oh yes!"). He is then raised high above everyone in the state and they acclaim him their king and all powerful.

The important roles of the Iyase and Ndichie begin at this stage and the rest of the investiture ceremonies are carried on with their co-operation.

Ijeozi Obodo (Performance of Domestic Services). The cheering crowd follow the king who is carried high to the Iyase's residence where the Ndichie are seated in the order of their rank. Before them, the Obi performs domestic services. He breaks some wood (nku), sweeps the floor (ezi), collects water (ichu mili), mends the roof (igba uno) in keeping with their tradition that he must render these services to the people for the last time. These services are to teach him that he is the servant of the people and must cater for their general interest as a dutiful wife does to the husband and her children. The ceremony inculcates humility.

Oath of Office.   After these services, he stands before the Iyase
and the other five Ndichie Ume also stand beside him. The Iyase
removes the white band which was tied on his head at the udo and
on which an eagle feather was fixed. He holds a red cap and asks
the Obi the following questions:

IYASE: Will you use your good office to govern well now that you
    will be crowned king?

OBI: Yes.

IYASE: Will you pervert the traditions of the people?

OBI: I will not.

IYASE: Will you suppress the poor and terrorise your subjects?

OBI: No.

IYASE: Will you respect the advice of your Ndichie for the good
    of the people?

OBI: Yes.

Ikpube Okpu.   The Iyase then raises the red cap and says:

> "This cap which I will place on your head will be the first step to
> your being made a king and I hope that from the moment this is
> done you will be worthy of this trust."

Placing the cap on the Obi's head the Iyase says:

> "Your reign will be good. I have surrendered into your hands the
> power that passed to me when the Obi died. May God (Chukwu)
> give you long life so that your reign with the Ndichie will be a
> peaceful one."

This ends the ceremony before the Iyase.

Return to the Palace.   The Iyase and Ndichie rise and proceed to
the ime obi (palace), where they occupy their seats as if in a council
meeting, waiting for the arrival of the Obi.

The Obi rises and the crowd follow. As he wends his way to the
palace, he follows a traditional path and on the way offers sacrifice
to various shrines by dropping nzu as he stops before the location
of each shrine. He informs the spirits of these shrines that he is now
the king and implores them to assist him in his reign.

Ewu Ono Egbo.   In front of every palace is egbo, a medicinal
cult which is protective in function. This is suspended on a pole which
is thrown across an arch made by two standing trees. The arch is
the entrance to the palace and is called onu egbo. As the Obi
comes near the onu egbo, a goat is slaughtered in front of this cult
and the cult is invoked to protect the Obi against any medicinal

charm from an enemy; and also to safeguard those who enter the palace and to neutralise any magic or dangerous medicines that any one might bring into the palace.

Idobo na Ukpo. The Obi then proceeds into the ime obi, the inner chamber, and the Iyase raises the Obi to the throne (ukpo) saying:

"Today I have raised you to the throne as the Eze (king) of Onitsha according to our traditions; you are made a king today by me."

Integrative Rituals

Public acclamation, and the feasting begin at the conclusion of this last ceremony. All members of the public are participants, for the periods of installation of kings are occasions of great festivities in the state. Their emotions are charged and they show this by the large attendance at most of the ceremonies.

Payment of homage. The Obi thus seated, the ufie (royal drum) and the egwuota are played and the huge crowd at the palace is in festive mood. The Iyase comes forward. He stands a little apart from the Obi, and extends his clenched right hand towards the Obi as he repeats each of the praise names one after the other. When he finishes, the other five Ndichie Ume come forward in their order of rank and each kneels and genuflects saying "Igwe! Igwe! Igwe!" with their foreheads on the ground as the words are repeated. The second and third grades come forward one after the other according to their rank. When the Ndichie have finished, the Agbalanze, the Ozo titled association, repeats this procedure and the then Agbala na Iregwu and other members of the public.

The Ofala. The Ofala festival then begins and the ceremonies described in Chapter 7 are performed except the preliminary stages of the ritual seclusion which in this case have already been performed in the udo ritual ceremonies.

ABO

At Abo, the ceremonies of investiture are the following:

Ibueze. The ceremony of installation begins with this act of carrying the king. Eight persons, four from Umudei and four from Ndichie carry the elect from his residence to the Isu Ani and the earth deity of Abo. These men represent the two political divisions. As they carry him along, the crowd follow and chant in great admiration.

Igo Ani.   Here the priest of the land offers sacrifice to the earth shrine and pleads with the spirit of the land to guide the new Obi and to defend him against his enemies. At the close of the ceremony, the eight men carry him again back to the uge (the palace) for the other ceremonies and place him on the throne (ukpo).

Igo Nze.   On his arrival at the Uge from Igo Ani, the Odua offers a sacrifice to the nze, the emblem of kingship, and then hands other emblems of office to the Obi. He gives the Obi the ofo ndi eze—the ofo of all the past kings, thus transferring political power and authority to the new king. Next he gives him the Ikenga Eze, the sword of office (nma eze), the staff (ngbachi eze) and then the Odua withdraws.

Ikpube Okpu Eze.   The Odua steps backwards and takes his seat. The Iyase comes forward, takes the crown (okpu eze) and places it on the head of the Obi. This completes the investiture ceremonies. The Odua performs the ritual acts while the Iyase performs the political ones. After the investiture the new Obi has to feast the public (Olili).

OGUTA

At Oguta any person of the royal lineage (ogbe) who is a member of the Ikwa Muo society and who can win the support of his lineage elders is eligible for the title and there is no bar on the number of Obi who can be appointed at any one time. The first to complete the installation ceremonies who is usually the oldest will perform the duties of the office and when he dies and his mortuary rituals have been completed he will be succeeded by the one who is next in ranking order and so on. No new installation rituals will be held until all the Obis in the set are dead and buried. The system which was introduced by the Umudei royal lineage is examined in greater detail in Chapter 9.

Seclusion Rituals
Ikwo omu.   This period of seclusion lasts for two native months and usually starts at the beginning of July until the end of August. During this period the Obi elect puts on a white cloth (abuocha) and is confined to the innermost chamber of his palace, ime ofe. A young girl of about twelve years cooks for him and he does not eat any food that has been left overnight. He offers daily sacrifice to the ancestors. This constant sacrifice is known as Izuonachi. During this period his praise name is Ogbobo but after

the crowning he is greeted as "Igwe". If he dies during this period of seclusion his funeral ceremonies will include some of the royal funeral rites such as the royal dance ufie and a catafalque (igbudu) at his public funeral.

Investiture Rituals

The investiture begins with the arrival at the palace of the Ezeukwu, the kingmaker. His position in the political system has been explained in Chapter 4. He is not from the royal lineage like Abo and Osomari, but comes from a non-royal lineage like the Iyase of Onitsha. His position in the political system resembles that of the Achadu, the kingmaker at Ida, who regards the king as his wife and "beats and abuses his wife" and sends the candidate for the throne to his senior wife for the ceremony of piercing the ears.[4] (It is said that when the Ezeukwu pays a courtesy visit to the Obi or Iyase, each vacates his throne until he enters and sits on it. They then sit beside him and the mat on which he sat and whatever is used to entertain him is taken away by him.)

On arrival, the following objects—a goat (ewu), mortar (ikwe), a pestle, iron needle (ndudu), a piece of eight yards of cloth (obuakwa), a mat (agini) which is spread on the throne where the Ezeukwu sits, cowries, kola nuts on a plate (formerly in a calabash)—are brought and placed beside him. Then the new king sits in front of the Ezeukwu. The Obi is without clothes so that the people will see his body and be satisfied that he is not deformed. The mortar is placed between his legs and in front of the Ezeukwu.

Oath and Rules of Office. The Ezeukwu then tells him the rules to observe: that he should not take the Ezeukwu's power from him, and should not seduce any person's wife; that he should not remove any property from him or any other persons and should not owe any debt; that he should not break the rules of society by committing any acts against the deities which are considered by the people to be "alu", an abomination. Then the Ezeukwu who, while reciting these rules, holds an ofo in his hand strikes it on the ground, saying: "If you break any of these rules let the ofo kill you."

Ikpuya Aboshi. After this, he places an aboshi plant in the Obi's mouth, and the goat is then held by three persons.

Ewu Ikwe. With the goat's neck on the mortar, the Ezeukwu takes the iron needle, pierces it through the goat's throat and they hold it firmly so that it will not resist. The blood is collected into the mortar and must not drop on the ground. If it does, then there is danger facing the Obi, but they make sure that it does not.

Ibueze.   This concluded, the Obi is carried to the second chamber and placed on the throne. He then retires into the room of his senior wife (Ishi Nwanya) who is automatically made the Odoba (praise name, Omodi) and elevated so that she can sit with the Obi on the throne throughout his reign. He is washed in the room and after this, he walks into his own innermost chamber. There, his agnates help to robe him.

Integrative Rituals
The Obi emerges for the final ceremony, Nni Eze, a ceremony repeated annually when he provides a feast for the people. He holds the ofo in his right hand, and the odu in the left. The bellman carries the bell and leads the procession from the inner chamber (ime ofe) by striking the bell announcing the arrival of the king. Two of his ogbungwogwa (bodyguards or acolytes), their bodies bare, with cloth tied round their waists and with chalk (nzu) rubbed around their eyes, and swords in their hands, stand one on the left and the other on the right.

OSOMARI

Initial Rituals
These are Ika Oge (fixing the date for the installation) and Igo Ife (sacrifice to the ancestors before the investiture ceremonies). The two form a single group. The selected candidate is presented to the Ugolo royal lineage and they confirm their selection. They convey this to him and normally obtain his consent even though he has previously indicated his desire to be selected.

Ika Oge.   The Ogene summons the Ndichie of the three political divisions and members of the public to his residence. The candidate is presented by the Ogene to the public for their approval, and when no objection is raised, he brings six bottles of gin and some kola nuts. These are shared into three and each division takes one of the shares.

Igo Ife.   They return to their divisions and the heads of the division offer these gifts of gin and kola to their ancestors' shrines asking them to assist the newly elect.

Investiture Rituals

Ibu Eze. After the ceremony at the Ogene's residence the Atamanya elect is carried shoulder high to his palace and the crowd
follow the carriers chanting "Isi ogu" (leader in war). On arrival
at the palace they place him on the throne which has already been
prepared.

Ritual sacrifices. These are elaborate at Osomari and in addition
to the sacrifices in the initial rituals the Ogene offers sacrifice before
beginning the investiture. Before beginning the investiture he brings
out the Ogene's ofo, together with the Ikenga (spirit of good luck)
of the ward and offers kola nuts and chalk, praying to the ancestral
kings to guide the new Atamanya, to give him strength and to
endow him with sacred and secular powers.

Ikpube Okpu Eze (crowning). The Atamanya elect goes into his
inner chamber accompanied by three men from the three lineages
in Ugolo ward. They pour water on him and wash his body. He
then puts on his royal robe and holds an odu or otulaka (elephant
tusk horn). He takes the okpu ododo or okpueze (red cap which
is the crown) and comes out to the outer chamber where the Ndichie
of the state are seated. He sits on the throne and places the okpu
ododo on it beside him. The Ogene steps forward and places it on
the Atamanya's head.

Nnoko Olinzele. The Atamanya invites the olinzele of the three
political divisions to the palace and three cows are slaughtered and
shared amongst them according to their rank, Ugolo first, then
Isiolu and then Umuonyiogwu.

Igbu Efi. After the investiture a series of sacrifices are made on
different days to the principal shrines of the land. The first is at
Onoje Oboli, located in Isiolu. The second is at Ani Ulashi, located
at Umuchi in Umuonyiogwu, the third is Efi Ala Ite, located at
Umuonyiogwu, the fourth is Efi Ohai Ndam, the cult of Osomari
women in Ugolo. Only the king and his agnates with the women
are present on this occasion and the Olinzele are not allowed to
attend. In each of these sacrifices, except that to Ani Ulashi, a
cow is slaughtered and shared into three, one for the people of each
division. In that to Ani Ulashi at Umuchi, the cow is divided into
two: the Ezeani, the priest of Ani Ulashi, takes one half while
the other half is shared into three.

Royal dances of elegede are played and the egwungwu (masquer-
aders) appear to represent the ancestors.

Iweofo. When the ceremonies are ended, the King, escorted by selected members of the royal ward, goes to the residence of the Oniha Ogene, who keeps the ofo. This is handed to him by the Ogene after he has offered sacrifice to it. The king on arriving home sacrifices a goat to this emblem of office and he does this annually.

DISCUSSION

We shall now consider the salient principles involved in these elaborate installation ceremonies. Fortes has suggested that rituals present the individual as the creation and possession of society or part of a society into which he is to be incorporated through the office. "Ritual mobilizes incontrovertible authority behind the granting of office and status, and thus guarantees its legitimacy and imposes accountability for its proper exercise."[5]

In our examination of the installation rituals of these kings, three salient points included in the statement above have emerged. First, there is the presentation of the individual king as the creation of society. This is evident from the general involvement of the entire community and even the deities in the affairs of the installation. Second, there is the mobilization of incontrovertible authority behind the office, and third, the guarantee of its legitimacy and the imposition of accountability for its actions.

But in addition, these rituals have the following meanings: firstly, some of the rituals are concerned with a formal indication of the candidate's intention to aspire to the office and the obtaining of the consent of the people. The Onitsha and Osomari ceremonies of Igo Muo, Igba, Okonti, and Ika Oge are concerned with the fulfilment of this principle. Secondly, some rituals are concerned with the purification of the individual, thus elevating him to sacred status, for example, the ceremonies of Imanzu and Ichendo at Onitsha and Ikwo omu at Oguta. Thirdly, some of the ceremonies involve communication with the ancestors, not only of the candidate's own lineage ancestors, but also the ancestors of the past kings. The ceremony of Ije Udo at Onitsha belongs to this category as well as those ritual ceremonies at the investiture. Fourthly, there are those ceremonies which involve sacrifice to the land and other deities, thus invoking their assistance for the preservation of the candidate and the institution during his reign, and also warding off dangers which might arise in the period of his office. Further, these deities add extra power to and bestow supernatural qualities upon the recipient. The series of sacrifices to the deities of Osomari, the offering of nzu (white clay) by the Obi of Onitsha as he walks from the Iyase's residence to the palace, the sacrifice of the Obi of Abo at Isuani, are all examples. Fifthly, some of the ritual ceremonies ensure a general continuity of the political power and authority of the office and its holder through the inheritance of the power from the ancestral emblems of office, for instance, the ofo and the regalia.

We find that these ceremonies have a number of common features which we can consider in greater detail.

Sacrifices

Most of the sacrifices embody two forms, firstly, personal sacrifices for the deconsecration of the candidate, to make him profane, and secondly, to make the profane candidate a sacred person.[6] The individual becomes through this series of 'rites de passage' a distinctive personality. In most of the sacrifices as we have shown, the candidate may not be the active participant, and other persons do so on his behalf until he wears the 'insignia' which then enables him to perform such a sacrifice by himself. The giving of the ofo, ikenga and nze at Abo by the Odua, and the ofo by the Ogene of Osomari, are illustrative of this statement.

In most of these sacrifices the victims used are animals and it is customary to select only domestic species, such as goats, bullocks and fowls, which are specifically reserved for the purpose.[7] These particular animals are reserved for this use except for the bullocks, which are substitutes for human sacrifices which were formerly offered on behalf of kings and chiefs. There has also been a change in the nature of the sacrifice as slaves were never eaten and cannibalism was forbidden in this area. Slaves, when killed and offered as sacrifice, were buried and a plant (akpu) was planted on the spot to record the ritual place and occasion.

These animal sacrifices are based on exactly the same principle of propitiation as the human, and with the same idea of substantiability to the spirits, who receive their due share of the spiritual essence of these offerings in the spirit land.

Most of the animals are slaughtered as follows: their heads are held over the shrines, then their throats are cut, and then the blood is sprinkled on the shrines. The animal meat is cooked and specific parts are placed on the shrines and later removed and shared among those present. Some meat is shared uncooked and the distribution follows the structure and the political hierarchy in the state.

The other objects that are used in sacrifices are kola nuts and palm wine, both of which are edible and of which the ancestors can also partake. The use of nzu (white chalk) symbolises purity, innocence and holiness. In most of the sacrifices, it is common for the body of the officiant and of the candidate to be smeared with nzu. The eyes and arms of the person on whose behalf the sacrifice is offered are decorated with this white clay by the officiating person. "Ihu eze ako nzu" (the king's face is never without white clay) is a popular saying.

The altars and places of sacrifice, in addition to being symbols of the spirits concerned, are also focal points of political unity.

The Ibu Eze Ritual

Another common feature in these ceremonies is Ibu Eze, the carrying of the king. This ceremony has a dual interpretation. First, once carried, he is regarded as above everyone, he becomes elevated and therefore is above all classes. Secondly, the journey to the throne, even though the distance is short, symbolises the people's entry to their political domain, an entry led by their ancestors the founder of the kingdoms of Onitsha, Abo, Oguta and Osomari, whose early kings led and defended them till they settled in their present abode. This ceremony of the re-enactment of entry is a common practice among the Nigerian kingdoms with whom they have political relationship distant or remote.[8]

The identification of this ceremony with the ancestor founder of the kingdom, and its first king, reinforces the claim of the royal lineage.[9]

Common Emblems of Office

The principal emblems and regalia are given in Table H opposite. The endowment of political power is associated with possession of such royal emblems. In all these states, the regalia of office are the exclusive possession of the kings, and these are objects that differentiate the king from the others. Most of these objects are sacred and have political significance. The investitures, as we have described, are marked by the placing of the most important regalia and emblems of office on the new Obi and once this is done, he assumes the sacred status and is ordained with political strength. The simple man of yesterday becomes a man who possesses the mystical power of kingship.

Most of these emblems are exclusive to the Obi though in some of the states the chiefs are allowed to wear or have some of the emblems as a mark of their identification with royalty. Each of them has its significance in relation to the power and position of kingship as an enduring power of the political system.

We shall explain briefly the meaning attached to each emblem that is common to the four states.

TABLE H
EMBLEMS AND REGALIA

ONITSHA	ABO	OGUTA	OSOMARI
Ofo Eze = emblem of power	Ofo Eze = emblem of power	—	Ofo Eze = emblem of power
Ufie = royal drum	Ufie = royal drum	Ufie = royal drum	Ufie = royal drum
Akpukpo Agu = leopard skin	Akpukpo Agu = leopard skin	Akpukpo Agu = leopard skin	Akpukpo Agu = leopard skin
Ada or Abani = sword	Nma Igbu = sword	Nma Igbu = sword	Nma Igbu = sword
Okpu Eze = the crown (a red cap)	Okpu Eze = the crown (a red cap)	Okpu Ododo = the crown (a red cap)	Okpu Ododo = the crown (a red cap)
		Afa Ocha = white robe	
	Afa Ododo = red robe	Afa Ododo = red robe	
Afa Ocha = white robe	Nkpo Ugo = eagle feather	Nkpo Ugo = eagle feather	Nkpo Ugo = eagle feather
		Nkpo Kolobibi = feather of the kolobibi bird	
		Oji = iron staff	Oji = iron staff
	Odu = elephant horn	Odu = elephant horn	Odu or Otalaka = elephant horn
		Okpu Omu = red cap	
Odu = elephant tusk horn	Esulu = coral anklets	Mgbiligba imi na Anya = special bronze bell with human face	
Nze = horse tail	Nze = Ofo Eze, Ikenga and other ritual objects	Olosi = special pillow made with leopard skin	
Okpu Ofa = ceremonial hat Aka and Esulu = coral bead armlets and anklets		Agunze = shrine of royalty	

The Ofo. Ofo eze, the king's ofo, is the symbol of ancestral authority and it identifies the present king with the founder of the royal lineage and the kingdom. Onitsha, Abo and Osomari kings possess the ofo of their first king, and this is one of the important ways by which continuity of the office is maintained. The Obi of

Oguta has a personal ofo but not an ofo eze—the ofo of the founder of the town, which in this case is held by the Ogene, the oldest male in the state.

The Ufie is the ancient royal drum and is possessed by every king in these Niger kingdoms. It is exclusive to the Obi and no other official in the state has it.

The Leopard Skin. All kings are likened to the leopard, which is believed to be the king of the forest. Just as the leopard reigns in the wild animal world of the jungle, so also does the king reign in his own domain. The Obi of Onitsha is greeted as "Agu".[10] Leopard skins are spread on his throne (ukpo). In fact, the Obi may not sit without one spread on his seat. When, therefore, any person kills a leopard, particularly at Oguta, the skin is given to the Obi. It is exclusive to him and to the Iyase.

The Sword. Oguta, Osomari and Abo call it "nma igbu", while Onitsha calls it "ada". Among the western Niger Ibos, it is called ada and it is also used by the Oba of Benin. Among the Yorubas this is also a common emblem of office. The Oba of Lagos also has an ada.

The sword means strength, and only persons who have performed extraordinary feats can be anointed by the Obi and given a sword. At Oguta, Osomari and Abo, the members of the Igbu society are allowed to hold a sword. The Ndichie Ume at Onitsha also possess the sword. In the three states, the Obi's identity with the Igbu is to reinforce the notion that he is the head of the military, and above the power of a leopard. The Obi holds it as a member of this society and also in his capacity as head and ruler of the state. The sword further conveys the idea that he, as the fountain of justice, holds the power of life and death. The king's subjects are reminded of this by the display of this emblem of power on all important occasions. Two royal servants known as "ogbu ngwogwa eze" (the executioners of the king) stand with bared swords on the right and left hand of the king. In former days these men were eunuchs.

Okpu Eze (the Crown). This is a red cap and is one of the most important regalia. It is exclusive to the Obi and once placed on his head he cannot appear without it. It is considered the consummation of the investiture, for once the crown is placed on the head, the political and mystical nature of the office is assured.

Robes.   White and red robes are common to all these states. White signifies purity and sacredness while red signifies power and authority. That the kings wear both indicates the combination of secular and sacred authority.

Nkpo Ugo (Eagle Feather).   Great importance is attached to the symbolic meaning of the eagle. It is a rare bird and is regarded as one of the superior birds in the bird kingdom. Eagle feathers are used by Obis and by officials and all persons who have received the Olinzele or the Ozo and Igbu titles.

Other Emblems.   There are other emblems special to particular states. The Obi of Onitsha uses the nze (horse tail) and it is exclusive to him. He also uses a fan made from the skin of an animal. He must not speak to the public and when he speaks to a visitor, he does so through the fan, hiding his mouth with it.

The nze at Abo comprises the ofo and ikenga and in fact all the regalia of office are collectively known as "nze". At Oguta, the king has the feather of a bird known as kolobibi. The kolobibi, according to this people, is the most beautiful and the king of birds. Wherever this bird is found in the forest, other birds surround it. The bird's feather is therefore used by the Obi, and no Oguta king will be crowned unless this bird's feather is found. The king combines therefore the emblem of the animal kingdom, the leopard, and the bird kingdom, the kolobibi.

The Obi of Oguta, like the Atamanya of Osomari, uses the oji, a special iron staff of office. These are also used by the Ndichie and Olinzele. They also use the odu, elephant tusk, at Onitsha, Abo, Osomari and Oguta, and in these latter two places, the Obis sound this horn every morning and on festival occasions. The Obi of Oguta uses the pointed end of the odu to test the ukpo to ensure there is no hole under the leopard skin spread over it. This is known as "ikpa odu", and originates from a myth that one of the Obas of Benin died by falling into a hole dug right underneath the throne. We have also referred to this myth in Chapter 10 in the case of the Obi of Abo.

The Kingmakers

The validity of the installation is only accepted by the people when specific functionaries, whom we shall refer to as kingmakers, officiate in these ritual ceremonies. In most of these Niger and Ada states the Iyase places the crown on the head of the Obi and it is correct to state that even though Onitsha people have recently modified this aspect of their ceremony, the general principle is that no Obi can crown himself. This is, for example, the case among the related Umuezechima kingdoms. An Obi can seat himself on the throne or in other places can be placed on the throne by others, but he cannot perform the critical act that validates his position.

At Onitsha the function of kingmaking is divided between the two political divisions of the state, the one selecting the candidate and the other investing him with the insignia of his office. These kingmakers are the Iyase, the priests (Eze Udo) and priestess (Ada Udo) of the Udo shrine and the Omodi of Umuasele, all of whom come from the non-royal division of Ugwuna Obamkpa. The initial duties of the Okpala of the lineage of the Obi elect are of minor importance and no person becomes accepted as Obi if he is not invested with the insignia of his office by these officials from the non-royal division.

At Abo the role of kingmaker is shared between the Odua of the royal division of Umudei and the Iyase of the non-royal division of Ndichie. Oguta has one kingmaker, the Eze Ukwu who does not come from the royal lineage, and at Osomari the Ogene (the oldest man) of the royal lineage, is the kingmaker.

However, where the succession may be in dispute some of the functions of these officials may be usurped or disregarded and the community itself decides which of these conflicting installations it will accept, a duty that has more recently been taken over by the colonial government and its successor, the regional government. In Onitsha, as we shall see in Chapter 9, two disputed successions in 1931–4 and in 1961–3 raised the following issues. At what point in the ceremonies did the candidate acquire the status of Obi? And which were the critical rituals, those performed by the priest and priestess of Udo or those performed by the Iyase? The uncertainty that now pervades the Onitsha ceremonies arises from the different interpretations given by the supporters of the rival candidates. In the first contest, the contention of the victorious party was accepted and the role of the priest and priestess of Udo was disregarded; in the second contest the position was reversed and the role of the Iyase was rejected. The recognised Obi did not perform the normal domestic service at the residence of the Iyase, but at the residence of his second in rank, the Ajie. The Obi desired to do the right thing, but as the Iyase was supporting another candidate, such an irregularity became the only possible course of action. The Obi placed the crown on his own head and his supporters argued that an Obi is crowned in the palace and not outside it; therefore the claim of the Iyase to place the crown on an Obi at the Iyase's residence was contrary to custom. The Iyase contended that historical precedent justified his action in crowning the Obi in his residence.

The Iyase also maintained that he alone could place an Obi on his throne, but the successful Obi and his supporters maintained that this was not the role of the Iyase and that an Obi ascends the throne by himself.

The King and the Law

As Mair has observed, there is little connection between the rituals of kingship and the qualities of justice and generosity that are ascribed to the ideal ruler. At the king's accession he may be admonished to rule his people justly, but the rites are not directed to ensure this end. These are concerned with making him strong and victorious[11] and to reinforce these political values the installation rituals we have been describing also endow him with the ritual power by transforming him into a sacred personage.

But this transformation does not mean that the king cannot be distinguished from the institution of kingship, for these rituals of installation have another essential meaning. They assert the permanency and rightness of the order which he symbolises. If the king errs he has offended against the sacredness of the institutions of kingship which it is his duty to defend and preserve. He becomes an ordinary person who has broken the rules of his society and, as we shall see in Chapter 10, he can be deposed just as in Ashanti, where if the Asantehene transgresses he is destooled.[12]

MORTUARY RITUALS

The funeral ceremonies of the Niger kings are performed in two stages. The first is the secret burial in which the actual interment of the body takes place and when the death is treated with absolute secrecy and never spoken about. The second stage is the public burial at which the death is officially announced to the chiefs and the public. During the intervening period before the public ceremonies, the affairs of the state are administered by the Iyase at Onitsha, the Odua at Abo, by the Udom at Oguta and the Ogene at Osomari until the funeral ceremonies are completed.

We shall describe these two stages of the ceremonies and conclude by examining the principles which these ceremonies convey to the people and their significance in the general framework of their institution.

THE FIRST STAGE (THE SECRET BURIAL)

Onitsha

The illness of the Obi of Onitsha is a guarded secret known only to the family, to a very few close agnates, to the Ndichie Ume and to the Olosi lineage of Ugwunaobamkpa. As soon as the Obi dies the Iyase (Onowu) is informed. The death is kept secret and is referred to euphemistically as "igwe ejie", the iron is broken. The Iyase assumes the authority of administering the state and becomes the regent.

Candidates from the royal division of Umuezechima who have begun the ceremonies of initiation into the Ozo title and have not completed them, lose their membership and have to begin again after the installation of a new Obi. The stages gone into are annulled and with this, the benefits which would have accrued to them if they had completed the process are withdrawn.

An Oniyiche (singular) who has not completed his Ndichie title is allowed to perform the remaining ceremonies required for full membership immediately and before the funeral ceremonies begin, failing which he loses what he has already spent and he cannot proceed to the title until after the crowning of a new Obi; and even then, only if he is appointed to the office by the new Obi.

A simple grave is then prepared in one of the palace chambers or near the ukpo (throne) and the burial takes place in the night. Only the immediate agnates and representatives of Olosi lineage in Ugwunaobamkpa, a lineage which derives from the senior daughter (Ada) of Chima, takes part in the burial.

Abo

As in Onitsha, the death of the Obi is a guarded secret. It is reported immediately to the Odua and Olinzele of both divisions and is announced by the most senior Olinzele with the words "Omuma Ejie", the stone has broken. The ufie is played every morning. The Odua and Olinzele take charge of the uge. Life remains normal, and all activities at the palace continue for three years as if the Obi were still alive.

A coffin (akpuluke) is secretly prepared. The body is put there for oge asa, twenty-one days, and throughout this period, umuigosi (women) dance daily at the uge as they usually do. Eight persons, four from the Umudei and four from the Ndichie divisions are selected to carry the coffin. This was the exact number that carried him during the accession ceremony of Ibueze. This notion of the figure of four and four is an emphasis on the duality of the political system. Before the coffin is carried, a staff (mkpisi) is struck on the coffin by one of the Olinzele, saying "choa umu mnei", meaning "seek your blood relations". As soon as this is done, the Umudei people are asked to lift the coffin. They try to do so but the corpse becomes too heavy to lift. This, according to them, implies that the deceased Obi does not want to leave his kinsmen upon whom he relied. Then the four Ndichie lift the corpse and it becomes light, indicating that they are not related to him. They carry the corpse and the other four Umudei assist them.

The body is carried to Ugboko, a thick forest where the Obis are buried. In the course of their journey to Ugboko, they do not carry the corpse through Ani Abo, the area of the earth deity, one of the places where sacrifice was offered during the installation of the Obi. It is taboo for a corpse to be carried across this shrine. The Olinzele and Ndi Igbu are all present. At the grave sacrifices are offered and in pre-British days, four slaves were laid in the grave. The coffin was placed on them and the grave was filled in.

Oguta

The death of an Obi is announced to the elders of the lineage (ogbe). Again, this is a close secret and they say euphemistically "Odibo jele uno", the servant has gone home.

The agnates begin to dig the grave in the inner chamber (ime ofe) of the palace. This is a very elaborate grave. There are seven steps leading down to the burial chamber. The grave is about ten feet deep measured by a person going into the grave and raising his two hands until they are not seen. The steps are constructed stage by stage. If in the course of digging they strike underground water, a white cock is offered as a sacrifice to the grave and according to them, the water will dry up and they will continue to dig until the last layer is prepared.

Inside this layer a throne is constructed and also a small raised platform where the deceased's shrines, ikenga, agu, and ofo are placed. A mat is fixed on top of this seventh layer to prevent anything falling on the corpse. The corpse is made to sit erect as if alive. It is fully dressed with all regalia and emblems of office. The throne underneath it is also fully decorated with cloths.

The Eze Ukwu himself or his deputy, the Uko,[13] arrives at the palace. All persons present remain silent. He shouts aloud, "Onye melulu nwunyem ahu!", who has injured my wife? He then sits down on a mat spread on the king's former throne. A big basin of water with money in it is placed before him. This money was formerly in cowries but now it is in Nigerian coins amounting to twenty shillings—ofu pam (one pound). He then dips his hands into the water, and wipes his face, symbolically indicating that he has wept for the death of the king, his "wife". The water is thrown out but he takes the basin and the money. Kola nuts and cowries, now equivalent to one shilling, are put on a plate and placed before him. The money is the fee for breaking the kola nut (ego ikwoaka oji), and he takes it after he has broken the kola nut.

The materials he used at the ceremony of installation are placed before him. He is led to the grave where the corpse has been placed. He does not go into the grave, but is given a long stick which can reach the head of the corpse. An Obi's agnate goes into the grave. The Uko holds this stick and with it he removes the crown from the head of the king saying:

"I have taken what I gave you! I gave you the crown in life and not as a dead person!"

The kinsman in the grave picks up the crown and replaces it on the king's head. The Uko repeats the same process and after the fourth time, the man in the grave comes out of the grave with the crown. He hands it over to the Uko who takes it back to the Ezeukwu. The Ezeukwu places it on his agunze shrine. He repeats the ritual of ewu ikwe as he did at the installation, and goes back with all the materials used for this ceremony.

After this he departs and the kinsmen place another red cap on the corpse's head and uma (slaves) in pre-British days were put into the grave. They roof over the sixth and seventh layers with planks of iroko wood and fill in the grave, leaving the surface rough and unfinished for the public funeral ceremony of ite ini.

The following day, the eldest surviving son of the deceased is recognised as Udom, the regent, ready for the public rituals. The ceremony of his installation as the Udom is similar to that of the head of a ward (ogbe), and all agnates attend. His regalia is also the same as that of the Okpala, but his status is higher. After his installation, he remains indoors for izu asa (seven weeks = one calendar month) and offers sacrifice to the ancestral shrines on every eke day. This seclusion is comparable to the seclusion period ikwe omu which the king passed through in the process of his installation.

On the completion of this period, the Udom goes to the houses of the heads of the various lineage segments of the ward, and in every house he enters, sacrifice is offered to the ancestors of the lineage. This is to enable the Udom to visit the house and sit on occasions. This ceremony of visiting heads of lineages is known as Iko Uko (buying the right of the Uko to sit before one's ancestors' shrines as sacrifices).

Before he performs the second burial of his late father, the Udom must have been initiated into the Ikwa Muo society. He must also have performed the minor rituals which give him a superior status in the age sets.[14] He also takes the Igbu title if he has not done so before, for it is only this that makes him eligible to represent his father who is all powerful and as great as the leopard in the animal world.

Osomari

Osomari people adopt the same secrecy in concealing the death of the Atamanya. The death is announced to the elders of the royal lineage alone. There is no wailing or mourning and anyone who raises an alarm is instantaneously made to pay a fine worth the price of a cow (efi). The body is washed by the Agana title members of the lineage and dressed in the full regalia and made to sit on the throne. All these things are done secretly.

The grave is then dug by the agnates. It is dug in the inner chamber of his palace. There are two chambers in the grave. They begin first by digging a single excavation about twelve feet deep. When this is completed, they dig a tunnel and expand it to form a second chamber. They dig this wide and construct a throne. The entrance to this second chamber is well constructed and a door made from iroko is affixed so that it can be closed. The roof of this second chamber is covered with mats (ute) so that no earth will drop on the corpse.

The body is taken down through the first chamber into the second chamber. It is made to sit on the throne and is held erect by a red cloth (ododo), which is tied across its mouth to a pole fixed behind the throne. The corpse holds an odu (elephant tusk) in its right hand and an ogbechi (horse tail whisk) in its left. It is made to sit on a chair placed on the throne, and its hands, holding the odu and ogbechi, are made to rest on its knees.

A cow and a goat are slaughtered in this chamber. Formerly two slaves were put into the chamber and tied to poles fixed beside the corpse. After the sacrifices the door is closed. The first chamber is then filled in. After the secret burial, the Odaje (Asi), the officer who attended the king and received his guests when he was alive continues his regular duties. The ufie is played every morning. A political assembly is held at the palace as before and the Odaje acts as the speaker. All the normal ritual duties of the Atamanya are carried on by him. The senior son (Diokpa) of the Atamanya is addressed as Odua until the new king is selected and crowned. He officiates in his father's place at the sacrifice offered to the king's ofo till the last day when it is taken to a new Atamanya. These things continue for three years until preparations are ready for the funeral ceremonies.

Summary

Oguta and Osomari grave chambers are similar and that of Oguta takes the form of a Benin grave dug in several chambers.[15] In both states the corpse is made to sit on a throne. Onitsha and Abo do not construct chambers and place the corpse in coffins. Onitsha, Oguta and Osomari bury their kings in the royal chambers while Abo does so in a special burial ground where all kings have been buried.

THE SECOND STAGE (THE PUBLIC FUNERAL)

Onitsha
As soon as preparations are completed for the funeral ceremonies and the period of mourning by the Ndichie is over, the public announcement is made. The intervening period varies and it spreads in most cases over six to nine months. Onitsha does not have any funeral ceremonies as such. Instead they perform the deceased Obi's Ofala festival ceremony for the last time. The next Ofala will be performed by the new Obi on his installation. At this final Ofala ceremony the Diokpa, the eldest son of the Obi, represents his deceased father and performs on that day the role that his late father performed in the Ofala rituals. This Ofala is considered the second burial ceremony.

On the funeral day the Ndichie are informed and a cannon is fired in the morning of this day. This is the official announcement of the Obi's death to the public, though officially the Obi is not dead and his son represents him. By this time affinal and cognatic relations and all important people in the surrounding towns are informed, and they come to the palace to pay their respects to the deceased Obi. The son dances as his father did. The ceremony as described in part I of this chapter comes to an end in the evening and the people begin to look forward to a new Obi who, at his crowning ceremony, will celebrate his first Ofala at the end of his installation ceremonies.

Abo
After the secret burial, the Odua and the Olinzele assume control for the period of aso ato, three years, and a special date is fixed on the completion of this period for the public announcement of the Obi's death. This official date is proclaimed by a series of cannon shots. The Olinzele and the public throng to the uge. A catafalque is made in which a mock coffin is placed and laid in state. It represents the deceased Obi and at the end of the ceremony is taken away by the agnates and buried in the bush.

Dancing groups stage a variety of dances and the most important dances are those in which they display military prowess on land

and on water. War dancers display with their swords, shields and guns. The old men display the way they manœuvred war canoes in former days. This is followed by a series of feasts in which eight cows are slaughtered, just as eight cows were slaughtered during the installation ceremonies. These slaughterings do not take place in one day. They are so arranged that they extend over a period of about one month. They begin with one slaughtered for the Olinzele, followed by one for the Igbu society then for the elders, for the Ikenga, for the Okwa Chi, for the Umuada (daughters of Abo), for Umuikoloba (the youths) and the eighth and last for the mother's agnates.

On each occasion the group invited to slaughter the cow are given eight kola nuts, eight yams, eight bottles of gin and eight shillings. From every cow slaughtered, the senior son Akpulosu takes ofu aka (a foreleg). The rest is shared into four equal parts for the representative from each Ebo. The group concerned will then share their own portion or cook it as they wish.

Osomari

We discuss Osomari before Oguta contrary to the order we have been following because the Osomari mortuary custom follows closely the same pattern as obtains at Onitsha and Abo. The notice for the public funeral is given on an Eke day by a member of the king's household. The Asimaha (Akwue) and Nzenabi (Okia) of Ugolo are asked to go to the heads of the other two divisions of Isiolu and Umuonyiogwu who are supposed to be ignorant of the king's death and inform them that the king is dead and ask them to go to the palace. When the messengers return, all Ugolo people assemble at the palace. An effigy of the king is prepared. Wine and kola nuts are offered and the Oniha (Ogene) of Ugolo, the political head at this time, offers prayers to the ancestors and breaks the kola nuts which are distributed to those present according to their age and seniority. Cannon shots and other guns are fired. The public on hearing these shots knows that the Atamanya is dead.

On Orie, the following day, the Agana title members arrive and a cow and a goat are given to them. Drinks are also offered. They perform the ceremony of Igbunye Akpu, a ceremony which is performed for every member of the society because every king must become a member[16] of the society.

On the third day, afo, the Ugolo royal ward stage their exclusive ogo dance at the palace. This dance is connected with the egungu, the masquerade that impersonates the spirits of their ancestors. The egungu and kingship are intertwined and it is believed that the masquerade originated from the spirits of the Atamanya.[17] They also stage the elegede royal dance and the dances continue till the following morning. A cow and goat are slaughtered for them, and throughout the dance women dance stripped to the waist for it is forbidden for them to dance with covered bodies before the king.

The Diokpa (Odua) the eldest son of the deceased instructs the Asanya Uzi, the head of Isiolu and of the Agana society, to summon Osomari people to the palace for the Ikpa Agana ceremony. At night the Olinzele and heads of the three political divisions and their members assemble and they stage the Ogene and other military dances. One division dances after the other and according to the political rank of each ebo in a division. Ugolo dances first, followed by Isiolu and then Umuonyiogwu. The autochthonous groups Umuoga, Umuchi and Ndam dance next and finally the three servile ebo dance last. This order emphasises the political status of the various groups and as Kaine put it, "an element of Osomari political domination is noted in this custom".[18] A special egungu masked figure represents the Atamanya. The other egungus that are displayed are regarded as the spirits of the other ancestors of the various lineages. The dance continues till the next morning.

In the morning the sons of the Atamanya stage their own dances and each of them offers two bottles of gin to each dancing group as a mark of appreciation for attending the funeral of their deceased father. A cow is slaughtered for the whole town. Isiolu, whose head is also the head of Agana, takes one part and the other half is shared among the other two divisions. At night time members of Isiolu alone return to the palace for a night vigil, icheabani. As heads of the egungu society, it is believed that throughout this night they are in communion with the spirit of the Atamanya and ancestors. They remain at the palace for five nights and on the fifth night they go on patrol of the whole town during which all members of the state are asked to keep indoors. Owners of domestic animals are asked to keep them in their pens.

Dances continue throughout these five days and on the last day a cow and goat are slaughtered and the meat cooked. The whole town partakes of this communal meal.

On the following day sacrifices to the shrine begin where the late Atamanya offered sacrifices during the installation ceremonies. A cow is offered on each occasion and the meat is shared as was done during the coronation.

After the completion of this, on a fixed date, the Olinzele are invited to the palace for the ceremony known as "Itikpo Ukpo", which means the breaking down of the ukpo (throne). It marks the end of the reign and since no king exists in that royal house, the ukpo is destroyed so that no person dares to sit on it any longer. The completion of this ceremony means that the Atamanya's spirit ceases to come to the palace and it is a rite of separation. His spirit is led to the other world where it joins the past Atamanyas.

The Diokpa offers the last sacrifice to the ofo eze in the presence of all royal agnates. One case of gin is given them on this occasion and after this ceremony, the mortuary ceremonies end, and the ofo eze is returned to the Ogene of Ugolo who assumes the role of full regent.

Oguta. Preliminary Public Rituals.

The public ceremonies at Oguta begin as soon as the secret burial is completed. The Udom (the eldest son of the deceased Obi) who now assumes his father's role, performs the following six mortuary rites and after their performance there is an interval of three years, as at Abo and Osomari, before the final second burial ceremonies. These rituals are:

Iwayiji na Aka. At this first ceremony yams are cut into two and placed in the left and right hands of a deceased male. This ceremony is followed by the sacrifice of a goat, but for the Obi a cow is used. For an ordinary man the ceremony is performed at the time of the burial, but in the case of the Obi it takes place now.

Ite Ini (scrubbing the grave).   A cow is slaughtered near the grave to complete the closing ritual of sending the spirit of the Obi to rest in peace.

Nni Unanine.   On the following day the Udom (Ajie) throws a feast for his age set and this is known as nni unanine. Other age sets of the same group as his own age set are invited. He also slaughters a cow and the meat is cooked and eaten by all present. Drinks of various types are served and the age sets dance all through the day.

Nni Eze.   This is soon followed by the royal banquet (Nni Eze), that is, a feast for the important age sets and for the Ndichie and Olilinzele in Oguta. A cow is slaughtered by the Udom and a great quantity of yam foo-foo is prepared. The meat of the cow is used for preparing the soup. They all partake of this communal meal and a great quantity of drink is provided. It is a feast similar to those of the royal festivals of Ibina and Omelife referred to in Chapter 5.

Itikpo Ukpo.   The fifth ceremony which follows is the Itikpo Ukpo when sacrifice is offered to the throne and the ancestors are informed that the king has ceased to sit on it in this world. The members of the state council—Ndichie and Olilinzele—are present and a cow is offered by the Udom and used for the sacrifice to the ancestors. All partake in a communal meal.

Itikpo Ufeshi Oko.   In the sixth ceremony the deceased Obi is separated from his yam deity (Ufeshi Oku). This cult is associated with the fertility of yams. A cow is used for the sacrifice in which this cult's deity is informed of the departure of its owner to the other world. His agnates and members of the state council are present at this sacrifice.

These series of sacrifices and feasts form the first stage of the public mortuary ceremonies. The Udom remains in office and performs all duties of the Obi, though he does not sit on the throne but beside it. The assemblies of the town are held in the palace if he is the Udom of the eldest Obi in the set. The state councils are held at the palace and he presides at these meetings. Judicial matters are also dealt with at the palace as before.

Oguta: The Final Ceremony. (Second Burial Ceremony)

Ibu Igbudu and dances.   Three years after the secret burial and accompanying ceremonies, the Udom and his agnates notify the Ndichie and Olilinzele of the day fixed for the second and final ceremony. The ceremony takes place in one day. An effigy (igbudu) of the king, which is a four-cornered object covered with various types of cloths is constructed. Inside it is placed a banana stem. The Igbudu is placed near the throne and the palace is decorated as was done on royal festival occasions. The royal dances opi and ufie are played throughout the day. At noon, the members of the council arrive and sit as they sat on the occasion of royal festival, and the Udom, who is dressed in his full regalia, sits beside the throne but not on it.

All the children of the Obi invite their age sets and the Udom entertains members of his father's age set with whom he, the Obi, had severed connections during his installation. Members of each age set stage their own dances and are entertained with drinks by the hosts. This is an occasion for dances and merriment.

At about four o'clock, four members of the late Obi's lineage each holding one end of the Igbudu lift it from the ground. Other agnates support them. The Igbudu leaves the late Obi's compound and is carried to the gates of all former Obi's compounds so that the deceased Obi greets all these royal compounds. When they come to the royal gate, they advance to the gate and return to another end of the open square facing the gate. They repeat this four times and proceed to the residence of another royal compound until they have completed the visits of these places. The Igbudu is returned to the Obi's palace and dismantled in the night. This ends the ceremony.

After the final funeral ceremony the Udom remains in office for izu asa, twenty-one days. On the last day, accompanied by some of his agnates, he goes to his mother's ward (ogbe) to the residence of the oldest male of the mother's lineage. The head of the lineage (Okei) sits before the ancestral shrines and the Udom sits on the ground. The Udom removes his cap, keeps the odu, removes the leopard teeth he wore on his neck and the bead (oka) on his wrist. Having divested himself of this regalia he rises and walks out from there as an ordinary man.

On his way back to the ogbe he greets as many people as he can remember in return for the greetings he received from them when he was in office and they reply to him using his former greeting name if they know it. He ceases to be greeted as "Ajie", the praise name of his Udom title. This ceremony of Iputa na Udom takes place at his mother's ogbe. This is because the Udom cannot deprive himself of the secular and ritual powers of the office he symbolises in his own, the royal lineage, which retains the office in perpetuity. Therefore an act which implies that he no longer represents the office must be performed outside the royal lineage, so that the successor to the office can symbolise the continuity of the office.

SUMMARY AND CONCLUSIONS

The death of an Obi is a terrible event. It creates a period of anxiety and insecurity, hence it must not be made known that the king is dead. At Onitsha when the king dies everything comes to an end, and so the prospective Ndichie and Ozo candidates have either to cancel their remaining ceremonies or complete them before the death is finalised. The death of the king is spoken of euphemistically and no one dares reveal that a king is dead. The king does not die. This notion reinforces their concept of the divinity of kingship. No one succeeds to the throne until the end of the funeral ceremony,[19] for in between the spirit of the king lingers and has not been finally separated from the office.

At the second or public stage the rituals begin by emphasising the continuity of the office, repeating most of the integrative rituals

o

originally associated with the Obi's installation. All groups in the state pay homage to their departing king, it is an occasion not of mourning but of rejoicing. The communal meals and drinks which feature in these ceremonies serve to incorporate the subjects with one another and sometimes with their king, in the same way that a chain that has been broken by the removal of one of its links must be rejoined.[20]. The summoning of chiefs and people to these meals, for example the banquets at Abo, Oguta and Osomari, or the staging of the Ofala at Onitsha, give these communal meals the character of a collective ritual.

The continuity of the king's personality is stressed. He is not dead but is passing into another world. Rituals which emphasise this are, for example, seating the corpse on the throne as if it were alive as at Oguta and Osomari; placing dead slaves and other property in the grave; the inclusion within the grave of all the ritual objects, shrines and regalia. The king's spirit is being associated with those of the ancestors, for example in the ceremonies of sacrifice to the shrines of the installation and in the funeral ceremonies.

The concluding rites mark the final separation of the deceased king from the living world. This is the meaning of the Ite Ini, Itikpo Ufeshi Oku and Ikpoko Ofo rituals which are practised at Oguta and Osomari. At Oguta there is the ceremony of the Eze Ukwu at the grave when he takes away the crown and says "I gave you the crown in life and not as a dead person".

At the same time the continuity of the institution of kingship is assured by, for example, the recognition of a regent as soon as the death is announced and when the final rituals have been completed. At Onitsha the Iyase and at Abo the Odua assume the role and at Oguta the position of the Udom is even more explicit. At Osomari during the first period the Odaje (Asi) shares the role with the eldest son of the deceased, the Diokpa (Odua) while the Ogene takes over the regency as soon as the public rituals are completed.

In all these states the senior son is the person who by right should perform his father's funeral ceremonies, though he does not normally succeed to the office. In most of the states he is assisted by his other brothers but in Oguta the Benin practice of the eldest son alone assuming the responsibility of burying his father is observed.[21]

NOTES

1 Cp. G. T. Basden, 1938, p. 138.
2 The controversy during the Harding Commission was centred on the exact stage in the ceremonies that this ritual took place. Writers like

Meek (1937), Milne (1933), Ifeka (1962) and Orakwue (1953) are unanimous that it should take place before the Ije Udo ceremony. The present Obi and his opponents did it after they had gone to Udo.

3　C. K. Meek, 1937, p. 186.

4　J. Boston, D. Phil. Thesis. 1964, p. 25. This role of the Ezeukwu as a special official responsible for the crowning of the Obi is peculiar to Oguta alone. The Achadu, the head of the Igala Mele, the non-royal clan of Igala has a status with privileges similar to the kingly officials at Oguta or Osomari.

5　M. Fortes, 1962, p. 86.

6　E. E. Evans-Pritchard, 1956, pp. 198-9.

7　Cp. A. Leonard, 1906, p. 451. He describes the elaborate methods of sacrifice as they apply in most Ibo areas.

8　This system appears in the Yoruba (P. C. Lloyd, 1960, p. 227), Benin (J. Egharevba, 1947, p. 28; also R. E. Bradbury, 1957, p. 40) and Igala (J. S. Boston, 1964, p. 118).

9　Cp. A. I. Richards, 1961, p. 135. Dr Richards' summary of the role of the royal lineages in those kingdoms are in most cases applicable to these kingdoms.

10　All Ada kings, the Obis in the Western Ibo division, are greeted as "Agu", meaning leopard, unlike the Obis of the Niger states who are greeted as "Igwe", with the exception of the Obi of Abo who is greeted as "Obonwe". The Obi of Onitsha is greeted as "Igwe" and also as Agu.

11　Lucy Mair, 1962, pp. 220-1.

12　K. A. Busia, 1951, p. 21.

13　Officials charged with special political or ritual duties can delegate their performance to a deputy called an Uko. An Obi or an Ezeukwu can employ an Uko for any of their ritual functions. Indeed, in some cases, e.g. funeral rituals, an Obi is debarred from performing them himself.

14　There are several feasts which a person must accomplish in order to obtain a certain position in an age set, and a prince must perform these so that no one can be above him in the status scale of the age set.

15　Cp. J. Egharevba, 1947, p. 71.

16　When a man becomes a member of the Agana title, three akpu trees are planted at a ceremony of initiation to mark his admission into the society. This ceremony is the rite of separating the man's spirit from those of the living.

17　The egungu is common among the Yoruba and Igala people. Osomari people reinforce the myth of their Igala origin by their great attachment to this egungu spirit masquerade which is performed at funeral ceremonies.

18　Isama Kaine, 1963, p. 80.

19　Cp. R. Hertz, 1960, p. 49.

20　Cp. A. Van Gennep, 1960, p. 164.

21　R. E. Bradbury, 1966, p. 133.

Chapter 9 The Dynamics of Kingship I

THE SUCCESSION

We now turn to an examination of the way in which kings are chosen. Succession to political office has been much discussed by various writers. In West African kingdoms, though the methods of succession are defined, there are still internal struggles for the choice of a candidate and these may lead to a redefinition of the accepted principle. In Benin, for example, the succession was formerly undefined and this resulted in contest for the throne between many princes. Successive rebellions and civil wars occurred until the eighteenth century when the principle of primogeniture was introduced. But as Bradbury has shown,[1] the Obas during the nineteenth century were not prepared to conform to the rule and define the heir during their lifetime, since they feared this might constitute a threat to their power. In Onitsha the contests for the throne give abundant examples of the ways in which rules of succession are modified in practice.

Succession to office among the Ibos is based on the principle of seniority and, in some areas, like Orlu and Awka, on the principle of primogeniture. In the kingdoms in our sample, the principle of succession to the Obiship is defined by facts of descent within approved royal clans or lineages. At Onitsha there are two opposing royal sub-clans or dynasties, and at Oguta and Osomari, there is a single lineage or dynasty in each state.

As Onitsha and Abo do not adopt the principle of rotation as is done among the Yoruba, Igala, Zazzau and Nupe,[2] the uncertainty over the succession has led to conflicts and the aim of this chapter is to discuss the issues arising from this.

All of these states set out general principles that govern the choice of a candidate. The following general principles are common to all the states: the candidate must be able to trace his genealogy to the founder of the royal clan or lineage; he must not be deformed (Eze Ada alu alu); his reputation must be exemplary by the community's standards; the candidate must not be a debtor; he must have given proof of his wealth by obtaining important titles or membership of a title society, without which he cannot be eligible for the office. At Onitsha it is compulsory for him to join the

194

Agbalanze society, that is, the Ozo title association. The Obi of Abo must have taken the Igbu title, and Osomari specifies that he must be a member of the Inyaakpa, Igbu and Agana title associations. Membership of these associations, besides being a good proof of wealth, has ritual significance because the initiation ceremonies involve a series of 'rites de passage' which elevate him from the 'ordinary' to the 'sacred'.

There are also other criteria which vary in different states. For example, Abo demands that the candidate's mother must come from another community and not from Abo, and Osomari has the same provision. Oguta on the other hand insists that the mother as well as the father of the candidate must be a citizen of Oguta. Onitsha in the past had no ruling on this point. In the recent dispute over the succession in 1961–3, however, those who opposed the candidate put forward by the Iyase and Ndichie claimed that he was ineligible as his mother was not a free-born of Onitsha but came from another town. The Ndichie, however, were able to show that at least five of the former Obis' mothers were foreigners of this sort. Oguta also insists that a candidate must not be childless; he must have a son who can act as Udom when the Obi dies.

ONITSHA

The royal clan, the Umuezechima, comprises the administrative divisions of Umuezearoli, Ogbeolu, Umudei (or Okebunabo), whose members reside in the Umuezechima division, and Ogboli-Olosi, whose members reside in the Ugwuna Obamkpa, non-royal division. For the purpose of contesting the throne, this clan provides two royal dynasties, Umuezearoli and Umudei (or Okebunabo). Onitsha kings have been supplied from particular lineages within these two dynasties.

Umuezearoli has remained a maximal lineage and, as shown in Table B at the end of the book, its four important lineages constitute one exogamous unit. Umudei, on the other hand, is split into two exogamous groups and its unity is not as apparent as the unity of Umuezearoli. The unity of Umuezearoli does not, however, mean that it is united in the period of contest for the succession. Candidature for the throne is restricted to those who are of direct agnatic descent from a true son of Chima. For this reason many of the lineages within the Umuezechima clan, though they share the honour of being regarded as Umuezechima, cannot supply an Obi. For example, the Ogbe Olu are a group of attached lineages within the Umuezechima clan, and Isiokwe, which is regarded as

I. SUCCESSION TO THE OFFICE OF OBI OF ONITSHA

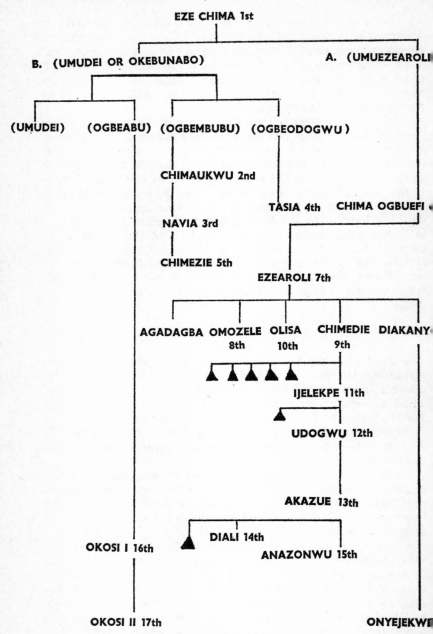

EZE CHIMA 1st

B. (UMUDEI OR OKEBUNABO)

A. (UMUEZEAROLI

(UMUDEI) (OGBEABU) (OGBEMBUBU) (OGBEODOGWU)

CHIMAUKWU 2nd

TASIA 4th   **CHIMA OGBUEFI**

NAVIA 3rd

CHIMEZIE 5th

EZEAROLI 7th

AGADAGBA   **OMOZELE 8th**   **OLISA 10th**   **CHIMEDIE 9th**   **DIAKANY**

IJELEKPE 11th

UDOGWU 12th

AKAZUE 13th

DIALI 14th

ANAZONWU 15th

OKOSI I 16th

OKOSI II 17th

ONYEJEKWE

(Lineage names are shown in brackets)

their senior lineage, is the original lineage to which the three other lineages of Obikporo, Ogbe-Otu and Umuikem were attached, and the lineages that constitute the administrative unit Ogboli-Olosi are also attached lineages.

The contest for the throne thus revolves around Umuezearoli and Umudei and these two dynasties look for support to the attached lineages in their sub-divisions. We can see how the pattern of succession has changed over time if we examine the genealogical diagram of the succession in Table I opposite.

The list of Onitsha kings as recorded in the sources and as obtained from my informants, who were members of the royal houses, varies from seventeen to eighteen. Jerry Orakwue[3] recorded eighteen, though he says that two "died as regents". The term 'regent' is not accurate but it is traditionally used to refer to an Obi whose accession is disputed and who therefore has not been properly elected. The actual person who acts as regent during an interregnum is the Iyase (Onowu). Onitsha people regard the two persons concerned, Tasia and Diali, as Obi. If we include the present Obi, the number becomes eighteen. My data, which include the founding ancestor (Ezechima) and the present Obi Onyejekwe, agrees with that of Harding[4] and are set out in Table I.

According to tradition, the office of Obi is vested in the royal division of Umuezechima, while that of the Iyase (Onowu), the second ranking chief, belongs to the non-royal division of Ugwunao-bamkpa. Reference, however, to the actual distribution of Obis and Iyase shown in Table J on page 214 and in Table K on page 228, indicates that, after the ninth Iyase, both offices became vested in Umuezechima. This suggests that after the ninth Iyase the royal division became all powerful. It is also clear from the diagram that whichever of its dynasties was the most powerful and united was able to retain the Obiship and that a dual division was brought about in Umuezechima whereby one dynasty, Umuezearoli, monopolised the succession to the office of Obi and the other, Umudei, the succession to the office of Iyase (Onowu).

After the death of the founder, Eze Chima the first, Umudei which today consists of four lineages, controlled the succession supplying the second, third, fourth and fifth Obis. This monopoly was then upset by the Umuezealori group which supplied the sixth Obi—Chima Ogbuefi. He was succeeded by his son Eze Aroli, who was succeeded by his three sons in rotation. Later his grandson Ijelekpe was crowned, and when he died, he was succeeded by his son Udogwu, who was succeeded by his son Akazue, who signed the treaties of 1863 and 1878. Akazue's son Diali succeeded his father but died in the same year and was eventually succeeded by his brother Anazonwu, who died in 1899. Thus for a considerable period, Umuezearoli controlled the throne.

The continuous line of Obis descended from Obi Chimedie gives the impression that this lineage virtually controlled the succession and had converted it into one of descent from father to son; tradition does not relate whether at the successions of these Obis other lines in Umuezearoli and Umudei put forward any candidates. Then, on the death of Obi Akazue, a conflict arose over the succession which ended in civil war. The two candidates were both from Umuezearoli, namely Diali, the son of Obi Akazue of the line of Chimedie, and Enendu of the collateral line of Diakanyo. The Chimedie line could represent Enendu's claim as contravening the convention of descent from father to son and as an attempt to weaken the unity of the Umuezearoli dynasty as against the opposing dynasty of Umudei, and they asked Enendu to withdraw in the interests of dynastic unity. It would have been more politic for Enendu to have done so but he refused and claimed the right as a descendant of Ezechima to contest the Obiship. This led to the civil war. The majority of Onitsha people supported Diali, who emerged the victor but died soon after. The Diakanyo lineage lost many lives in the fighting and were in no position to recontest the succession. Holding Enendu responsible for their losses, they told him to commit suicide, which he did, and Diali was succeeded by his brother Anazonwu.

We shall now examine in greater detail the three conflicts for the throne which occurred in the twentieth century when records are more adequate. This will enable us to show the nature of the struggle and the role of the Iyase and Ndichie Ume in maintaining and in modifying the installation rituals. It will also indicate the way in which competition for the throne tended to reinforce the value set on kingship and served to unite the society.[5]

What occurred, after 1899, was that the competing candidates were supported by political blocks,[6] each making efforts to have its own candidate crowned. This led to their seeking to bypass some of the rituals of coronation outlined in Chapter 8 and attempting to justify their action by falsifying the rules. At the same time each block would seek to defeat the candidate supported by any other block by claiming that he had failed to perform the prescribed coronation rituals. The successful candidate was the one who was eventually able to win the support of the majority of Onitsha people.

By the end of the nineteenth century, Onitsha was under British control. The missionaries had been well established (the Church Missionary Society in 1857, and the Catholics in 1885), and trading firms had acquired a permanent position at the waterside though the seat of government was still at Asaba.

In these three contests people were no longer able to resort to force to settle the matter. They could only hope to achieve their ends by building up sufficient support for their candidate and by political manœuvring and intrigue to create a situation of sufficient gravity to force the colonial government and its successor in 1960 to intervene and decide the issue in favour of their candidate.

The 1899–1900 Succession

In 1899, Obi Anazonwu, the fifteenth Obi of Onitsha, and the tenth from Umuezearoli, died. This provoked a contest and the Umudei dynasty decided to recapture the throne from Umuezearoli. This was difficult because the long and unbroken reign of the Obis from Umuezearoli had given them a considerable advantage. Their royal houses had become rich, particularly during the period when the trading companies had been established and were paying tribute to the Obis; this prosperity was enjoyed from 1857 to 1889. The Resident, who acted as arbitrator in the 1935 contest, summed-up the relative advantage of the Umuezearoli in these words:

'It is reasonable to assume that once a member of a kindred had been an Obi, that kindred would in the course of time be stronger and better off than at the beginning of a reign and so more able to secure a successor from its own ranks. This might well explain the succession of eight Obis from Ezearoli. Moreover in as much as an Obi's family would have time and opportunity to canvass the Ndichie and the Umuezechima in favour of the dead Obi . . . It might well follow, that when a public announcement of the death was made the people would be faced with the fact of a presumably properly appointed successor.'[7]

In the 1899–1900 contest Umuezearoli assumed that they would supply a candidate to the throne, but Umudei put forward a candidate in the person of Samuel Okosi from Ogbeabu. He was a Christian and a follower of the missionaries, which was to his advantage for he was the 'good candidate' of the zealous Catholic mission authorities. The colonial government had to intervene in the dispute and the matter was disposed of by a judicial commission of inquiry held in 1900 at Asaba by Commissioner Bedwell.[8] He pronounced in favour of Samuel Okosi, who became the sixteenth Obi of Onitsha. But he was crowned without conforming to the traditional rules of succession. According to Harding,

"In 1900 all traditional methods of selection and many of the traditional requirements were arbitrarily disregarded. Okosi I was recognised because of the superior force of government, and the natural consequence was dissatisfaction and non-acceptance by many of the clan . . ."[9]

Obi Okosi, having secured the throne by the decision of the Bedwell Commission, began to build up the strength of his political group, the Umudei dynasty and its supporters to ensure that the succession would remain in this line. He did this in two ways.

When the Iyase Ofala died, Okosi appointed his own half-brother Gbasuzor to this office. The reason for this was the need for Ndichie support when competing for the Obiship. The Iyase was the head of the Ndichie chiefs. The fact that such an appointment would result in losing the support of the Ugwunaobamkpa division could be disregarded as the office had in fact been held for a considerable period by men from the Umuezechima division.

Secondly, Okosi disregarded the rule that Ndichie Ume appointments should be shared out evenly between members of the various ebo and he conferred an unduly large number of these appointments on members of the Umudei ebo of the Umuezechima division. The opposition of the Ugwunaobamkpa division could be weakened if the Ndichie at the head of ebo in this division were men who were themselves members of the Umuezechima division. The situation was only likely to become critical if the Ndichie at the head of ebo in Ugwunaobamkpa were prepared to support the opposition of this division by boycotting the Obi's council and refusing to co-operate with the Iyase, and this would not be likely to happen if these Ndichie were themselves members of the Umuezechima division and of the Umudei section of it.

The 1931–35 Succession

Obi Okosi died early in 1931 but his death was not announced until December of that year and Gbasuzor, the Iyase, was able to take full advantage of this. Umudei and Umuezearoli both put forward candidates, but Umudei, following the procedure established by their rivals (Umuezearoli) on previous occasions, presented only one candidate in the person of James Okosi, the son of the deceased Obi Okosi. Umuezearoli were too disunited to present a single candidate and four candidates put themselves forward for selection, namely, A. S. Nzegwu, J. Egbunike, S. J. Nzekwu, and the Onya of Onitsha, an Ndichie Ume.

Onitsha custom stipulates that on the death of a king, the Iyase (Onowu) acts as regent but that members of Umuezechima should select a candidate and present him to the Iyase and Ndichie. The candidate is then presented by the Iyase and Ndichie to the six political divisions (ebo) of the state and each ebo is given a present of one cow. The members' acceptance of the gift signifies that the candidate is acceptable to them. After this, the Iyase and Ndichie present the candidate to the whole community.

The crucial issue in the contests of 1931–35 and of 1961–63, however, was who had the right to select the candidate—the Iyase and Ndichie, or the Umuezechima clan. Evidence from many informants and written records show that the members of Umueze-chima clan have the collective right to determine who the candidate should be. But it is in this process of the selection that conflicts arise because each royal dynasty is interested in supplying a candidate and, moreover, this division of the royal clan into two opposing blocks intensifies the competition, and divides the Ndichie who come from the Umuezechima division. Thus, in 1931, when Obi Okposi I died, Gbasuzor acting as the regent rallied the Ndichie to his side, but only with the greatest difficulty because the Ndichie of Ugwunaobamkpa (the non-royal division) were not prepared to support his candidate unless an undertaking was given in writing that this candidate, if appointed, would rectify the situation created by his late father by appointing the Iyase (Onowu) from Ugwunao-bamkpa, and by distributing the Ndichie offices in an equitable manner so that all major political sections of the community would have a representative in the Obi's council.

At a meeting held on 25th August 1932, the Ugwunaobamkpa people resolved:

"That in accordance with our ancient custom, the Obi designate of Onitsha should agree to sign the following resolution before we can support him.
1.   That the office of Onowu (Ndichie Ume) shall in future be held exclusively by Ugwunaobamkpa as was originally intended by our ancient rulers.
2.   That the present holder of the office of Onowu must be made to confine himself to the recognised privileges attached to the Onowu as Ndichie Ume, and that he should never again be allowed to usurp the rights and privileges attached to the office of Obi as during the lifetime of the late Obi Okosi.
3.   That the six offices of Ndichie Ume shall be equally divided between Umuezechima and Ugwunaobamkpa, that is to say, three being held by Umuezechima and three, including the Onowu, held by Ugwunaobamkpa.
4.   That the Obi is never to act arbitrarily in any matter affecting the welfare and ruling of Onitsha people but should in all public matters consult the Ndichie and Elders . . ."[10]

Gbasuzor, an astute and clever man, was bent on securing the full support of the Ugwunaobamkpa in addition to the support of

202 STUDIES IN IBO POLITICAL SYSTEMS

the Umudei Ebo, thus leaving Umuezearoli in the minority. He therefore advised the candidate, his nephew, to accept the points made by Ugwunaobamkpa but to deny that he (Gbasuzor) was influencing him, and urged him to accept and respect the principles set out in resolutions 1, 3, and 4 but to deny resolution 2, as this would be a serious indictment of Gbasuzor's reputation and would prejudice his political manœuvring. Influenced by his uncle, the candidate accepted the terms of Ugwunaobamkpa people, who then gave the new Obi their massive support; thus all the Ndichie of this division of Onitsha were solidly behind Gbasuzor.

The four candidates of Umuezearoli spent their time slandering each other and weakening the position of their sub-clan, Umuezear-roli. Iyase Gbasuzor, considerably strengthened by the support of the Ndichie of Ugwunaobamkpa, went further and solicited the mass support of the Agbala na Iregwu, i.e. of the Ozo titled people, and of the influential age-sets. He eventually rallied those from the Olosi and Umudei ebo of Umuezechima and the three ebo from Ugmnaobamkpa.

Gbasuzor had three advantages which he exploited to the full. Firstly, his position as Iyase made him ipso facto the regent and head of the state. He was thus in control of the situation from the time of the death of the late Obi until the time of the announcement of the death, burial and the selection. Secondly, his rights as a member of Umuezechima division entitled him to take part in the selection of a candidate. Thirdly, his right as the Iyase (Onowu) entitled him to crown the Obi. He reinforced these advantages by persuading many sections of the community to support his right to select and to crown.

The legality of this coronation became, throughout this period, a matter of controversy. The questions that arose were: Who had the right to crown the Obi? What were the valid rituals involved in this crowning and were these rites observed?

The right of the Iyase to assume the role of the regent and to rule with the Ndichie until a new Obi was appointed was not disputed. In this contest, and in the succeeding one, however, those who disapproved of the new candidate argued that the Iyase had no right to crown the Obi, or that if he had, he took advantage of being the next of kin to the Obi in order to violate the rules of succession to the kingship.

Gbasuzor, having won the support of a large section of the town, proceeded to crown James Okosi the Obi. This he did by taking him to the Udo; then on coming out from the Udo, he placed him on the throne and crowned him.

The opponents felt that Gbasuzor had no customary right in this matter, but it was nevertheless recognised that the Iyase was the next title to the Obi, and, as the official mouthpiece of the people, he usually presided at all the general meetings of the Ndichie and Agabala na Iregwu, and communicated their decisions to the Obi. Furthermore, he had the right to appoint and install Ndichie in the absence of the Obi and, after his death, to crown the new Obi.[11]

To defeat those challenging his right to crown the Obi, he persuaded a large section of the community to petition the Resident to accept the legal validity of his act. They wrote on 6th May 1932 accordingly and stated, inter alia:

"We would respectfully lay great stress on the fact that the Iyase Onowu in his capacity, when he throned a successor to the office of Obi, with the customary homage, his ceremonies are considered absolutely legal and unquestionable, his subordinates are bound by the custom to follow suit by paying the same homage in order of rank to the new Obi which is a sign of recognition."

They went further to cite precedents of Obis crowned by former Iyase.

"We would further clearly state for your information, that the late Obi Anazaonwa was installed by the late Iyase Osili, and the late Obi Okosi was installed by the Iyase Ofala . . ."[12]

Having obtained public support for his role in the coronation, Gbasuzor proceeded to challenge the action of the other contestants, two of whom had already gone to Udo to assume the role of the Obiship. They had already performed the ritual ceremonies of the Ije Udo and the Ofala festival, which are exclusive to the Obi.

According to custom, when the Obi elect is led to the Udo shrine, which is a place of seclusion where the Obi communicates with the ancestral spirit of the first Obi, he is taught the duties of kingship by the head of the Obio lineage who officiates as the priest of Udo and helps in the offering of sacrifice to the Udo shrine. This priest must be an Agbalanze, that is, a member of the Ozo society.

One John Ezeocha from Obio claimed that he was the "head of Obio and the priest of Udo" and that in the full capacity of "my father Ezeocha Igwe", he had performed the installation ceremonies of the Obiship of Onitsha for Akunne Samuel Nzegwu. He then enumerated the eleven shrines to which sacrifices were offered and how specific animals (sheep, goat, fowl, dog) and also kola nuts and palm wine were used. Since Mr. Nzegwu had evidently procured the services of this man to install him as the Obi, Gbasuzor did not hesitate to act. He challenged the validity of this act on the grounds that according to custom once a candidate had gone to Udo and the ufie gong was sounded no other person was entitled to do so. In his petition to the Governor, Sir Donald Cameron, dated 20th September 1934, Gbasuzor argued:

> "It is against the custom to go to the ceremonial Bush 'Udo' when the rightful candidate (of royal blood) has first gone and the ceremonial gong ufie is proclaimed for the new Obi . . ."

He stated that James Okosi (his candidate) was the first to go to "Udo", that he went on the 2nd April 1932 and returned on the 24th of that month. Mr. Samuel Jideofo Nzegwu who was a native court clerk and one of the candidates from the Umuezearoli sub-clan, went on the 25th April 1933 and returned on the 26th of the month; while police sergeant James Egbunike, another of the Umuezearoli candidates went on the 3rd September 1932 and returned on the 4th of that month.[13]

By these arguments, Gbasuzor tried to solicit government support. It should be pointed out that the Government was reluctant to take part in this second contest, having been accused of bias in that of 1899–1900. The Resident of Onitsha, Captain O'Connor, stated clearly that:

> "From the outset Government declared that it would not interfere in what appeared to be a domestic matter—in spite of repeated appeals for such interference . . ."[14]

In the earlier times it had been customary to mark the acceptance and recognition of a new Obi for the candidate to send some of his servants to slaughter a human being as a sacrifice in each of the nine ebos of Onitsha thus indicating their acceptance of his installation. This prospective Obi must now send a cow and refreshments to each of these nine ebos to be slaughtered and feasted upon by the Ndichie of each ebo. Gbasuzor explained this traditional custom before the government and argued that his candidate had fulfilled this obligation on the 24th April 1932. Of these nine ebos in Onitsha, eight of them, he explained, had accepted their cows and drinks.

The only exception was Umuezearoli which remained divided and none of their candidates would withdraw, more especially as three out of four of them had already been allegedly crowned. In March, efforts to make Umuezearoli come to an agreement to present a candidate seemed fruitful, but none of the four candidates would withdraw. This lack of unanimity disgusted the rest of Onitsha. It also made Gbasuzor's group (Umudei) remain united in the hope of winning, and they were supported by Ugwunao-bamkpa. (At the initial stage they had wavered because of their grievance against Okosi I, a situation which was rectified by the acceptance of their demands by the Obi elect.) Ogbo-Asato, an influential age-set class, gave their support to the Umudei candidate. As the issue dragged on, the Ndichie rallied around Gbasuzor and by 1935 three of the Ndichie Ume, and nine of the Ndichie Okwa, followed by four of the Ndichie Okwareze, accepted James Okosi unconditionally. The remaining Ndichie—one Ndichie Okwa, one Ndichie Okwareze and two Ndichie Ume—refused to accept him. One of these Ndichie Ume was the Onya, who was himself a candidate. The Government however had to intervene to see that the town's government was in good order, and it did so to avert what would have led to bloodshed.

At the meeting, held with the Resident in March 1935, the Government records state that "it was made clear that, with very few exceptions, the gathering was in favour of the Umudei candidate" (Okosi II). The principal representatives from Ugwunaobamkpa stated that as they were all tired of the disputes in Umuezearoli, they were prepared to acknowledge support for an Umudei man.[15] Further efforts were made to unite Umuezearoli, but the four candidates each continued to petition the government while the rest of Onitsha continued to rally around Gbasuzor's candidate.

At an open meeting in which most of the Umuzechima of Onitsha were present, they were invited by the Resident to express their opinion. Almost seventy per cent of them called for James Okosi. The Government weighed all the conditions and petitions and proceeded on 8th November 1935 to recognise James Okosi as the successor to his late father Obi Okosi I, and it was agreed that in future the Obiship should be rotated between the two dynasties of Umuezechima. The Obi had already agreed that the Iyase (Onowu) title should in future be awarded to an Ugwunaobamkpa candidate.

The role of Iyase Gbasuzor in this conflict showed the value to a candidate of having a close kinsman in this office. The lesson was not lost on the new Obi, Okosi II, who, on the death of Iyase Gbasuzor, went back on his undertaking to Ugwunaobamkpa, and appointed despite stiff opposition, Obinwe, another member of his lineage of Ogbeabu, to the office. However, when Obinwe died in 1960 the office passed to Ugwunaobamkpa.

The 1961–63 Succession

In 1961,[16] Obi Okosi II died and it was the turn of the Umuezearoli dynasty to supply a candidate in accordance with the agreement mentioned above. But the conflict was now within the Umuezearoli themselves, owing to the fact that Umudei decided to honour the 1935 concordant, and did not present a candidate.

The points at issue in this contest can be narrowed down to six, namely: who had the right to choose the candidate? who had the right to crown him? who were the right priests and which were the right ritual places or emblems in the case of the Udo cult, the ofo eze, and the Imanzu rituals? and finally, what were the descent and affiliation requirements for the office? We shall treat them in this order.

The right to choose a candidate.   In the 1931–35 contest it was evident that the choice of a candidate must be that of the Umueze-chima royal clan. But a decision was reached only after Iyase Gbasuzor had taken advantage of the complete split in the Umuezearoli ranks when the Ndichie of all grades, sixteen out of twenty, rallied to his side.

In this case the Iyase and Ndichie held the view that since it was the turn of Umuezearoli to select a candidate, they alone and not the entire Umuezechima had the right to approve this selection and to present the candidate to the Agbala na Iregwu and crown him Obi of Onitsha. Some Umuezearoli initially adopted the candidature of Joseph Enweuzor, the principal contestant from the Diak-anyo lineage of Umuezearoli, but there was opposition from several people in Umuezearoli who wished to contest and they submitted their names direct to the Iyase. This act of submitting their names to the Iyase was regarded by the Iyase and Ndichie as a recogni-tion of the fact that they had the power to confirm a candidature and to crown him accordingly.[17] Eleven candidates applied, but by the time the commission was held there were only four potential candidates. These were J. O. Onyejekwe, J. J. Enweuzor, M. M. A. Odita and J. M. Onyechi. Onyejekwe and Enweuzor, however, were the two principal contestants. They had already, before the holding of the commission, performed the ritual ceremonies of accession, and had each been declared by their supporters as Obi.

One section of Umuezearoli was supported by the Iyase, by three other Ndichie Ume (the Odu, the Onya, and the Owelle), by four Ndichie Okwa (second grade), and by four Ndichie Okwareze (third grade). They argued that the candidate they had selected was Enweuzor and that they would consider any opposition to this as a breach of the traditional custom. But two Ndichie Ume, the Ajie and the Ogene, contradicted this and decided to oppose the action of their colleagues. According to the ranking order of Ndichie Ume, the Ajie is the next in rank to the Iyase and the Ogene is the fourth in rank, so that the Ajie felt he had the right to oppose the

Iyase, his immediate senior, and he and the Ogene circumvented the Ndichie and some of the Umuezearoli people and convened a conference of the entire clan of Umuezechima.

This was the beginning of the crucial issue in the contest. Two politically opposing blocks had been set up, and the major question between them was to decide whether Umuezechima as a whole should select and recognise an Obi or whether the Umuezearoli alone should do so. This conference of the Umuezechima clan, which now constituted the new block, comprised the entire royal sections of Umuezechima, including Umuezearoli. Onyejekwe, the closest rival of Enweuzor, was also from the same Diakanyo lineage of Umuezearoli, and had supporters among them, while the two other members of Umuezearoli rallied to the side of Onyejekwe and joined with Okebunabo to accept him by majority decision as the fit Obi elect.

So, in short, the two leaders of the community, the Iyase and the Ajie, divided the state into two blocks, and the Ajie manipulated the majority of the Umuezechima against the Iyase, who was now a member of the Ugwunaobamkpa division.

The Ajie was successful in winning the support of Umudei but his opponent, the Iyase Anatogu, like the Iyase Gbasuzor, firmly secured the support of most of the Ndichie of all sections of Umuezechima and Ugwunaobamkpa (sixteen as against four). These Ndichie considered that as traditional leaders of the state and its political elite, the people were bound to accept their decision. As in their statement to the Commission:

> "The Ndichie are the traditional pillars upon which rest the framework of the executive and administration of the town. In other words, by virtue of their social and political status the Ndichie supremacy in matters affecting the destiny of the town cannot be rescinded or challenged by Agbala na Iregwu or the minority splinter group."[18]

The Iyase led one block, assisted by the Onya, the political head of Umuezearoli administrative ebo, by the Odu, the political head of the Odoje ebo, and by the Owelle, the political head of Ogbeolu ebo. Thus, of the heads of the six administrative units of the state, four were on the side of Enweuzor, and they were backed by eight of the lesser Ndichie.

The other block was led by the Ajie, the head of the Ogboli-Olosi administrative ebo and the Ogene, the head of the Umudei sub-clan. Had the issue been resolved by civil war, the military organisation of the state (described in Chapter 4) could have meant that the commanders of two major divisions of the militia would be

P

behind Enweuzor against one supporting Onyejekwe. In such a case, however, what would have determined the strength of the military force of the Iyase and the Ajie would have been their ability to recruit supporters into their units. But the majority of the young people from whom they could have recruited their militia was on the side of the group led by the Ajie.

The Right to Crown.   The two political blocks of the Iyase and the Ajie now proceeded to install their respective candidates by performing the traditional ritual installation ceremonies. The interpretation given to these rituals differed.

In 1931–35 the people upheld the view that the Iyase and Ndichie had the right to crown an Obi, that is, to place him on the throne and put the red crown on his head; and that various services must be performed at the residence of the Iyase (Onowu) after the Obi has come from the Udo. In 1961–63 the people argued that the Ajie, the next in rank to the Onowu, had the right to perform these duties. Thus, they accepted as valid the services performed by Onyejekwe at the residence of the Ajie, disregarding the services performed by Enweuzor for the Iyase. This implied that the precedent set at the installation of Obi Anazonwu by Iyase Osili, of Obi Okosi I by Iyase Ofala and of Obi Okosi II by Iyase Gbasuzor was no longer accepted.

The Udo Rituals.   In the 1931–35 contest the question arose as to who should officiate as the priest of Udo. One John Ezeocha, who claimed to be the priest of Udo, performed the Udo ritual functions for Nzegwu, one of the opponents of Obi Okosi II. The people rejected the role of this Ezeocha because he had not taken the Ozo title. Another priest (a usurper, as Ezeocha regarded him) performed these rituals for Obi Okosi II and the people felt that this was legitimate.

In the 1961–63 contest, this same Ezeocha who had by now taken the Ozo title, performed the rituals for Onyejekewe on behalf of the Ajie block. The Iyase block secured the services of another person. From his cross-examination of the witnesses, the commissioner was rather of the opinion that the Iyase had tried to secure the services of Ezeocha but was unable to do so, implying that both sides recognised the right of Ezeocha to officiate as the priest of Udo.[19] Members of the Iyase block did not confirm this during my interviews with them, but it would appear that Commissioner Harding was right in his observation.

Another aspect of this Udo ritual controversy was that both factions chose different spots as the location for the Udo shrine, each side making sure that there was an ant-hill on the spot, for according to the Ndichie, there should be an ant-hill through which the candidate could become inspired by the spirits which haunt ant-hills.[20]

The submissions offered at the commission show that the Udo shrine which was recognised was the one attended by Onyejekwe and not his opponent Enweuzor, and, because the exact place of location and offering of sacrifice must be the same Udo where all the previous Obis have performed the rituals, symbolising continuity with the ancestral kings, Onyejekwe scored on this point even though the other ceremonies connected with the Iyase and Ndichie were denied him because of the dispute.

This acceptance of the priest rejected in 1931–35 is the second change in the continuity of the ritual, though both factions still accepted that the Obio lineage was the legitimate lineage to provide a priest for the Udo ceremonies.

The Ofo Eze. When Umuezearoli lost the throne in 1900, the family of their last Obi (Anazonwu) held the traditional ofo Ezechima which was brought from Benin and which was handed on to each new Obi to symbolise the transmission of political authority to rule the state as ordained by their ancestor Chima. Okosi I did not inherit this ofo, and the Umuesele lineage group had to prepare a new ofo for him. Okosi I was asked by the Catholic priest to burn his new ofo, which he did; hence the people attributed all the dissensions in his reign to this act of sacrilege. A new ofo was again made and given to his son Okosi II.

In 1961–63, what was alleged to be the original ofo Ezechima, held by the fifteen Obis down to Obi Anazonwu, was restored and given to the rival candidate Enweuzor during his installation ceremony, and refused Onyejekwe, who had to obtain a new ofo from the legitimate ofo-making lineage of Umuasele in Ugwunao-bamkpa.[21]

The break in continuity in the bestowing of the ofo upon Okosi I, Okosi II and Onyejekwe (the eighteenth Obi), is the third variation in these rituals. The people explain this break in the tradition of continuity, by asserting that once the ritual of consecration of a new ofo has been performed by the appropriate head of the Umuasele family, the new ofo becomes a valid receptacle for the spiritual powers of the ancestral kings which are automatically transferred to it. But the issue then is that continuity has been lost through failure to transfer the ofo of Okosi II to Onyejekwe.

Another argument produced by the supporters of Onyejekwe to explain his failure to obtain the ofo of Obi Anazonwu is that it was not the original ofo Ezechima. This they say was never transferred from Obi Ijelekpe to his successor Obi Udogwu, as Udogwu's mother would not allow him to use it, since she believed it would endanger his life.

The Imanzu Rituals. This ritual purification of the candidate in preparation for the rituals of office was a point of controversy in both the 1931-35 and 1961-63 issues. The importance of this ceremony was to make sure that the person who aspired to the Obiship should be able to trace his genealogy to the founder of the royal lineage group to which he belonged. He had to be a citizen of Onitsha by descent. The Okpala of his own major lineage group who officiated as the priest at this ceremony also had to be a true male descendant of the founder of the lineage. No one could deputise on behalf of the candidate. He had to be present at the ceremony. On this issue there was no contradiction. Controversy arose, however, when in one ward, as in Umuezearoli, several candidates aspired to the Obiship. An example of this is the case of three of the Chimezie lineage—Onyejekwe, Onyechi and Odita. The issue is one of determining which of the Okpala is the legitimate priest to perform the ceremony of Imanzu.

It was not clear who was the rightful Okpala to perform this ceremony at this period and in the memorandum submitted by the Umuezechima Conference, the members although expressing their doubts, stated:

> "The Committee discovered that the Oreze family of Obikporo is the Spiritual Head of Umuezechima, but has recommended that the Spiritual Head of each particular section of the sons of Chimaeze and Dei from where a candidate has been selected for appointment as the Obi of Onitsha should have the function of Imanzu to perform."[22]

In the light of the uncertainty about who was the rightful priest to officiate, it is difficult to know what had been the traditional procedure. With such uncertainty about the rightful priests and the traditional ritual one is left with the conclusion that the accepted procedure becomes the one performed by the successful candidate.

The Candidate's Geneaology. The question of the geneaology of the officiant and of the candidate also arose in the Igo Muo rituals. In these the candidate must go to the Okpala of his major lineage group to perform this ritual sacrifice to the ancestors. The Okpala can only inherit the ukpo (office) if he is the direct blood descendant of the founder lineage, and he should only perform this ritual for a person whose genealogical line of descent cannot be questioned.

The opponents of Enweuzor questioned the genealogy of his mother, who was not of Onitsha descent, but his supporters showed that a precedent had been created by the previous acceptance of candidates whose mothers were not of Onitsha origin. According to them, Obi Ezearoli's mother came from Igala, Obi Omozele's from Oze, Obi Chimedie's from Oze, Obi Udogwu's from Akiri and Obi Ijelekpe's from Ibuzo.

The argument shifted from the determination of the genealogical ancestry of the mother to that of the father, and opponents of this candidate contended that his grandfather migrated from another town and was absorbed into one of the lineage groups of Diakanyo in Umuezearoli. He did not lose the contest on this point since it was difficult to prove, and it was established that the foreign ancestry of an Obi's mother should not be a handicap. But in 1931–35 the Ogbo Isato age class, whose recommendations guided the activities of 1961–63, were emphatic in stating that both parents of a chosen candidate must be true descendants of Onitsha. Obi Onyejekwe satisfied this condition. If this has now become the accepted convention then it supersedes the one established by the four previous Obis whose mothers did not come from Onitsha.

Commissioner Harding eventually advised the government that J. O. Onyejekwe "has the best claims to recognition"[23] and it recognised him as the eighteenth Obi of Onitsha.

Summary

In the past the struggle for the throne was determined by force. In the present period (from 1899–1963) as we have shown, it was decided by an appeal, first to the new British Authority, as was the case during the Bedwell Commission of 1899, then by an appeal through the British Resident to the Governor in 1931–35, and then to the regional government in the 1961–63 contest. In each of these cases the government was asked to support the traditional usage, while the government commissioners based their decisions on a majority decision. Bedwell tried to introduce the principle of rotational succession by supporting the claim of Umudei, maintaining that the Umuezearoli's exclusive monopoly of the office was unconstitutional. He favoured rotation which was eventually accepted after the contest of 1931–35 and put into practice in the 1961–63 selection. In the subsequent contests of 1931–35 and 1961–63, both sides sought to support their claims by reference to traditional usage, but the precedents accepted in the case of the succession of Obi Okosi II were disregarded in the succession of Obi Onyejekwe. In Okosi II's case in 1931–35, the principle was accepted that Umuezechima had the right to select and the Iyase and Ndichie had the right to crown. The 1961–63 contest was based on a majority decision of the people supporting the action by a minority group of Ndichie (Ajie and Ogene) against the Iyase and the majority of Ndichie. Again, in 1931–35, Ezeocha was rejected and in 1961–63 was accepted as the legitimate priest of Udo. In the case of the bestowing of the ofo Ezechima, this was dispensed with from 1899 onwards and every succeeding Obi had a new ofo prepared for him.

The parties involved in the dispute were different in both contests. In the Obi Okosi II case, it was the Umudei ebo, versus a divided Umuezearoli ebo. In the most recent contest the principle accepted was that the candidate should come from Umuezearoli and the dispute was between the Ndichie who were split into two factions. One was led by Iyase (Onowu) Anatogu from the non-royal division of Ugwunaobamkpa and supported by the majority of the Ndichie, all of whom supported one candidate (J. E. Enweuzor), and the other faction was led by the Ajie and a few Ndichie who supported another candidate (Onyejekwe). Both groups divided the community into two political blocks. These instances show that the ritual performances of the successful candidate tended to be accepted as the new rules and norms of kingship.

In the traditional system, following the Benin pattern, the royal division of Umuezechima supplied the Obi and the non-royal division of Ugwunaobamkpa supplied the Iyase. But subsequent Obis sought to alter this by retaining both the offices for the same royal division, and the two dynasties of Umuezearoli and Umudei shared the offices of Obi and of Iyase between them. In 1935 a new principle was accepted, that the office of Obiship should be rotated between the two dynasties and in 1960, the original position of the Iyase was restored when the title was given to a person from the Ugwuaobamkpa division.

ABO

The royal clan collectively known as Umudei is divided into four sub-clans. Each of these four sub-clans can present candidates to the Odua and Olinzele who have the right to choose the best candidate. Because the final decision is made by the Odua and the Olinzele it implies that the contesting candidates must command enough influence among the Olinzele in the community, the most popular and powerful eventually winning the contest. In this competition for the Obiship, the candidate draws his support from his own sub-clan, from his affinal kinsmen, and from members of the Igbu society.

Abo judged a candidate's prowess by the standard of his military might. This criterion was decisive in the past, and military power was measured by the booty brought by a person in the raids on the Niger. The booty was often given as a tribute to the Obi and in those days heads of captives obtained in these raids were used for the Igbu title; the more heads a person could secure the greater his position.

In putting forward candidates, lineages ensured that they put up the most powerful and influential person who could command the support of the Olinzele and the community. A candidate whose position was sufficiently powerful in the state to become an inevitable choice saved the Odua and the Olinzele the difficulty of making a choice, but where several strong candidates appeared, competition could be tense and only controlled by the persuasion and firmness of the Olinzele, if necessary by the threat of subduing by force a rejected candidate who dared oppose their selection. Every such contest at Abo involved serious tension which left sources of political enmity that only faded away in the second generation.

The Abo people claim to have had sixteen Obis. Table J overleaf shows the four royal sub-clans of Umuojigbali, Umuobi (or Umuozegbe), Umuossai and Umuogwezi, and one of these, Umuobi, has tended to control the succession of the throne. Umuobi has produced eight Obis, Umuojigbali four, Umuogwezi three, and Umu Ossai one Obi. After Ogwezi I, Ojigbali, the senior son of Ogwezi, occupied the throne as the second Obi. When he died Obi Ossai from Umu Ossai sub-clan ascended the throne as the third, and when he died the Obiship passed to Umuobi. Umuobi supplied the fourth, fifth and sixth Obi and in the seventh contest the Obiship passed to Umu Ojigbali when Obi Enebeli won the contest from Umu Obi. Umu Ogwezi won the eighth contest and retained the office in the ninth. So that in the seventh, eighth and ninth contests, both Umuojigbali and Umuogwezi were the rival sub-clans.

But Umuobi wrested the office again in the tenth and eleventh contests and lost to Obi Olisa of Umuojigbali in the twelfth. The twelfth contest was a bitter one and when Umuobi lost, they defied the decision of the Odua and Olinzele and demonstrated their opposition by preventing the new Obi from entering the uge, the royal palace. The Olinzele and the community therefore built and used another uge. When Obi Olisa died, Umuobi again secured the throne and supplied the thirteenth, fourteenth and fifteenth Obi, who resided in the original uge. They lost the office again in 1916 when Obi Oputa, from Umu Ojigbali, was chosen and crowned as the sixteenth Obi of Abo. The new Obi preferred to live in his own private uge because he considered the original uge dangerous for

J. SUCCESSION TO THE OFFICE OF OBI OF ABO

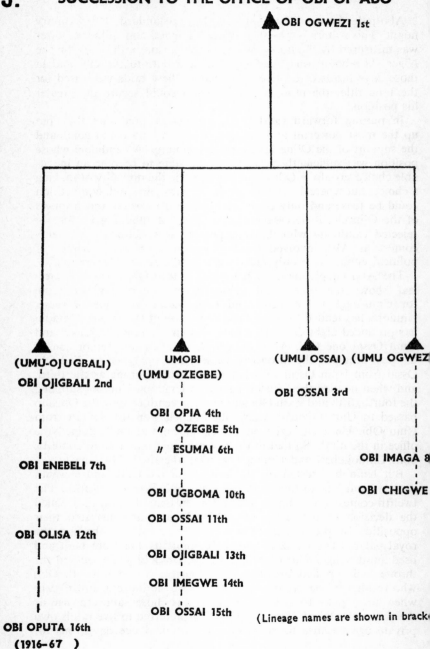

OBI OGWEZI 1st

(UMU-OJUGBALI)
OBI OJIGBALI 2nd

OBI ENEBELI 7th

OBI OLISA 12th

OBI OPUTA 16th
(1916–67)

UMOBI
(UMU OZEGBE)

OBI OPIA 4th
" OZEGBE 5th
" ESUMAI 6th

OBI UGBOMA 10th

OBI OSSAI 11th

OBI OJIGBALI 13th

OBI IMEGWE 14th

OBI OSSAI 15th

(UMU OSSAI)

OBI OSSAI 3rd

(UMU OGWEZ

OBI IMAGA 8

OBI CHIGWE

(Lineage names are shown in brack

people of his lineage. This was a condition he made with the Olinzele before he accepted the office.

There was an interregnum from 1897–1905 when it was too dangerous to select an Obi. The Odua with the support of the Olinzele continued to act as regent to avoid a civil war because they dared not choose between the two candidates. These were two powerful war chiefs who were ready to plunge the state into a civil war should their rival be accepted as a candidate. Both were wealthy and each had a large following. One of the contestants migrated to a new area and mobilised his army in readiness for attack if his opponent was conceded the throne. Eventually one of them died and his death resolved tension in the state, and in 1906 a new Obi was selected from Umuobi.

Umuobi is made up of two segments, one producing five Obis and the other three. When they succeeded to the throne, Obis from this ruling house accumulated wealth, followers, and influence, and could persuade the Odua and the majority of the Olinzele to accept another candidate from their group. From this royal sub-clan, powerful candidates emerged who during the period of each reign had acquired qualities of leadership and diplomatic abilities, and who extended their influence in the neighbouring Ibo kingdoms and up to Igala. These princes of the reigning house thus won a distinct position in the state. Wealth which accrued to the throne was used to establish the princes by the taking of titles and buying of slaves and in amassing military strength and power not only in the state, but outside it. Most of them were diplomatic emissaries to Osomari, Onitsha, Oguta, Asaba, Ida and places with whom Abo had diplomatic relations and also military contests. The Obis from Umuobi were determined to control the succession and the whole ruling sub-clan was united at every contest. They presented the most able candidate irrespective of which segment within the sub-clan he came from.

Obi Ossai (11th) was a king whose influence was paramount along this section of the Niger. He ascended the throne at the period of European contact. When the Landers were captured at Asaba, they were handed to him, and he in turn handed them to the Delta traders who gave them up to the British traders at the coast. He was also the first Obi of Abo to meet English naval officers and missionaries and traders. He met them on board the *Albert*, which with the *Wilberforce* and the *Soundan* were travelling up the Niger in August 1841 and signed a treaty between the representative of Her Majesty Queen Victoria and the Abo Kingdom in August 1841. Crowther took pains to describe the regalia of this king in this manner:

"He is a middle-sized man, between the age of forty and fifty; his countenance is soft, and he appears to be of a peaceful temper. Today his dress, as I was told, was very plain. He appeared in calico trowsers of a country make, and an English-made jacket of the same stuff: it would have been more respectable had they been cleaner, especially as he had no shirt on. He had on his neck three strings of pipe coral, as large as a man's small finger; two of which were short, and close to the neck, while the third extended to the navel. As far as we could count from the feet of his trowsers, when he moved, each of his feet about the ankles was ornamented with eight strings of coral; a dull old brass-button closing each string, and two leopard's teeth attached to the strings of coral on each foot. He had on a red cap; over which was a marine's cap, decorated with brass scales and other pieces, and coloured cords. His Majesty was not a little proud of this new equipment from the Commander of the Expedition."[24]

Obi Ossai had several wives, about one hundred as described by Trotter. It was through diplomatic marriages, characteristic of monarchies, that these Obis maintained their relative strength in the kingdom and far beyond. It was usual for them to marry into the houses of the powerful men and through these affinal ties created by such marriages, the Obis built up support for their sons or nephews when the throne fell vacant.

With time, the population of this ebo grew and some sections moved to another site at Abo known as Ogbe Ukwu and formed a new settlement. The descendants of Obi Ossai occupy the Umuobi quarters and are near the Onu Obi Ukwu, the residential palace of the Obis of Abo already referred to as uge. The size and importance of this sub-clan of Abo explains their having produced half of the recorded Obis of Abo. This was due to the accumulation of wealth, power and population.

The net advantage has been that the most important ritual cults and objects have been located in this ebo. These include the uge, the royal palace, the Ekwuru, the place where the spirits of Muo appear (it is in this important spot that Igbu title officials hang their omu palm leaves, used for the celebration of their annual Igbu ritual, which means that they go to perform the ceremony of Ikpu Omu after a new member has completed the rites appertaining to the title); the shrine of Nguru (the tutelary deity for the whole of Abo who is an alushi (spirit) with three faces (isu ato) and the Obi appoints a priest who officiates when sacrifices are offered to it); the Nne Dei, a pond where the wives of the Obi wash including the ngbala oto eze (eunuchs of the palace); and the Isuani, the shrine of the earth deity of Abo.

OGUTA

Three maximal lineages (ogbe) have been successively accepted by the chiefs and the people as the legitimate royal lineage with the right to fill the office of Obi. The first was Ogwuma, the second Ngegwu and the third Umudei, after that the throne went back to Ngegwu. The traditional history validated the right of Oguta people to depose their kings and to determine which ogbe should have the right to provide an Obi.

This "approved" lineage (ogbe) selects the candidate after considering most of the factors already raised, but they must consult a diviner (dibia) to make sure that the choice is accepted by the deities of the land and by the ancestors, and that his reign would bring prosperity to the whole community. As stated in Chapter 4, their choice is not limited to a single candidate, and a number of candidates, usually three, can be selected and crowned at the same time.

Once they have made their choice the members of the royal lineage inform the Ogana, the head of the Olinzele, the Ogene, the head of the Ndichie (Ndi Okpala), the Iyasara, the Ndanike, the Ezekoro and the Eze Ukwu who alone has the right to perform the rituals of installation.

The Ogwuma Royal Lineage. The first king came from the Ogwuma maximal lineage (ogbe), which was asked by the Oguta people to supply the king. This maximal lineage is made up of the three major lineages of Umu Isama Onyeuna, Odogwu, Umuegbua. The two remembered kings from this ward came from the major lineage of Umu Isama Onyeuna. Oguta people say that the first Obi was Eze Nkpo who was succeeded by his son Eze Ogwuala. The latter was a war-like man and during the lifetime of his father waged private wars against neighbouring people. When he ascended the throne it was thought that he would be of good behaviour but he continued to behave irresponsibly by concealing his actions from the state council and the people. He was the Obi that led the people during their journey from Benin to Illa and then to Obodo Akpuleukwe, where he eventually betrayed them and as explained in Chapter 10, he was deposed and the office given to another lineage (ward).

Umu Isama Onyeuna lost the right to the throne, but they retained some royal privileges. Firstly, the Okpala of this ward is the only Okpala in the whole town who can wear the red omu cap, which is the special prerogative of the Obi. The third royal lineage, Umudei, which we shall discuss at a later stage in this section, challenged the right of the Okpala of Ogwuma to use the red cap, and in 1930 instituted an action in the Native Court against the Ogwuma people. Obi Adikea, from Umudei, gave evidence in the court in favour of the Ogwuma people stating that it had been the custom since they lost the Obiship for their Okpala to put on the omu cap. The Umudei lost their action. Secondly, the Okpala of Ogwuma alone of all the other Okpalas can use the ibom gong to summon his agnates to a meeting, another prerogative exclusive to the Obi. Thirdly, when the Okpala of Ogwuma wants to offer a sacrifice to their ancestral shrine, he places an omu cap on the shrine to remind his agnates that their ancestors once put on the red cap thus symbolising their royal connection. Fourthly, Ogwuma people have in their custody the royal wooden dish, agini, which was used by their Obis on ceremonial occasions.

The Ngegwu Royal Lineage.   When Ogwuma lost the right to the throne, the office passed to Eroa, of the ogbe of Ngegwu, which then became the second recognised royal lineage. This ogbe is made up of five major lineages, each being founded by a son of Ngegwu, the founder of the ogbe. Only one, Umuoga, has the right to the Obiship. Umuoga further divides into five minor lineages, each of which can present a candidate for the Obiship.

Umuoga lineage produced three successive Obis and two Omus (candidates accepted for the office). The first was Eroa and he was succeeded by Osaka from the fifth minor lineage, that is, the succession shifted from the fourth to the fifth. When Obi Osaka died his elder son Agadagba succeeded him, and when he was deposed (the cause of which is treated in Chapter 10), the two omus Ojigbani and Oboduagwu from the second and first minor lineage groups within Umuoga died while performing the initial ceremonies for the installation, and thereafter no other Obi came from this ward.

Eze Agadagba was deposed, but the Ngegwu royal lineage was not, like Ogwuma, deprived of the right to the kingship. The two omus would have been crowned, if they had not died prematurely. Their deaths seem to have instilled fear in the minds of other lineages in the ward, and it seems that the kingship lapsed in their ward and Umudei the third royal lineage, soon to be discussed, monopolised the right to succession until 1958 when the conflict of Obi Ojiako (see Chapter 10) and the Ngegwu ward against the rest of Oguta people, led to his deposition and the return of the right to the throne to Ngegwu. They presented Mberekpe to the Oguta people and he was crowned and recognised by them as the Obi of Oguta.

The Umudei Royal Lineage.   Umudei is made up of three major lineages of Umunikwu, Umuezenwanya and Umuakata. The latter is further segmented into Umu Odua and Umuezeyiche, both being Umunne and acting together in matters relating to the selection of an Obi and in policy-making affecting the larger units. Each of these major lineages constitutes a royal house. There are thus three royal houses, and at every reign three or occasionally four Obis were selected, one from each of them.

The man who won the throne for the ward was Nkweke from the major lineage of Umunikwu. But he did so with the support of his other agnates, and in order to compensate them, he decided that the collateral major lineages should each supply a candidate, and that all of them should be crowned simultaneously. The senior Obi, namely himself, should become the recognised head of the state. By this policy he united the entire ward, for each major lineage had an interest in the kingship, and this interest in the right to the throne was thence shared and not moopolised by any particular segment.

Multiple Succession.   From the time that they acquired the right to the throne, Umudei institutionalised this principle of crowning three or four Obis at once, the eldest being recognised as the senior Obi.[25] When Nweke died, the second in seniority of age took his place, but only after his Udom (regent) had completed three years in office and performed the final funeral ceremonies for his father. When the last Obi of the group died, and his regent had completed the three years period of regency, other candidates were selected and simultaneously crowned.

The number of Obis supplied has usually been three, as the Umuakata lineage has usually supplied only one candidate who was chosen from either of its two sub-divisions. Thus competition for the throne is minimised because of the fact that every major lineage can supply a candidate, though this did not entirely preclude internal jealousies, intrigues, and in some cases the use of sorcery among aspirants within the same lineage segment. The choice of a candidate was determined by internal secret realignments within each major lineage, between the various minor lineages that make up the major lineages.

For purposes of comparison with other succession lists I consider it best to treat such a group of Obis who are crowned at the same time as a single unit of succession, taking as the period of their reign from the time the first Obi of the unit began to rule up to the time the last one's funeral rituals had been completed (including the period of his Udom's regency).

At the Commission of Inquiry held in 1961 to determine the status of the new Obi of Ngegwu, the Umudei people submitted to the Commissioner, Mr. Harcourt, a list of thirty-nine Obis to support their claim to the absolute right of the throne. They showed from this list that only three Obis were crowned at a time, thus giving thirteen units of succession. There was not enough evidence from their list to show the correct order of succession, nor did they show the exact number that came from each major division of the ward.

However, from the 1880s when the Royal Niger Company was established at Oguta, there was a succession unit which ended with the death of the last of the three Obis, namely Obi Ohanyere. Ohanyere had been crowned with Orisha and Adigwe, but Adigwe and Orisha pre-deceased Ohanyere who continued till his death in 1924, a long reign which lasted for forty years or more.

In 1926, another set of three, Adizua, Adikea and Ijoma, son of Ohanyere, were crowned. The eldest, Adizua, died in 1934, Adikea in 1936 and the youngest, Ijoma, remained on the throne till 1941. The period of their reign lasted for fifteen years. In 1947, another succession unit, Ezediaro, Nsofor and Ojiako was crowned. Both Ezediaro, the eldest, and Nsofor died shortly after, and Ojiako was on the throne until his replacement by Eze Mberekpe. Thus from 1880 to the present Obi, three succession units to the throne occurred.

If we use this system as our guide, we can reduce the claim of thirty-nine Obis of Umudei to thirteen periods of succession to the throne in the Umudei royal lineage. The reign of each unit becomes equivalent to that of an Obi at Onitsha, Abo and Osomari, or comparable to the situation when the former royal wards of Ogwuma and Ngegwu supplied one Obi in one succession instead of three.

There have therefore been nineteen succession units beginning with the Ogwuma lineage which supplied the first two Obis. Ngegwu supplied the third, fourth, and fifth. Umudei took up from the sixth until the 1947 succession unit which would count as the eighteenth. A single new Obi from Ngegwu was installed in 1958 and became the nineteenth in succession. This suggests a return to the former rule of one king at each succession.

It could be observed that the period that lapsed between one unit of succession and another varied. Though we do not have evidence for all the successions, the three recorded, of which the third has not ended because one of the Obis is still alive, show that the succession gap after the 1880–1924 unit was two years, for the succeeding unit were crowned in 1926. This unit finished in 1941, and the third was crowned six years later, in 1947.

OSOMARI

The Ugolo royal ebo is made up of three major lineages of Ada, Ulasi and Olo, and their right to the throne is recognised by the two brother ebo of Isiolu and Umuonyiogwu.

The two brother ebo, Isiolu and Umuonyiogwu are equally interested in the type of candidate to be presented. When the Atamanya dies and the last funeral rites have been completed, a time lag is given to enable Ugolo members to select the most suitable candidates. The three major lineages of Ugolo have a competing interest in the succession to the throne and Ugolo people sort out the best one from the candidates who put themselves up for selection.

If Isiolu and Umuonyiogwu feel that Ugolo is wasting too much time in selecting a candidate, they both summon the Ogene and the Ugolo ebo to a meeting at which they ask them to present a candidate. In the interim the Ogene performs a dual political function. One such function is that he becomes, after the completion of the funeral ceremonies of the last king, the head of the state, acting as regent and performing all the political functions of the Atamanya until a new one is installed. A second function is that he becomes the political head of the Ugolo division, retaining his normal ritual function as the spiritual head representing the ancestors of the ward.

Because the offices of both the Ogene and Atamanya are located in the same ebo, and this is the ruling ebo, there is no difficulty in the administration of the state between the period of the death of an Atamanya and the succession of the next. The Ogene is, in this respect, equivalent to the Odua of Abo who is also the oldest male from the Umudei royal clan, the difference being that at Abo the demand for immediate succession to the throne is accelerated by the fact that there are four competing royal ebo, the sub-clans of the royal clan, as opposed to one at Osomari.

In the three states already discussed, the list of kings is on average eighteen but Osomari maintain that they have only had nine Atamanyas, and of these they can only remember five. I obtained two more names, one of which occurred on the Treaty of 1885, making the number seven. These five came from either the Ulasi or Olo major lineages, but none from the Ada. It shows that three came from Ulasi and two from Olo. If their list is correct, Ulasi supplied the first three, after which succession passed to Olo.

According to Osomari tradition Ada has never produced an Atamanya. This means that the remaining four Atamanyas come from either of the other lineages. However, Ada has produced four

Ogenes an office which is not based on wealth but on age, and both divisions of Ulasi and Olo have also provided Ogenes.

Candidates are selected purely on merit which all other segments in the royal lineage accept as a prerequisite for the post. Ugolo people try to ensure that they maintain their solidarity and defend their royal status and privileges. A conflict over succession within the ebo could weaken their internal solidarity, and they resolve their differences so as to select a candidate unanimous to the ward, and acceptable to the other wards. The status of the candidate and his popularity also enhance the prestige of the ward.

The Olinzele of the two other political divisions of Isiolu and Umuonyiogwu must approve the candidate selected. He must command a following among all grades of Olinzele. The popularity of the candidate in the state helps Ugolo people to determine the manner of selection, and it appears that this fact of public acceptability of the candidate does constitute an important guide for them. If, therefore, many candidates are interested in the throne, Ugolo sort out the right candidate by feeling the pulse of the other political divisions.

Conflict can arise if two candidates consider that they are strong and command popular support but the fact that they have to obtain the support of both of the other two political divisions usually means that only one will be powerful enough to succeed.

One important point to make about the shortness of the list of the kings is that because the Ogene can perform the role of a king as already explained, it makes Ugolo reluctant to select a candidate immediately the funeral rites of his predecessor are completed. The continuity of kingship is maintained by the fact that the Ogene continues to act as the political head until a new king is chosen and installed. The last Atamanya, Awogu, died in 1954 and his funeral rites were completed in 1956, but Osomari is still ruled by the Ogene. The two non-royal political divisions have been impatient about the delay of Ugolo people in selecting a candidate, and at the Annual Convention of the Osomari Improvement Society held in December 1963, this matter was raised by the delegates in a notion which stated:

> "This House in conference assembled hereby calls upon Ugolo village to elect an Atamanya within six months from January 1964 and present same to Osomari people."[26]

This motion, the minutes state, "was unanimously carried except that there was a division as to the time factor, which was then sent to the elders to settle. The elders amended the motion by reducing the time to four months".

There is no difficulty in this instance over the selection of a candidate. The choice has already been made; but the man selected is a devout Catholic and President of the Catholic Society of Nigeria. The issues involved are how to waive some of the rituals connected with the coronation ceremonies and whether the Odaje Asi, the official who is always by the king, could perform all ritual functions associated with the Atamanya's office even in the absence of the king who has a building in Ugolo suitable for a palace, but resides mostly at Onitsha where he can effectively carry out his Catholic and other Nigerian duties.[27]

It is over ten years since the last Atamanya was buried, and no Atamanya has been installed, but the ritual functions of an Atamanya are being carried out by the Oniha Ogene. This is the longest interregnum in the four states in our sample.

At a date not specified by the tradition, the custom that Isiolu and Umuonyiogwu should be content with keeping their titles of Iyase and Odobo respectively and accept the right of Ugolo to the throne was challenged by two notables from the two divisions. Feeling themselves wealthy, influential and able, one Okwuosha from Umuonyiogwu, and Nwafuo from Isiolu decided to challenge the candidature of Oniha Obieka of Ugolo. Each of these contenders to the throne with the support of their wards insisted that they had the right to monopolise the throne. In circumstances like this, people often falsify the traditional history (ntita egbeli) to justify their claim to the office, and false stories were spread to raise some doubts concerning the right of Ugolo to the throne. These maintained that the other wards have not cared in the past to test this right of Ugolo because it was not worth their while to do so or that because they had not produced people of the calibre of those who were now challenging the candidate from Ugolo. They tried to set aside the 'mythical charter' of kingship as handed down to them by their ancestors. None of the candidates was prepared to withdraw, for each felt that he was equal to the other. They were each crowned by their respective divisions and Osomari had at this unrecorded period, three Atamanyas.

This supports our contention that the segmentary nature of the Osomari state depends on the will of the people. Where willingness to combine is lacking the structure becomes very susceptible to disintegration. This contest revealed the weakness of the state. There was not a single state, but three independent political units. The constitution of the state was changed completely. The inability of Ugolo to enforce its will showed again its minority position in the state, and it would appear that the other two persons who assumed the role of the king had no fear of spiritual sanctions.

On the death of these three Atamanyas Osomari reverted to the original position when Isiolu and Umuonyiogwu accepted the primacy of Ugolo.

It is crucial to note that the threat against the throne came from outside and not from inside the royal ward, which avoids any effort to break its unity through internal disagreement as to the right person to select.

NOTES

1   R. E. Bradbury, 1967.
2   Cp. J. S. Boston, 1964, for Igala; M. G. Smith, 1960, for Zazzau; S. F. Nadel, 1942, for Nupe; P. C. Lloyd, 1963, for Yoruba.
3   Jerry Orakwue, 1953.
4   R. W. Harding, 1963.
5   Cp. P. C. Lloyd, 1965, p. 80.
6   The word "block" is used in the sense that Barth used it in his analysis of Swat Pathan Systems. F. Barth, 1959.
7   Resident Captain D. O'Connor, *The African Advertiser*, December, 1936, p. 19.
8   No copy of the Commission's report is available in the Government Archives or office. My account is based on local oral information and from reference to it in other government documents such as the Harding Report.
9   R. W. Harding, 1963, p. 177.
10 Ibadan National Archives Paper C526/293 79. Vol. I.
11 J. Orakwue, 1953, p. 57.
12 Ibadan National Archives Papers C526/29379 Vol. I. Extracts from petition of Agabala na Iregwu, second grade Ndichie from Olosi, Umudei, Eka na ube and Ugwunaobamkpa, dated 6th May 1933.
13 Ibadan National Archives Paper, op. cit.
14 Captain Resident O'Connor, 1936.
15 Ibid., 1936.
16 I was in Nigeria when Obi Okosi II died. When I arrived in 1963, the Commission of Inquiry had been held and I interviewed all the Ndichie, the opposing blocks, Obi Onyejeke, and important heads of the respective lineages to check the material from the report and to make my own anthropological evaluation. I read accounts of the controversies in the local press and spoke to most of the young men who took part in these controversies.
17 Memorandum submitted by Ndichie Ume to Harding Commission, 1963. On Onitsha Dispute.
18 Ibid.
19 R. W. Harding, *Report*, 1963, p. 134.
20 Cp. C. K. Meek, 1937, p. 156.
21 A section of Umuasele objected to the ceremony and did not recognise its validity because they were not united, on this occasion, in the granting of this ofo.
22 R. W. Harding, *Report*, 1963, p. 126.
23 R. W. Harding, *Report*, p. 203.

24 Samuel Crowther in *Journals of the Rev. James Frederick Schön and Mr Samuel Crowther* . . . 1942, p. 282; 2nd edition, with a new introduction by Professor J. F. A. Ajayi, Frank Cass, London, 1970.

25 G. I. Jones, *Report*.

26 Osomari Improvement Society, Minutes of the Annual Conference, December 1963.

27 Since the civil war, the Atamanya elect has returned to Osomari and is preparing to be crowned King.

Chapter 10 **The Dynamics of Kingship II**

THE KING AND HIS CHIEFS

In the third and fourth chapters we described the manner of recruitment and functions of offices in the state. We pointed out the number of official titles in each state and distinguished between titles in each state that are hereditary in particular lineages and those that are open to competition among all the citizens. At Abo and Onitsha we showed that the king has power to appoint all titled officials. At Oguta and Osomari the king cannot appoint persons to the hereditary titles, that is, titles vested in particular lineages, but can appoint people to the non-hereditary titles of Isugbe at Osomari, and Olilinzele at Oguta.

In the Onitsha and Abo system one might be misled into thinking that the Obis, who recruit and appoint these titled officials, cannot be challenged by them when they have cause to do so. But an Obi is not considered above the law. He is expected to conform to the customs of the land and to the conventions of the constitution and, if he does not, there are various means of disciplining him. The Obi should listen to the advice of his leading chiefs; they can take action on specific issues against an Obi who abuses his authority and they can mobilise the people against him. His position naturally gives an Obi advantages in situations of conflict with his chiefs particularly in Onitsha and Abo and he is able to minimise the consequences of his unconstitutional actions by fomenting conflict between segments of the community and between their leaders. But if the chiefs cannot always discipline a recalcitrant Obi the converse is also true, the Obi cannot always control a powerful chief or titled man who is in some cases able to defy both the Obi and the constitution. Nevertheless the conventions of the constitutions are valued highly and any flagrant or repeated violation of them either by the Obi or by his chiefs will rally public support to the side of those who can represent their actions as being in defence of the constitution and of the values attached to the kingship. We hope to provide specific illustrations of this in the rest of this chapter.

ONITSHA

The Office of the Iyase (Onowu)

Probably the most interesting example of the abuse of his constitutional power by an Obi is that concerned with the appointment
of the Iyase. This has already been referred to in the previous
chapter as an illustration of how a constitution can be changed to
accommodate changing political developments. What is of interest
here is the way in which the Ugwunaobamkpa division was, after
a lapse of several centuries, able to force the Obi to revert to the
original convention and restore the office to this division.

The Onitsha constitution specifies that the Iyase, the head of
the Ndichie and next in office to the Obi, should come from the
non-royal lineages of Ugwunaobamkpa. This dual division of the
political structure is an important aspect of the system, and the
concentration of power in the hands of a royal lineage is avoided
by this rule that the Iyase, the most important official after the
Obi, should come from the non-royal division.

The actual derivation of the nineteen Iyases remembered in
Onitsha traditions is given in Table K below. A comparison of
this table with that of the succession of Obis of Onitsha (Table I
in Chapter 9) shows that the early Obis, who came from the
Umudei dynasty of Umuezechima division, adhered to this rule.
This was followed by a period when the office rotated between the
Umuezearoli dynasty of Umuezechima and Ugwunaobamkpa.
Thereafter from the time of the tenth Iyase onward the office was
held by the Umudei dynasty while the office of Obi was held by
the Umuezearoli dynasty. When in 1900 Obi Okosi I of Umudei
regained the Obiship for his dynasty he also retained the office of
Iyase for Umudei by conferring the title on his half-brother
Gbasuzor. This brought protests from Ugwunaobamkpa which he
sought to appease by appointing people from this division to an
undue number of other Ndichie titles, mainly at the expense of
the Umuezearoli dynasty of Umuezechima who should have received
a fair share of them.

In 1931, when Obi Okosi I died, Ugwanaobamkpa headed by the
Odu, the senior Ndichie Ume in Ugwumaobamkpa, asserted their
claim and before they agreed to support the candidature of his
son who became Obi Okosi II, they made him sign an undertaking
that he would not follow in the footsteps of his father. In the
resolution of 25th August 1932, already referred to in the issue on
succession, Ugwuaobamkpa specified that:

"The office of Iyase Onowu (Ndichie Ume) shall not in future be
appointed for the purpose of proper administrative function in the

same quarter in which the Eze of Onitsha has been appointed, that is to say comprehensively, that no appointment to the office of Iyase Onowu, after the present holder of office Onowu, shall be made within the Okebunabos family, or alternatively, the Umudei family, during the whole of any office as the Eze of Onitsha."[1]

They made the Obi sign this on the 23rd April 1933. However, in 1948, on the death of his uncle Iyase Gbasuzor, he broke this pact by appointing Obinwe, another agnate of this minor lineage as Iyase and Ugwunaobamkpa took the following actions against the Obi.

TABLE K
DISTRIBUTION OF THE OFFICE OF IYASE (ONOWU)

| UMUEZECHIMA ROYAL DIVISION | | UGWUNAOBAMKPA NON-ROYAL |
UMUDEI	UMUEZEAROLI	DIVISION
		1st Iyase Ovo
		2nd Iyase Ile
		3rd Iyase Ndoke
		4th Iyase Nsu
	5th Iyase Ebo	
		6th Iyase Ula
	7th Iyase Chima-Ukwu	
		8th Iyase Okwugbali
		9th Iyase Ugboma
10th Iyase Ugbogulu		
11th Iyase Achusim		
12th Iyase Okpuno		
13th Iyase Okagbue		
14th Iyase Ugani		
15th Iyase Osili		
16th Iyase Ofala		
*17th Iyase Gbasuzor		
*18th Iyase Obinwe		*19th Iyase Anatogu

* [From S. Ifeka, 1962. His list corresponds to the list which I collected.]

They refused to attend the Obi's court and respond to his summons; they usurped the Obi's ritual duty of slaughtering cows at funeral rites: and all the Ndichie of Ugwunaobamkpa boycotted the Obi's palace and also his annual festival of Ofala. This boycott was not relaxed until December 1958. Iyase Obinwe died two weeks after the settlement and the nineteenth Iyase, Anatogu, was appointed from the Ugwunaobamkpa division.

OBI OKOSI I AND HIS CHIEFS

The succession of Obi Okosi I marked a radical break with tradition. In the first place he owed his appointment to the support of external agencies, the Roman Catholic mission and the colonial government. In the second, his qualifications were inadequate (he was not for example an Ozo titled person) and the traditional rituals of installation were not observed as the candidate was a Christian. Once on the throne and secure in his recognition by the government as the rightful 'Native Authority' of Onitsha, the Obi was able to consolidate the position of his dynasty by disregarding the accepted conventions relating to the distribution of political offices. What is interesting here is the way in which those Ndichie who opposed him and who therefore championed the traditional values of the constitution were able to mobilise public opinion behind them and eventually secure the restoration of all the rules and rituals which Obi Okosi I had set aside.

His succession to office was considered by a section of the Ndichie to be contrary to the principles of the rules of kingship. He was a Catholic and was backed by the Roman Catholic Church, which showed interest in controlling the spiritual 'soul' of the kingship. The Bedwell Commission appointed by the government to investigate the succession issue may have favoured the idea of rotation of the kingship, considering that because Umuezearoli had previously monopolized the throne, Umudei should now have their share: but it is also likely that they felt it was in their best interests to recognise an Obi who was inclined to support British administration and the missionaries.

The Obi was careful to retain their support. Having accepted the Roman Catholic faith, he sent away some of his wives, and did not use the ofo ezo, the symbol of office; he is said to have burned it. He also attended mass, contrary to the rule that he could only leave his palace on state occasions. Between 1919 and 1921 the colonial government made a division between the new Onitsha waterside community and the old inland town, the former being converted into a township. The inland town was to be grouped into a new province of Onitsha together with other Ibo communities in the area. The government obtained the support of the Obi for this change but the Ndichie viewed with disapproval this merging of their state (the inland town) with people who, they felt, belonged to a different political system and culture. The Ndichie were angry and for several years the Ndichie and community of Onitsha boycotted the Obi. They refused to attend his palace or to hold courts there, they usurped his ritual roles, and they boycotted his annual festivals. The Ajie next in seniority to the Iyase led the revolt of the Ndichie against the Obi. The then Iyase, being the Obi's half-brother, was in no position to do so.

While keeping in with the government and missions Obi Okosi I was also building up the strength of his dynasty regardless of the effect this would have in consolidating opposition against him. He is said to have "made Ndichies surreptitiously and without regard to proper representations of all the kindreds. Of the twenty Ndichies today eight were Okebunabo (Umudei), nine from non-kingly families (i.e. Ugwunaobamkpa), and only three are from Umuezearoli".[2]

The Ndichie of the Umuezearoli dynasty were aggrieved that Obi Okosi I concentrated the offices in his own section of the division, and gave the Ndichie Ume title, which should have gone to Umuezearoli to Ugwunaobamkpa, while this non-royal division of Ugwunaobamkpa was angry that the Obi usurped their office of Iyase. Thus the reign of Obi Okosi I was marked by constant agitation stemming from this abuse of office and the failure to perform the sacred rituals of kingship.

Politically this policy was successful and secured the succession of his son Obi Okosi II, but the Ndichie who were opposing him were completely successful in securing the restoration of the traditional rituals of seclusion and installation. All candidates in the 1931–35 and 1961–63 successions took care to perform them and the value attached to them by the Onitsha people, both progressive and conservative, could be seen in the controversies which arose over their correct performance.

Over-powerful Chiefs

To be successful in his office, an Obi needs the support of his Ndichie and when this is lacking we can expect to find influential chiefs asserting their power and defying the Obi and the constitution. This was not only the case during Obi Okosi I's reign, it also occurred during that of his predecessor. For example, tradition relates that about 1890 one Ezeoba, a powerful man of rank, usurped the right of the Obi to celebrate the Ofala festival and performed this festival. It was according to them a successful event and "he came out unquestioned",[3] for as he had a considerable following in the state, he was not prosecuted by the Obi and the Ndichie for this breach of the law.

A similar case of usurping the Obi's exclusive right to celebrate the Ofala festival occurred during Obi Okosi I's reign when the Ogene, who came from Umudei, celebrated this festival. He too was not punished. In the case of Ezeoba he became so powerful that he and a certain Modozie Odu of Umudei waged a protracted civil war against each other and thus created a situation that was regarded as menacing to the British maintenance of peace in the area. He was arrested by the Royal Niger Company on 14th May

THE DYNAMICS OF KINGSHIP II 231

1898, and deported to Asaba. He died on 2nd June of the same year and his body was brought to Onitsha for burial.[4] However, if a powerful person acts in a way that not only challenges the Obi's authority but also offends against the accepted values of the constitution, even an unpopular Obi can expect to receive the support of his chiefs in disciplining him. For example, in 1920, while the political tension arising from the Obi's support of the British administration and his injudicious appointment of Ndichie had not subsided, the Ogene, an Ndichie Ume chief, died. The office thus became vacant and the Ndichie felt that the Obi should adhere to the conventions when appointing another Ogene. But he again conferred the title on a member of his sub-clan of the royal division and did not award the title to Umuezearoli sub-clan who considered that it was now their turn to hold the office.

In answer to this, Odita, the Ajie (who was next in rank to the Iyase) supported by the Ndichie of Umuezearoli, usurped the authority of the Obi to appoint persons to Ndichie office and conferred the title of Ogene on Chima Akunne from Umuezearoli, and thus Onitsha had two Ogenes. The dispute, which started in 1925, dragged on until 1928. The Obi first took action in the Supreme Court against Odita, the Ajie. The judge however refused to hear the case on the grounds that the case disclosed no cause of action, and that he had no jurisdiction to hear it. The Obi then referred the matter to the Native Court, where the Ajie was charged and fined ten pounds and the judgement was confirmed by the District Officer. The Ogene Chima whom the Ajie had installed was ordered to hand over his regalia of office to the Obi in the District Office.

Though the Obi was unpopular with his chiefs, yet the action of the Ajie was considered contrary to the constitution and was regarded as a challenge to the office of Obi, and they collectively applied social sanctions against the Ajie by ostracising him. His house was boycotted by the Ndichie and he was further prohibited from attending their meetings and enjoying the privileges attached to his office, such as performing with others the annual festival rites. When he died, his agnates had to perform on his behalf the ritual of absolution, known as "ikpu alu", before the funeral rites appropriate to his office were performed.[5]

Between 1938 and 1942 the Onya, Obiozo, of the Ndichie Ume grade, was impeached in the Obi's council for taking fees for permission to play the "egwu ota" at a mortuary ceremony contrary to the decision of the council, which said that this permission if given should be free. This was regarded as an abuse of a privilege which the Ndichie enjoyed. As already shown, the egwu ota is a dance exclusive to them. The Ndichie instructed the Ogbo-na-achi-ani, one of the age classes vested with executive authority, to take action against him. He was prosecuted in the Native Court, found guilty and fined. In the same way, one Chude Adazie, a second grade Ndichie Okwa, and another man, Nwosa Oziziani, of the same grade, contravened the rule which stipulated that specific animals should be used for the mortuary rites of certain categories of people. The mortuary rules say that a goat (ewu izuzu) should not be killed for the mortuary ceremony of a woman. Chude Adazie violated this rule and performed this mortuary rite of an ewu izuzu on behalf of a deceased woman. Further, the rules say that a cow should not be used for the mortuary rites of a woman unless she had bought a slave (igba ohu), had a son who had taken the Ozo title, or had herself taken the female title known as Igbu Odukwu, a wealth title in which the woman wears on her hands and legs costly ivory bracelets and anklets purchased to display her wealthy position in the society. Nwosa Oziziani violated this rule by slaughtering a cow for the mortuary rites of a woman who did not have the prerequisite qualification entitling her to this mortuary privilege. In both cases, this age class was instructed to take action against them. They were both prosecuted in the Native Court and found guilty and fined.

ABO

An Abo myth reminds the Obi every morning of what happened to a former king who ruled unconstitutionally. According to the legend, one Obi Ozegbe (nicknamed Eze-anya Oku, the irascible king) was very despotic and cruel. His cruelty became unbearable, and, because Abo custom does not allow the deposition of an Obi, they planned another way to remove him. Two acts of his provoked this plot.

First, he asked his people to recover an alligator pepper (ose oji) which he had dropped in the Niger. This was an impossible proposal and many people were drowned when attempts were made to recover it. However, a thoughtful man put an alligator pepper in his mouth, dived in in search of the king's pepper, came to the surface, and presented the one he had put in his mouth as the Obi's pepper. This satisfied him and the people were relieved from this tortuous adventure.

Second, not content with this, he again asked the Olinzele to instruct the people to cut down a big iroko tree by the palace and to carve a canoe out of this tree for his use. The people proceeded to cut the tree, but when he saw that the tree was about to fall, he asked them not to allow it to reach the ground, but rather all should hold it when it was falling. In trying to carry out the order many people were crushed by the tree.

The Olinzele and the people therefore plotted to remove him. The only way to achieve this without shedding the blood of the "anointed head of state" was to secure the assistance of the palace eunuchs and Idibo, so that all should help to construct a tunnel from one of the rooms in the uge direct to the ukpo which would be covered with a mat, without the knowledge of the Obi. They did this, and when the Obi sat on it he fell into the hole. He was left to suffocate and was covered up and buried. A few days later the Olinzele announced that he was dead.

By this method of assassination, no blood had been shed and the ancestors and deities of the land could not hold anyone culpable as would have been the case if the blood of a "sacred person" had been shed. Again, it eliminated any notion of open revolt, or dethroning of an Obi which could have created a dangerous precedent in their constitutional history. Milder social sanctions could have been applied, but in the case of Obi Ozegbe, his acts were brutal to the point at which mere boycott of his palace could not have changed his attitude.

The ofo of this Obi is kept separately and not mixed with the ofo of the other deceased Obis of Abo. This is chained to an Ikenga (a representation of the spirit of good fortune) and the people believe that the chain is to control his roving spirit in the other world. From this legend began the sounding of a warning, every morning, to the future Obis of Abo.

At about five o'clock in the morning (when the cock crows) the drummer plays the following expressions on the ufie drum three times:

OBONWE! OBONWE! OBONWE!	KING! KING! KING!
Kwulu Wuzo Kwulu Wuzo	Abo once punished their king.
Abo meni Eze wa mbu!	Adamgbu gbu (the despotic ruler)
Adamgbu gbu mele ife ana aka	did what is often remembered.
Adamgbu gbu anala Abo aha	Adamgbu gbu did not prevent
Obonwe! Obonwe! Kwulu wu zo.	Abo from fighting back.
	Obonwe Obonwe stop and look (watch your ways).

The Obonwe (praise name) of the Obi is called three times by this talking drum. This myth reinforces the notion that an Obi should not rule without the consent of his people.

Although the chiefs and people of Abo cannot constitutionally depose their king they are not without legal means of controlling him. They can, as at Onitsha, disassociate themselves from the Obi and can boycott the palace. The constitution provides in the person of the Odua (whose office has been described in Chapter 3) an official who can preside at council meetings in the absence of the Obi and who can, when the need arises, summon the Olinzele to meet in his house instead of in the palace. It is possible, however, for an Obi to become an Odua as well if he survives long enough. This is the case with the present Obi Oputa who is now the oldest male in the royal clan.

The Olinzele can also, in addition to boycotting the Obi's council meetings, bring pressure on him by refusing to perform their special palace rituals; but the Obi can counter this by getting his Idibo titled wives to carry out these rituals in their stead.

An individual Olinzele would not normally refuse to attend the palace for this is tantamount to rebellion. When an Obi sends for an Olinzele through his servant, it is imperative for the Olinzele to follow the servant immediately. This servant carries a special staff to which a red cloth is tied at one end. On arriving at the residence of the Olinzele, he thrusts the staff into the ground indicating that the king demands the presence of the official.

If he refuses to follow him, the servant returns and reports to the Obi. The Obi then summons the rest of the Olinzele to the palace. The ufie drum is played. They all quickly respond and on assembling at the palace the Obi thrusts his sword to the ground indicating that he has declared war. He then explains to them what has happened, and they all prepare for a collective attack on the rebellious Olinzele.

The constitution also provides less drastic methods of disciplining an Obi. He can be impeached 'indirectly' before the council. The charge is never made against the Obi directly but against his 'servant' who in this case is the Akpulosu. For example, Obi Oputa was found to have awarded the title of Igbu to a politician who was not a member of the society, and not a citizen of Abo and therefore did not qualify for holding that office, despite the fact that his position in the country gave him a rank which in the modern context could be rated far higher than the Igbu title of Abo. This to them did not matter, and they felt it was derogatory and wrong for a non-Abo man to receive the title from their honoured Obi whose ancestors conquered all ethnic groups around them including, they implied, those of the person on whom this title was conferred.

The language of the speakers at the gathering was strictly conventional, the charge was made against the Akpulosu, the Obi's son and against the Iyase and when the case was proved they made the Obi and the Iyase pay fines for this act. My informants confirmed that this was a general practice adopted whenever the Olinzele or the Igbu, of which the Obi is the head, brought charges against his person for abuse of his office.

The Obi may also have to take the blame for actions which he is powerless to prevent. For example the introduction of direct taxation by the Nigerian government in 1927 led to a great conflict in the state and shook the confidence of the Olinzele and the people in the Obi. The Obi was suspected of supporting the idea of taxation which the British administration was introducing in the area. The aims of taxation were not explained to them, and they thought that the Obi conspired with the District Officer to extort money taxes from the people. The Obi in his position as a sole Native Authority was ordered to enforce the collection of taxes within the area of his jurisdiction, and since in the tradi- tional way, he should consult with the Olinzele in all he did, they felt that he was no longer willing to do so and was usurping their right to be consulted. In protest they refused to pay the taxes and asked the people not to do so.

The Government backed the Obi and was determined to enforce taxation. A detachment of police was sent to Abo and the leading Olinzele of the Umudei and the Ndichie and heads of various lineages were arrested and placed under guard. An irate crowd broke into the court room and released these notables. Police reinforcements were despatched from Warri and they re-arrested more people than before, including the persons released by the crowd. They were sent to Warri, tried at the Magistrates' Court and sentenced to various terms of imprisonment, and taken to Sapele prison to serve their sentences.

Eighteen Olinzele from the four ebo, six from Umuogwezi, seven from Umojigbali, two from Umuossai and three from Umuobi were involved. When they completed their terms of imprisonment and returned to Abo some of the older ones died. This left a very deep scar in the hearts of many people and affected the position of the Obi in the state.[6] With the passing of time the bitterness seemed to have lessened, but people still remember the incident which brought them into open conflict with the Obi.

OGUTA

The position of the Obi vis-à-vis the Council of the State and the people reveals that he is a constitutional monarch whose power is circumscribed by rules and precedents. The people look to the Obi and council as the mainspring of their political life. All political segments (ogbe) are represented on it by their respective heads, either ritual (Ndichie) or secular (kingly officials and Olilinzele) and they must act together if the unity of the state is to be maintained. The council has to deal not only with over-powerful or recalcitrant Obis, it has also to maintain a balance of power between the Obi and over-wealthy kingly officials and prevent particular wards from expanding their prerogatives at the expense of others less privileged. This position is manifested in the rules that guide the Obi's conduct with his council, in the ways that some of the powerful chiefs can usurp his privileges of office, and in the disputes which can lead the wards (ogbe) to oppose actions regarded as denying their representatives their political privileges.

The Oguta constitution differs from that of Onitsha and Abo by providing for the deposition of an Obi who has lost the support of his people and this is accompanied by transferring the right to the kingship to another ward.

In Chapter 8 we referred to three wards of Ogwuma, Ngegwu and Umudei as royal wards. In this section we shall examine the reasons why this situation has been created. Oguta myths validate this convention that the Obi is subject to deposition if he goes against the rules of the constitution. Three instances of deposition have occurred and each led to the transfer of the right to the throne from one ward to another. The depositions of the Obis from Ogwuma and Ngegwu happened in the distant past, but the myths which record them become their document of precedent,[7] and served as a precedent for the deposition of the Obi in 1958.

Obi Ogwuala of Ogwuma

The episode which led to the deposition of Obi Ogwuala and the subsequent loss of the throne by his ward is narrated by the elders as follows. There was a fierce war between Igala and Abo. Oguta was on friendly terms with both kingdoms, and as the war became protracted, the Obi of Abo wanted Oguta people to arbitrate and restore peace between them. Abo offered a gift to Obi Ogwuala to summon his council and inform them of the plea of Abo for the mediation of Oguta people in the war. Obi Ogwuala received the gift, regarded as fees for settlement, but did not inform the council and the community. Oguta, Abo and Igala attended one central market at Ubom Oshimili (a sand bar in the Niger) and there the news of Abo's bid for peace was made known to Oguta traders. Also, Igala, knowing of Abo's move, offered a gift to Obi Ogwuala for the same purpose, but he again accepted this without informing the council and the people of Oguta.

Both Abo and Igala having waited in vain for him to arrange

a meeting between them decided to stop the war on their own. They learned that Obi Ogwuala had not conveyed their plea to his council and people of Oguta, and both states therefore decided to wage war against Oguta.

According to the local rules of war, it was customary for an attacking nation to send a declaration of war to the people to be attacked and the Ata of Igala notified Obi Ogwuala that they would wage war on Oguta. Obi Ogwuala instead of notifying the council and the people so that the military officials would mobilise and prepare for war, concealed this from them, and instead asked his own agnates to prepare to leave the town before the attack occurred. They all prepared and secretly migrated to Ukwuani in the Western Ibo division where they now constitute the Ogwuma ward of Ukwuani.

But the secret plan and migration of Ogwuma people was revealed by one of the wives of the king. This woman, from a major lineage group of Umuoga of Ngegwu ward, went and told her father Eroa about the impending attack of Igala and Abo, and that the Obi and his people were beginning to move to Ukwuani. Eroa summoned members of Ngegwu and informed them. They organised their defence of the town and passed the information to the council. Oguta mobilised for war under the leadership of Eroa and his agnates who occupied a vulnerable area of the town. In the war that followed, Oguta people were victorious and Igala and Abo were driven off. Eroa was recognised as Obi. Thus Ogwuma lost the right to the throne and it was shifted to Ngegwu.

By this time Obi Ogwuala and his people had left but there remained a certain woman, a wife of an Ogwuma man who stayed behind with her two sons in her natal lineage. No one knew about this, and Oguta people thought that all Ogwuma had left the town. An incident occurred and the council sent a delegation to consult the Chukwu oracle of Arochukwu, and Chukwu revealed that there were some Ogwuma people still living at Oguta. This caused great anxiety and the woman and her sons were brought out, but the Chukwu oracle told the people of Oguta to recall Ogwuma and they were brought back and allotted land in the middle of the town. Some of them stayed where they were and today they form the Ogwuma ward of Ukwuani. The Ogwuma ward of Oguta still maintains cultural ties with Ukwuani.

Obi Agadagba of Ngegwu
Obi Eroa and his successor Osaka were both strong kings, but the reign of Obi Agadagba created another political crisis.

According to tradition, Obi Agadagba was performing the Okwukwu Eze midnight ceremony. This takes place once a year at the end of the royal yam festival referred to as Omelife. At the end of this, the king goes out at midnight naked and greets all the alushi (spirits) in the town. No one is supposed to see the king naked, so all persons are expected to stay indoors after dusk. There must be no noise and all lights in the town must be extinguished. The king carries his igbu knife, he is completely naked and with the whole town in perfect silence, he moves round and offers kola nuts, palm wine and nzu (white clay) to the shrines, praying for the life of his subjects. This still happens today.

It happened that as Obi Agadagba was celebrating his Okwukwu Eze rituals a child of less than one year old, whose father was Nkweke, in Umudei ward, cried aloud in a room and this was heard by the Obi. He did not bother about this, but as he was returning from the trip, he again heard the cry of this child. He then went to the gate of the child's ngwulu uno (compound) and knocked. They opened and he demanded that the child should be handed to him, which they did and he killed the boy.[8] The homicide of this boy caused great indigation in the town, and Nkweke, his father, was backed by the four major lineage groups that make up this ward of Umudei and they demanded that the king should commit suicide or be executed as he had acted unreasonably.[9]

The council assembled and went to the Obi for explanation. Nkweke's ward of Umudei gathered and prepared for a feud against the Ngegwu ward. The Ndichie (elders) who constitute the judges in the Obi's court, were faced with the problem of determining what was reasonable or unreasonable in the action of Obi Agadagba. They could not accept the demand of Umudei for the execution of the king, for "ishi eze bulu ibu", the king's head is great; "ana atu eze onu", you cannot measure the king with any being. The idea of execution was ruled out. The council suggested that a daughter from the Obi's family be given to Nkweke, but the Umudei people refused. They had their eyes on the throne, and began to win over a section of Oguta to this demand.

The council considered that in this case any action of the king should be that of a reasonable person. The life of a young innocent child was important, because according to custom, the great desire of a man is to beget a son. Children are known as innocent people, umu muo, children of the ancestors, and harsh treatment towards them is repudiated by society. An infant is innocent because it cannot differentiate between right and wrong (omadife). For the king to have executed this child was considered an unreasonable act. It was depriving the child that was new in the world of his destiny (ekelechi).[10]

They decided therefore that Obi Agadagba had acted unreasonably, that homicide by itself was a serious crime, particularly on the part of an Obi, and that Nkweke, the father of this boy, should be compensated by being given the kingship, for Obi Ogadagba by his action had desecrated the kingship and should no longer hold the office. Ngegwu, however, did not lose the right to the throne, as already explained.

Obi Ojiako of Umudei

In this third example, we are concerned with an agitation against an "autocratic" king whom the people decided to depose after all other measures of restraining him had, according to them, failed. The parties in this case were the council representing the rest of Oguta against the Obi and his ward, the Umudei royal ogbe. The issues in dispute led to the eventual 'deposition' of the Obi Ojiako and the restoration of the right of succession to Ngegwu royal lineage from whom Umudei had originally taken it. The role of the Umudei royal lineage was not, according to the people, commendable, for they and the Obi were united against the council and also the people, who by this century had been awakened by the influence of modern education. The new elite, organised into the Oguta National Union, rallied around the council of the state to defend the institution of kingship against the 'onslaught' of the Obi Ojiako and his royal agnates.

The Obi was charged by the council with offences considered inimical to the best interest of his subjects. We shall not be concerned with the personal motives of the accusers nor the personally motivated arguments of the royal lineage against these accusations, rather we shall discuss some of those accusations so as to bring out the theoretical issues involved.

The following were the principal charges made against him:

That he conferred the Olilinzele title on persons not eligible for it. In the first place he conferred this title on some of his agnates. An Obi may not do this for a number of reasons. For instance, by doing so he would upset the balance of the state council by packing it with his relatives. He could make this number sufficiently large to counterbalance the other two colleges, and to the exclusion of the representatives of the various other wards. Again, an Olilinzele in receiving the title accepts the superior position of the Obi and is by this his servant and adviser, but an Obi's agnate is himself a potential candidate for the throne and should not receive a title

R

subordinate to an Obi since he might himself one day become Obi. The office of Olilinzele should therefore be reserved exclusively for persons from those non-royal wards whose heads cannot be senior officials of the state. It should be noted in passing that a precedent for this award had already been created by a previous Obi. The Obi Ijoma conferred the title on one of his agnates who was a very wealthy oil trader, as was his wife, who commanded a great following in the town. The other title was conferred by Obi Adizua and again on a rich trader. This man was subsequently crowned as one of the Obis in the set headed by Obi Ojiako in 1947. He and the other Obi in this set died soon after, leaving Obi Ojiako the sole survivor in the set.

In the second place he conferred the Olilinzele title on a man from an Osere ward. The constitution of Oguta vests the right to provide the three ritual officials called Osere in three particular wards. The office is one that is ascribed to the oldest man in the ward, thus any man in the ward who lives long enough can become an Osere. As already explained in Chapter 4, an Osere's installation ceremonies include the performance of his funeral rituals to enable him to commune with dead members of the Ikwa Muo society of which he is the head. When an Olilinzele dies he must have the special mortuary rituals which belong to his office. Should a man from an Osere ward be made an Olilinzele and live long enough, he might well become its Osere, in which case he would not be able to have the funeral rituals associated with the office of Osere. In the case of the Umunarukwu ward which supplies the Osere for the Ugwu ukwu division of Oguta there is a further complication. The Osere from this division may not attend assemblies at the Obieze (palace) which is in the Ugwunta division as he must avoid meeting the Osere of this division. It is believed that if they did meet the Osere of Ugwunta would die. Thus if a man from the Umunarukwu ward was appointed an Olilinzele and if he subsequently became Osere he would not be able to answer the Obi's summons to attend meetings in the palace, as he would run the risk of meeting the Osere of Ugwunta there. The Obi should not therefore appoint to the office of Olilinzele a person from any ward that provides an Osere. However, Obi Ojiako defied this rule and conferred this title on a man from Umunarukwu ward.

In the third place he conferred the title on a person not ritually qualified for it. In Oguta the first important initiation ceremonies which a man performs are the rituals of the Ikwa Muo society connected with the funeral of his father. Once a man's father is dead and the senior son has completed the funeral rites, he joins this society with his other brothers. If he does not, he has no status in society and is called an ofeke, a man of less substance. One of the things he may not do is to take the Olilinzele title, since this title can only be conferred on those whose fathers' funeral rituals have been completed and who have thus been initiated into the Ikwa Muo society.

Oguta people say that such a person "bu onu oto", has no string on his neck, and that his father is in the same shameful position in the other world. A person who has failed to be initiated has no respect for his father, and his ancestral ceremonial father. When sacrifices are offered to the ancestors his father will not partake of the meals because his son cannot offer sacrifices to him because of his son's non-membership of the Ikwa Muo. Besides conferring the title on his immediate kin, Obi Ojiako did so on a man whose father had died some years previously but who, it was alleged, had not performed the Ikwa Muo funeral rituals.

That he took a partisan attitude in the affairs of the state by supporting a factional body known as the Anidima Fraternity against the majority of his people. The significance of this accusation is not that the Obi disregarded the opinions of the new elite organised as the Oguta National Union, but that rather, the participation of the Obi in the politics of the Anidima Fraternity alienated him from a harmonious relationship with members of his council.

Members of the Fraternity, from my discussion with some of them, bound themselves into an oath of secrecy and loyalty to their leader. The Obi, by accepting an active and secret association with this society, was standing in opposition to the traditional council. It was his association with this society, they argued, that led him to violate the principle governing the distribution of the Olilinzele title. Two of the members on whom he conferred this title were members or supporters of this society, and this meant that he was acting not on the advice of the council, but on the advice of the Fraternity.

That the Obi was becoming financially embarrassed. In the rituals of installation, the kingmaker, Ezeukwu, administers an oath to the Obi forbidding him to owe any debt because this disgraces the position of the Obi. There is another ritual aspect of this oath. In this community there are certain cults already referred to as alushi (spirits). These cults are localised and owned by various lineages and one of the functions of such cults is to visit with illness the family of those who by debt or other offences have wronged members of their ward. These alushi are active on behalf of their owners, and the Obi being in debt might find himself exposed to their attack. That is why it is forbidden for an Obi to be in debt, for a visitation against his person might indirectly threaten the anger of the deities connected with the kingship, one of which is the Agunze shrine which is the symbolic deity of power and authority of the Obi in the state.

The Obi Ojioko was accused of placing himself in an embarrassing position, by refusing to refund money entrusted to his care by the Association of Ferry Women (Ndi Efere). In the circumstances in which this act was allegedly committed, it would normally be considered a private matter, but the people brought this charge since the position of the Obi was estranged because of the tension generated by his abuse of his office.

That the Obi and his lineage tried to alienate land belonging to the community. The twenty-seven wards each have their own locality, and land in these areas is owned by the wards, and, in the case of residential land, it is divided among the various subdivisions within each maximal lineage (ogbe). Wards have their farm land in other areas outside the town where they build their farm hamlets, and the principles governing the tenureship in their residential land govern also the farm land. The original dwellers of Oguta, the Awa, vacated their land when the people of Oguta arrived. But the autochthonous Obeagwa group who own land at the Okposha site acted as the priest (Ezeani) of the land, and performed the rituals necessary for the leasing of the land.

In the early thirties, the people decided to declare the whole land lying behind their residential area communal land for the purpose of creating a new township layout. The allocation of land for building was made with the consent of a committee acting with the authority of the Obi and council, and members of this committee were selected at the Obieze by the people and charged with the responsibility of allocating land to indigenes of Oguta. When it came to dealing with outside agents such as missionaries, proprietors of schools and the government who wanted to acquire land for a school, a post office, a police post and a demonstration farm, the Obi and council signed the lease on behalf of the people.

After several years of this development a land dispute arose. A neighbouring village, Egwe, claimed that part of this communal land belonged to them. While this case was being heard in the High Court at Aba, the Obi's agnates prepared a counter action against this village claiming that the land in dispute belonged to them, and according to the Obi, that part of it was royal hunting ground.

This action of the Obi and his agnates was felt to be undermining the legal action of Oguta people against Egwe village.

When the action of the Obi became known, the council on behalf of the community demanded that the Obi should explain the cause of his action. The Obi's action which caused suspicion in the minds of the people was his silence in the High Court when he was giving evidence on behalf of the people. He remained mute on being asked under cross-examination, "Are you claiming that the land Okwu Oru belongs to Umudei Umuezenwanya?" The Commissioner, Mr Harcourt, remarked during the inquiry that "among the alleged offences of the Obi therefore it is only his connection with the land case against Egwe that can perhaps be condemned as contrary to the interests of Oguta people as a whole".[11]

Alienation of the land under his custody without the knowledge and consent of the council was the last straw, and these four offences consolidated the people against him. The Obi no longer commanded the respect due to the office and obedience to his commands was therefore withdrawn. Opposition was directed against the person of the Obi and because his agnates were culprits and collaborated in some of his actions, as was the case of the former Ogwuma ward, they were included in the people's action against the Obi.

The Umudei royal lineage defended the Obi, and both he and his agnates gave the impression that the Obiship belonged to this ward. This attitude alienated them from the people and the council withdrew its support and gave the Obi time to recant and declare his position with them vis-à-vis the people. Since he could not rule with the council, it meant that the sanctity of his office, which rested on the basic notion of the traditional authority handed down through the ages, was no longer valid. In August 1958 the people assembled at the house of the Ogene and the council, on behalf of the majority wards, asked Ngegwu people to select a candidate, which they did. They passed a resolution 'deposing' the Obi and they called on the Ezeukwu to crown Mberekpe, selected from Ngegwu ward as the new Obi.

The 'deposed' Obi and the Umudei ogbe petitioned the regional government which found itself obliged to intervene to try and settle the matter. In 1960 it appointed a commission of inquiry to settle the dispute.[12] Its report, published in 1961, ruled in favour of Obi Ojiako and against the new Obi appointed by the Oguta chiefs in council. The regional government upheld the ruling and appointed Obi Ojiako to the Eastern House of chiefs as a first-class chief but the Oguta council and all the ogbe except Umudei refused to recognise him and defied the Government and recognised the new Obi Mberekpe from Ngegwu, whom they had crowned in August 1958 before the Commission was appointed.

They argued that the dethroning of an Obi was in keeping with the precedents of their history. They therefore refused to recognise the Obi of the government's choice. They proceeded further to apply vigorous social sanctions against the Obi and his agnates. The royal lineage was excluded from all societies such as Igbu and Ikwa Muo, and from age sets, and were deprived of the privileges of these offices. They were prohibited from visiting friends and relations in all the twenty-six wards and were confined to their own locality. The funeral rites of their members were boycotted, and daughters of the other wards who had married unto Umudei were not allowed to visit their agnates. When they died, their corpses were buried by Umudei and this applied to the daughters of Umudei who had married into Oguta wards. The Obi's festivals were boycotted. The loyalty of the people was transferred to Obi Mberekpe. They held staunchly to their traditional belief that they had acted constitutionally and therefore defied the government.

After seven years of this boycott the Government was forced to review the matter. They appointed a committee headed by one of the junior ministers, the Hon. Ukuta. This Committee heard evidence from both sides, and recommended:

> "That the attempt to increase arbitrarily the number of Olilinzele should stop.
> "That Oguta people should accept and recognise Obi Nnani[13] Ojiako and that after him Oguta people should have the right to select and crown their Obi and that the Obi Ojiako should recognise the subordinate Obi."
> "That the Obi should perform acts and celebrate festivals with the people and other Ezeigwe."[14]

This was in September 1965 and in the following year the government appointed the new Obi Ndokwu as the President of Oguta Urban Council, after Oguta people had pledged that they would withdraw their sanctions against the Obi Ojiako. They did this, and today both Obis are recognised by the government and allegiance to them now depends on Obi Ojiako fulfilling some of the terms of the settlement.

CONCLUSIONS

These three instances of deposition give us a clear idea of the constitutional position of the Obi in the political system. First, there is a clear notion of what the position of a monarch is in the political framework. Secondly, sovereignty of the people expressed through the assembly recognised in the state is supreme and binds both the Obi and the people alike. Thirdly, the presidency of the Obi at the Council sitting is a matter of constitutional routine, since assemblies can proceed without him, as was the case, but decisions bind him automatically. Fourthly, the determination of the action of an Obi and the interpretation given to it depends on the considerations arising out of each action and the gravity with which the assembly view it. Fifthly, established precedents which serve as case laws can guide decisions at any particular period.

In the three instances, the offences committed by each of the reigning Obis were not similar, but they have been classified as offences which threatened the welfare of the community.

The interpretation of such offences is the prerogative of the Council who are the repository of custom. The charges brought against these Obis amounted to criminal charges and therefore involved obligatory intervention of the entire people to remedy the situation. In matters where only disciplinary measures are taken, as we shall show later, such offences are considered civil.

There is another fact which emerges from these depositions. Each Obi lost his office, but the throne continued to be honoured as the symbol of political unity. The action of the people cannot be termed rebellious for they were raising constitutional issues, and the rebellion differed from Gluckman's and other concepts of rebellion, but retaining the principle of regarding offences as against the person of the king and not the institution itself. Further, while in the case of Gluckman's Barotse the deposed king is replaced by another member of his lineage, here, at Oguta, the group is held responsible and the kingship is given to another group. The two kings Agadagba and Ogwuala lost their office and their lineages also lost (in the case of Ogwuala) the right to the kingship. The office and the royalty were transferred because the principle of hereditary kingship in Oguta differs from the societies referred to by Gluckman. In Oguta as we have seen, princes who provoke rebellion may jeopardise their position, since such rebellion may lead to the loss of the throne by the ward.

The people of Oguta look upon the Obi and his Council as the mainspring of their political life and the bond which keeps the balance of political power. The various segments of Oguta are represented by their ritual and political heads, and this framework provides that all actions should reflect the true nature of the segmentary representative nature of the constitution. These officials of the Council who represent the political segments of the state must act together, for they are regarded as able and competent leaders because on specific important issues they are guided by the moral political principle of the land. They hold the Ofo of their respective ancestors and they are collective defenders and guardians of the territorial earth deity, which again unites the people ritually and territorially. Weber sums up the position by his statement that "the exercise of traditional authority is normally orientated to the question of what the chief and his administrative staff will normally permit, in view of the traditional obedience of the subjects and what will or will not arouse their resistance. When resistance occurs, it is directed against the person of the chief or a member of his staff. The accusation is that he (the servant, as Oguta people euphemistically say) has failed to observe the traditional limit of his authority. Opposition is not directed against the system as such.

The constitutional precedents that arise from these depositions are firstly, that any act which affects the public morality and evokes the feeling of the people, can eventually lead to the loss of the sacred influence of the king and make him lose the support of the Council and the community, and be denounced by them. Secondly, any act that implies a desertion of the people in the face of a danger of attack by an enemy, such as threatening their physical well-being, could lead to deposition. Thirdly, any act which the people consider a threat to their common property—which in our example is land—could lead to deposition. Fourthly, when an Obi participates in factional politics, that is, by supporting one faction against another in order to gain political advantage against the Council and the people, he has committed an act which leads to the loss of his position as father of the state. Fifthly, any violation of the sacred taboos which he must observe in the interest of the community might draw public anger against him. Lastly, when the Obi flaunts the constitution as he did by wrongfully awarding Ofilinzele titles, he is subject to discipline.

These six principles are conventional rules that have been deduced from the incidents which have occurred within the political structure.

Correction of an Obi

A disagreement between the Obi and the council begins by a report being lodged with the Ogana, the head of the college of Ofilinzele. He summons the Ofilinzele who are closest to the Obi and they discuss the issue with the representatives of the segments within the royal lineage, and try to resolve the issue. If at this stage they fail to resolve the issue, then the Obieze, the assembly of the council and the people, is summoned. At this assembly, the matter is fully discussed, reference being made not to the Obi directly but to "his servant" (odibo), and if this public assembly finds that the odibo has erred, for the Obi cannot err, the Ogana, the chief speaker at the assembly, will state that "odibo dala iwu", the servant has erred.

Two forms of punishment can be imposed. One form is a fine called "ikpuchi afala". The Obi puts a certain amount of money that he considers appropriate into a plate. This is covered and brought out and placed before the council. The council cannot tell the Obi the exact fine that he should pay and they must accept what he gives, though it is understood that a man of his status should pay something substantial. Another form of fine is known as "igbagbu efi". That is, a cow is shot and the Obi pays the owner whatever is deemed to be the price.

Evidence of conflicts between some Obis and the council occurred in every reign. From about 1880 till the revolt of 1958 there are instances of disagreements between the Obis and their councils which substantiate the fact that Obis can be fined by the council when they err.

In 1923 Obi Nnani Ohanyili, who has been revered as one of the most influential Obis for several decades, collected tolls from traders who were selling their goods in the market, contrary to the rule that markets are free and tolls should not be imposed. This action was further considered a violation of the royal role, for an Obi should not indulge in acts that go against the interest of his subjects. The council met and found his action improper and he was fined. About the same time he visited the house of one Obedike Mazi who was feasting his age set of which the Obi was a member. This was contrary to the law, for having once become a king, he has abandoned his association with his age set, and should not pay any private visits to anyone. The council similarly protested and the Obi was made to pay the cost of a cow killed by them in protest against his conduct.

Obi Adikea passed most of his life at Osomari, with his mother's lineage. He thought he belonged to that lineage and therefore had the right to compete for political office there and was entitled to all jural rights of this lineage. However, when the throne of Osomari was vacant and he thought he was qualified to compete, he was reminded that he was an adopted member and was only eligible for the Obiship of Oguta. During his reign (1926–36), Obi Adikea inadvertently made a statement in the court which implied that he was the king of Osomari. Again the council rallied and challenged his statement, and he was fined.

Over-powerful Chiefs

In Oguta, as at Onitsha, it is possible for a powerful chief to challenge the Obi by usurping some of the prerogatives of the king. Two instances have occurred in Oguta history.

The Iyasara Igwulu Enefua. According to Oguta tradition, this Iyasara was one of the richest Iyasara of his day. He was known as Eze Ihulu Ife, a king who dealt in two hundred units. He had two hundred wives, two hundred slaves and bought things in two hundred units. Wealthy and powerful, he felt that he should extend his own privileges of office by usurping those of the Obi. According to tradition, the Obi uses the ibom (a metal-made gong) for summoning people to the palace and this is exclusive to him. An Iyasara uses a hand bell. Iyasara Igwulu Enefua usurped the Obi's privilege by using an ibom to summon Oguta people to the annual feast at his palace. The Iyasara's messenger went around proclaiming that the people were summoned by the Iyasara and on reaching Umudei ward, Obi Ebonwu ordered that the messenger be arrested and the ibom seized. This was done. The Obi sent his own messenger with an ibom to go round the town and proclaim to the people what had transpired. On reaching Umuenu, the ward of this Iyasara, Igwulu Enefua ordered the Obi's messenger to be arrested and the Obi's ibom to be confiscated. This was immediately carried out by his people, who were anxious to retaliate.

Tension arose, and both began to show their might by going further to prove that they could usurp each other's rights. Obi Ebonwu conferred the Iyasara title on one Eyiche Odinibe, a wealthy man from Abatu. This meant that the Obi transferred the Iyasara title to another lineage contrary to the rule, for the Iyasara, as pointed out in Chapter 4, is a title hereditary to the Umuenu and Umunkwokomoshi wards. The Iyasara Enefua retaliated by raising himself to the status of the Obi by assuming the full privileges of the Obi. Having done this he conferred the office of Obi on one Animene Iwaeze Oguti from Umopu ward, a ward forbidden to take the title, as it supplies the Osere, the priest of the Ikwa Muo cult. A male from this ward cannot take an Olilinzele title, as we have explained earlier in this chapter, and it was even worse to make him an Obi. This action of Iyasara Enefua was calculated to debase the status of the king, and to punish the royal lineage.

The council of the state intervened and after a series of meetings, the solution reached was that the candidates so crowned, the Iyasara Eyiche and the Obi Animene, should take an oath to surrender their titles after death, and that no one should ever take the title again in their lineages. This was done and the rift was settled.

The Ndanike Obua Ajukwu.   Towards the end of the last century Oguta had one Ndanike Obua Ajukwu of very great power and influence. His military strength was great and his influence extended to all the Niger Ibo kingdoms where he fought and won many battles. He was to begin with an active supporter of the early missionaries and of the Royal Niger Company, both of whom recognised his influence and felt safe to carry on business with him. Like Iyasara Enefua, Ndanike Obua purposely defied the authority of the Obi by debasing the status of the office. This he did by crowning one of his slaves as king. He made him wear a king's regalia and perform the formalities of an Obi. He sent him round the town parading with a crowd of his slaves around him and showered praises on him.

Ndanike Obua then feasted a large number of people and placing this slave on the throne made the audience come forward and greet him as if he was an Obi. By equating the title of Obi with that which a slave bears, he made a mockery of the office. By doing this, his intention was to show that the office of Ndanike which he bore was superior to that of the Obi. With the military might he had no one could challenge his improper action, and he got away with his mockery of the significance of the kingship.

But as he continued to molest the peace of the town, the council of the State was relieved when he challenged the authorities of the Royal Niger Company and was deported by them to Calabar in 1902. The Ndanike title has remained vacant since then.

Disputes between Ogbe

Royal and Iyasara Wards vs Ndichie Wards.   In 1949 other Oguta wards felt that the privileges of their representatives, the Ndichie, were threatened, and they rose with one voice to protest against the efforts of the royal ward to usurp the privileges of the Ndichie. In that year, the Iyasara ward of Umuenu in collaboration with Udom Obi Ezediaro of Umudei, issued a proclamation curtailing the prerogatives of the Ndichie. The edict was meant to deprive the Ndichie of their regalia of office. These royal wards felt that some of the Ndichie regalia were the same as those of their offices (Obi and Iyasara) and therefore proclaimed that the Ndichie be forbidden:

"To wear eagle feathers in front of their official cap (okpu omu). That no person in the town should wear the ododo (red gown) cloth, which is exclusive to the Obi and Iyasara. That no Okpala should rub white clay (nzu) around his eyes. That no elder should wear around his neck the teeth of the tiger (eze agu)."[15]

These were part of the traditional regalia of every Okpala.

The non-royal wards, being incidentally more numerous, felt that this was a challenge to their heads, the Ndichie, and the entire members of these wards rallied around these officials who constituted one of the colleges of the council. They were summoned by the Ogene, the head of the Ndichie, to a meeting at one of the constitutional places for assembly, the Akpatakwuma. There they unanimously decided to apply sanctions, namely, the boycott of the royal and Iyasara wards. The Ogene assumed the leadership of the town and they issued the following resolution:

"That we unanimously agree that we should remain separate from them, and we bind ourselves with the following laws, the violation of which by any individual or quarter shall be punished by a fine of five pounds (£5).

(a)   Nobody from us should answer the Obieze call.
(b)   No cases should be settled at Obieze.
(c)   The annual royal dinner (nni eze) should be boycotted together with his festival of Iluma Chukwu, installing the deity of the High God in honour.
(d)   That the royal feasts at Ibina and Omalife should be boycotted.
(e)   That anyone who killed a leopard should not take it to the Obi's residence, but to Akpatakwuma where it will be butchered in the presence of Ndichie."[16]

This last law was formerly the prerogative of the Obi who was entitled to take the teeth and the skin of the animal.

The resolution, which was written and interpreted at the meeting, was adopted. The Ogene Azogu Ezeanyibala and the Ogene Nwanya Nwoji Akapati (head of the council of female elders) put their thumb impressions on behalf of the Ndichie of both sexes. They resolved that the Ogene's messenger should summon the people for meetings with a bell. After weeks of tension and complete boycott and isolation of the royal lineages, they pleaded to the council and the matter was resolved by the intervention of some of the Olilinzele chiefs, and the Obi and Iyasara rescinded their proclamation.

The Umudei Royal Ward and the Ezeukwu.   Another instance, which occurred in 1940, was the effort of Umudei ward under Udom Obi Ijoma to curtail the privilege of the kingmaker Ezeukwu by trying to deprive him of his right to his regalia of office. Umudei prosecuted this important official of the state for wearing the red robe, which the royal ward argued was exclusive to the Obi. After the installation of the Ezeukwu it is customary that he should go to the Egbenuka shrine at Ngegwu to offer a sacrifice. He does so fully robed in his regalia of office. Six weeks after the Ezeukwu's installation he prepared for this sacrifice, and because the shrine is located at the northern limit of the town he had to pass through Umudei royal ward. These people, it was alleged, were ready to halt him on his way past their ward and take the robe from him. He did go by, however, and no one of the Umudei had the courage to do what they planned. According to my informants, the people attributed this to the amulet that the said Ezeukwu wore, which made every member of Umudei fear.

They then resorted to court action and brought a suit against him twenty-four miles from Oguta, in the magistrates' court at Owerri, the headquarters of the province named after it. The magistrate felt that he had no jurisdiction to try such a case and ordered that it be taken to the native court (customary court). The judges in this court were drawn from the thirteen neighbouring village groups (obodo) that make up the Oguta Native Administration, now Oguta County Council. Oguta judges were also represented, and in the interpretation of the customary rule of kingship, the Ezeukwu ward felt that such a mixed court with persons who did not know about the rules of kingship was not competent to interpret the law or to determine the issue involved in the suit.

According to them, the people of the Umudei royal ward were able to manœuvre the majority of judges who eventually awarded judgement in their favour. The robes of the Ezeukwu were confiscated, but put in the custody of the court. The Ezeukwu ward did not give up, and put up petitions and appealed against the judgement. The case dragged on for about one and a half years, when the decision of the court was rescinded, and the Ezeukwu was given his robes back to use them for his official duties without molestation.

OSOMARI

The segmentary nature of the Osomari state makes for internal autonomy within each of the political divisions of the state. The relationship between one unit and the other is clearly defined, though the two divisions of Isiolu and Umuonyiogwu often dispute their respective seniority. This dispute as to who is the next in rank to the Atamanya often arises but is not one that has resulted in conflict. While I was in the field each division tried to emphasise the seniority of their divisional head over the other, but they could not remember whether such claims of seniority had ever led to an open rift in the state. What has led to open conflict is the situation where when one head of a division tries to usurp the political privileges of the other. Again, if conflicts occur within a division, it is likely that the personalities involved in such conflicts will appeal to other neutral segments and seek to involve them. Thus conflicts which originated in a single division have come to involve the entire community. To illustrate these points we can cite two examples.

The first was the efforts of two personalities from the non-royal divisions of Isiolu and Umuonyiogwu to usurp the office of the king by crowning themselves Atamanya[17] with the support of their agnates, which has been discussed in Chapter 9.

The second was the internal struggle for succession to the office of Iyase in the Inwala lineage of Isiolu. In 1937 a crisis developed when two candidates Onwodi and Egonu contested the vacant office of Iyase and this contest raised a constitutional problem in the state. The two candidates enlisted the support of the Olinzele of the various divisions. Their mothers belonged to two major lineage groups in Ugolo royal ward. Both were therefore Nwadiani (sisters' sons) of Ugolo. Ugolo ebo was thus drawn into a conflict that began in another division. Onwodi's mother came from Odogwu Mafe lineage and Egonu's from Alabo. Each of them appealed to his mother's agnates. Egonu was a man of wealth and relatively younger, and not, under the principle established for succession to the office, eligible for the office. But because he was a wealthy person and could buy the support of other people his intention was to win the contest so as to change this principle of succession based on seniority of age, and throw the title open to men of wealth and influence, placing it on a par, in this respect, with the method of the choice of the Atamanya and the Oniniogwu titles of Ugolo and Umuonyiogwu respectively.

He was backed by his matrikinsmen and the majority of Isiolu ebo, his own agnates. Supporters from both divisions carried him to his residence (ibu eze) and crowned him Iyase.

Onwodi's supporters from Ugolo rallied around him and from the residence of the Edogu Ajie of Isiolu they carried him to his residence and crowned him Iyase, claiming that only their rituals were legitimate.

Since neither would vacate the throne for the other, nor be destooled, the people waited for both to die before deciding on the principle of succession to be adopted. Iyase Egonu, the younger man died first, and of course, some attributed his early death to his violation of the custom. When the other Iyase died the men of Inwala lineage of Isiolu who had the right to the title decided to reaffirm the principle of succession based on seniority by age. It has remained so till now, though no Iyase has been crowned at the moment.

CONCLUSION

The foregoing analysis of the conflicts between the chiefs and the kings shows that the constitutional framework imposes specific checks on the king and the chiefs, and they are required to conform to the rules of the constitution. The kings in their coronation rituals are made to take the oath of office to abide by the rules of the constitution, and to rule the people well. So also the chiefs are admonished through their oath of office to serve the interests of their people. This applies to all these states.

There are, however, variations in the methods of dealing with the abuse of constitutional authority in these states. At Oguta it is done by deposition of a recalcitrant Obi. At Abo it is done by a rebellion in which the king is killed according to their myth which is daily reaffirmed every morning by the voice of the talking drum that reminds the Obi of this past myth. The chiefs can withdraw their support by boycott. This obtains in the four states. The boycott is by a group not by an individual. Obis can also be punished by a fine at Oguta and Abo.

The practice of vesting major titles in particular lineages at Abo, Oguta and Osomari, and not allowing all the titles to be the gift of the Obi is another way of checking his power. Powerful chiefs are also able to set themselves up against the Obi in exceptional circumstances. The only historical record of it occurred during the nineteenth century with the economic development which arose in connection with the palm oil trade. It enabled some men to acquire wealth and to use it for political purposes as shown by the examples at Oguta and Onitsha. The examples of wealthy traders at Onitsha and Oguta illustrate how wealthy men can challenge the authority of the constitution and go unpunished.

It is also possible for ogbe, as at Oguta and for political divisions as at Onitsha and Osomari to withdraw from general activities with the rest of the community, or to seek to enforce their rights against other sections of the community by the use of the boycott and similar sanctions.

NOTES

1 Memorandum submitted by Ndichie, 1963.
2 From an Intelligence Report written in 1935 and quoted in Harding, 1963, p. 24.

3   M. O. Ibeziako, 1937, p. 9.
4   Ibid.
5   Memorandum submitted by Ndichie, 1963.
6   Charles Obi, *History of Abo*.
7   Max Weber, 1947, p. 342.
8   There is a similar myth, recorded by Boston, in connection with the succession of Amachoto, the kingship at Idah. J. S. Boston, 1964, p. 121.
9   Oguta judges in most cases behave like Barotse judges and apply the concept of 'reasonable man' in their verdicts. M. Gluckman, 1955. Chapter III, 1963, Chapter VII, p. 183.
10 Cp. M. Fortes, 1959, p. 38.
11 H. N. Harcourt, Report of Inquiry 1961, p. 10.
12 The Harcourt Commission, 1961.
13 Oguta call their Obi "Nnani", father of all.
14 Ukuta Report, 1965.
15 Resolution of twenty-four wards of Oguta, 1949.
16 Ibid.
17 E. Agha, *Ijoma* (date not stated), p. 10.

Chapter 11 Summary and Conclusions

To avoid a dogmatic approach to the classification of the kingdoms we have studied we shall examine their systems by comparing their similarities, and by noting the special characteristics common to any group of them as revealed by our findings.

In these kingdoms there are some structural units and associations (e.g. title societies) which have political significance, and others which are social and not political. There are associations based on age without power and those based on age with political power. There are titles with priestly functions which carry political as well as ritual functions. These social groupings are found in one form or another in each state, but frequently are used for performing a particular function in one state and used differently in another.[1]

Our first concern then is to distinguish how each state uses particular variables which appear common to all of them, and then we shall show the similarities peculiar to any group of them.

COMMON CHARACTERISTICS

BENIN AND IDAH INFLUENCES

These states fall within one cultural environment and, as riverain people, they share common riverain activities such as fishing, agricultural pursuits and trading along the River Niger. There were basic elements of cultural contact and borrowing in their political organisation, even though each kingdom resisted outside domination.

They all attributed their origin to outside kingdoms, either to Benin or Idah, and they derive their system of government to some extent from the political structure of the capital of these older kingdoms. For example, apart from Oguta they share the same features of division of the state into royal and non-royal. The king comes from the royal division, a situation that confers prestige upon the royal division; this is balanced, however, by the recruitment of the next most senior official from the non-royal division. The kings, as in these older kingdoms, appoint titled

255

chiefs who perform particular functions, many of which are performed by the chiefs in the older kingdoms. But although they borrow these title names from the older kingdoms, they vary both the names and the functions of the office. Thus, a title in a higher grade in one state may be relegated to a lower grade in another. A title which bears the same name has a different function in one state from that which it has in another. There are titles and praise names associated with them but what is regarded as a title in one state, could be only a praise name in another state and vice versa. Titles may be limited in one state and elaborate in another.

In all these changes the variations in grade and rank reflect the variations in the functions of these borrowed titles. Thus we find that Benin titles like Oniha, the head of the Uzama chiefs in Benin (found in Onitsha, Abo and Osomari), Edaikan, the title of the Oba's heir in Benin (Ndanike at Oguta and Abo), Iyase and Asagba (found in the four states), and Osuma (found in Onitsha) carry different statuses and roles in these four states.

Though Onitsha and Abo are closer to the Benin and Igala model in the dichotomy between royal and non-royal divisions, Oguta and Osomari clearly distinguish the position of the royal lineage in the political system. The royalty is emphasised by the establishment of royal palaces and palace officials, which we find in all them, though the palace officials at Benin and Idah are more elaborate than those of the Niger kingdoms. The Obi of Abo, however, has Idibo titles which we find at Idah, and he awards these titles to his wives, as the Oba of Benin does to his senior wives. These have ritual functions as have the Idibo of Abo. Oguta and Osomari confer titles on the senior wife of their Obi, but no such equivalent title exists in Onitsha.

The principle of primogeniture in the choice of a successor to the crown does not apply in these states. At Osomari the royal lineage is an adaptation of the Igala system in which, as Boston has shown,[2] the royal clan superimposes this political system on the Igala Mele, the non-royal division, as the Osomari Igala stock has done by superimposing their own political system on the autochthonous clans of Ndam, Umuchi, and the later migrant group of Umuoga. They also follow the Igala model of having separate offices for each political group. Abo adopts also this system, though in a different way, but Onitsha and Oguta do not. Osomari also models its political organisation according to the Igala political organisation at Idah (the capital), where a sub-royal group is divided into three divisions, each having its own head and titles.

SOCIAL AND POLITICAL ORGANISATION

All the kingdoms studied in this thesis have a political organisation based on a constitutional monarchy, the king being the focus of political unity, and the royal and non-royal groups play particular roles in connection with the position of the king.

The personnel of these states is grouped into political segments which are based on descent, and these segmentary structures coincide with the administrative units of the state. Each level of the segmentation constitutes a policy-making group, or council, the highest being that of the State Council composed of the Obi and his chiefs.

These administrative units consist of the ebo—six at Onitsha, four at Abo, nine at Osomari (which are grouped into three primary political divisions under Isiolu ebo, Ugolo ebo and Umuonyiogwu ebo) and none at Oguta. The component units of these ebo are, except at Osomari, the ogbe (twenty-two at Onitsha, sixteen at Abo and twenty-seven at Oguta), and constitute the base of the political pyramid. At Osomari the ebo are equivalent to ogbe.

These ebo and ogbe administrative units coincide with the descent system. They are patrilineages and, as Fortes has pointed out, in societies of this type the lineage is not only a corporate unit in the legal or jural sense, but is also the primary political association.[3]

However, those descent units (ebo and ogbe) are subordinate to the state council, which consists of the Obi as the head, and the grades of chiefs are ranked according to specified order, and drawn from these various administrative units of the state. The power to direct the affairs of the state resides in this council, and the degree of centralization rests also on the specific status and roles of the composition of its members and the constitutional position of the king in the states.

In all of them the state council is the focus of political activity and becomes the factor that unites its various political segments. Hence, at Onitsha and Abo, it should balance the position of the chiefs representing the royal and non-royal divisions; and at Oguta and Osomari, it brings together the chiefs from the different political segments (ogbe, ebo). It becomes the centralizing power structure which is used to hold the various segments together and carry out the activities of government.

The degree of centralization varies in the different states. Thus at Onitsha and Abo we have an inner council which we styled the privy council. (Ndichie Ume at Onitsha, and the senior first grade Olinzele of both divisions at Abo.) They constitute the core of the power structure. Oguta and Osomari do not have privy councils of this sort.

All these states have, besides a state council (Izu Ndichie or Olinzele) a general assembly, known as Izu Obodo, in which the chiefs, the political class, consult the general public and obtain their opinion and also communicate the council's decisions to them so that the public will be in a position to approve and to help carry them out. The frequency with which the state council or the privy council uses this sort of policy-making body varies from state to state, but its structure is a common feature in all the kingdoms.

We find, therefore, at the state level, two common organisational structures: the state council and the general assembly. Below these councils are the councils organised in the administrative units of the ebo or the ogbe.

RECRUITMENT OF CHIEFS

In the states under discussion kings have the prerogative of appointing some (Oguta and Osomari) or all (Abo and Onitsha) of the chiefs. Those so appointed pay title fees to the kings and to the chiefs of the same and higher grades in the hierarchy. These chiefs are grouped into a number of grades in each state. There are specific qualifications and rules regulating the appointment of chiefs which vary from state to state. The chiefs so appointed enjoy particular privileges of office such as specific regalia and elaborate mortuary rites and other special social distinctions, though the degree of these privileges depends on the prestige scale of the office in relation to the grades of officials in each state.

Their selection is based on two principles: a plutocratic principle i.e. on a basis of wealth and power; a gerontocratic principle i.e. on a basis of age. Three of these states—Abo, Oguta and Osomari —recognise both principles of selection, and Onitsha, except in the case of ritual offices (Okpala), emphasises only the principle of selection based on wealth.

THE JUDICIAL SYSTEM

The organisation of courts in these states corresponds to their administrative structure. All the courts are hierarchically graded, the lowest being the minimal unit of the political administration, the ogbe, the highest being the court of the Obi. Their judiciary system is centralised in the hands of the Obi and members of the council.

Besides these units, they also include other judicial bodies, by allowing the senior chiefs to organise courts of their own to dispense justice, so as to ensure that there are no difficulties for the people to seek redress on judicial matters. At Abo, the Odua, who holds a key position in the state, is allowed to organise his own court to which he can invite members of the Olinzele to assist as court judges. At Oguta the four kingly officials (the Iyasara, the Ndanike, the Ezeukwu and the Ezekoro) are allowed to hold courts at their palaces to which members of the other colleges of Olilinzele and Ndichie can be invited. Furthermore the Ogene, the head of the Ndichie, can also organise a court at his palace which is attended by the Ndichie and the Olilinzele.

EXECUTIVE AGENCIES

All the states have agencies through which the administrative officials carry out or enforce their activities of government. The age grades, corporate lineages, women's organisations, ritual associations and title associations are all social groups whose members are charged with specific functions by members of the State Council. These agencies carry out obligatory and non-obligatory functions. They resort to the chiefs to seek redress against any infringement of the rules of their group, as well as bringing pressure to bear on the chiefs to ensure that they do not abuse their constitutional position.

WAR ORGANISATION

Because of this cardinal principle of the supremacy of the state in matters of defence, each state has developed an elaborate system of defence. The unity of the state is emphasised during times of war, and is expressed in the organisation of the units of defence in ways that minimise opposition or differentiation between the political segments within it. The war chiefs are able to recruit their military contingents from the rank and file of the population. Women are not excluded, and war, as we have explained, becomes the concern of the whole state. It emphasises the value of the statehood and affirms sentiments of national solidarity. Victory in war implies greater status for the king and the chiefs, and the material rewards of war are commensurately enticing for the military officials who endeavour, in each state, to discharge their obligations and duties to the interest of the state and to the glory of their office.

THE KINGSHIP

In Chapter 7 we showed that all these states have myths that validate the office of kingship and rituals that consecrate their political systems. Their kings perform specific duties to sustain the ritual of the office. These duties also impose specific obligations which must be fulfilled in order to sustain the institution. These include secular notions such as elaborate praise names, as at Onitsha; special insignia of office with specific secular and ritual meanings; specific national festivals which are exclusive to the kings and which reintegrate people with the office; accession rituals which are special to them and validate their office; and special mortuary rites that integrate and emphasize the myth of continuity of the office.

In all these states the king is the head of the society. He presides at the council meetings and on social and ritual occasions. The officials of the state assist in the course of his performing these state duties, hence at the state and general assemblies, the Iyase at Onitsha and Abo, and the Ogene at Oguta, and the Odaje Asi at Osomari act as deputies and speak on behalf of their kings.

Succession to the Office. There are similar rules governing the succession to the kingship and the candidate must satisfy specific conditions which can qualify him for this election. The selection body is restricted to the royal lineage, but the approval of the person chosen is the concern of the chiefs, for the choice becomes the concern of the whole people.

During the interregnum all have a system of regency, though this varies from state to state.

Investiture. The importance of the office is further demonstrated by the way the people adapt their constitution through the distribution of the role of the kingmakers among the political divisions of the state, particularly the two divisions into royal and non-royal groups. The making of their king is a national concern. These officials must play their part so as to validate the legal sanctity of the office holder. Though, as in the case of the Onitsha, it is not often that they support the same candidates.

There are stages in the rituals of accession (Chapter 8) which must be followed and the completion of these stages validate the office holder. They endeavour to adhere to the fulfilment of these ceremonial stages and where a person who assists in any of the stages is ignored because of a dispute arising from succession, as at

Onitsha in 1931–35 and in 1961–63, they accept alternative personnel to perform any of these stages.

In the course of the investiture of their kings, the regalia of office, as explained, are significant to all of them, and these carry symbolic meanings which demonstrate the secular and ritual positions of a king in the political system. The chiefs may share some of this regalia with their kings, particularly the senior chiefs at Oguta, Onitsha and Osomari, but their emblems of office are never rated higher than those of the king. He must not be surpassed by any of his subjects.

Mortuary Rituals.   The mortuary rites discussed in Chapter 8 are elaborate. In all of them the secular and ritual aspects of kingship are emphasised. Some of these rituals emphasise the continuity of the office by a repetition of the same aspects of rituals conducted at the installation ceremony. This is more noticeable at Oguta and Osomari than at Onitsha and Abo.

In all of them they observe the secrecy of a king's death. His death is spoken of euphemistically, for the king never dies. It is a calamity to the nation, and at Onitsha all political titles are stopped until the completion of the mortuary rites. The chiefs mourn for the death of the king.

At the mortuary rites of kings their eldest sons play important roles which confirm the notion of their fathers' continuity. At Onitsha the senior son assumes the role of the father by impersonating him at the annual ceremony of the Ofala, which marks the last stage of the mortuary rites. The senior son of the Obi of Oguta assumes the role of the regent (Udom) and also officiates during the mortuary ceremonies of his deceased father. Abo and Osomari do not follow this procedure, but the Odua at Abo and the Ogene at Osomari are the regents, and the senior son of the Atamanya continues to offer regular sacrifices to the ofo until the funeral rites are over and the Ogene becomes regent. Onitsha makes the Iyase regent.

Balance of Power.   The kings are not despotic monarchs. There are checks and balances in each constitution which regulate the conduct of the monarch. Their oaths of office bind them to abide by the rule of the land, to consult the chiefs and to rule wisely. The right of an Obi to appoint chiefs does not imply that he is free to do so without restrictions. At Onitsha he is specifically required to appoint the highest senior official from the non-royal division, and must be judicious in distributing the officers between the various divisions and sub-divisions of the state. The Obi of Abo has to appoint officers of the state from within the political division to which the offices belong. At Oguta he is confined to the appointment of Olilinzele. Even in this sphere he shares this right with the Iyasara. Further, he is restricted from distributing these titles as he wishes, for he may not distribute them to specific lineages, including his own lineage. We have shown in Chapter 10 how the violation of this rule led to a deposition of a king.

Chiefs have the right to oppose a recalcitrant monarch who abuses the rule of kingship. This right is exercised in different forms in each state. At Onitsha they can boycott the palace; alternatively, a section of the chiefs can deprive the king of his ritual roles. At Abo the chiefs can also boycott the palace and can impose a fine on the king, though the charge is made overtly against his chief minister, the Iyase and the Obi's senior son, the Akpulosu. The myth of the despotic Obi which is repeated every morning by the royal drum, ufie, reminds the Obi that he can rule only with the consent of his chiefs, and must therefore remember the despotic king who suffered for not abiding by the rules of the constitution. At Oguta, the king's position is less secure, and each instance of deposition has been cited as a constitutional precedent in their history. We have shown how these have been applied in the case of three deposed kings. Oguta chiefs can boycott the king and resort to another place for meetings; and decisions reached at these meetings are binding on the Obi. The king can be fined and also reprimanded, though not overtly—the charge has to be directed against odibo (his servant). At Osomari the king can be boycotted and/or reprimanded, but there has been no case of deposition. In all of these states, the errors of the kings are referred to euphemistically and indirectly; for, in theory, a king cannot err.

The realisation of the fact that powerful chiefs can usurp the role of a king is another important check on a king's power. This, however, occurs frequently in the states where the king does not appoint all the chiefs. That is why at Oguta, as we have shown, a kingly chief has on occasion assumed the role of an Obi. Such incidents have also occurred at Onitsha, as we have seen, and also at Osomari when two powerful persons from the non-royal ebo assumed the office of the king.

It is not only in this way that powerful chiefs can oppose a recalcitrant Obi; the chiefs themselves are a source of power which can be used to counterbalance the authority arising from the constitutional position of the king. At Onitsha the position of the Iyase is that of an opponent of the Obi and he leads the Ndichie of the first and second grades in opposition against the king. The Ndanike at Abo also plays the role of leader of the opposition to the Obi, and the Odua who is not appointed by the Obi holds a specific position in the constitutional arrangement. Since courts can be held at his residence and he can consult with the chiefs and also act as the regent, his position is of a restrictive nature vis-à-vis the Obi.

At Oguta the kingly chiefs not appointed by the Obi are neutral whenever there is a dispute between the Obi and the Ndichie who are the representatives of the political segments of the states. The leader of this opposition is the Ogene, the head of Ndichie, and they sit separately. At Osomari the two kingly officials are, as at Onitsha and Oguta, not bound to support all the actions of the Atamanya, but the younger chiefs, the Isugbe, constitute a forward block within the council. The tripartite balance in the council indicates that the Atamanya's position is regulated because each political division could opt out if they felt the Atamanya had broken the conventions of the constitution.

An Obi can exploit his prerogative to award titles as a way of strengthening his position. An Obi protects his position by balancing the forces of opposition within the council. Through the distribution of titles within each political division, he is able to recruit into the division persons who are disposed to support him so that eventually power, concentrated in the council, can be wielded by an Obi through his supporters in the council.

In Onitsha, more than anywhere else, the Obi uses his power of appointment to secure political support. He can do this by concentrating particular offices in one division of the state, thus winning its support on a particular occasion. He can also use the award of titles within each division to win over a section of that division to his side, thus weakening any opposition to his power within the rest of the division.

At Abo the Ndanike, head of the Umudei Olinzele, leads the opposition, but the Obi counters through the Iyase, who together with the Olinzele of the Ndichie division, of which he is the head, defend the Obi. The Obi's son, the Akpulosu, supports him. The Umudei sit on the Obi's right, the Ndichie on his left. I have no instance of a breakdown in the constitution of Abo. The Obi is able to avoid the ritual consequences of a boycott of his council by all the Olinzele by the fact that his wives are given similar titles and are therefore able to perform the ritual duties associated with the Olinzele.

At Oguta the Obi counters the opposition of the Ndichie by using the Olilinzele whose head is the Ogana, the Obi's officer. This officer is appointed by the Obi. This prerogative of appointment is vital to the Obi since, in making this choice, he chooses a person favourably disposed towards him, and influential enough to command a hearing among the members of the Ndichie. The Olilinzele lobby members of the Ndichie and thus temper their attitude towards the Obi, thus affecting settlements of disputes between him and the Ndichie. When the Olilinzele and the Ndichie unite, the Obi has either to accede to the wish of the chiefs or face deposition.

At Osomari, where there is a tripartite balance, the seating arrangements at the state council in which the officials from the three divisions are intermixed, ensures that a form of consensus is arrived at in the state council or the assembly. In as much as the status of the head of the state is recognised by the other divisions, the state council continues to be united under the Atamanya, and his position becomes secure.

As long as a king continues to follow the rules of kingship, his sacred and secular status will remain the symbol of the people's admiration for him. The opposition from his chiefs must therefore have sufficient support from the people to be effective, and a popular king is often defended by his subjects against his chiefs.

SPECIAL CHARACTERISTICS

THE ONITSHA AND ABO MODEL

As pointed out elsewhere, various efforts have been made during the past twenty years to create particular models so as to distinguish particular political systems from the others.[4] Each classification is an attempt to analyse the material known to the author and it is only in this respect that we can accept that the model created is to reflect the 'latent' aspect of the society after the 'manifest' has been described (Morton).[5] A model becomes necessary as a means to explain political processes, and not in the sense of an idealized or simplified description of the structure or any particular kingdom in its totality (Lloyd).[6]

In the first part of this chapter we noted the common features characteristic of these kingdoms. But they show variations also in those institutional aspects which distinguish some of them as against others. We can, from our study, discern two political models which we can classify as the Onitsha and Abo model on the one hand, and the Oguta and Osomari model on the other.

Onitsha and Abo share greater common characteristics in the following respects:

Recruitment of Chiefs

In both these states the king recruits almost all the chiefs and recognises his position in respect of this vital fact; that he alone can confer the rights of chieftainship. The Obi of Onitsha appoints fifty-one chiefs from all members of the state, and even though he is supposed to accept various conventions in doing so, he is able, as we showed in Chapter 10, to disregard them to a considerable extent. Although he may provoke some political agitation through not obeying these conventions, he can get away with it when it does occur by splitting the members of the council and by balancing the opposition within it.

At Abo the same principle of recruitment obtains, even though there are two classes of title. The Obi has the prerogative of appointing all of them with the exception of the Odua, whose position, as explained above, helps to create a balance in the power structure. This, however, does not mean that an Obi cannot be an Odua. Obi Oputa (1916–67), was both king and the Odua by virtue of his being the oldest man of Umudei. He thus combined both offices. Like the Obi of Onitsha, he was able to manipulate members of his council in the way we have explained above, and thus balance the opposition.

In both states the chiefs are hierarchically graded into three groups, and constitute a distinct political association or class.[7] The most senior of these three groups is the elite who consult with the Obi in the day-to-day activities of the state. Below the Obi the most senior individual in the political hierarchy is selected by the Obi as his right-hand man, yet in both states, the Iyase at Onitsha, and the Ndanike at Abo, these officials are not only the right hand of the Obi but opponents of his authority and help to curb his powers. The Ndanike of Abo, who is the head of the chiefs of the royal division, performs the role of the Iyase of Onitsha in this connection but the Iyase at Abo is the Obi's right-hand man in the true sense.

The relative positions of both kings are differentiated in that while at Onitsha, the chiefs are recruited at random, irrespective of the distinction between the royal and non-royal division, at Abo the offices are restricted to one or the other of these groups. The Obi of Onitsha can, by this more open method of recruitment, pack the council with chiefs from a particular division. The Obi of Abo enjoys the other advantage of being able to use the chiefs of the non-royal division as his supporters, and he can by judicious distribution of titles within the royal division split the ranks of the royal group so as to weaken the forces of the opposition against him. Both kings are thus able to use the prerogatives of appointment to their own political advantage despite the checks and balances inherent in the constitution.

266 STUDIES IN IBO POLITICAL SYSTEMS

The Royal Lineage

At Onitsha and Abo the position of the royal division in terms of numbers can be a great advantage. In both states the royal division consists of several large corporate co-operative lineages which, when united, are able to act with disregard to the interests of the non-royal division. These royal lineages are relatively strong and wealthy, and at Onitsha they were so strong that for several decades and even as late as the 1940s (as we noted in Chapter 10) they retained the office of the Iyase which belonged to the non-royal division of Ugwunaobamkpa. Some of the Obis deliberately concentrated more of Ndichie Ume offices in the royal division. In both states, however, what strengthened the position of the non-royal division was that the royal lineages tended to break up into competing segments, each of which sought support from the other division. This occurs particularly in the period of succession. This point was discussed in Chapter 9.

In both states the members of the royal lineages are not debarred from taking a chiefly title. At Abo, the titles of the royal lineage are considered superior to those of the non-royal lineage. Furthermore, Abo ensures that the Iyase (the head of the non-royal Olinzele) must be the son of a daughter of the royal division, and this maternal tie is to make him remain faithful to the Obi.

The Balance of Power

The degree to which the constituent units of the state can act together determines the degree of centralization of the state. In both of these states they share the common feature that chiefs cannot act independently of the state council, headed by the Obi. All wars are waged in the name of the king and the chiefs pay tribute to him.

At Onitsha, however, the political divisions of Umuezechima and Ugwunaobamkpa can, in times of crisis, act separately. One way in which the chiefs of the Ugwunaobamkpa can check the power of an Obi is to unite in protest when an Obi abuses his power. When this occurs, as we explained in Chapter 10, the chiefs of the non-royal divisions assume a distinct political position, and take separate action boycotting the Obi's council. In this respect, the relative position of the Obi of Onitsha is weak compared with that of the Obi of Abo. At Abo the two political divisions are not territorially divided as at Onitsha, and the chiefs of both divisions have their own separate offices. This ensures that there is no conflict arising from the usurping of the office of one division by the other. This separation of titles has preserved Abo from the sort of agitation that is typical of the Onitsha system.

SUMMARY AND CONCLUSIONS 267

As we explained in Chapter 3, a common area of residence at Abo means that the duties allotted to the component segments of the state, the Ebo and Ogbe, are shared collectively by the chiefs of both divisions: they are members of the same corporate groups. Though Ndichie are members of lineages attached to particular Umudei lineages, they are both part of the same corporate residential groups and share all the jural rights of the group. Since the chiefs of these descent units are members of the state council and constitute not only a class but an interest group by itself, they tend to subordinate their lineage loyalty to that of the state of which they are a dominant power-cum-authority controlling body.

Lineage matters which conflict with state matters are in most cases avoided; where this avoidance becomes impossible, elements of instability tend to confront the state. That is why, in order to preserve the centralized authority of the state, the judiciary and the military structure are hierarchically organised and controlled by these chiefs who constitute the apex of the political hierarchy. All subordinate groups are controlled by them. The fact that both states concentrate more power in a smaller core of the senior chiefs, whom we styled members of the privy council, indicates the degree of centralization of power and authority in the state. Though the component lineages might have rights over land, and some ritual rites, the ritual functions of the king and the chiefs predominate. The chiefs levy taxes on behalf of the king and the subjects pay these levies to the chiefs as superior officials.

Onitsha and Abo share these institutional characteristics mentioned above, and conform to the theory formulated by Fortes (1953) that the more centralized the political system the more the corporate strength of the descent groups is reduced.[8] Fallers (1956) also indicates that in such situations conflict could arise if the lineage loyalty was not subordinate to that of the state, or if the lineage rights were usurped by the state.[9] Greater stability in Buganda, he maintains, "would appear to be associated with the fact that, at the level of the rulership, the lineage principle gives way to the state structure". This applies to Abo and Onitsha. The conflicts at Onitsha where the chiefs of one division boycotted the Obi, were conflicts arising from the ways the power of the state had been abused and not the usurpation of rights that belonged to a particular lineage, for legal and political status are conferred by the allegiance to the state and not by descent.[10]

The Succession

Succession conflicts at Abo and Onitsha are the result of the structural organisation of the royal lineages. The fact that in both states the rule of succession is not clearly defined means that there is no definite rule which ensures that every lineage within the royal division can supply an Obi.

The rule for the rotation of the office was forced upon Onitsha in 1899, but was rejected in 1931–35, and re-adopted in 1961–63. This acceptance of the principle of rotation, however, does not imply that conflicts in the period of succession no longer arise. It is on occasions like this that the political loyalty of the chiefs is expressed in terms of the loyalty to the state and the institution of kingship, and not to the lineage principle. Thus there is in both states the formation of blocs or alliances during the period of succession. Rival candidates seek political allies in other lineages. Corporate descent ideology is no longer considered and becomes negative, and one finds the formations of blocks which cut across lineage loyalties and alliances so as to achieve one's political ambition. The Onitsha example illustrates this. In the 1931–35 contest, four candidates from the Umuezearoli dynasty, which regarded itself as a corporate descent group, competed against each other, each seeking alliance outside the corporate group. None was ready to give way to the other. In 1961–63, when the dynasty of Umudei withdrew from the contest, four candidates from Umuezearoli again repeated the same action. Opponents might be one's own agnates or members of ones own dynasty. But lineage loyalty does not matter, for what is paramount is the individual's choice of strategic allies to enable him to achieve as Barth put it in his study of the Swat Pathans, his own aggrandisement.[11]

These political blocs emerge from the dissension among the chiefs. It is from these chiefs that contesting candidates seek support and they aggregate their own units of supporters within their blocs. At Onitsha, the two political blocs in 1931–35 were organised by two powerful chiefs, the Iyase Gbasuzor, and another senior chief of the Ndichie Ume grade. In the 1961–63 contest the same thing happened. The Iyase and the Ajie, both of the Ndichie Ume grade, with their numerous supporters, constituted two political blocs. At Abo, the candidates had often come from the royal dynasties of Umuojigbali and Umuobi. In both cases the support of a majority of Olinzele was an advantage, and it meant that the Olinzele as a group were divided at each contest between the two royal dynasties. Where there was a balance of power, as was the case in the 1905 contest, this balance was maintained by the unity and neutrality of the Olinzele who supported neither candidates.

Unlike the Pathans where land is the major 'booty' for bloc formation and forms the basis for conflicting political interests, the office of the Obi in these states is the fundamental interest, as a successful candidate distributes offices by awarding titles to his supporters. The potential political opponents are those of one's own lineages or dynasty who have the same interest in the office. The Obis of Onitsha distributed offices to appease an opposing royal dynasty, and also to buy the support of the non-royal division. This, though not clear from the data, might also have occurred at Abo. The stronger bloc, however, is that which ultimately wins the support, not necessarily of the majority of the chiefs, but of the majority of the population. At Onitsha in 1931–35, the bloc led by Iyase Gbasuzor and the majority of the Ndichie won, but only because it commanded the support of the people. In the 1961–63 contest the political bloc led by the Ajie and the minority of the Ndichie commanded the support of the majority of the members of the public and won, but the bloc led by the Iyase Anatogu, who had the support of the majority of the Ndichie but of a minority of the public, lost.

THE OGUTA AND OSOMARI MODEL

Oguta and Osomari share certain common characteristics and we will compare these common features in terms of the four variables that we used for Onitsha and Abo.

Recruitment of Chiefs
While the Obis of Onitsha and Abo can appoint all the chiefs, the position is different in Oguta and Osomari. The kings of these two towns do not appoint all the chiefs. The Obi of Oguta cannot appoint the four kingly chiefs but only members of the Olilinzele chiefs. Furthermore, he shares this prerogative with the Iyasara. The four kingly chiefs are located in specific lineages. Their titles, like that of the Obi, are acquired through the distribution of wealth. In both states again there is a category or grade of chiefs, Ndichie at Oguta, Ndichie Ume at Osomari whose titles are ascribed on the basis of age. At Oguta the Ndichie are the Ndi Okpala of their respective ogbe and represent them on the state council. At Osomari the Ndichie Ume are the senior ranking chiefs of their ebo.

At Oguta the Obi can select and appoint Olilinzele chiefs from any ogbe except those whose heads are forbidden from holding this office, and the Olilinzele respresent their respective ogbe in the State Council. The Ndi Okpala of ogbe possessing an Osere do not rank as Ndichie and do not attend the state council. In Osomari the Atamanya can only appoint chiefs of the Isugbe and from within his own ebo. He is merely notified of the titles which are awarded or ascribed in the other ebo. Thus in both states the position of the king is weak in relation to the chiefs, the position of the Atamanya being weaker in this respect than that of the Obi of Oguta. The kingly officials, the Ndichie and other senior chiefs do not owe their appointments to the king and this makes them more independent and provides a potential for opposition to the king by a powerful chief.

The Royal Lineage

While the royal clans at Onitsha and Abo consist of many lineages whose members are wealthy and populous, the royal lineages at Oguta and Osomari are limited each to one single descent group (ogbe at Oguta, ebo at Osomari) out of all the wards in the state. At Oguta only three ogbe at particular periods in their history have supplied the Obi, out of a total of twenty-seven. This makes the Obi's position weak and dependent on the goodwill and consensus of the chiefs and the public of the other ogbe. The king may not confer the Olilinzele title on any of his own agnates, thus he cannot pack the council with them. This relative position of weakness of the royal lineage (and ward) contrast with the size and power of the royal clans in Onitsha and Abo.

At Osomari the royal lineage (ebo) is in an even weaker position, not only because it is one of three political divisions, but also because the heads of each of the other two divisions are supported by grades of chiefs who are of equivalent hierarchies to that of the royal division. In other words, the fact that each of the three political divisions constitutes a semi-autonomous unit makes it possible for them either singly or jointly to establish their own political organisation in opposition to that of the royal division. The royal lineage depends, therefore, on other methods—for example, marriage to women from the non-royal lineages. Alternatively, daughters are used as diplomatic emissaries to gain the support of powerful chiefs and personnel in the non-royal wards. Whilst this occurs also at Oguta its use at Osomari is more vital for the preservation of the position of the royal ward. This was argued in Chapter 10. Again, its political position rests on the ability of its members to maintain a general consensus and balance of power in the political system.

The Succession

Oguta and Osomari do not, however, express the same kind of political conflict which arises from the choice of a successor to the throne, as in the Onitsha and the Abo model. Internal manœuvring goes on in the period of selection, but only within the royal lineage so that the solidarity of the lineage is maintained.

This solidarity is necessary because of the royal ward's relatively weak position in the state.

At Oguta, when the Umudei royal lineage was awarded the right to the throne, they resolved the problem of open conflict which might have arisen in the choice of a candidate by adopting the system already described in Chapter 9. According to this method every major lineage in the ogbe was allowed to supply an Obi, the most senior being the person recognised by the state, the others acting in a subordinate position. The Ngegwu royal lineage limited its choice to one major lineage; the brother collateral lineages had no hand in the presentation of a candidate. This, I think, led to their indifference when the incident of Eze Agadagba occurred (see Chapter 10).

The weak position of the royal lineages in both states forces their kings to rely on the support of their agnates. This dependence on the support of their agnates also tempts them to forget that they are the heads of state. The two instances of deposition at Oguta support this latter statement. In the case of Eze Ogwuala from Ogwuma, he fled with his agnates to Ukwuani and did not confide in the Ndichie and Olilinzele. The security of these royal agnates appeared more important to him than the security of the state. In the second case of deposition, Obi Ojiako relied on his agnates and refused, after warning by the Ndichie and Olilinzele, to support their policy and dissociate himself from that of his agnates. He decided, rather, to support his agnates.

In the Onitsha and Abo model on the other hand the royal agnates are many and a king can operate on a wider scale, soliciting the help of the non-royal ebo. It is to the king's advantage to exercise his prerogative to appoint powerful people from other lineages as state officials, and a king continues to exercise his influence in the state council even when his own agnates are hostile to him. The fact that they do not rely solely on the agnates for their offices, makes them attach more weight to the interests of the community as a whole as against the narrower objectives of their dynasty. It does not, however, mean that the royal agnates do not have an important role in the affairs of the state.

The Balance of Power

Oguta and Osomari have another structural feature in common. In the first model the grades of chiefs are hierarchically differentiated with power and authority concentrated in the highest grade. In the second model, power is more evenly distributed between the three grades of chiefs, the kingly chiefs, the Ndichie and the Olilinzele at Oguta, and the kingly chiefs, the Ndichie Ume and

T

the Isugbe at Osomari. For instance, the two grades, the kingly chiefs and the Ndichie, share the same position in terms of recruitment and office in each state, while the other grade, the Olilinzele at Oguta and the Isugbe at Osomari, who are in both cases appointed by the king or the kingly chiefs, are open titles both in the manner of recruitment and almost in the similar functions they perform for their kings, and in Oguta they form a group which counterbalances the group of Ndichie.

The kingly chiefs are selected and appointed in the same way as the king. They share common privileges of office and are equally respected and deferred to by the other chiefs. The Olilinzele of Oguta and the Isugbe of Osomari are attached to the kings or chiefly officials to whom they owe their appointments and are separated from and in a different relationship to the Ndichie and Ndichie Ume—chiefs whose offices are not acquired through the expenditure of wealth but ascribed by virtue of their age. Thus the chiefly hierarchies of these two states combine gerontocratic and plutocratic principles. At the same time the segmentary structure inherent in the system is expressed by the fact that these chiefs are also the heads of their respective segments (ogbe, ebo) and are able to represent the interests of these segments in the state council.

In other words, the constitution specifies that every major segment of the kingdom is represented at the state council by a chief. Those who lack the right to supply kingly chiefs are represented by their lineage heads, some of whom are priests who perform specific ritual functions (the Osere and Ezechioha at Oguta and the Ezeani in both states). Thus at Oguta the twenty-seven wards (ogbe) are represented just as the six ebo at Osomari are also represented. But in the first model this representation does not involve every ogbe. The Obi of Onitsha is not duty bound to distribute the fifty-one offices of the state to members of the twenty-two wards, nor is the Obi of Abo bound to do so with respect to the sixteen wards at Abo.

The principle we deduce from this analysis is that the Oguta and Osomari states are more decentralized and segmentary, and are, as Southall put it: "Fragile structures of great flexibility".[12]

How are these segments articulated in the functions of the state? Here we have to examine the degree to which the segments can act independently of the central authority. We shall use two structural elements—the right to wage war and the right to administer justice in the state to answer this question.

The war chiefs at Oguta and Osomari could wage external war independent of the king and the state council. Space does not permit us to record the military activities of the Iyasara Eyiche and the Ndanike Obua Ajukwu at Oguta, nor those of the war chiefs at Osomari. They had their war canoes and military units and waged war by themselves against other kingdoms on the Niger. Both the Iyasara Eyiche and the Ndanike Obua Ajukwu on some occasions jointly planned their campaigns. The Iyasara Eyiche waged war alone against the convoys of the Royal Niger Company.

In both states, the kingly chiefs are allowed to hold their own courts even though they are not allowed to try cases of homicide. They can summon the two grades of chiefs to their courts. This does not happen in the Onitsha-Abo model, for the courts at the ebo level are confined strictly to the chiefs from the particular ebo. This is distinguished from the kingly courts which chiefs from other political segments, particularly at Oguta, can attend. The fact that the ebo courts at Osomari consist of the two grades of chiefs in the ebo courts does not raise them to the same status as the ebo courts at Abo and Onitsha. Here their powers are more limited because of the dependence of their chiefs on the authority of the Obi, but in the model we are discussing, this relationship does not exist. The Ndichie at Oguta can also hold their own courts at the residence of their head, the Ogene, and members of the Olilinzele can attend.

The centralizing factor in both states is based on the principle that the Obi's court is the highest court to which all cases in the lowest court can be appealed. Decisions here are final. The centralization of the court system in both cases, nevertheless, indicates the level of the sharing of the state functions among the officials of state.

In both states policy-making is the concern of the segments. At Oguta the Ndichie can hold an assembly at the residence of the Ogene and also in front of the Akpatakwuma shrine. The kingly chiefs might not attend such an assembly but are bound by decisions reached at this assembly. This institutional arrangement means that the state council—the Obi's council—could share its policy-making rights with the council of Ndichie. This is a situation which does not exist at Onitsha and Abo. There the senior Ndichie and first grade Olinzele constitute a standing committee of the political association of the chiefs and co-ordinate and control the activities of the state (see Chapter 5). At Osomari also, the political divisions could hold their own meetings. Their decisions become binding on members of their divisions, and the state council cannot oppose such decisions.

The principle of segmentary systems as developed by Southall applies in these two states to a greater degree than in the Onitsha

T *

and Abo model. Both Osomari and Oguta recognise the territorial sovereignty of the centre and the internal autonomy of the segments. At Osomari this segmentation is highly flexible and the acceptance of the power of this state council is based merely on the existing consensus among the grades of chiefs who make up the state council (see Chapter 4). At Oguta the conflict between the Ndichie and the kingly chiefs is more of a segmentary conflict, for here the kingly chiefs represent their own segments in the political organisation of the state. The tendency is for members of a political segment to defend and support its chief. Where, therefore, the chiefs divide their loyalty and subordinate the interests of the state to that of their lineage, instability will occur.[13] This is what happened in the case of the two Obis of Oguta, and at Osomari where particular individuals with the support of their political divisions, assumed the office of the Atamanya.

We find, therefore, that the state council depends upon the delegation of authority to it by the component units in each case, without any stable recognition of the right to enforce or maintain this by coercion. Both the council at Osomari and Oguta can only act if the chiefs within the council are united, in which case they play their role as members of their political class, defending the interest of the state. The councils in both cases cannot act independently of the units represented on it. The Obis of Onitsha or Abo can by consulting the senior chiefs act with any section of the chiefs and enforce their decision. The Obi of Oguta or the Atamanya of Osomari cannot do this. In both these states, therefore, the flexible aspect of their segmentary system is more distinct and the working of this system is possible only through consensus among its members. Such consensus implies that the chiefs who represent the political segments are acting both as members of the council and as representatives of their people, and on the understanding that their actions are accepted by their people.

CONCLUSION

We can conclude by saying that while all the four states have segmentary structures, the Oguta and Osomari model is more fragile than that of Onitsha and Abo. It is also more decentralized than that of Onitsha and Abo. Nevertheless, all the states have the component elements that qualify them for classification as states. This is the view which we have tried to verify and establish throughout this study.

NOTES

1 For example, age grades and title associations are more developed and used as basis of government in Asaba and Aguleri, which have not been included in the present study. Age grades and title associations are subsidiary to the council of chiefs in the four states studied in this volume.

2 J. S. Boston, 1964.

3 M. Fortes, 1953, pp. 17–41.

4 e.g. the classifications into "state" and "stateless societies" (M. Fortes and E. E. Evans-Pritchard, 1940); "unitary" and "segmentary" states (A. Southhall, 1953); "despotic", "regal", "incorporative", "aristocratic" and "federal" states (J. Vansina, 1962); "open" (representative government and "government by political association") and "closed" (government by royal aristocracy) (P. C. Lloyd, 1965).

5 R. K. Morton, 1957, p. 16.

6 P. C. Lloyd, 1965, p. 63.

7 The Ndichie Olinzele at Abo have four grades while the Umudei Olinzele have three grades, the last being again sub-divided.

8 M. Fortes, 1960, p. 173.

9 Lloyd Fallers, 1956, p. 236.

10 M. Fortes, 1960, p. 173.

11 F. Barth, 1959, p. 11, 1955, Chapter 9.

12 A. Southall, 1953, p. 260.

13 M. Fortes, 1953; Lloyd Fallers, 1956.

Bibliography

OFFICIAL DOCUMENTS

(*a*) *Reports*
Committee on Bridal Prices, Report of. Enugu, 1955.
Harcourt, H. N. Report of Inquiry into Oguta Chieftaincy Dispute. (Official Document No. 19. Government Printer: Enugu, 1961.)
Harding, R. W. The Dispute over the Obiship of Onitsha. Report of the Inquiry. Official Document No. 6 of 1963. Government Printer: Enugu, 1963.
Jones, G. I. Report of the Position, Status and Influence of Chiefs and Natural Rulers in the Eastern Region of Nigeria. Government Printer: Enugu. Date not given (circa 1956).
Ukuta Peace Commission, Report of the.

(*b*) *Parliamentary Papers*
Milne, W. R. T. Intelligence Report on the Town of Onitsha in Papers Relating to the Instrument Establishing Onitsha Urban District Council.
Instrument Establishing the Oguta Urban District Council. Eastern Regional Government Law No. 238 of 1959.
Slave Trade No. 2, Vol. LXIX, 1880. Correspondence relating to the Bombardment of Onitsha. London, 1880.
Western Region, Local Government Law No. 344 of 1955.

(*c*) *Archival Material, Memoranda etc.*
Harcourt Commission, Memorandum submitted by the Ndichie and people of Oguta. 1961.
Harding Commission, Memoranda submitted by the Ndichie Ume. Onitsha, 1963.
Jones Commission, Memoranda submitted to.
Obi Okosi I. Papers relating to the Dispute over the Succession. National Archives, Ibadan. C526/293 79, Vol. I.
Onitsha Urban District Council, Papers relating to the Instrument establishing the. Government Printer: Enugu, 1956.
Ugwunaobamkpa, Memorandum of 25th August 1932. National Archives, Ibadan. Paper C/526/293 79, Vol. I.

JOURNALS AND PERIODICALS
Church Missionary Intelligencer.
Church Missionary Record, 1870.
African Advertiser, December 1936.

PRIVATE DOCUMENTS
Osomari Improvement Society. Minutes of 1963 Annual Conference.
Resolution of 24 wards of Oguta against the Royal Lineages of Umudei and Umuenu, 1949.

BOOKS AND ARTICLES

Allen, Capt. W. and T. H. H. Thomson. *A Narrative of the Expedition sent by Her Majesty's Government to the River Niger, in 1841*, Vols. I and II, London, 1848; reprinted Frank Cass, London, 1968.

Baker, Earnest. *Politics of Aristotle*. Oxford, 1952.

Barth, F. *Political Leadership among Swat Pathans*. University of London Press, 1959.

Barth, F. 'Segmentary Opposition and the Theory of Games; A Study of Swat Pathan Organisation'. *Journal of Royal Anthropological Institute*, Vol. 89, 1959.

Basden, G. T. *Niger Ibos*. London, 1938; reprinted with a new bibliographical note by John Ralph Willis, Frank Cass, London, 1966.

Bailey, F. C. *Decision by Consensus in Councils and Committees*. ASA Monograph No. 2. Political System and the Distribution of Power. Tavistock Press: London, 1965.

Beattie, J. M. H. *Bunyoro: An African Kingdom*. Holt, Rinehart and Winston: New York, 1960.

Beattie, J. M. H. 'Bunyoro: An African Feudality'. *Journal of African History*, Vol. V, 1960 or 64?

Beattie, J. M. H. 'Checks on the Abuse of Power in some African States'. *Sociologus*. 1952. No. 2, pp. 97–115.

Bohannan, P. *Social Anthropology*. Holt, Rinehart and Winston: New York, 1963.

Boston, J. S. *The Igala Kingdom*. Ibadan and Oxford University Press: London, 1968.

Boston, J. S. 'Notes on the Origin of Igala Kingdom'. *Journal of the Historical Society of Nigeria*, Vol. II, No. 3, Ibadan University Press, 1962.

Boston, J, S. 'Notes on Contact between the Igala and the Ibo'. *Journal of the Historical Society of Nigeria*, Vol. II, No. 1, 1960.

Bottemore, T. B. *Elites and Society*. Watts: London, 1964.

Bradbury, R. E. *Some aspects of the Political Organisation of the Benin Kingdom*. West African Institute of Social and Economic Research: Ibadan, 1952.

Bradbury, R. E. 'The Benin Kingdom and the Edo Speaking Peoples of Southern Nigeria'. *Ethnographic Survey of Africa*. Western Africa Part XIII. International African Institute: London, 1957.

Bradbury, R. E. *Fathers, Elders and Ghosts in Edo Religion. Anthropological Approaches to the Study of Religion*. ASA Monograph No. 7. Tavistock: London, 1968.

Bradbury, R. E. 'Benin Kingdom in the 19th Century' in Forde and Kabery (eds.), *West African Kingdoms in the 19th Century*. Oxford University Press, 1967.

Bradbury, R. E. *Continuity and Discontinuity in the Pre-Colonial and Colonial Benin Politics*. ASA Monograph No. 7. Tavistock: London, 1968.

Busia, K. *The Position of the Chief in the Modern Political Systems of Ashanti*. Oxford University Press, 1951; reprinted Frank Cass, London, 1968.

Busia, K. *The Challenge of Africa*. Pall Mall: London, 1962.

Dike, K. O. *Trade and Politics in the Niger Delta*. Clarendon Press: Oxford, 1966.

Easton, D. *The Political System*. Knopf: New York, 1959.
Easton, D. 'Political Anthropology' in B. J. Siegel (ed.), *Biennial Review of Anthropology*. Stanford University Press, 1959.
Egharevba, J. *A Short History of Benin*. Ibadan University Press, 1960.
Egharevba, J. *Benin Law and Customs*. Lagos, 1947.
Eisenstadt, S. W. 'Primitive Political Systems. A preliminary comparative analysis.' *American Anthropologist*. 1961; pp. 200–20.
Evans-Pritchard, E. E. *The Nuer*. Clarendon Press: Oxford, 1940.
Evans-Pritchard, E. E. *Nuer Religion*. Clarendon Press: Oxford, 1956.
Evans-Pritchard, E. E. 'The Divine Kingship of the Shilluk' in *Essays in Social Anthropology*. Faber and Faber: London, 1962.
Evans-Pritchard, E. E. with M. Fortes. *African Political Systems*. Oxford, 1940.
Elias, T. O. *Nigerian Land Law and Custom*. Routledge and Kegan Paul: London, 1951.
Fallors, Lloyd. *Bantu Bureaucracy*. Heffer: Cambridge, 1956.
Flint, J. E. *Sir George Goldie and the Making of Nigeria*. Oxford University Press, 1960.
Forde, Daryll. 'The Yoruba Speaking Peoples of South Western Nigeria'. *West Africa*. Ethnographic Survey of Africa, Part IV. International African Institute: London, 1951.
Forde, Daryll and Jones, G. I. 'The Ibo and Ibibo-Speaking Peoples of South Western Nigeria'. *West Africa*. Ethnographic Survey of Africa, Part III. Oxford University Press: London, 1950.
Fortes, M. *The Web of Kinship among the Tallensi*. Oxford University Press, 1940.
Fortes, M. *The Dynamics of Clanship among the Tallensi*. Oxford University Press, 1945.
Fortes, M. 'Structure of Unilineal Descent Group'. *American Anthropologist*, Vol. LIII, 1957; pp. 7–41. Reprinted in S. Ottenberg, *Culture and Societies of Africa*. Random House: New York, 1960; p. 173.
Fortes, M. *Oedipus and Job in West African Religion*. Cambridge University Press, 1959.
Fortes, M. 'Ritual and Office in Tribal Society' in Max Gluckman (ed.), *Essays on the Ritual of Social Relations*. Manchester University Press, 1962.
Fortes, M., and E. E. Evans-Pritchard. *African Political Systems*. Oxford University Press, 1940.
Frazer, J. G. *The Golden Bough. A Study in Magic and Religion* (abridged edition). Macmillan: London, 1925.
Gennep, A. Van. *The Rites of Passage* (translated by Monika B. Vizedom and Gabrielle Caffee). Routledge and Kegan Paul: London, 1960.
Gluckman, Max. *The Judicial Process among the Barotse of Northern Rhodesia*. Manchester University Press, 1955.
Gluckman, Max. *Custom and Conflict in Africa*. Blackwell: Oxford, 1955.
Gluckman, Max. *Order and Rebellion in Tribal Africa*. Cohen and West: London, 1963.
Gluckman, Max. *Politics, Law and Ritual in Tribal Society*. Blackwell: Oxford, 1965.
Gluckman, Max. *The Ideas of Barotse Jurisprudence*. Yale: New Haven, 1965.
Gluckman, Max., ed. *Essays on the Ritual of Social Relations*. Manchester University Press, 1962.

Goody, J. *Death, Property and the Ancestors*. Tavistock: London, 1962.

Goode, W. J. 'Contemporary Thinking about Primitive Religion' in Morton H. Fried (ed.), *Readings in Anthropology*, Vol. XI. Cultural Anthropology. Thompson Y. Cromwell Co: New York, 1959.

Green, M. M. *Igbo Village Affairs*. London, 1947; 2nd edition, with a new introduction by the author, Frank Cass: London, 1964.

Gulliver, P. H. *Social Control in an African Society*. Routledge and Kegan Paul: London, 1963.

Hertslet, Lewis. *A Complete Collection of the Treaties and Conventions between Great Britain and Foreign Powers*. London, 1850 onwards.

Hertz, R. *Death and the Right Hand* (translated Rodney and Claudia Needham). London, 1960.

Ibeziako, M. O. *The Founder and Some Celebrities of Onitsha. Some Aspects of Ancient Civilisation*. Onitsha, 1937.

Ifeka, S. 'Onitsha Social Heritage. Historical Synopsis'. *Nigerian Spokesman*. Onitsha, 19th May–30th June 1962.

Ijoma, Agha. *A Short History of Osomari*. Ude Press: Onitsha (date not stated).

Irstam, T. U. H. *The King of Ganda*. Statens Etnografiska Museum. New Series No. 8. Stockholm, 1944.

Jones, G. I. 'Dual Organisation in Ibo Social Structure'. *Africa*, Vol. XIX, 1949; pp. 150–6.

Jones, G. I. 'Ibo Land Tenure'. *Africa*, Vol. XIX, 1949. pp. 309–13.

Jones, G. I. 'Ecology and Social Structure among the North Eastern Ibo'. *Africa*, Vol. XXXI, 1961.

Jones, G. I. *The Trading States of the Oil Rivers*. Oxford University Press, 1963.

Kaine, Isoma. *Osomari Historical Sketch*. Onitsha, 1963.

Kuper, H. *An African Aristocracy*. Oxford University Press, 1947.

Leach, E. R. *Political Systems of Highland Burma*. Bell & Sons: London, 1954.

Leach, E. R. *Rethinking Anthropology*. University of London Press, 1961.

Leonard, Major A. *The Lower Niger and its Tribes*. Macmillan: London, 1906.

Lloyd, P. C. 'The Traditional Political System of the Yoruba'. *South Western Journal of Anthropology*, Vol. X, 1954; pp. 366–84.

Lloyd, P. C. 'Sacred Kingship and Government among the Yoruba'. *Africa*, Vol. XXX, No. 3, 1960.

Lloyd, P. C. *Yoruba Land Law*. Oxford University Press. London, 1962.

Lloyd, P. C. 'The Political Structure of African Kingdoms: An exploratory model' in ASA Monograph No. 2. *Political Systems and the Distribution of Power*, pp. 63–112. Tavistock: London, 1965.

Lloyd, P. C. *Conflict Theory and Yoruba Kingdoms*. ASA Monograph No. 7. Tavistock: London, 1968.

Mair, Lucy. *Primitive Government*. Penguin Books, 1962.

Manoukian, Madeline. 'Tribes of the Northern Territories of the Gold Coast'. *West Africa*. Ethnographic Survey of Africa. Western Africa, Part V. International African Institute: London, 1952.

Maquet, J. J. *The Premise of Inequality in Ruwanda*. Oxford University Press, 1961.

Meek, C. K. *Law and Authority in a Nigerian Tribe*. Oxford University Press, 1937.

Middleton, J. and D. Tait (eds.). *Tribes without Rulers (Studies in African Segmentary Systems)*. Routledge and Kegan Paul: London, 1958.

Mockler-Ferryman, Lt. Col. A. F. *Up the Niger*. George Phillip & Son: London, 1892.

Morton, R. K. *Social Theory and Social Structure*. Glencoe, III, 1957.

Nadel, S. F. *A Black Byzantium. The Kingdom of Nupe in Nigeria*. Oxford University Press, 1942.

Nwakuche, G. *A Short History of Oguta*. (unpublished).

Nzimiro, F. I. *Family and Kinship in Ibo Land. A Study in Acculturation Process*. Cologne, 1962.

Nzimiro, F. I. 'Social Mobility among the Ibos of Southern Nigeria'. *International Journal of Comparative Sociology*, Vol. VI, No. 1. Leiden, 1965.

Nzimiro, F. I. 'Oguta' in *Nigeria*, No. 80. Lagos, 1964.

Oberg, K. 'The Ankole' in Fortes and Evans-Pritchard (eds.), *African Political Systems*. Oxford, 1940.

Obi, Charles. *The History of Abo* (unpublished).

O'Connor, Resident D. 'The Obiship of Onitsha'. *The African Advertiser*, December 1936.

Okojie, C. E. *Ishan Native Laws and Customs*. Lagos, 1960.

Radcliffe Brown, R. R. *Structure and Function in Primitive Society*. Cohen and West: London, 1952.

Richards, Audrey I. 'African Kings and their Royal Relatives', *Journal of Royal Anthropological Institute*, Vol. XCI, Part II, 1961; pp. 135–90.

Schapera, I. *Government and Politics in Tribal Societies*. Watts: London, 1956.

Smith, M. C. *Government in Zazzau*. Oxford University Press, 1960.

Smith, M. C. 'On Segmentary Lineage Systems'. *Journal of Royal Anthropological Institute*, Vol. LXXXVI, No. 2, 1952.

Southall, A. *Alur Society*. Heffer: Cambridge, 1953.

Southall, A. 'A Critique of the Typology of States and Political Systems' in *Political Systems and the Distribution of Power*. ASA Monograph 2. Tavistock: London, 1965.

Vansina, J. 'A Comparison of African Kingdoms'. *Africa*, Vol. XXXII, No. 4, 1962.

Weber, Max. *The Theory of Social and Economic Organisation* (translated by A. M. Henderson and Talcott Parsons). Collier-Macmillan: London, 1957.

Index

Abo, xiv–xv, 5; government, 38, 56–64, 264–68; history, 11–14; judicial system, 118–125; kingship, *see* Obiship; legislative process, 109–10; palace organization, 158–59; political elite, 95–96; religions, 131; social organization, Chapter 2; social structure, 56–58; war organization, 135–53, 137–38; war with Igala, 236–37

Adikea, Obi of Oguta, 218, 247

Adizua, Obi of Oguta, 220, 240

Agadagba, Obi of Oguta, 218; reign, 237–39

Agbalanze Society (Onitsha), 45, 54; membership a pre-requisite for Obiship, 195

Agbanta society (Oguta), 66–67, 76

Agbor, 7

Age grades: Abo, 64; Oguta, 68, 76, 113, 123–24, 139; Onitsha, 55; and law enforcement, 128

Aguleri, xiv–xv, 5

Ajie (Onitsha), 229, 231; duties, 136; installation of Obi, 208; selection of Obi, 206–07

Ajukwu, Obua, Ndanike of Oguta, 249

Akazua, Obi of Onitsha, 9, 197–98

Akiri tribe, 12

Allen, 12

Ameshi clan, 15

Anatogu, Iyase of Onitsha, 228

Anazonwu, Obi of Onitsha, 9, 198–99, 208

Anidima fraternity (Oguta), 241

Anyafuru, Atamanya of Osomari, 18

Arochukwu, 237

Asaba, xiv–xv, 5

Ase, 15

Atamanyaship of Osomari, 17–18; constitutional safeguards, 251–53, 261–64; installation rituals, 161–64, 172–76; judicial functions, 120–24; legislative functions, 114–16; mortuary rituals, 185–86, 187–89; origins, 147; palace organization, 160–61; praise names, 148; qualifications for, 194–95, 221–22; regalia, 176–79; relations with chiefs, 271–74; rights and privileges, 81–2; ritual duties, 151, 156; status, 78–80; succession, 270–71

Atani, 5

Attah, King of Igala, 17

Awkuzu, 9

Awogu, Atamanya of Osomari, 222

Bedwell, Commissioner on the Niger, 199, 211

Benin, 43, 58, 71, 139, 147, 157, 194; influences on the Niger states, 255–58

Bombardment of Abo, 1862, 13–14; 1883, 14; of Onitsha (1879), 9–10

Bride price, Onitsha, 106–07; Oguta, 116

Catholic Missions, Onitsha, 198–99

Chiefs, *see* Ajie (Onitsha), Ezeukwu (Oguta), Iyasara (Oguta), Iyase, Ndanike, Ndichie, Odu (Onitsha), Odua (Abo), Ogene, Olinzele, Oniniogwu (Osomari), Oririnzre (Oguta), Owelle (Onitsha)

Chima legend, 7–8

Chima Ogbuefi, Obi of Onitsha, 197

Chimedie, Obi of Onitsha, 198, 211

Church Missionary Society, 9, 198

Citizens, see Nwadiani

Councils, see General assemblies, Intermediate councils, Local councils, Privy councils and State councils

Courts, see Intermediate courts, Lower courts, and Supreme courts

Crowther, Samuel Ajayi, 9, 14, 18

Dike, K. O., xi
Divorce, Onitsha, 107

Egbema, 15
Egbunike, J., 200, 204
Egungu, see Spirit societies
Enebeli, Obi of Abo, 213
Enefua, Igwulu, Iyasara of Oguta, 248
Enweuzor, J. J., 206-11
Eroa, Obi of Oguta, 218, 237
Esumaiukwu, Founder of Abo, 11-12
Europeans, 5-7, 9-19
Eze Aroli, Obi of Onitsha, 197, 211
Eze Chima, see Chima legend
Eze Nkpo, Obi of Oguta, 217
Ezeoba, 230-31
Ezeocha, J., 203, 204
Ezeukwu (Oguta), 70-71; death of this Obi, 183-84; installation of the Obi, 171, 180
Ezi, 7

Festivals, 151-56, 227-28
Forde, C. D., xiii, 3
Fortes, M., xi
Free-born, see Nwadiani

Gbasuzor, Iyase of Onitsha, 200-05, 227-28, 268-89
General assemblies, 258; Abo, 109; Oguta, 111-12; Onitsha, 104-06; Osomari, 114-15
Goldie, Sir George, 9
Goody, J., xi

Hausa, 16
Hopkins, David, 18

Ibina festival (Oguta), 154
Ibos, cultural areas, 3; religion, 3; social structure, 21
Idah, 147, 255-56
Igala, 15, 17, 86, 88, 157, 194, 211; influences on the Niger States,

255-56; wars with Abo and Oguta, 236-37
Igbu title society: Abo, 34-36, 64, 153; Oguta, 76; Osomari, 79; prerequisite for kingship at Abo and Osomari, 195
Ihiala, 135
Ijaws, 5
Ijelekpe, Obi of Onitsha, 197, 209, 211
Ijoma, Obi of Oguta, 220, 240, 250
Ikwa Muo society (Oguta), 240-41
Illah, 15
Imanzu rituals (Onitsha), 210
Imegwu, Obi of Abo, 14
Intermediate councils, 97-98; Onitsha, 102-03; Osomari, 114
Intermediate courts, Abo, 125; Oguta, 126; Onitsha, 124-25; Osomari, 126
Inyi community, 15
Isele, 7
Isuama (Orlu Ibos), 17
Iyasara (Oguta), 67-70; appointment of Olilinzele, 72; duties, 139-40; origins, 256; relationship with the Obi, 248; selection of this Obi, 217
Iyase (Abo), duties, 62, 109-10, 120, 137-38; installation of the Obi, 170, 180; installation of Olinzele, 61-62; origins, 258
Iyase (Onitsha), xviii; appointment and status, 227-28; disputes, 227-28; duties, 50, 104-05, 120, 136; installation of Ndichie, 47-48; installation of the Obi, 167-69, 180, 202-03, 208; origins, 256; selection of Obi, 197, 200-11
Iyase (Osomari), duties, 114-15; Isiolu ward, 91-92; disputes, 252-53; origins, 256; status, 78-79, 81-82
Izu (councils), see General assemblies, Intermediate councils, Local councils, Privy councils, and State councils

Jones, G. I., xi, xiii, 3
Judicial processes, see under State

Kalabari, 16
Kingmakers, see Eze Ukwu (Oguta), Iyase (Abo, Onitsha), Odua (Abo), Ogene (Osomari)

Kingship, *see* Atamanyaship (Oso-
mari), Obiship (Abo, Oguta,
Onitsha)
Koenig, R., xii
Kwale, 12, 237

Laird, Macgregor, 9, 12–13, 18
Lander, John, in Abo, 12
Lander, Richard, in Abo, 12
Law enforcement agencies, 128–29
Leach, E., xi
Local councils, 96–97; Abo, 109;
Oguta, 110–11; Onitsha, 101–02;
Osomari, 114
Lower courts, 127

McWilliam, J. O., 13
Marriage laws, Onitsha, 106–08
Mau, *see* Spirit societies
Mberekpe, Obi of Oguta, 220, xviii,
218, 243–44
Meek, C. K., xii
Missionaries, 5–6; Onitsha, 9, 198

National Africa Company, *see* Royal
Niger Company
Ndanike, Abo, 58, 137; Oguta, 71,
138, 217, 249; origins 256
Ndi Okpala (Lineage heads), Abo,
63–64; Oguta, 65–66, 217; Onitsha,
55–56, 101; Osomari, 77; and law
enforcement, 129–30; and Onitsha
kingship installation; rituals, 164–
66
Ndichie (Oguta), composition, 74;
duties, 74–75; privileges, 75
Ndichie Nta (Osomari), 79–80
Ndichie Okwa (Onitsha), composition, 44–45; duties, 51, 120, 136;
installation rituals, 47–49
Ndichie Okwareze (Onitsha), composition, 45; duties, 51–52, 105,
120, 136
Ndichie Ume (Onitsha), xviii;
appointment, 45–46; composition,
42–43; duties, 49–52, 103–04, 120;
installation rituals, 46–49; mortuary rituals, 52–53; privileges and
distinctions, 52–53; relations with
the Obi, 230–32; succession to
Obiship, 200–01; titles, 44
Ndichie Ume (Osomari), 79–80
Nembe, 16

Niger Delta, 5
Njaba River, 15, 18
Njoku, Eni, xi
Nri, xiv
Nupe, 16, 194
Nwachukwu, Aja, xi
Nwadiani (citizen), composition, 23;
rights and privileges, 24
Nzegwu, A. S., 200, 204
Nekwu, S. J., 200, 204

Oath-taking, 122–23
Obamkpa, 7
Obazome, Prince of Benin, *see*
Esumaiukwu
Obinwe, Iyase of Onitsha, 228
Obio, 7
Obiship of Abo, appointment of
Olinzele, 60–62, 265; constitutional safeguards, 233–35, 261–64;
installation rituals, 161–64, 169–
70, 173–76; judicial functions,
120–24; legislative functions, 109–
10; mortuary rituals, 182–83, 186–
87; origins, 147; palace organization, 158–59; praise names, 148;
prerogatives, 149; qualifications
for, 194–95, 212–13; regalia, 176–
79; relations with chiefs, 162–64,
234–35; ritual duties, 150, 152–
54; succession, 267–69
Obiship of Oguta, constitutional
safeguards, 235–50, 261–64; disputes, 220, 242–44; installation
rituals, 161–64, 170–72, 174–76;
judicial functions, 120–24; legislative functions, 111–13; mortuary
rituals, 183–84, 189–91; multiple
succession, 219–20; origins, 15,
147; palace, 159–60; praise names,
148; prerogatives, 149; qualifications for, 194–95, 217; regalia,
176–79; relations with chiefs, 171–
74; ritual duties, 150, 154–55;
succession, 270–71
Obiship of Onitsha, appointment of
Ndichie, 45–53, 265; constitutional
safeguards, 227–32; disputes, xiv,
xviii, 104, 108, 180, 195, 198, 211;
installation rituals, 161–69; 173–
76, 208–10; judicial functions,
120–24; legislative functions, 103–
09; mortuary rituals, 181–82, 186;
origins, 7–8, 147; palace, 157–58;

praise names, 148; prerogatives, 149; qualifications for, 194–95; regalia, 176–79; relations with Iyase and other chiefs, 227–30, 261–64; ritual duties, 150–52; succession, 194–211, 267–69

O'Connor, Resident of Onitsha, 204

Odita, M. M. A., 206, 210

Odoekpe, 17

Odu (Onitsha), duties, 136; selection of Obi, 206–07

Odua (Abo), 59; duties, 125; installation of Obi, 169–70, 180; interregnum (1897–1905), 215; relations with Obi, 234–35

Ofala festival (Onitsha), 151–52, 227–28

Ofo, in kingship installation rituals, 166, 209; in Ndichie installation rituals, 48

Ogbaru Ibos, xiv, 3; government, Chapters 3–4; history, 6–19; legislative process chapter, 5–6; occupations, 4–5; social structure Chapter 2

Obosi, 9

Ogene (Oguta), 75–76, 111–12, 120; selection of the Obi, 217

Ogene (Onitsha), 136; disputes, 231; origins, 256; selection of Obi, 206

Ogene (Osomari), 84–85, 90; installation of the Atamanya, 180; origins, 256; regency, 222–23

Ogidi, 9

Oguta, xiv–xv, 5; government, 38–39, 65–76, 269–74; history, 14–16; internal strife, 248–51; judicial system, 118–24, 126; kingship, see Obiship; legislative process, 110–13; palace organization, 159–60; political elite, 96; religion, 131; social organization, Chapter 2; social structure, 65–67; war organization, 134, 138–41, 272

Oguta National Union, 113, 124, 132–33, 241

Ogwezi I, Obi of Abo, 213

Ogwuala, Obi of Oguta, 217; reign, 236–37

Ohanyere, Obi of Oguta, 220, 247

Ohu, see Oru

Ojiako, Nnam, Obi of Oguta, xviii, 218; reign, 239–44

Ojigbali, Obi of Abo, 213

Okagbue Ofala, Obi of Onitsha, xviii

Oko, 17

Okosi I, Obi of Onitsha, 104, 107, 158; accession, 199–200, 208; government, 228–30

Okosi II, Obi of Onitsha; accession, 201–05, 208, 227, 230

Okposi festival (Osomari), 156

Oldfield, 12

Olilinzele chiefs (Oguta), appointment, 72; duties, 73, 110–12, 126; privileges, 73–74; relationships with the Obi, 246–47; selection of the Obi, 217

Olinzele chiefs (Abo), composition and hierarchies, 58–60; duties, 62–63, 109–10, 125, 137–38; installation rituals, 61–62; interregnum (1897–1905), 215; privileged, 63; relations with Obi, 162–64, 234–35; selection and appointment, 60–61

Olinzele chiefs (Osomari), 85–93; selection of the Atamanya, 221–22

Olisa, Obi of Abo, 213

Olisa, Charles, xii

Olisa, R., King Elect of Osomari, xii

Omelife festival (Oguta), 154–55

Omozele, Obi of Onitsha, 211

Omu (queen) of Osomari, 83

Onicha Olona, 7–8

Onicha-Ugbo, 7

Onicha-Ukwu, 7

Oniha, see Ogene

Oniniogwu (Osomari), status, 78–79, 81–82

Onitsha, xiv, xv, 5; government, 37–38, 41–56, 264–68; history, 7–11; judicial system, 118–25; kingship, see Obiship; legislative process, 100–09; palace organization, 157–58; political elite, 95; religion, 130–32; social organization, Chapter 2; social structure, 41–46; war organization, 135–37

Onitsha Improvement Union and bride price legislation, 106–08

Onono, 15

Onowu, see Iyase (Onitsha)

Onyechi, J. M., 206, 210

Onyejekwe, Obi of Onitsha, xviii; accession, 206–11

Oputa I, Obi of Abo, xvii, 14, 213–15

Orakwue, J., 197

Oranye, F., xii

Orashi River, 6, 15–16, 18

Oreze, Founder of Onitsha, 8, 104

Oru (slaves), 24; abolishment (by law), 28; origins, 25; status and rights, 26–28

Osaka, Obi of Oguta, 218, 237

Osomari, xiv–xv, 5; government, 39, 76–93, 269–74; history, 17–18; judicial system, 118–24, 126; kingship, see Atamanyaship; legislative process, 113–17; palace organization, 160–61; political elite, 96; social organization, Chapter 2; social structure, 76, 78; war organization, 141–43, 272

Osomari Improvement Society, 28

Ossai, Obi of Abo, 12–13, 32

Ossai II, Obi of Abo, 14, 215–16

Osu, see Oru

Owelle (Onitsha), 136; selection of Obi, 206–07

Oze, 8

Ozo title society, see Agbalanze Society

Petri, H., xii

Privy councils, Abo, 109–10, 257; Onitsha, 103, 257

Purvis, J. C., 18

Regents, xviii

Richards, A., xi

Ritual sanctions, 130–32

Rituals, see under Atamanyaship, Ndichie Ume, and Obiship

Royal clans, 29–39; Abo, 212–15, 266; Oguta, 217–19, 270; Onitsha, 195–99, 266; Osomari, 221, 270; see also Umudei (Abo) and Umuezechima (Onitsha)

Royal Niger Company, Abo, 13–14; Oguta, 16, 141, 220; Onitsha, 9–10

Schon, J. F., 13

Slaves, see Oru

Social sanctions, 132–33

Spirit societies, Onitsha, 55

State councils, 257; Abo, 109; Oguta, 111–12; Onitsha, 103; Osomari, 114–15

Supreme Courts (of Abo, Oguta, Onitsha and Osomari), composition, 120; fees, 120–21; judgement, 123; oath-taking, 122; procedure, 121; relationship with government, 123–124

Title societies, 94–95; regulations at Osomari, 115–16; royal families and, 33–36; see also Agbalanze, Agbanta, Igbu, Ozo

Treaties, Abo, 13–14; Oguta, 16; Onitsha, 9, 46; Osomari, 18

Trotter, H. D., 12–13

Udo shrine (Onitsha), Obiship installation rituals, 166–67, 180, 202–04, 208–09

Udogwu, Obi of Onitsha, 197, 209, 211

Ugwunaobamkpa (Onitsha), 42–43, 166, 201, 204–08, 266–67

Ugwuta, founder of Oguta, 15

Uje festival (Abo), 152–54

Ukwuani, see Kwale

Ulashi River, see Orashi River

Ulo festival (Osomari), 156

Umudei (Abo), 28–29, 56–60, 212–15

Umuezechima (Onitsha), 7–8, 29–30, 41–42, 194–211

United African Company, see Royal Niger Company

War organization, 134–35, 259; see also under individual states

Warrant chief system, xiii, 14

Women's organizations: Abo, 64; Oguta, 76; Onitsha, 55, 105; Osomari, 83; and law enforcement, 129–30

Yoruba, 194

Zazzau, 157, 194